HD
9697
.T694
A232
1998

HWBI

D1220294

ABB

THE DANCING GIANT

Creating the globally connected corporation

Kevin Barham

and

Claudia Heimer

FINANCIAL TIMES
PRENTICE HALL

PEARSON EDUCATION LIMITED

Head Office:
Edinburgh Gate
Harlow CM20 2JE
Tel: +44 (0)1279 623623
Fax: +44 (0)1279 431059

London Office:
128 Long Acre, London WC2E 9AN
Tel: +44 (0)171 447 2000
Fax: +44 (0)171 240 5771

First published in Great Britain 1998

© Financial Times Professional Limited 1998

The right of Kevin Barham and Claudia Heimer to be
identified as Authors of this Work have been asserted by them
in accordance with the Copyright, Designs, and Patents Act 1988.

ISBN 0 273 62861 5

British Library Cataloguing in Publication Data
A CIP catalogue record for this book can be obtained
from the British Library.

All rights reserved; no part of this publication may be reproduced,
stored in a retrieval system, or transmitted in any form or by any means,
electronic, mechanical, photocopying, recording, or otherwise without either
the prior written permission of the Publishers or a licence permitting restricted
copying in the United Kingdom issued by the Copyright Licensing Agency Ltd,
90 Tottenham Court Road, London W1P 0LP. This book may not be lent,
resold, hired out or otherwise disposed of by way of trade in any form
of binding or cover other than that in which it is published,
without the prior consent of the Publishers.

3 5 7 9 10 8 6 4 2

Typeset by M Rules
Printed and bound in Great Britain by
Biddles Ltd, Guildford & King's Lynn

*The Publishers' policy is to use paper manufactured
from sustainable forests.*

ABOUT THE AUTHORS

Kevin Barham is former Director of the Ashridge Centre for Management and Organization Learning and a founding partner of the Global Development Partnership. His research has focused on the development of leaders for global business – an issue which is a major priority for ABB. ABB has itself participated in Kevin's previous research in this critical area. An early opportunity to get an inside view of ABB's 'action recipe' (to use Finnish researcher Rolf Leppänen's phrase) came when ABB participated during 1990–91 in an Ashridge research project studying the competences of successful international managers. This research provided an early opportunity to learn from the inside about the early challenges that the company faced in restructuring its operations, integrating its many new acquisitions in different countries, introducing its global matrix and securing cross-border cooperation among previously independent national companies.

ABB has led the way for Western firms interested in investing in the emerging economies of Central and Eastern Europe. Kevin had a further opportunity to learn about ABB from the inside and about the challenges it faces in these regions, when, in 1994, he researched and wrote a case study about ABB Elta, a power transformer and electrical equipment plant that ABB had acquired in Poland some two years earlier, and where the ABB turnaround process was in full swing.

Claudia Heimer is Business Director and a member of the management team of Ashridge Consulting where she has been interested in the cultural, strategic and IT implications of globalization.

Claudia first met ABB in the early 1990s, when Robert Feller, ABB's Vice-President for Corporate Management Development, participated in a seminar which the authors ran to share the outcomes of the research on international management competences and to create the authors' approach to developing global managers. Ever since, she has had occasional interactions with people at ABB based in places from Finland to India. She works with large group processes which involve hundreds of people interacting to create momentum and move a company forward. ABB participated in one of her assignments to bring the outside world into the room and show people what is possible. There was no better challenge than the reality of what other people had achieved! She has been struck ever since by ABB managers' generous willingness to share their stories and take time out from their busy schedules to reflect on their experiences.

To Christine, Katie and Claire
with thanks and love.

To Franz-Wilhelm.

CONTENTS

PART I

THE BIRTH OF A MODERN GIANT

PART II

GIANT STEPS TO THE GLOBALLY CONNECTED CORPORATION

PART III

REAPING THE HARVEST

ACKNOWLEDGEMENTS

This is an independent book and we are therefore especially grateful to the ABB managers who have given time to talk with us: Robert Feller who supported us in our initial approach to ABB; Göran Lindahl who agreed to take the book on and whose concern that we paint a true picture was an important motivator for us; Percy Barnevik who gave generously of his time and unique insights and who also provided a wealth of material; Fred Bystrand; Jean-Pierre Dürig; Eric Elzvik; Beat Hess; H.K. Mohanty; Arne Olsson; Jan Roxendal; Bengt Skantze; A.K. Thiagarajan. All provided invaluable perspectives on the development of ABB.

We would also particularly like to thank John Fox and Iwona Jarzębska of ABB Corporate Communications for their considerable help in arranging interviews and handling feedback on the draft of the book.

We need to say thank you also to those other managers in ABB with whom we have talked over time both in the course of this research and in previous projects including our research on the competences of international managers and those managers who talked with us in the course of completing the ABB Elta case study.

Other people to whom our gratitude is due include Christian Berggren of the University of Linköping for meeting with us in Stockholm and commenting on early drafts of the book; Christopher Conway for contributing to some of the early ideas in Chapter 6; Karen Ward of Ashridge Consulting Ltd for commenting on the draft of Chapter 6; Christine Barham for continuing encouragement and for careful reading of our various drafts; Stephen Tallman of the University of Utah and Cranfield School of Management for ongoing debate on global strategy and organization; Ariane Berthoin Antal of the Wissenschaftszentrum Berlin and the Europa-Akademie for permission to draw on the ABB Elta case study.

We appreciate very much the support provided by our publishers at Financial Times Management. Richard Stagg has been an excellent coach with whom it has been very motivating to work. Elizabeth Truran has been a most diligent project manager.

We also wish to thank our Ashridge colleagues – Michael Osbaldeston, Chief Executive, and Andrew Mechelewski of Ashridgeís Learning Resource Centre.

INTRODUCTION

Behind the master plan

In June 1987, Beat Hess, head of the Legal Department of the world-famous Swiss electrotechnical firm Brown Boveri and Company (BBC), was about to take his family on a well-earned week's holiday to Italy. He was suddenly told by BBC's Chairman, Fritz Leutwiler, and Chief Executive, Thomas Gasser, to prepare a full draft agreement for the 'unthinkable' – negotiations for a merger with long-time rival ASEA, the Swedish power engineering firm that had been gaining ground on BBC ever since a new CEO, Percy Barnevik, had taken over in 1980. If it came off, this would be the largest cross-border merger in history.

Despite the enormity of this move, Hess was not entirely surprised as Leutwiler and Gasser had told him about the possibility of such a merger some weeks previously. None the less, it was a huge challenge to write an agreement for merging two very large, internationally active firms, headquartered in two different countries – especially as he was told that it had to be done fast and in absolute secrecy. He was told to go ahead with his holiday if he wanted to but that the agreement had to be completed by the first week in July. The handwritten draft, with its coffee and suntan lotion stains, that Hess brought back from Italy was to be the basis for what has now become a legend in corporate history.

Of course, the merger – while a highly dramatic event in a world where the concept of 'globalization' had not yet taken root – was only the beginning. The newly merged entity, under Percy Barnevik as CEO, went on to catch the imagination of both managers and business gurus with the boldness of its restructuring, its adoption of a novel form of global matrix structure and the pace of its expansion into Eastern Europe and Asia.

If we hadn't written this book, we would have been dying to see someone else do so. Whenever one reads about ABB in the management literature, there is a 'no questions asked' attitude of 'if ABB has done it, why can't you? It must be the right thing to do. This is the way to do it, this is what ABB has done.' It is almost as if there is an ABB doctrine that fascinates both scholars and managers. Why is ABB so interesting to managers and business gurus alike? Why is it the world's favourite case study? Why is Percy Barnevik possibly 'the most influential manager in the world' (according to *The Observer* newspaper)?

Certainly, the numbers relating to ABB are more than impressive. In ten years, it has grown to its present position as the leading power engineering company in the world. It is now a $31 billion corporation, employing 220,000 people in 50 or more countries, including all the major markets, around the globe. It consists of some 35 business areas – each a global business in its own right – with 5000 profit centres, or what the new CEO, Göran Lindahl, calls '5000 perceived companies', each with, on average, 50 people and $7 million in business. It is the largest Western investor in Central and Eastern Europe, where it has 30,000 employees and orders received have grown from $200 million in 1989 to $2 billion today.

And some of the numbers impress because of their smallness. While ABB's global employment figures are enormous, it employs no more people than absolutely necessary. It runs this vast organization with a very small head office (150 without counting business area staff who relocated to Zürich in 1993). It is famous for being allergic to bureaucracy and for the way that it has slashed head office staff using Barnevik's 30 per cent rule. Before he created ABB, he had already reduced ASEA's head office from 2000 people to 150 since 1983. At Strömberg in Finland, which ASEA acquired in 1986, the head office shrank from 880 people to 25 people in 3 years. And in the two years after the merger, the staff of the former BBC HQs in Switzerland and Germany went down from 4000 to 200 and 1600 to 100, respectively.

How can we make sense of what ABB has achieved? The company's success, in one of the most fiercely competitive industries in the world, is all the more remarkable because it has been pioneering a new form of global organization to meet the new challenges. Percy Barnevik has described the paradoxes that ABB has tried to resolve as the simultaneous attempt to be 'global and local, big and small, and radically decentralized with central reporting and control.' In essence, Barnevik and his senior colleagues at ABB have tried to resolve these contradictions by creating what we call a 'globally connected corporation', a loose–tight network of processes, projects and partners that can only be held together by highly committed people and strongly held principles. This is an organization that fosters sharing and collaboration between its operations in different parts of the world, and links closely with clients, suppliers and the countries where it is present. Its combination of 'multidomestic' local presence and coordination by means of a global matrix organization is a unique response to the 'think global, act local' imperative.

Is ABB a model for other organizations? In 1990, business journalists were already pointing to ABB as the organizational archetype of the future. For example:

From headquarters in neutral Zürich, ABB's élite corps of stateless managers shuffle assets around the globe, keep the books in dollars, and conduct most of their business in English. Yet the companies that make up their far-flung fiefdom, tailor ABB's turbines, transformers, robots, and high-speed trains to the local market so successfully that ABB looks like an established player. Barnevik predicts such corporate ingenuity is the blueprint for the future (Kapstein and Reed, 1990).

Indeed, Percy Barnevik does have particular views on this question. In an interview in India, he said:

More and more companies will see the need to develop this multidomestic combination for global coordination. The big American companies used to have a domestic and an international division. You cannot have an international division. In my company, the word does not exist because if you are foreign, you are foreign everywhere. The whole meaning of being domestic or foreign has lost its meaning. When I am sitting here in India, I am not an Indian citizen, but I represent an Indian company just like I represent a Spanish company when I am in Spain. People have difficulty in perceiving that. When I was with the French Prime Minister the other day, I tried telling him that we were a French, English-speaking company. He said 'No, you are not a French company!' I do not want to be preposterous and say that this is the solution for all companies. Each company has to find its own way. And I will honestly say that we have had our setbacks and difficulties too (Skaria, 1995).

Leaders of tomorrow

The leaders of tomorrow are the ones who today think about the next big ideas that will give us growth in the future. Those leaders see the consequences of the second Industrial Revolution that is now taking place in the emerging world with ten times more people involved and moving five times faster than the first Industrial Revolution. They also see the tremendous opportunities of the IT revolution on products, processes and how you organize in a new 'borderless' world. They see the new environmental demands and they adapt their organizations to the new global competitive scene and make them fast and responsive to unforeseen changes.

Percy Barnevik

Eberhard von Koerber, who in his time has served as ABB's country manager for Germany, president of the company's European region, and is now Senior Adviser to the CEO and corporate management, says that other companies can learn from ABB's experience, but that ABB itself can do much to improve its effectiveness:

In a fast-changing world, where regional partnerships are growing, where local customers want local suppliers who can deliver world-class performance, where technology leadership will continue to be a key source of competitive advantage, the high achievers will be those who:

- **build long-term partnerships with their customers** *being present everywhere as a local partner, giving customers their full attention at both the top management level and the operational level;*
- *will be **energetic and fast movers** in response to new regional markets and changing customer needs;*
- *will deliver **world-class expertise** in technology and low-cost supply at identical standards worldwide;*
- *will **have the skills to make it work fast and profitably.***

This has been ABB's approach to business, one that has so far brought us success . . . At the same time, we know that we have a long way to go. There are still huge untapped potentials in the areas of improving customer relations, cycle time reduction, standardization and modularization, concurrent engineering, and global supply. To realize them, we must continue to adopt a culture of continuous learning and change, where ever-higher targets and constant transition are seen as normal and positive, not threatening and negative. We will make it happen only by instilling a creative entrepreneurial attitude in all of our employees who welcome change as a challenge (von Koerber, 1996).

Is ABB a model for nations? Warren Bennis, Professor at the University of Southern California and an expert on leadership, edited a collection of interviews carried out by the *Harvard Business Review* with top executives. This included the 1991 interview that Percy Barnevik gave to the *Harvard Business Review*, on which many researchers and commentators on ABB (including ourselves) have drawn. In his preface, Bennis says:

The ability to align, create, and empower will characterize successful leaders well into the twenty-first century. But there is another theme that surfaces provocatively in some of the interviews . . . , most notably in the remarks of Percy Barnevik of ABB. That is the emergence of federation as the structure uniquely suited to balancing the seemingly incompatible drives toward global cooperation and the putting down of deep local roots. This paradox is evident in world politics, where intense ethnic and national identities coexist with the widespread recognition that new economic and political alliances must be forged outside one's borders. I'm convinced that 'federation' will be the watchword of the 1990s. And I can imagine a time when corporations such as ABB that are simultaneously global and deeply rooted in local cultures serve as models for nations that aspire both to survival in an international economy and to national self-expression (Bennis, 1992).

So, what are the lessons that other organizations and managers facing the challenges of globalization can learn from ABB's experience so far? We think that there are many lessons that are both explicit and implicit throughout this book. However, we asked Percy Barnevik for his views. He says:

I do not believe that you can mechanically copy what another company has done. ABB itself has several variations on its organization and management depending on products and customers. You handle $10 electrical products differently than $1 billion plants. Some businesses are highly local, like service shops and installation, while others are highly global and demand another structure. However, there are some important general principles to learn from and adapt to your own business: the need to be global–local, big–small, and decentralized–central control.

We also asked Percy Barnevik why he thought ABB had become the world's favourite case study. His explanation is that ABB came along at just the moment when both organizations and business schools were looking for new ideas and models for an increasingly globalized world. Certainly the gurus fell in love with ABB very quickly. Tom Peters calls ABB a 'buckyball organization' and says that Percy Barnevik has concocted 'what may be the most novel industrial firm structure since Alfred Sloan built "modern" GM in the 1920s' (*Liberation Management*, Macmillan, 1992). Manfred Kets de Vries, who has described the challenge of managing ABB as 'making a giant dance', goes further and declares that ABB is a new organizational concept, a 'new prototype' that is in line with the needs of the post-industrial age, and which can discharge us from Sloan's model of the 'modern organization' (*European Management Journal*, Vol. 5, 1996). Sumantra Ghoshal and Christopher Bartlett describe ABB as an 'individualized corporation' made up of a portfolio of entrepreneurial, integration and renewal processes. While it may not be a *model* for every other company, they say, it is certainly an *example* of what most companies can achieve (*The Individualized Corporation*, Heinemann, 1998).

While ABB is certainly fascinating from a conceptual standpoint, what is perhaps most striking about it is the sheer pragmatism of its approach. The company often uses striking catchwords to describe its management philosophy (as shown throughout this book). These catchwords are not just theoretical, they have a deep practicality behind them. To the paradoxes that Barnevik famously describes, we would add that ABB is simultaneously complex and simple.

Percy Barnevik cut to the heart of the challenge in a recent interview with the *Financial Times* when he talked about what globalization means to ABB:

Too many people think you can succeed in the long run just by exporting from America or Europe. But you need to establish yourself locally and become, for example, a Chinese, Indonesian or Indian citizen. You don't need to do this straight away but you need to start early because it takes a long time. It can take ten years. Globalization is a long-lasting competitive advantage. If we build a new gas turbine, in 18 months our competitors also have one. But building a global company is not so easy to copy (Financial Times, 8 October 1997).

We were intrigued by the gloss and the immaculate PR image of ABB and wanted to see what is behind it. This book gave us the exciting opportunity to look through the keyhole and talk to some very interesting people around ABB, both in the corporate headquarters and locations in Europe, the Americas and Asia. We have carried out research in ABB before, when researching the competences of international managers (K.A. Barham and S. Wills, *Management Across Frontiers*, Ashridge Management Research Group and the Foundation for Management Education, 1992), but this gave us an opportunity to go back and take a broader view. We were also very curious about the heritage of Percy Barnevik, and how the company is doing now that he has passed on the role of CEO to a successor and divides his attention between various Swedish companies that are part of the Wallenburg sphere. Barnevik has almost come to personify the company and the spotlight has mostly been on him. He has certainly been an excellent spokesman for the company, but we wanted to look behind his image and public statements and find out what other people in the company think, how they experienced the merger and what life is like for them in the organization.

A key figure in ABB today is the new CEO, Göran Lindahl, a tough international sales negotiator and engineer by background – 'deep in the technology' as he describes it. Determined, energetic and impatient to see changes in ABB, he has taken on the major challenge of following Percy Barnevik's brilliant track record. In a seamless transition, the man who has been a vital part of the ABB success story since the days of the merger has quietly taken control of the company and set out to consolidate and renew ABB. What are the concerns that he needs to address? His predecessor says:

> ABB has virtually finished building its global structure. The main task now is to bring more executives from emerging countries in Eastern Europe and in Asia into the higher levels of the company. We have 82,000 employees in emerging economies. We have to bring the best of these to the top. Building a multinational cadre of international managers is the key ... Very rarely would you get a global manager from the outside. Of course, companies such as Shell and IBM have such people, but there are very few available to hire (*Financial Times*, 8 October 1997).

When we talked to Göran Lindahl about the future of the company, he told us that one of his major aims is indeed to 'globalize' the leadership of ABB. When he called us back for an update on the restructuring that he announced in August 1998, this concept became clear. He was not talking about a soft issue relating to the competences of ABB leaders. By fine-tuning the matrix, he has begun a significant shift of power away from the countries towards global interests. Decentralization and self-organization inside the matrix are still key principles. And yet the shift becomes clear in his statement: 'If in doubt, the global interests should prevail'.

In 1996, Financial Times Management approached us to write this book. We had both been working together on international change issues since 1992, and had developed a practical approach to identifying and developing international management competences, based on Kevin's earlier research (K. Barham and C. Heimer, 'Identifying and Developing International Management Competence', in Stuart Crainer (ed.) *Financial Times Handbook of Management*, 1995). The invitation seemed a great opportunity to find out what had really happened in ABB since the merger.

Our objectives in writing this book have been to:

- document the story of the merger, ABB's growth and global expansion;
- catch more than a glimpse of the real story behind the company's ongoing success;
- raise some key questions for the future of ABB;
- highlight some lessons from ABB's experience for managers in other organizations facing international and global challenges.

We have drawn on a wide range of sources, including the many articles that have been written about ABB in the international business press, the analyses of ABB offered by leading business academics and our own interviews with ABB managers. Part of our intention has been to bring together the different perspectives offered by these different observers. We have, for example, concentrated one chapter on the views of some of the leading 'management gurus', such as Tom Peters and Sumantra Ghoshal and Christopher Bartlett. We have also brought in the research of lesser-known academics and writers, such as Professors Staffan Brege, Ove Brandes, Christian Berggren, Rolf Leppänen and Edwin Rühli, who offer valuable insights into ABB, not least because they come from its original home countries. We have also drawn on the corporate history of BBC written by Swiss journalist Werner Catrina that was published just after the company merged with ASEA.

As we wrote this book, we were clear about our bias. We are both generalists who have developed out of specific areas of expertise in international management development and organizational psychology. We have looked at ABB from different angles and, without claiming to have produced the most exhaustive or critical coverage of the company, we have tried to give you, the reader, some rich insights into its story so far. The structure of the book reflects this.

Part I describes the early days of ABB. In the first chapter, we tell the story of the two companies that came together to form ABB – ASEA of Sweden and BBC of Switzerland. We describe how they reached the point of merging to form ABB, from their respective foundations at the end of the nineteenth century.

Chapter 2 moves on to give an account of one of the most dramatic events in recent corporate history: the 1987 merger that created ABB and set a standard that is still to be matched today. We give you an insight into the details of the merger talks, the high emotions involved and the way that Percy Barnevik drove the negotiations to a successful outcome.

What *was* the masterplan behind this incredibly ambitious gambit – the biggest cross-border merger to have happened at that time? Chapter 3 outlines Percy Barnevik's concepts regarding the strategy, structure, control mechanisms and people development of the new company. Barnevik talked about ABB's strategy after the merger in terms of a two-stage rocket – restructuring and then growth.

Part II looks at ABB's global expansion and the company itself through a number of different lenses. In Chapter 4, we recount the way it has sown the seeds of its global 'triad' by building a presence in each of the three 'superregions' of the Americas, Europe and Asia. Like the merger, this restructuring exercise has been characterized by speed and decisiveness. In Chapters 5 and 6, we look at ABB as the 'globally connected corporation' and we set ABB in the context of the global transitions that more and more firms are having to make to compete in a globalized world. As noted above, ABB has inevitably attracted the attention of the world's business scholars and consultants. In Chapter 7, we give an overview of four of the most important analyses of ABB that have been made by leading management gurus.

Part III looks at the organization a decade after the merger to find out how the masterplan has worked out to date and at how ABB has started to reap the harvest resulting from all the hard work it has put into building its structure and implementing its strategy. Chapter 8 looks more closely at why ABB has become the world's favourite case study and why it is an example of that rare organizational breed, a successful cross-border merger. One measure of ABB's success is also the extent to which the creation of ABB led to a fundamental restructuring of the electrotechnical industry. We take a look at the fallout in the rest of the industry and at what happened to those competitors caught in the blast.

Chapter 9 looks at the payback from ABB's strategy of multidomesticity. Chapter 10 asks how ABB's global matrix has worked out so far and describes the changes and refinements that the company has made to the matrix. It also enquires how ABB's strategy and structure have translated into financial performance and considers Percy Barnevik's assertion that 'long-term shareholder value' is the ultimate measurement of corporate performance.

The company has consistently been among the most admired European companies in recent years, but what is it like to work for? What does it mean to be a global manager in ABB and how does it go about developing them? What other tricks has ABB got up its sleeve for the future? Göran Lindahl, who took over from Percy Barnevik as Chief Executive at the beginning of 1997, says that two of the major priorities for ABB in the future are innovation in human resources and information technology, so Chapters 11 and 12 look more closely at what ABB is doing in these areas.

Anyone who has followed the company's development will be asking, 'What will life be like after Barnevik? What are Göran Lindahl's plans? What is his personal style as a manager and leader?' Percy Barnevik has said that every company with global aspirations now needs to be an 'IT company'. What are ABB's plans in this regard? Is it preparing another revolution? Chapter 11 gives some answers to these questions, but we expect to be continually surprised by Percy Barnevik, who has gone on to direct the industrial holdings of one of the world's wealthiest families. In the meantime, we ask how is Göran Lindahl preparing ABB for the next millennium?

We conclude with our summary of how to become a global organization and a memo to Göran Lindahl setting out some thoughts about the future of ABB.

We write this book ten years after the creation of ABB, when the company has fully established itself. The timing coincides with a development cycle the company has followed from the beginning. Percy Barnevik told us about five-year cycles, during which the company is left undisturbed in terms of its formal structure, before a significant review of the organization is undertaken. As we write, ABB is completing its current reorganization, again about five years after the last one. It will be interesting to follow the pattern into the second decade of its existence.

Although we were, of course, interested in the value of ABB's experience to other people, we must qualify the validity of the lessons for anyone who has not gone through the experience themselves. There is a paradox in offering learning to those who have not had the opportunity to experience the kinds of transition described in this book. Are you willing to take on the challenge and discover which insights the book can reveal to you? Find out what it takes to create a global company. Find out what living in a globally connected corporation is like. Find out if the globally connected corporation is really for you.

Kevin Barham
Collonges-sous-Salève, France

Claudia Heimer
Freiburg-im-Breisgau, Germany

EDITOR'S NOTE

There are a number of unreferenced quotes throughout this book which originate from the authors' personal communications with the following interviewees. Please note the titles of the interviewees are as at the date of interview:

Percy Barnevik, Chairman, 13 May 1998, Zürich.

Göran Lindahl, President and CEO, ABB, 7 April 1998 and 31 August 1998, Zürich.

Fred Bystrand, Vice-President, Group Information Systems, ABB, 10 February 1998, Zürich.

Jean-Pierre Dürig, former Corporate Controller, BBC and ABB, 28 January 1998, Zürich.

Eric Elzvik, Vice-President, Corporate Development, ABB, 17 December 1997, Zürich.

Robert Feller, Vice-President, Corporate Management Development, ABB, 23 January 1997, Zürich.

Beat Hess, Senior Vice-President, General Counsel, ABB, 17 December 1997, Zürich.

David Hunter, Group Senior Vice-President, Head of Central and Eastern Europe, ABB, 21 November 1997, Zürich.

Volker Leichsering, Senior Vice-President, Corporate Communications, 17 December 1997, Zürich.

Arne Olsson, Senior Vice-President, Corporate Staff Management Resources, ABB, 20 November 1997, Zürich.

Jan Roxendal, President, ABB Financial Services, 21 November 1997, Zürich.

Bengt Skantze, Senior Vice-President, ABB, 17 November 1997, Zürich.

A.K. Thiagarajan, Managing Director, ABB India and H.K. Mohanty, Vice-President, Corporate Personnel, ABB India, 17 May 1997, New Delhi.

THE BIRTH OF A MODERN GIANT

ASEA and BBC – milestones on the way to Europe's most admired company

As ASEA came up, BBC went down, year after year.
Jean-Pierre Dürig
former Corporate Controller, BBC and ABB.

When the merger of ASEA of Sweden and BBC (Brown Boveri and Company) of Switzerland was announced at simultaneous news conferences in Stockholm and Baden in Switzerland, it came as a total surprise. Business analysts had known that ASEA had been looking for suitable acquisitions for some time, but the sheer scale of the biggest cross-border merger since the Royal Dutch Petroleum Company linked up with Shell Transport and Trading in 1907 caught them totally unawares.

How did the former arch-competitors ASEA and BBC come to merge together to form one of the world's mightiest power engineering groups? What did they each bring to the party? To understand this, we need to go back into the history of each of the companies and understand the nature of the power engineering industry. We need to do this not just because the histories are fascinating, which they certainly are, but to ask ourselves what other managers who are faced with the challenges of globalization can learn from the story. Does such a move, for example, mean giving up your identity? How do you learn to work with colleagues who do things very differently to you? How do you become the acquirer rather than the acquired?

To answer such questions, we need first of all to take you two steps back. We need to understand how two technologically strong and admired corporations rose to leading positions in their industry, but were then almost outpaced by changes in that industry and by the globalization of their business. Ask yourself what you can learn from their evolving global strategies and the processes of corporate transformation that they have endured in order to survive and prosper in a fiercely competitive global market. We also need to look back for another reason. Observers and ABB insiders themselves sometimes describe

ABB as a young company. That is not entirely true. It is, in fact, an old company, the heritage of which continues to strongly influence the way that it approaches its business challenges and from which it derives many of its distinguishing strengths.

ASEA – the history of a Swedish dynamo

Sweden has strong commercial and business roots. These go back at least as far as the Vikings who pioneered trade routes down the Volga and Dnepr rivers to Byzantium, founding the city states of Novgorod and Kiev. Later, Europe's oldest chartered company, Stora (now a forest products company, but originally, as Stora Kopparberg, a mining concern), was established in Sweden under the patronage of the Swedish monarchy in the thirteenth century.

Despite these antecedents, Sweden industrialized late compared with the rest of Europe and the United States. Although it was a slow starter, it entered the scene at a favourable moment when economic development in the rest of Europe had raised international demand and paved the way for Swedish products. These products inherited a legacy of simplicity and practicality derived from the Swedes' need to survive a hard northern climate and exploit what natural resources were available in the form of forests and minerals. Out of this need, grew stolid values of humility and diligence coupled with inventiveness and an entrepreneurial spirit. These, in turn would give rise to an industrial culture based on technical skills and a sense of quality.

When industrialization did start in the late nineteenth century, the country produced an extraordinary range of inventions considering that it had a relatively small population. At the small end of the scale, there has been the zip fastener, safety match and adjustable wrench. Other inventions led to the creation of some of today's major Swedish corporations. Alfred Nobel invented the explosive he called dynamite and his earnings enabled him to create the Nobel Foundation and the Nobel Prize, awarded for important contributions to science and the arts. Lars Magnus Ericsson invented the first table telephone and, in 1878, founded the L. M. Ericsson company, now one of the world's leading telecommunications companies. Gustaf Dalen, a pioneer in the use of gas, founded the Aga Company, a manufacturer of industrial gases. Baltzar von Platen invented the gas-driven refrigerator, which was made and marketed by Electrolux, now a global company and the world's largest manufacturer of domestic appliances. Sven Wingquist perfected the modern ball-bearing and, in 1907, founded SKF, also to become one of Sweden's global giants.

The common factors among these companies – as management researchers Peter Lawrence and Tony Spybey point out – were high added value potential and a strong export orientation (Lawrence and Spybey, 1986). The profits from exports generated the capital that industry needed for growth. Sweden's developing industries could also take advantage of one of its major natural resources – hydroelectric power. The abundance of rivers and waterfalls in the north of the country were to provide cheap electricity, which, in turn, lowered the costs of industrial production and raised international demand for Swedish products. ASEA was to be no exception to the high value-added, strong exportability rule. It would itself make a major contribution to the development of the power industry on which other Swedish manufacturers depended.

As in other industries, the dawning of the electrical age at the end of the nineteenth century produced some important innovators in Sweden. In 1883, Swedish entrepreneur Ludwig Fredholm founded the forerunner of ASEA in Stockholm – Elektriska Aktiebolaget – to manufacture electric dynamos based on the innovative designs of a young engineer called Jonas Wenstrom. The venture proved successful and, in 1890, Fredholm decided to expand the business by merging his company with an electrical firm founded by Wenstrom's brother, Göran. Göran Wenstrom became joint President with Fredholm of the new company, Allmanna Svenska Elektriska Aktiebolaget (Swedish General Electric Company), becoming sole President after Fredholm's death in 1891.[1]

The aim of ASEA – which set up its factory and head office in Västerås, a town 100 km west of Stockholm – was to provide electrical equipment for Swedish industry. As the industrial and domestic use of electricity grew in Sweden, it was to become a pioneer in industrial electrification. Its installation of electricity at a rolling mill for metal-forming in the town of Hofors was said to be the first of its kind in the world, and, in 1893, ASEA built one of Sweden's first power transmission lines. In 1897, ASEA produced Sweden's first electrically powered locomotive.

In 1896, one of Sweden's leading inventors and industrialists, Carl Gustaf de Laval, acquired a 50 per cent interest in ASEA, ousting Wenstrom in a management reorganization. Sad times for ASEA ensued as reputed mismanagement by Laval drove the company into severe financial difficulties – it fell deeply into debt and lost a large part of its market share in Sweden. In 1903, however, the Stockholms Enskilda Bank (predominantly owned by the Wallenbergs, Sweden's famous industrial family) helped to remove control of the company from the hands of Laval. The bank agreed to guarantee the salary of J. Sigfrid Edstrom – the former manager of the Gothenburg Tramways Company who had a reputation for sound management – if he would take charge of restoring the company's fortunes.[2]

Under Edstrom, who remained in charge until the Second World War, the company recovered its financial health and resumed its growth, establishing subsidiaries in Denmark, Great Britain, Russia and Spain during 1910–14. Some of these subsidiaries were set up to avoid trade restrictions, a forerunner of the 'insider' approach to global strategy that ABB would later pursue. It had also been early ASEA policy to buy up its competition whenever possible, and, in the early years of this century, the company had bought up all its main Swedish competitors – another policy that ABB would also apply in its local acquisitions around the world. While Sweden stayed neutral during the First World War, the conflict had a mixed impact on ASEA. A shortage of coal encouraged the further development of electricity, including the firm's first major railway electrification project. However, eventually, ASEA lost most of its European markets.

Edstrom's cautious spending policies enabled the company to weather the post-war recession and put ASEA back on the path to growth and profitability. The rebuilding of war-torn Europe favoured Swedish industry as it had an intact labour force and undamaged production facilities. In the 1920s and 1930s, ASEA provided locomotives and other equipment for Sweden's national railway. In 1932, it built the world's largest self-cooling three-phase power transformer. In 1933, it became one of Sweden's largest electrical equipment manufacturers by buying its rival Elektromekano from Ericsson. In the same year, ASEA bought a large minority stake in Fläkt, a manufacturer of ventilation equipment. A statue in the centre of Västerås shows a group of ASEA workers of the inter-war period walking and cycling to work. It captures the ASEA values of diligence and hard work. It also reflects the importance of ASEA to the town as the main employer of its citizens.

It was during this period, in 1929, that the Wallenberg family – the main owners of the Enskilda Banken, one of Sweden's most important banks – acquired a large stake in the company. The Wallenbergs had been shaping Swedish business since the mid-nineteenth century and had built up control of many of its leading companies. They were to play an important role in the future of ASEA and would be one of the major backers behind the creation of ABB 50 years later.

The Wallenbergs – the power behind Sweden's industrial throne

The Wallenberg influence goes back to 1856 when a former Swedish naval officer, André Oscar Wallenberg, founded the Stockholms Enskilda Banken (later merged into the Skandinaviska Enskilda Banken, the biggest bank in the Nordic region). Over the years, and particularly between the two world wars, the family had built up a 'sphere' of leading Swedish companies. André Oscar's grandsons, Marcus and Jacob, bought into ASEA in 1929. They rescued Ericsson from financial difficulties and, in 1932, averted a national economic crisis by saving Swedish Match after the financial collapse of the match empire of entrepreneur Ivar Kreuger (who controlled three quarters of the world's match industry). Marcus Wallenberg became a business legend and went on to found Scandinavian Airlines System (SAS) and build up substantial holdings in blue-chip firms such as Astra (pharmaceuticals), Atlas-Copco (air compressors), Electrolux (domestic appliances), Saab-Scania (automobiles and aerospace), SKF (bearings) and Stora Kopparberg (forest products). In addition to their banking and industrial holdings, the Wallenbergs also developed interests in hotels, television, newspapers and trading. Their portfolio eventually accounted for more than 40 per cent of the Stockholm stock market's total capitalization. 'Imagine', said one observer, 'that IBM, General Motors, General Electric, Ford, Exxon, Amoco, Philip Morris and Citicorp were all controlled by the same American family. This mythically powerful clan would still not wield as much clout as the Wallenberg family has enjoyed in Sweden for decades (*The Economist*, 23 June 1990).

Part of that power derived from the varied sharholding system, developed by Marcus Wallenberg, that prevented Swedish companies from falling into foreign hands. The Wallenbergs were able to keep their industrial empire intact by means of their ability to create different classes of shares with weighted (that is, unequal) voting rights and curbs on ownership of Swedish firms. This limited their vulnerability to takeovers (although it often meant that otherwise-admired Swedish companies were relatively lowly rated on stock markets abroad). Under Swedish law, foreign investors had to get government approval to hold more than 10 per cent of a Swedish company's shares. Swedish firms were also able to keep restricted A shares for themselves, while giving B shares, with lesser voting rights, to foreigners. Thus, for example, the Wallenbergs were able to control Electrolux with 16 per cent of the equity as it translated into 95 per cent control. In Ericsson, 4 per cent of the equity gave the Wallenbergs 40 per cent of the votes. Protection was also provided by the system of cross-shareholdings as Wallenberg companies owned shares in each other, such as the holding that ASEA held in Electrolux.

The Wallenberg sphere was not totally invulnerable as it was often held together with only small minority shareholdings. However, Marcus Wallenberg was able to rule by virtue of the sheer weight of his personality. The sphere was both an advantage and disadvantage for the firms it controlled. On the one hand, it made it possible for managements to concentrate on investment and growth, rather than worry about hostile takeover bids. On the other hand, it removed the market as the judge of economic efficiency and could lead to a resistance to change.

None the less, the group of multinational companies that the Wallenbergs controlled helped to transform Sweden into an industrial power and generated much of the wealth that built its famous welfare state after the Second World War. They became the main economic pillar of modern Sweden and can take credit for Sweden's status as a country that is home to more multinational companies proportionally than any other. Through their companies' investments outside Sweden, they also exercised considerable power abroad.

In the 1990s, a spate of deregulation in Sweden opened up its protected stock market to foreign investment. Wallenberg sphere firms such as Astra and Ericsson became key targets for foreign buyers of Swedish stocks. Weighted voting rights in many cases ensured the continuance of Wallenberg control, although the situation was more volatile. In 1994, the Wallenberg position was strengthened when it gained effective control of auto manufacturer Volvo, Sweden's biggest foreign investor and exporter, after a shareholder and management revolt against the company's plans to merge with Renault of France.

If many of the firms in their sphere did not have to worry too much about takeovers, it placed great responsibility on the Wallenbergs as the ultimate arbiters of economic efficiency for those companies. The family's historical ties with some of its companies sometimes made it difficult to take corrective action and the family has admitted that it has sometimes been too patient when the performance of some firms fell behind. On the other hand, one of their main strengths was their ability to choose skilled managers who, in turn, benefited from working for dedicated owners who understood international markets and invested for the long term. On the whole, the Wallenbergs saw themselves as 'hands off'-type owners, although they admitted this did not exclude 'moments of hands on'. They preferred to select strong managers with a low profile, 'with a bit of dirt under their nails, as opposed to banking types' (*Financial Times*, 21 November 1988). Percy Barnevik – the man they picked to wake up ASEA – certainly fitted this bill.

References

Financial Times (1988) 'Sweden: the FT talks to Peter Wallenberg, head of Sweden's leading industrial dynasty', summary of original article dated 21 November, 52.
The Economist (1990) 23 June.

Although Sweden remained neutral again during the Second World War, the Swedish economy was badly affected and, once more, ASEA's operations in Europe were curtailed. After the war, however, fast-growing domestic demand for power stimulated the company's revival, despite initial shortages of materials and industrial relations problems.

In 1947, ASEA broke into the American market, signing a licensing agreement with the Ohio Brass Company for the local production of electrical surge arrestors. In 1954, it received substantial orders for equipment for the huge Aswan Dam project in Egypt. Also in the 1950s, the company produced the world's first synthetic industrial diamonds and supplied the first permanent high-voltage, direct current transmission, linking the island of Gotland with the Swedish mainland.

In 1961, Curt Nicolin became ASEA's new president (he was later honorary chairman of ABB). He reorganized the company and formed an electronics division, starting the transition of ASEA from a heavy electrical equipment manufacturer to a high-tech electronics company. The US market became increasingly important, with ASEA supplying equipment for the Tennessee Valley Authority and a major power project on the West Coast. Also in the

1960s, ASEA built Sweden's first nuclear power station, although a national referendum in 1980 later voted to phase out nuclear power programmes over a period of 25 years. In 1973, the company produced the world's first high-performance, microcomputer-controlled industrial robot.

In the 1970s, ASEA's overseas expansion took it into the complicated world of international alliances when it joined some of its competitors in the nuclear field to develop an improved nuclear boiling water reactor. The collaborators – including GE, Toshiba, Hitachi, and KWU (Siemens) – shared their upstream R&D on a global basis, but kept downstream construction and local customer relationships to themselves. ASEA thereby had early experience of a type of collaboration that the globalization of business has made more and more common – that is, companies that may be competing fiercely in certain products or markets joining forces in other areas. ASEA's rival GE summed it up thus: 'We are very much the type of company where companies around the world might be our competitor in the morning, our customer at lunch, and our joint venture partner in the afternoon' (Barham and Devine, 1991).

By 1980, ASEA was well-respected as one of the world's ten largest electrical engineering companies, with 40,000 employees, 30,000 of them in Sweden. Its technical ability was recognized as being world class and it was a leader in modern manufacturing planning and control systems, but its markets were by now suffering from excess capacity and weakened demand. While the world consumption of electricity had been growing at 7 per cent a year up to 1973–74, after that date growth had fallen to 4 per cent a year. Like many other utility and power companies, ASEA's growth and profitability had declined. Although the company had long operated internationally and about 50 per cent of turnover was exported, it was still highly dependent on the low-demand, high-cost Swedish and other Nordic domestic markets. Its international expansion was also constrained by increasing protectionism that had inhibited the growth of world imports into industrialized countries.

Although ASEA was technically very competent, it was let down by poor integration and cooperation between its different functional departments and between head office and the international operations. It was described as 'centralized, authoritarian and bureaucratic' (Brege and Brandes, 1993). Although it had advanced accounting systems, only a few people were able to interpret the information they provided. The culture was technocratic and emphasized technical development, contracting and production at the expense of market orientation. Managers were selected on the basis of their technological competence rather than their business acumen. ASEA also took a patriarchal approach to its employees and had not laid people off since the 1930s, even maintaining this policy during the difficult late 1970s. The company did have some product areas that were growing and profitable, but the time had come for change.

It was clear to Marcus Wallenberg, a major shareholder and the honorary chairman, that conditions now demanded a strong new leadership with a very different way of thinking, both strategically and organizationally, who could transform this large, slow-moving organization. The way in which Wallenberg now interceded, against top management opposition, to appoint a new, radically different chief executive, is indicative of the influence the Wallenbergs wielded over Swedish business.

Percy Barnevik – on the way to global mastery

Marcus Wallenberg's choice of Percy Barnevik as the new CEO of ASEA was both surprising and unorthodox. At that time a vice-president at Sandvik, a Swedish specialized steel and tool company, the 39-year-old Barnevik was virtually unknown in Swedish business, partly because he was managing the Sandvik operations in the US from 1975–79. Those who *were* acquainted with him knew, however, that he had a strong analytical capacity and rare ability to cut to the essence of a problem, an unusual capacity for hard work and a demanding approach to his fellow managers. The German business magazine *Bilanz* once called Barnevik 'Ritter Percyfal' – an allusion to Parsifal, the knight who set out on the quest for the Holy Grail. There is certainly something of the missionary about Barnevik.

Percy Barnevik was born in 1941 and brought up in Uddevalla, a town on Sweden's rocky, inlet-carved western coast, 70 kilometres north of Göteborg (Gothenburg). Manfred Kets de Vries and Raoul de Vitry d'Avaucourt of the international business school INSEAD, who have carried out some of the most extensive research into the development of Barnevik's leadership style, describe how his early upbringing shaped his values. This impressed on him a Lutheran work ethic and he learned the virtues of a lean management style, working long hours with his parents and brother and sister to help out in his father's small family company, a printing shop employing 10–15 people. Barnevik's belief in human-sized small units that achieve high performance as a result of individuals taking more responsibility stems from this early experience. Barnevik says that the firm was 'small enough for everyone to know who had a hangover, who was getting married, what job was urgent that day' (Caulkin, 1998). His parents valued thrift and disapproved of waste and inefficiency. Early on, he learned the value of commitment, speed, meeting deadlines and customer service. He has drawn on these lessons to inform his perfectionist approach to business ever since. Barnevik saw how employees pitched in and worked on weekends when necessary.

> The workers understood that, if they didn't come in on a Monday morning, there was going to be trouble. They were really needed. Standing at the printing press, they knew it if a customer got a bad product. So you got a sense of engagement and responsibility in every employee. You won't get the same sense of responsibility in a workshop with a few thousand people. The whole process becomes anonymous, The person becomes a small component in a huge piece of machinery (Kets de Vries, 1994).

Barnevik says that this early experience has made him obsessed with decentralization throughout his career.

Seeing that work environment where everyone had to pitch in, gave me a feeling of the importance of small teams. When I was 10–15 years old, I grew up with my father wishing that I would look after it. He was sort of disappointed that I went in for another career (Skaria, 1995).

Many of the traits that Barnevik later demonstrated as a top manager were evident in his younger years. At school, he was known for his desire to be the best in his class, an intolerance of timewasting and a concern to be well-prepared in advance with his classwork. When, like all young men in Sweden, he had to complete 15 months of military service after school, his doggedness in achieving objectives led him to be made platoon commander. At the age of 19, he was admitted to the exclusive Gothenburg School of Economics. He tackled his studies there with the same energy, determination and perfectionism.

On completing his university course, he enrolled for a Licentiate in Philosophy – a degree that might have taken him into an academic career. While undertaking a compulsory internship at Mölnlycke – the Swedish pulp and paper company – however, his work so impressed a group of American consultants from the Stanford Research Institute that he was offered a scholarship at Stanford Business School in 1965–66, where he specialized in business administration and computer science. Barnevik's studies in operations research at Stanford gave him an appreciation for systems analysis. Looking at organizations as systems meant understanding their components and their relation to one another and identifying ways to optimize their potential for a given set of environmental conditions (Leppänen, 1994). His studies at Stanford convinced him that he did not want an academic career and he gave up his Licentiate studies to join a fast-growing, new consulting company, Datema.

During his three years at Datema, he built an extensive network of contacts and assumed more and more responsibility until he was asked to manage systems development for the Axel Johnson Group, a Swedish conglomerate, thereby effectively becoming a member of the company's senior management team. Once again, Barnevik was noted for his perfectionism, long working hours and ability to assimilate large amounts of information. This facility for absorbing data supported him in his arguments with colleagues and clients, and enabled him to work at a very fast pace.

In 1969, Barnevik was consulted by Sandvik, a Swedish tool and specialized steel company, which was having problems with its information systems. When Barnevik very quickly produced major recommendations to solve the problems, Sandvik offered him a full-time job so that he could implement his ideas. He accepted on the condition that they allowed him freedom to select his own team. Sandvik gave Barnevik his first major experience of managing organizational change and a further opportunity to develop his skills at analyzing problems, devising solutions and convincing people of the necessity for change. His role was to develop new information systems and rationalize the administrative functions, but he soon expanded it into troubleshooting and restructuring Sandvik companies around the world. This expanded role was officially acknowledged when he was made group controller in 1973. Barnevik's experience at Sandvik gave him, in particular, a deep appreciation of the control function in an international company – something he would later apply at ASEA and ABB.

In 1975, Barnevik was made CEO of Sandvik's US subsidiary, which had been having trouble breaking into the big US market. Barnevik, determined to turn the company round, achieved his aim. He tripled sales to $250 million in 4 years and took market share from tough US competitors such as US Steel and General Electric. He introduced a matrix organization and also applied his ideas on decentralization by establishing a rule that no workshop should be bigger than 250 people. His ten years at Sandvik gave Barnevik a strong appreciation for results and a sense of action. The US experience also taught him the importance of being able to operate in a large, open market that was not hemmed in by artificial boundaries. Barnevik said of his US experience:

The impulses that I got at Stanford, then the five years with Sandvik in America, were extremely educational. I felt those huge, unlimited opportunities to penetrate the country, coming out of this chopped-up European continent. The possibility to be able to build distribution in such a huge market was extremely stimulating (Klebnikov 1991).

Sandvik remained strong in Barnevik's affections and he would later become the company's chairman while CEO of ABB (he still is chairman of this $5 billion company).

One of the major skills that Barnevik developed in these years was his ability to synthesize and build on the ideas of those working with him. Arne Olsson, now in charge of management development at ABB, describes his approach as that of a 'hub in a wheel':

When Percy starts something, he asks people to give him some ideas or write a paper. He works like a hub in a wheel. He has a number of spokes and works with and via those spokes. He sends signals out through the spokes and gets information back and uses different spokes as appropriate. Being in the middle of this wheel, he gets a fantastic view. With his computer-like skills, he then processes all this information and out comes something very good.

In 1979, Barnevik returned to Sweden to take charge of finance and administration for the Sandvik group with the possibility of becoming CEO in a few years' time. However, his performance in the US had caught the attention of Marcus Wallenberg. Within a year, Barnevik was offered the job of CEO at ASEA.

References

Caulkin, Simon (1998) 'Swede dreams of going truly global', *The Observer*, 22 March, 2.

Kets de Vries, Manfred (1994) 'Making a giant dance', *Across the Board*, **31**(9), 27–32.

Klebnikov, Paul (1991) 'The powerhouse', *Forbes*, 2 September, 46–50.

Leppänen, Rolf (1994) *ABB Action Recipe: Strategic Management in the Growth and Restructuring of a European Enterprise*. Helsinki: International Networking Publishing INP Oy.

Skaria, George (1995) 'Interview with Percy Barnevik', *Business Today* (India), 22 February–6 March, 100–5.

The turnaround at ASEA

The prospects were not clear when Percy Barnevik, the new chief executive chosen by Marcus Wallenberg, took up the reins at ASEA. The appointment of an external graduate economist to run a highly technology-oriented corporation met with a lot of surprise and scepticism within the company. Some thought that his experience in the US might have tainted him with American short-termism. Although he might know about marketing, could he appreciate what it took to achieve engineering excellence? Would he respect research?

Barnevik realized that he would have to move quickly. The challenges were to change the complacent attitude of the workforce, create a lean and efficient company that could survive in a highly competitive global market and reposition the company to take advantage of the expected upturn in the heavy electrical engineering industry. The organization needed a fundamental shake-up to shock it into action. A long drawn-out change would only create too much uncertainty and prevent the company refocusing quickly. Barnevik only accepted the job of CEO after having first obtained the Board of directors' promise to give him total support for the radical changes he believed were required. One thing in his favour was the poor economic situation as this meant that the climate in the company was more open to change than in the past.

As it turned out, Barnevik's turnaround of ASEA was, in many ways, a test-run for the corporate transformation that he would later achieve on a global basis for ABB. In the next eight years, he was to hone his approach to building a lean and keen organization that could compete with the best internationally. Some clear principles in Barnevik's approach were already apparent.

Refocus on the customer

The first thing that Barnevik did was apply one of his earliest lessons about the central importance of the client. He says, 'I remember coming to inspect ASEA for the first time in 1979 and seeing that huge glass and plastic building with 4000 engineers, each in their room, and I wondered whether they ever saw a customer' (Kets de Vries, 1994). A first step, therefore, was to reorganize the company so that people would focus more closely on customer needs. He did this by splitting the central plant engineering sector into new product divisions where, for the first time, production and contracting were brought together with marketing people under one division manager for each product. Eventually, the divisions were made into legally independent companies with separate profit and loss statements and balance sheets. As one manager described the process of creating ASEA's drives business (later ABB drives), 'We took the motors and the converters from two different organizations and put them together because that was what the customer needed; it was a customer-oriented organization.' From the perspective of the late 1990s, Barnevik's drive for a greater customer orientation may seem an obvious strategy. Nearly 20 years ago, however, many organizations were far from understanding the customer imperative. Barnevik was ahead of the game. He also understood that merely urging people to pay greater attention to customers would not produce the required change in thinking and acting – a structural solution was needed.

Restructure into profit centres to create profit awareness and accountability

For the first time, too, the company was to operate with profit centres that would have virtually total responsibility for their performance. As Barnevik saw it, the 40 new profit centres that he created made it easier to formulate and follow up objectives, increased the delegation of authority and responsibility, enabled functions such as R&D and production to be better coordinated with marketing and gave people a better overview and team spirit. Separate profit centres made performance more visible and management feel more directly responsible for results. An important longer-term result of decentralization to profit centres was that it provided a training ground for a new generation of Swedish general managers who would later assume leading roles in ABB.

Reduce excess capacity and bureaucracy – apply the 30 per cent rule

Some other first steps were painful as they involved cutting the number of jobs. Excess production capacity in Sweden had to be reduced so Barnevik set about closing unprofitable plants and weeding out unprofitable products. On one occasion, this resulted in a mass lobbying of the Swedish parliament when he effectively closed down a town by shutting a loss-making steel plant. Believing that bureaucracy creates waste and that what was needed were self-contained business units situated as close as possible to the end customer, he also took the pruning knife to ASEA's head office. In a drastic reduction, he cut the numbers of headquarters staff from 2000 people to 200 by applying what he called the '30 per cent rule'. Thus, 30 per cent of head office staff were spun off into separate and independent profit centres, 30 per cent were transferred to the operational companies as part of their overhead, and another 30 per cent of head office jobs were eliminated. The result of this was that just 10 per cent remained to staff the corporate centre.

Barnevik later reflected on the difficult decisions he had to make during this period, including one of the steel plants that he had closed in Sweden:

That was tough. People crying and some of them had to sell their houses; it was a hopeless situation. But there was no way we could rescue that steel plant. You can't shrug it off. You have to take it like a chess move. But toughness per se is not what

I stand for. You have to be decisive and be ready to swallow the criticism and hul-labaloo that may surround unpopular or difficult decisions. However, if you lack empathy for people affected, you are not suitable to handle a close-down of a plant (Skaria, 1995).

Emphasize the need for commercial hard-headedness

Barnevik also changed the principle of employment security regardless of the economic situation. The traditional desire to maintain production volume to protect employment had led to a number of unprofitable and marginally priced business deals. Barnevik stopped such deals, reviewed the pricing system and renegotiated unprofitable contracts. The resulting media attention helped to bolster his position in the company, where he was still regarded with suspicion by some managers.

Identify and activate idle or hidden assets to provide bridge financing

Barnevik the economist could not stand waste or idle resources. In addition to the closure of unwanted factories and product lines, he set about tightening up ASEA's financial management. He concentrated on using working capital much more efficiently by, for example, cutting inventories and putting strong pressure on debtors. A senior manager at ASEA's UK business recalled how he had previously thought it a tightly run operation – that is, until the visit of ASEA's vice-president for finance who, within one week, had found half a million pounds lying dormant in the business. Corporate turnarounds are resource-demanding ventures and activating unused assets provides vital finance to bridge the gap until recovery is really under way.

Reorientate to a 'multidomestic' international strategy

ASEA's 'once-and-for-all contraction' boosted its earnings five times in 1980–83 but Barnevik knew the company had to make new investments to secure its future. At the same time that he applied short-term surgery and tightened financial disciplines, he therefore presented a long-term vision and strategy for what he called 'The new ASEA'. The underlying argument was that the increasing costs of maintaining a leading position in R & D demanded growth in volumes and profitability. This, in turn, required the company to strengthen its position in selected international markets. Barnevik's vision was to move the company from an export orientation to being a multinational company with strong marketing and production operations abroad, including North America. This initially involved building up local sales organizations and, as one manager described it, 'moving our knowledge from Västerås to various parts of the world.' The challenge was to 'train and educate the salespeople so that they were talking about customer demands and the customer language – not about motors and converters themselves, but about where they are used.' The next step was to establish local production facilities, perhaps sending a Swedish manager to set up a joint venture with a local company. The company's 'multi-domestic' approach to overseas markets was to be summed up in the slogan 'To be an insider, not an invader'. This meant that, to compete in large, government-protected markets, ASEA required an acquisition strategy of buying established local companies rather than pursuing organic growth, which would not give 'insider' status and would also take longer to implement. This would also avoid adding more capacity in an industry where there was already overcapacity.

Dominate carefully selected international niche markets

Barnevik also introduced a number of strategic principles – the promotion of 'spearhead technologies', rather than offering the complete range of heavy electrical engineering products, and the dominance of carefully selected international niche markets. Like the early Swedish entrepreneurs, he steered the company into faster growing higher value-added products such as transportation equipment and financial services. He also built on ASEA's electronics capability to move more strongly into high-tech products, such as robots.

Balance control and planning with speed and action

The new management called for more attention to be given to financial control and strategic planning. This partly depended on the timely provision of information that people could understand and use. Barnevik put in place improved systems for gathering data about markets, sales and profitability and transmitting it fast to the decentralized managers who needed it. Formal strategic planning was to be an important means of communication between the top management team and division managers and of giving the strategic initiative to the divisions. Barnevik hand-picked a central group of 'highly analytical' ASEA managers, drawn from various functional areas and recognized within the company for their competence, to act as his personal consultants and catalysts. Known as 'Percy's boys' (although one of them was a woman), the job of the 'President's Investigation Group' was to assist the CEO in analyzing the issues confronting the company. They were also to provide economic and strategic support to the divisional managers and eliminate time-consuming investigations and overly detailed reports in the interests of speedy action and results. 'Better quick and approximate than slow and precise', said Barnevik.

Reorganize around an international matrix

A second reorganization in 1981 introduced an international matrix structure. Barnevik had learned about the matrix organization when he was studying at Stanford and had introduced it at Sandvik. His experience convinced him that it was the most appropriate way to coordinate ASEA's international operations. There was already some support for this type of organization. Professors Staffan Brege and Ove Brandes from the Linköping Institute of Technology in Sweden, who in the early 1990s studied what they called the 'successful double turnaround of ASEA and ABB', suggested that Barnevik made use of the 'Bennborn effect' (Brege and Brandes, 1993). His prompt action in starting the turnaround process would not have been possible, they say, without the contribution of ideas from a small number of managers who sympathized with his ideas. Arne Bennborn, an ASEA vice-president, had presented ideas for a matrix to ASEA's top managers seven years before, but they had not supported it.

Under the new matrix, ASEA's operating divisions were overlaid by country managers and product managers in the subsidiaries abroad now reported both to product division managers and to the country managers (see Figure 1.1). This tied the subsidiaries abroad closer to the parent company divisions and gave the divisional managers responsibility for allocating production resources among the international network of production units. It also projected the company as local wherever it operated. The matrix, by its nature, created tensions between managers and was to make considerable demands on them. Division managers had to change from being mainly functionally based specialist managers to being general managers with profit responsibility. The managers of the foreign subsidiaries had to coordinate their operations with the division managers. Also, although the structure had been formally decentralized, the matrix kept the centre involved in decision making as the top management team had to intervene to hold the organization together. The matrix brought other demands. One issue that would continue to cause problems was the need for internal price negotiations between the divisions.

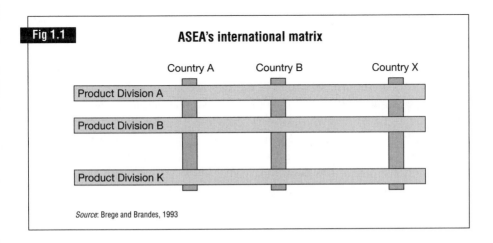

Fig 1.1   **ASEA's international matrix**

Country A   Country B   Country X

Product Division A

Product Division B

Product Division K

Source: Brege and Brandes, 1993

Upgrade management skills and change the mindset

These new challenges meant that more attention had to be given to management training and development to 'upgrade' the managers in the subsidiaries and ensure that the profit centres had managers with the required new market-oriented skills and mindset. Barnevik also brought in some new managerial blood from outside, although the new people sometimes had problems in integrating into the organization.

Confront the doubters – communicate the need for change intensively

In the early days, when the progress of Barnevik's overhaul was uneven, both managers and unions wrote to the Board condemning the restructuring and the short-term profit orientation. Some called for his dismissal. Barnevik countered with intensive and continuing communication. He took care to communicate what he was doing and why to as many people as possible, including trade union leaders and politicians. This contrasted with the style of the company's previous top management, which had regarded such people as threats rather than stakeholders. Barnevik learned, in particular, that early, open contact with the unions was vital to the success of the change process. He also understood the value of skillful public relations in creating international goodwill. In 1983, he took advantage of ASEA's centenary celebrations to bring thousands of guests from abroad to Västerås to see the company and its exciting new products, such as the robots. And he kept up a relentless pace of travel to take the message around the organization, keeping a suitcase permanently stationed inside his office door.

Keep up the pressure

'I am just a consultant', Barnevik told *Fortune* magazine in 1985 (Tully, 1985), although his managers knew there was another side to the story. Barnevik was ready with advice, but he also kept the pressure on by setting them tough financial targets. Divisional heads were expected to achieve an average annual return on capital of 25 per cent over 5 years. As one ASEA manager said, 'Now you think twice about taking a bad order or hiring an extra person' (Tully, 1985). Barnevik was also said to have banned the words 'I think' at meetings. 'Either you know or you don't', he demanded. He certainly demonstrated typical strength of determination throughout the change process. Bengt Skantze, who had worked with Barnevik at both Johnson and Sandvik and was to become ASEA's head of corporate development, says that Barnevik had implemented many of the basic ideas at Sandvik. 'There was a tremendous resistance to this non-technician coming in. It gave Percy strength because he knew it could work.'

The Vikings are coming – ASEA expands internationally

With the restructuring and reduction of excess capacity of mature businesses, ASEA's performance started to improve. By the mid 1980s, its international strategy of dominance and market leadership in niches also began to pay off – assisted, it is true, by two devaluations of the Swedish krona, which increased the competitiveness of its products. The first priority had been to become a Nordic group. Having expanded in neighbouring countries to make the whole Nordic region a home market, Barnevik had then set his sights on markets further afield. Sales increased in Western Europe, Japan and other rapidly developing countries in Asia, although the biggest gains were in the USA where ASEA invested heavily in local production.

The Japanese had identified the new ASEA as being a threat early on. Japanese robotics companies Matsushita and Fanuc tried to underprice ASEA's still young robotics division, but Barnevik counter-attacked with a robot sales drive of his own in Japan. He made plant managers cut costs by 10 per cent a year and halve the time it took to bring out new robots. ASEA became Europe's leading robot producer by the mid 1980s and would eventually lead the world market.

Barnevik also continued ASEA's involvement in international alliances where firms that are competing in one market or product sometimes find themselves collaborating in other areas. For example, while ASEA's robot division competed head-to-head for first place worldwide with GMF – a joint venture between General Motors and Fanuc – ASEA also cooperated with General Motor's Electro-Motive division to design a high-speed railway locomotive for Amtrak, the US passenger train system. In the late 1970s, it had beaten GE to supply locomotives for the Metroliner between New York and Washington. As Barnevik later described it, 'That win caused quite a stir. It was the first time in 100 years that an American railroad bought locomotives from outside the United States. We won because we could run that track from Washington to New York, crooked and bad as it was, at 125 miles an hour' (Taylor, 1991). Barnevik may have instilled a greater marketing orientation in his managers, but he still depended on their engineering excellence. All told, Barnevik's international moves attracted growing attention from the international business press. 'ASEA is attacking foreign markets like a flotilla of Vikings', said *Fortune* magazine in 1985, calling Barnevik a 'goateed go-getter' (Tully, 1985).

Barnevik's reputation was now growing abroad and he was becoming a sought-after speaker at international business conferences. At the 1984 annual conference of the European Foundation for Management Development, for example, he described the restructuring and international expansion of ASEA. He told the delegates about the way in which he was trying to create a preparedness for change among employees by giving line managers the tools to analyze their own situations, making them learn about the competition and relate to it in a way that they had not done before and meeting 'prejudiced views'. He also talked about his aim of achieving 'critical mass' – the need to make high investments of time and resources to achieve the high earnings that, in turn, make high investments possible. ASEA's strategy for market development was to invest to develop, or to retain and expand its position, in highly attractive markets where it was above critical mass, or where critical mass was within reach. In markets that were less attractive and where the company's position was below critical mass, it would 'act opportunely'. How to achieve critical mass on a global basis was to be a central concern for Barnevik and his top management colleagues over the next three years.

By 1987, ASEA's turnover quadrupled, its earnings increased 8 times and its market capitalization multiplied 20 times, or 2.5 times the stock exchange index during this 8-year period. It had established leading positions in power transmission, especially high-voltage DC transmission (originally an ASEA invention), railway electrification and the electrification and automation of industry. Barnevik had done 'an extraordinary job in turning ASEA from a dull Scandinavian electrical power company into a nimble international player', as one commentator described it (Hindle, 1989). He had stilled his internal critics and was now famous in Scandinavia as a 'master of restructuring', emerging as 'one of the leading management talents of his generation' (*Financial Times*, 1987).

Inevitably, Barnevik's dynamism did not endear him to everybody. A Swedish executive who had known Barnevik for years summed him up as follows: 'He comes from the west of Sweden, where the work ethic is a kind of religion. He is not very social. He has this beard. He's too aggressive and ambitious. There is his American training and his time with the steel company in the US. He is different from most Swedes' (Klebnikov, 1991).

Different or not, the unknown Sandvik manager of 1980 had established himself among the élite in the Wallenberg sphere and, in 1987, he was appointed to the Board of Providentia, one of the two investment companies through which the Wallenbergs then controlled their financial empire. It was a mark that he had been accepted into the inner circle of not only Sweden's most powerful industrial grouping, but also one of the most important conglomerations of industrial power in the world.

The future still held many challenges and uncertainties, however. Bengt Skantze, who was ASEA's head of corporate development at that time, says:

You have to understand the background. The business environment in this industry was extremely tough. The power engineering industry was like the steel industry – no growth, crowded with competitors, extreme overcapacity, and very protected. Countries considered it a strategic industry which had to be protected and you could not export into European countries. Everything was exported to developing countries and everybody was fighting over their parts of the business. There were discussions about whether it was good or bad to be in the power industry. Percy himself talked with a smile about one of his 'road shows' to the US to talk to investors about the company and its activities and how they came up afterwards and said they liked the fact that ASEA was in robotics, but this was only 1 per cent of our business! The fact that our main business was with the utilities was bad news. We had to grow ASEA somehow.

ASEA had greatly improved its position compared with its competitors, but it too could yet succumb to industry difficulties. Demand in the power engineering sector was still weak and many markets remained closed to imports. Barnevik realized that 'the handwriting was on the wall. The European electrical industry was crowded with 20 national competitors. There was up to 50 per cent overcapacity, high costs, and little cross-border trade. Half the companies were losing money' (*Harvard Business Review*, 1991). He had transformed ASEA, but it had become clear that, to continue to grow, the company needed to take some big international steps. ASEA was still atypical for large Swedish firms, most of which had 80–95 per cent of sales outside Sweden. ASEA had in 1980 only 50 per cent of sales outside Sweden although this increased to 70 per cent in 1987. Furthermore, it was operating in a saturated market. It was very profitable, but it had to go for growth.

As margins thinned, the need to achieve efficiencies via large-scale operations was becoming increasingly important. Barnevik saw that a major shake-out was impending in the electrical engineering industry and that only those companies with sufficient size and presence – the all-important critical mass – would survive to take advantage of the upturn he expected in the market. ASEA needed to expand dramatically and internationally, but where could he find the acquisitions that he needed?

As early as 1981, ASEA attempted to acquire a major part of the ailing German company AEG but this was blocked by the Germans and ASEA still had internal problems to solve. When Barnevik tried to strengthen ASEA's position in the USA by buying businesses from competitor General Electric, GE's CEO Jack Welch set a price that was too high. ASEA eventually decided to become a large Nordic company first by reaching out from Sweden to the other Nordic countries, then to Europe and, ultimately, to the whole world.

The purchase and turnaround of the Finnish company Strömberg and the Norwegian company Elektrisk Bureau in 1986–87 fulfilled ASEA's Nordic strategy. The acquisition of Strömberg was a particularly significant move as it set the example for the way in which ABB would later persuade other proud national companies to adopt a new mission as a partner in the new group. Bengt Skantze, who was in charge of the acquisition, says:

ASEA had tried unsuccessfully to acquire Strömberg before in the 1960s. It had reached an agreement but Strömberg's engineers threatened to leave. When we tried to do it again in the mid 80s, it was therefore a very sensitive thing and it was very important to do it right. Percy invested a lot of time to talk to all the important people including politicians. We went out of our way to make them feel an equal partner. This included moving products from Sweden to Finland – which upset the Swedes and there were some high noise-level discussions!

Strömberg had a very large range of products, but operated out of a restricted home market. ASEA (and soon ABB) persuaded it to shift its sights to become ABB's worldwide centre of excellence for a key group of products – electrical drives. Barnevik says, 'Strömberg could not be a broad-based electrical engineering company working out of Finland for the whole world. We had to convince them that the merger was necessary for the change in Europe, and then give them a new mission – to provide the world's biggest, most profitable, most successful technology in a particular field. Better to be the king of AC drives than be a peasant in generators and transformers' (Kennedy, 1992).

Barnevik's vision at this time was also influenced by the announced intention of the then 12 member states of the EU to create a European single market at the beginning of 1993. Europe was littered with numerous subscale manufacturers. Across a range of industries, there was growing awareness of the need to restructure to become competitive in world markets. Barnevik was one of a number of top managers who realized that European industry needed to achieve European domestic scale, if it was to compete with US and Japanese companies. A number of new international deals, including the purchase by France's CGE of ITT's European business and Volkswagen's acquisition of a 75 per cent stake in SEAT of Spain, were giving a new impetus to cross-border mergers and acquisitions. In ASEA's own industry, changes in public procurement regulations, an integral part of the single market programme, would mean a substantial drop in the price of turbines and railway locomotives. Sweden itself was increasingly worried about being locked out of the EU and set up a governmental working party to explore how the country should respond. For Barnevik, the portents were clear. When ASEA's attempted deal with GE fell through, he decided to approach another competitor – the Swiss company BBC Brown Boveri – with an offer that, in hindsight, they could not refuse.

This time Barnevik was not thinking about acquiring and integrating a smaller company – a process at which he was now a past master. He was going for a much bigger challenge – nothing less than a full-blooded merger of his own company, a Swedish national institution, with another huge organization that was also a national monument in its own country, Switzerland (and also to some extent in Germany where it had a large independent German subsidiary company). It was an unprecedented move, full of political and managerial complexity that would shake the electric engineering industry to its foundations. The restless Barnevik relished the new challenge. What was he taking on? What kind of company was BBC? Why would it be attracted to a merger with its arch-rival ASEA? What were the strengths that a new, merged entity could build on? And what would need to change, if such a merger were to succeed?

BBC – a Swiss powerhouse that nearly ran out of steam

Like Sweden, Switzerland has also produced an extraordinary range of internationally successful companies, given its size. Its central location on Europe's major trading routes, its early development as a commercial and financial centre and its political neutrality, allowed it to maintain commercial relationships with most of the important economies in Europe. The Swiss, as a multicultural and multilingual society accustomed at home to the need for compromise between very different perspectives and interests, have also enjoyed some advantages in working with different nationalities while expanding internationally.

BBC was, in 1987, the third largest company in Switzerland after food manufacturer Nestlé and chemicals company Ciba-Geigy. It, too, was a result of the electrical revolution at the end of the nineteenth century. It was formed in 1891 as a limited commercial partnership – Brown Boveri et Cie – in Baden, near Zürich in the northern, German-speaking part of Switzerland. Why does the name of a company that was to become a Swiss national institution, and later a Swedish–Swiss global corporation, contain an English surname? As it happens, neither of the founders of the company were directly Swiss in origin.

In the middle of the nineteenth century, Charles Brown, a young English engineer from Uxbridge (near London) decided to seek his fortune on the European continent, unlike many of his contemporaries who took themselves to India and the colonies of the growing British Empire. He made a name for himself in Switzerland working in engineering companies in the towns of Winterthur and Oerlikon (now a suburb of Zürich and the location of ABB's head office). His two sons, Charles Eugene Lancelot and Sidney William, both inherited his technical aptitude and grew up in Winterthur where they graduated from the technical college. When, in 1887, his father returned to take up a job in England (before moving on to work in Italy and later retiring to Switzerland), the younger Charles Brown took over his job as manager of the electrical engineering department of the Oerlikon Engineering Works, although he was only 22 years old at the time.

Brown, who throughout his life was interested in daring designs and inventions, soon pioneered some outstanding electrical innovations, including, in 1891, the transmission of electricity at a voltage of 25,000 volts – previously regarded as impossible – over a distance of 110 km between the German towns of Lauffen and Frankfurt-am-Main where an international electrical engineering exhibition was being held. Brown believed that the ability to transmit energy over long distances by using high voltages offered unprecedented opportunities for industry.

At Oerlikon he had hired a young German engineer from Bavaria, Walter Boveri, who shared his vision of the industrial potential of electricity. Together the two decided to set up a partnership that would combine Brown's technical abilities and Boveri's business acumen and organizing skills. They chose the small spa town of Baden – perhaps an unlikely location for a new industrial venture, but the land for a factory site was cheaper there than in other more industrialized towns and the owners of the town's new power plant promised to give them an order to produce generators, if they would locate the factory nearby.[3] The concerns of client power producers for reliability and service were already important drivers in the power engineering industry.

Starting with 100 workers and 24 salaried staff, BBC set out to produce electrical generating equipment that could exploit water power from Switzerland's rivers. Its early products also included electrical components, such as electrical motors for locomotives and power-generating equipment for railways. While Brown strove continually to improve the performance of his machines, Boveri saw the manufacture of power stations as an opportunity to achieve competitive prices by implementing batch production methods.[4]

Because of the limited nature of the Swiss market, the company was forced to export from the start. The timing was perfect. As with ASEA, industrialization and the development of railways throughout Europe led to heavy demand for its products. A significant early success was an order, in the face of stiff competition from German companies, from the power station of Frankfurt-am-Main, which stipulated that the company should erect a repair shop nearby. A similar clause was imposed by Mannheim when it ordered power generators in 1898, this leading to the establishment of BBC's branch there. Mannheim eventually became the head office of BBC's large German operations.

Although Brown's designs found a ready market abroad, heavy customs duties imposed by the industrialized countries, together with insufficient protection against foreign firms copying their designs and the difficulties of obtaining the necessary raw materials in Switzerland, led the company to found subsidiary companies abroad and grant manufacturing rights under licence to foreign companies. Brown and Boveri recognized the significance of international markets in an important decision that they made in 1900. Having built some 40 hydro power plants, they realized that many other countries relied on fossil fuels and had little in the way of hydro-electric resources. They saw an opportunity to produce steam power plants and decided to become the first company in continental Europe to produce a steam turbine. This was an important turning point because they also recognized that the absence of coal and oil meant that it was unlikely they would sell steam turbines in Switzerland. The company would now be heavily dependent on its export business and would have to fight in very competitive markets abroad. In a sense, Switzerland would just become additional geography. That Brown and Boveri were able to make this fundamental decision was undoubtedly due, at least in part, to the fact that both had backgrounds that naturally made them look abroad – internationalism was in the very genes of the company.

Brown's solution to the technical problems involved in producing the much faster-running generators needed by steam turbines gave the company a clear lead over its competitors and became a model for all turbo-generators produced elsewhere. In 1904, the company supplied Europe's first marine turbine system. In the early years of this century, it also established companies in Germany, France and Italy to produce and distribute its steam and gas turbine equipment. In 1919, BBC signed a licensing agreement with the British engineering firm Vickers, which gave this British company the right to manufacture and distribute Brown Boveri products throughout the British Empire and some parts of Europe.

Brown retired from the company in 1912, although Boveri continued as its president until his death in 1924. The verdict on their achievements presented by a company history applies equally to the founders of other electrical engineering firms, such as ASEA and Strömberg:

> We make use of electricity nowadays, as a habit, without even pausing to think of the faith, optimism, daring and conviction its introduction and taming once involved. Even when electrical engineering finally began its irresistible advance, the new machines and equipment did not fall into our fathers' laps as mature designs. Behind every invention and development were often years of hard, dedicated work (Reideknecht, 1966).

BBC continued to build on these achievements as it expanded abroad. The growth of Italy's railway system in the first decades of this century gave a particularly strong stimulus to BBC's Italian subsidiary. The large German market also fed the growth of the company's German operations, which eventually generated considerably more business than the Swiss parent. BBC's French subsidiary became another large operation. After the Second World War, the company took part in the post-war reconstruction of Europe, receiving large orders from State-owned utilities for power-generation and distribution equipment. It diversified into nuclear power-generating equipment and also benefited substantially from electrification projects in developing countries. High international demand for its power equipment led BBC to concentrate on this sector, which came to dominate its other activities, such as electrical equipment for railway locomotives, control equipment and electronics. It established BBC companies in Brazil, Mexico, South Africa and India. In 1967, it purchased the Swiss electrical machinery company Maschinenfabrik Oerlikon, which gave it the site that would later become ABB's head office in the Oerlikon suburb of Zurich.

Problems of international coordination

BBC's international growth presented it with problems of international coordination. As it expanded, BBC found itself with subsidiaries, like the one in Germany, that were much larger than the parent company. Each subsidiary developed individually as if it were a domestic company in the country in which it operated, and was usually managed by local nationals.[5] It is important to understand how this came about as it had ramifications for today's ABB.

Up until 1970, BBC was not a unified group as such. Rather than creating fully owned subsidiaries, the BBC company in Baden had expanded abroad by taking minority or majority shares in companies around the world. Where these were manufacturing companies, they were also licencees of BBC in Baden. These companies manufactured for their home markets but were not permitted, as BBC licencees, to do business abroad, unless special permission was granted by BBC (which it was reluctant to give). The main subsidiaries were quoted on their national stock markets. BBC also maintained a fully owned sales network, with offices in countries around the world that carried out sales and marketing operations and, sometimes, service and maintenance. BBC had a 56 per cent majority shareholding in its Mannheim-based German affiliate, which was larger in both sales and numbers of employees than the mother company. In France, on the other hand, the third biggest operation, BBC had a clear minority holding. The companies were run by the delegation of executives to the company Boards, whose role was essentially to agree the year end accounts and collect the dividends and licence fees payable to the mother company. BBC's own executive committee had a geographic focus, with each of the five members being responsible for a major country or region. The allocation of resources reflected the independence of the subsidiaries. Apart from R&D projects and key contracts, which were discussed in the executive committee by the heads of the geographical groups and the chairman, decisions about resource allocation were made at the level of each group and there was little overall coordination. A corporate strategic planning group was based in Switzerland, but most planning took place within the geographic groups.

The autonomy of local activities originally made strategic sense on the grounds that local management was best situated to negotiate with State-owned utilities and railways, as locally based companies had access to national export credits, and as trade and foreign exchange restrictions required local manufacture. The resulting fragmentation meant that the company as a whole had no uniform reporting across its operations and did not produce consolidated accounts. It did not even publish a list of its subsidiary companies. Although not allowed to trade in BBC products outside their own borders, the subsidiary companies could acquire other activities in their countries and through these could do business abroad, if doing this did not conflict with the mother country. The German company in particular grew significantly by means of this route, acquiring activities in such sectors as cables, computers, white goods and low-voltage adaptors for domestic installations. (Such activities did not participate in dividend contributions to the mother company.) One negative effect of BBC's fragmented stance was the wasteful duplication of R&D across the subsidiaries, sometimes with local subsidiaries developing different solutions for the same customer need.

BBC's difficulty in maintaining control over its larger subsidiaries was particularly complicated in the case of its German affiliates because of German corporate law. This has very strict rules to protect minority shareholders. Any action dictated by the majority shareholder must be neutral or to the advantage of the minority holder. And it was the *Vorstand*, or Board, of Mannheim that had the right to decide whether an action by the parent company was positive, neutral or negative for them. This prevented any attempt by BBC in Baden to rationalize products or allocate markets, for example, as these could be judged by Mannheim to be detrimental to their interests as a minority shareholder. At the same time, the situation was compounded by tax law, which made transfers of profits impossibly expensive. Germany's *Mitbestimmung*, or codetermination law, also required agreement with the German company's works council, which fought hard to defend local interests.

The end of the 1960s saw a big increase in the Swiss company's export business and, in 1970, this prompted the then chairman Max Schmidheiny to carry out a large-scale reorganization in an attempt to restore control. This, for the first time, created a BBC Group and divided the company's subsidiaries into five groups (German, French, Swiss 'medium-sized' – the seven manufacturing operations in Europe and Latin America – and Brown Boveri International – the remaining operations). Markets were opened up for all countries within the group. The aim was that, for the first time, BBC in Baden should fulfil a real holding company function, with central staffs for such functions as finance, control, planning, marketing and technology. The parent company started to implement a group accounting and reporting system that allowed the company to produce consolidated accounts (although these were still not published) from 1972 on.

Despite the reorganization, the problem of control persisted. As one senior ABB manager later recalled: 'This Mickey Mouse nonsense went on for decades, with the German daughter refusing to take instructions on industry from a parent based in a country that many Germans regard as a tourist centre' (Arbose, 1988). There was one possibility for change. Under German corporate law, it is possible via a so-called 'domination agreement' to 'neutralize' the rights of minority shareholders by offering to buy their shares at a fair price (as evaluated by an independent major accounting firm). For those who do not want to sell, the company is obliged to retain for ever at least the equity they had at the date of the agreement and also guarantees that, for as long as they hold the shares, they will be paid a yearly dividend of the same amount as the year before the agreement. This legally neutralizes the opinion of the minority shareholder as they have equity and a guaranteed dividend and means that the majority shareholder can instruct them to carry out their wishes. BBC's finance staff in Baden wanted to take advantage of this legality (and, in 1978, prepared an agreement) but BBC's top management refused to act, fearing that it would damage relationships with major clients in Germany, such as the German railway system Deutsche Bundesbahn and the large German power producers. The proposal would remain in the drawer until a new chairman arrived in 1985–86.

BBC was used as a classic example of a 'nationally responsive' business by C. K. Prahalad and Yves Doz in their 1987 book *The Multinational Mission* (Prahalad and Doz, 1987). Noting that career paths, incentive systems and control systems were all nationally-oriented, they said:

> *While intersubsidiary product teams, business committees, and steering groups abounded, their role in coordination was made impossible by the strong orientation of data management and managers' management tools toward national responsiveness alone. As a result . . . they could share information and develop a world view in favour of integration, but no individual manager would see it sufficiently in his interest to pursue such a view in action, except on mundane matters* (Prahalad and Doz, 1987).

As an example of an unsuccessful 'strategic redirection' change process, Prahalad and Doz describe how, in 1972, when faced with severe competitive attack, BBC's small electrical motors business tried to formulate a rationalization plan for plant specialization and coordinated product development among its plants in France, Germany, Italy and Switzerland. All the managers involved agreed intellectually with the need to integrate manufacturing across Europe, but, by 1976, while joint development had proceeded reasonably well, manufacturing remained largely national:

The original understanding was not sufficient to trigger collaboration and integration in the absence of changes that would much more strongly affect the power of managers. Division managers in Germany and France were still measured and evaluated on their own short-term results and had little incentive to help their Italian colleagues (Prahalad and Doz, 1987).

The integration plan aborted, and the small motor business was eventually divested after heavy financial and employment losses. As Prahalad and Doz say, 'Intellectual agreement on a new world view and a new strategy is likely to have no consequence unless the managers' self-interests and the balance of power among them are modified' (Prahalad and Doz, 1987). (ABB would later take this lesson to heart by seeking to measure people's careers not only by their own bottom line, but also by how they contributed to group development.)

A noble old lady

Meanwhile, BBC had continued to grow its international operations. In 1974, its acquisition of the British controls and instrument manufacturer George Kent stirred up fears in the UK about foreign ownership of highly sensitive technology. The deal went through, however, with the support of George Kent's own workforce who were more fearful of takeover by Britain's General Electric Company (GEC). The new acquisition was renamed Brown Boveri Kent and gave BBC a presence in Britain – the only major European country where it did not have any industrial activities.

Despite its international expansion, the company never managed to establish a strong presence in the important North American market. In the 1970s, it tried to negotiate a joint venture with Rockwell – the US aerospace manufacturer – but the deal fell through when the prospective partners were unable to agree on financial terms. Although it managed to attract some large US customers, such as the Tennessee Valley Authority and American Electric, North American sales continued to represent only 3.5 per cent of total sales. The company kept up its search for a solution to its American weakness, but was distracted by strong demand from the Middle East for its power-generating systems and from oil-rich African countries such as Nigeria, which sought its electrical engineering know-how in developing its own manufacturing industries. BBC's business boomed in the 1970s and continued, despite the oil crisis, until 1976–77. (Producers of power equipment were traditionally late in the business cycle. As it could take two to four years to produce a power plant, BBC was still delivering power stations ordered in 1973 before the economic crisis.)

When the second oil crisis hit and demand from the developing regions fell in the early 1980s, BBC's sales levelled off and profits declined, and were further struck by the slump in the nuclear power industry. Faced by a failing market and growing competition, BBC's policy of concentrating on its core power business ran into trouble. Attempts to diversify in the USA to create new market opportunities were unsuccessful and led to large losses. Although demand recovered for BBC's German subsidiary in Mannheim – now representing half of the entire company's sales – the company needed a strong dose of rationalization. As one observer put it, 'The group was increasingly gaining the character of a noble old lady whose best days are past and who is beginning to feel the pinch' (Leppänen, 1994).

BBC was still highly respected for its advanced technology and the almost academic level of its R&D – it was sometimes called the 'Nobel prize company' – and it was still able to draw first-class professionals to Switzerland from all over the world. It was now out of tune, however, with the changed business environment. It was heavily overstaffed in some areas. Traditionally tied to State power authorities, its managers took few risks and were afraid to cut jobs. Like ASEA before 1980, the company's policy of keeping its highly skilled workforce with its know-how intact led it to accept loss orders. The company defended this by pointing to an expected upturn in the power market. BBC's structure of autonomous national companies, which had once made sense when it was mainly selling power equipment to public authorities in their home countries, had now become a major problem.

With saturated markets in the industrialized countries, the national subsidiaries were now competing with each other in export markets. The company's medium-voltage business, for example, in which it had a large market share, developed and produced equipment at nine different locations in five countries. The company's setbacks in the late 1970s and early 1980s nearly paralyzed the company's top managers, who were unable to take corrective action. BBC's key managers, says one observer, were:

> unable to incorporate a global view into their management practice and to understand the system of new complex worldwide organizations . . . The straightforward culture of BBC was unable to respond to new types of organizational challenges created by worldwide operations: to complexity, tensions, the need for quick response, etc. (Leppänen, 1994).

Cost-cutting in 1985 temporarily improved the German company's performance, but price competition in international markets and unfavourable exchange rate movements wiped out the effects of increased orders. Although the Italian and Brazilian subsidiaries turned in good results, overall earnings dropped 11 per cent in 1986 and profitability stood at a mere 1.5 per cent of sales. Like ASEA six years before, the time had come for change and the company's Board took a big gamble in appointing an outsider as chairman – Dr Fritz Leutwiler – a former president of the Swiss National Bank and a Board member of other big Swiss companies, such as Nestlé and Ciba-Geigy.

Leutwiler – highly respected for his achievements as a central banker and described as 'the most influential person in Switzerland' – was prepared to take risks and listen to the advice of those BBC executives who had been urging change, but had previously been ignored. His first comment on the company was 'BBC makes 10 per cent too little turnover and has 10 per cent too many people' (Catrina, 1991). A bold first action was to initiate the domination agreement with the company's minority shareholders abroad. Sensing a new determination and spirit in Baden, Mannheim agreed with the move, at least on the surface, as it was eager to retain its position, but its management team was not happy and at least one or two senior executives resigned as they did not want to work for a completely controlled company. Implementing the agreement with shareholders was, in retrospect, a highly significant act for, without it, the 1987 merger with ASEA that created ABB could never have occurred. The German company would always have been able to question whether or not such a move was in the interests of the minority shareholder.

Leutwiler also took over the chief executive's role and, in his first few months in office, reorganized the company to give it a more clear-cut organization with 24 worldwide business divisions, each with a general manager responsible for strategy, product line and profitability. He sought to cut out loss-making activities and make BBC more responsive to customers' requirements. He also tried to emulate Percy Barnevik's strategy by moving into faster-growing areas in transportation, electric traction and process technology for manufacturing industries. Leutwiler's actions made BBC much more attractive as a partner. In general, he instilled a much more positive, open and aggressive spirit in BBC and publicly announced some very ambitious profit targets for the group. These had a very strong impact on the stock market evaluation of the company. Again, this would be important during the merger when equality of stock market evaluations of the two partners was a crucial issue in the success of the negotiations. In fact, without Leutwiler's attempts to revitalize the group, it would probably have been very difficult for BBC to negotiate a merger (as opposed to a takeover).

In 1986–87, the company struggled to implement the rationalization programme, which looked as though it would ultimately be successful, but its currently poor financial performance meant that it was forced to pass its dividend in those two years. Profits in 1986 increased only slightly. In March 1987, Leutwiler brought together BBC's 450 top executives to review the company's progress and set targets for the future. Participants raised many questions and expressed their fears about the future at this conference. The new strategy and the new products needed time and investment. Resources for investment were available, but time was running out. And BBC lacked the managers who could make a more globally oriented organization work effectively.

At this time, ASEA came into view. Leutwiler said, 'I was not looking for a company to merge with, but for different firms to cooperate within problematic areas. When I first heard the name of ASEA, I thought of something Asiatic. After I learned better, I took their annual report in hand and soon found out that they were largely doing the same we were, only commercially more successfully' (Catrina, 1991). Ironically, back in the early 1980s, when ASEA was still in poor shape, BBC's controller, Jean-Pierre Dürig – an advocate of change who would be a strong supporter of the 1987 merger – semi-jokingly suggested to colleagues that BBC should consider making a takeover bid for ASEA 'instead of investing in things in the USA which did not work'. As he says, thereafter, 'as ASEA came up, BBC went down, year after year.' Dürig later told a Swiss journalist who had been commissioned to write a corporate history of BBC, 'I felt like a flight engineer sitting behind two self-righteous pilots. I saw the threatening data on my instruments and knew that we were flying in the wrong direction in the fog and that the treetops were getting closer and closer because the fuel was running out. But there was nothing I could do' (Catrina, 1991).

Table 1.1 Key figures for four competitors 1975–84

	BBC	Siemens	ASEA	GEC
Order intake	+ 14	+ 129	+ 350[1]	[2]
Turnover	+ 45	+ 142	+ 359	+ 218
Turnover per person	+ 48	+ 125	+ 229	+ 283
Earnings	+ 29[3]	+ 133[4]	+ 396[5]	+ 367[6]

Notes

1 Period 1978–84
2 GEC did not publish order figures
3 Cash flow
4 Yearly annual profit
5 Earnings inclusive of financial items
6 Profit after taxes

Source: based on tables in Catrina (1991), Leppänen (1994)

Looking back ten years later, Barnevik admits that, 'If anyone had asked me in 1980 would you have merged with BBC I would have said BBC is a big company, ASEA is a small Swedish company. People would have been laughing at me, because we would have been swallowed up!' A comparison of the performance of ASEA with that of BBC in 1986 shows how far the Swedish company had come since 1980 under Barnevik's guidance, however, and how far BBC had slipped. In 1980, BBC's turnover was twice that of ASEA and its stock market value was four times greater. By 1986, however, the turnover of the two companies was roughly comparable, while ASEA's market capitalization was double that of BBC's. BBC earned profits of $135 million on sales of $8.79 billion in 1986, while ASEA earned $380 million on sales of $7 billion in 1986. ASEA's profits represented 5.5 per cent of sales compared with BBC's 1.5 per cent of sales. ASEA, with 71,000 employees, was achieving nearly 10 per cent more turnover per employee than BBC with its 97,500 employees.

A marriage made in heaven?

So why did the dynamic Barnevik approach the by now venerable BBC? The answer is business logic. ASEA could no longer go it alone. It needed scale, but it recognized that it could not do everything by itself everywhere. A partnership with BBC would offer both sides what Rosabeth Moss Kanter calls 'collaborative advantage' (Moss Kanter, 1994). The potential partners certainly fulfilled some vital principles of successful collaborative advantage. Both were individually excellent – they were strong and could contribute something of value to the relationship. The relationship was important to both sides and fitted the long-term strategic aims of both sides. As *The Wall Street Journal* would say when the deal was announced, the merger was 'born of necessity, not of love' (*The Wall Street Journal*, 1987). Both realized that, if they remained isolated, they would have to allow themselves to be bought out or shut down. 'We are condemned to succeed,' Percy Barnevik said. The merger therefore also met the criterion of interdependence – neither partner could accomplish what both could do together. In partnership, they would represent a major force in global terms, capable of competing with the US and Japanese giants of the industry.

The two companies certainly had a number of useful similarities that would help the integration process. They had a similar background and engineering tradition. They also had similar accounting procedures and followed similar reporting practices.

ASEA was less international than BBC and was essentially a Swedish company. Only two of its top managers had worked abroad. BBC was Swiss, German, French, Italian and more. ASEA had the edge in management and performance, but the companies complemented each other in many respects. First, they fitted together very well geographically in terms of market coverage. ASEA had a strong presence in the Nordic countries and northern Europe. BBC had a worldwide presence. In Europe, it was strong in Switzerland, and had an insider presence in West Germany, France, Austria and Italy – a strong presence in each of the major national markets for power engineering in Europe was important because of the protectionist nature of the industry. BBC's one-third share of the important German market was particularly enticing because ASEA's presence there was relatively minor; BBC's sales in Germany were 12 times larger than ASEA's. A merged company would also have a much stronger presence in the new Single Market in Europe. Together, said Barnevik, they would be an EU company, a Nordic company and also a company that was active outside Europe.

The fit was also good technically. Both invested more in R&D and valued their engineers better than many other electrical engineering companies. Both realized that innovation was essential for the future. BBC probably had the edge in terms of technology – it was strong in basic research – while ASEA had concentrated on applications-oriented research 'We need both – ASEA's for quick results and BBC's to ensure our future in 20 years,' said Barnevik (Arbose, 1988). In many areas, the company's products were also complementary rather than competing:

- ASEA specialized in small gas and steam turbines while the addition of BBC involved it in all sizes of equipment;
- both firms developed nuclear reactors – BBC was well known for its high temperature reactors; ASEA specialized in light water reactors;
- both firms developed high-speed trains. BBC's strengths in railway traction were in alternating current equipment, while ASEA's strengths were in direct current: 'They fit hand in glove', said Barnevik who also looked forward to exploiting the growth in demand for urban mass transit systems around the world;
- ASEA invented high direct current transmission and held more than half the world market – BBC was much smaller in the field but was strong in medium-voltage equipment;
- BBC was stronger than ASEA in industrial equipment and electronics – ASEA had substantial robotics (it was the market leader in Europe) and financial services businesses that Brown Boveri lacked;
- there was a major overlap in power transmission, but restructuring and consolidating the operation to cut costs would give them a strong lead in size and competitiveness, enabling them to increase their market share (even here there were complementarities – ASEA was strong in hydro-electric and nuclear power plant and BBC was better known for its expertise in thermal power stations burning coal or oil);
- BBC's technological base was still solid – better in some ways than ASEA's – and its particular strength lay in the big power plant markets where some big opportunities were thought to be developing;
- against ASEA's superior profit performance, BBC had a relatively stronger order book: 'For the first two years, BBC will dig into ASEA's pockets, but after that it will be otherwise' said Fritz Leutwiler at the time of the merger's announcement (Arbose, 1988).

The merger represented an opportunity to draw on the experience of the two companies and select the best from the two worlds. It meant that long overdue actions could be taken, particularly in the case of BBC's business. (It has been suggested that one of BBC's hopes for the merger with ASEA in 1987 was that it would help the company to reassert authority over its international operations.) It also enabled the organization to appoint the most qualified people to top jobs. In sum, the merger represented a major opportunity to build on the combined strengths of the two companies.

The fundamental reason for the merger was the need to be large – producing the next generation of advanced power plant would cost five to seven times more than the current generation. A merger would create a stronger company because the two would be able to merge their expensive R&D efforts and eliminate production overlaps. Combining the complementary parts of the two companies would promote a 'one stop shop' image with clients. Together, they could offer customers around the world any type of power station they wanted *and* all the parts, including turbines, boilers, electrical switchgear and controls. Achieving this market offer would mean, however, extensive rationalization on both sides.

Just as important as the market and technological issues, however, a Swedish–Swiss corporate marriage also avoided one of the 'black holes' in cross-border mergers that often accounts for expectations not being met – the question of cultural fit. When new partnerships are put together, all too often more consideration is given to financial, market or technical issues than organizational or human factors. Yet, different approaches to management and differing deep-seated assumptions in the corporate and national cultures involved can undermine even the most strategically logical partnership.

Barnevik chose a partner that, in many ways, was not too culturally distant from that of ASEA. In fact, there are cultural similarities between the Swedes and the Swiss that help to avoid temperamental flare-ups. The top managers of both sides came from small, politically neutral countries acutely aware of their economic vulnerability and they had enough international experience to know that they were dependent on the world for the survival and prosperity of their companies. This could help to avoid ethnocentric or insensitive behaviour. The merger was not without its cultural problems, however. The Germans in BBC's subsidiaries in its biggest market would not be happy about being dominated by the Swiss. Barnevik was aware of the problems in the most important home market in Europe: 'If we don't succeed in Germany,' he said, 'we won't succeed at all.' Germany, in particular, would need sensitive handling.

One former BBC manager who became a senior executive in the merged company described the strengths of both sides:

BBC had two very strong points – technology and a very broad international network. ASEA had a very strong management, young and enthusiastic, who had a very tough, controlling and transparent approach to business whereby you could see the results of all the profit centres. The combination of these two companies resulted in a tough management, which was business-oriented with a control of the figures, and was based on solid technology. Tough management is the ability to take difficult decisions, make them fast and to make sure that things happen – that there is not only a good decision but also a strong follow-up.

There was going to be plenty of strong follow-up in the years to come.

Notes

1 Around the same time that ASEA was created, the Finnish entrepreneur Gottfrid Strömberg founded an electrical company in 1889 in Finland, then part of the Russian Empire. The Strömberg company would, in time, become one of Finland's top companies. It was purchased by ASEA in 1986, and is now a leading member of the ABB group of companies.

2 Laval was more successful with other ventures. He invented the centrifugal cream separator in 1878 and the steam turbine in 1890. The separator led to the mechanization of the world's dairy industry (reducing the demand for farm labourers and so transforming agriculture) and the steam turbine revolutionized the powering of ships and power stations. The Alfa-Laval company became one of Sweden's leading international corporations.

3 The Pfister brothers were members of a leading Baden family who wanted to bring new industries to the town. Having visited the World Exhibition in Paris in 1889 with its sensational illumination by Edison lamps, they were convinced that Baden must have its own power station to attract new industries. Hence their approach to Brown and Boveri. The decision to locate BBC's new company in Baden created, in the words of a company history, 'a curious mixture of health resort and industrial centre, such as would be difficult to find in any other part of the world' (Reideknecht, 1966). Although ABB's modern offices and plant are a strong presence in Baden today, the town, with its medieval tower and its ruined castle on a hill above the river, retains much of its old charm.

4 Charles Brown senior disapproved of this approach to production. On a visit to his son's factory he declared: 'This form of work must be very boring. One should always try to design something new' (Reideknecht, 1966).

5 In the UK, the fact that the company's name incorporated the very English surname 'Brown' added to the impression that it was a British company.

References

Quotes without references originate from the authors' personal communications – see page xviii for details.

Arbose, Jules (1988) 'ABB: The new energy powerhouse', *International Management*, June, 24–30.

Barham, Kevin and Devine, Marion (1991) *The Quest for the International Manager: a Survey of Global Human Resource Strategies*, Special Report no. 2098. London: Economist Intelligence Unit, January, 73.

Brege, Staffan and Brandes, Ove (1993) 'The successful double turnaround of ASEA and ABB – twenty-one lessons', *Journal of Strategic Change*, August, 2, 185–205.

Carnegy, Hugh and Brown-Humes, Christopher (1994), 'The family firm fights back', *Financial Times*, 1 September, 23.

Catrina, Werner (1991) *BBC: Glanz, Krise, Fusion*. Zürich: Orel Füssli Verlag, 223.

Caulkin, Simon (1998) 'Swede dreams of going truly global', *The Observer*, 22 March, 2.

Euromoney (1988) 'Review of 1987 – preview of 1988', *Euromoney*, (2)25.

Financial Decisions (1988) 'Swimming against the stream', *Financial Decisions*, May, 45–9.

Financial Times (1987) 'The *Financial Times* has published a profile of Mr Percy Barnevik, the 46-year-old chief executive of the Swedish engineering group ASEA', summary of original article dated 15 August, 6.

Financial Times (1988) 'The *Financial Times* takes a brief look at the Wallenberg family, which controls one of the most powerful industrial spheres in Sweden', summary of original article dated 11 March, 18.

Financial Times (1988) 'Sweden: The *FT* talks to Peter Wallenberg, head of Sweden's leading industrial dynasty', summary of original article dated 21 November, 52.

Financial Weekly (1987) 13 August, 7.

Garnett, Nick, Dodsworth, Terry, Done, Kevin and Wordsworth, William (1987) 'The ASEA-Brown Boveri deal: Joining up in the battle to beat the blues', *Financial Times*, 11 August, 12.

Hindle, Tim (1989) 'ASEA Brown Boveri: Full of Contradictions', *Eurobusiness*, July, 24–7.

International Directory of Company Histories, (1990) (vol. II). Chicago and London: St James Press.

Kennedy, Carol (1992) 'ABB: Model merger for the new Europe', *Long Range Planning*, **25** (5), October, 10–17.

Kets de Vries, Manfred (1994) 'Making a giant dance', *Across the Board*, **31** (9), 27–32.

Kets de Vries, Manfred, F. R., de Vitry d'Avaucourt, Raoul and Morcos, Raafat (1994) *Percy Barnevik and ABB*, INSEAD case study, Fontainebleau, France.

Klebnikov, Paul (1991) 'The powerhouse', *Forbes*, 2 September, 46–50.

Lawrence, Peter and Spybey, Tony (1986) *Management and Society in Sweden*. London: Routledge & Kegan Paul.

Leppänen, Rolf (1994) *ABB Action Recipe: Strategic Management in the Growth and Restructuring of a European Enterprise*. Helsinki: International Networking Publishing INP Oy, 95.

Löhrer, G., and Peters, M. (1982) 'Ritter Percyfal', *Bilanz*, February, 48–57.

Management Today (1988) 'Inside management', February, 16.

Moss Kanter, Rosabeth (1994) 'Collaborative advantage: the art of alliances', *Harvard Business Review*, July–August, 96–108.

Panni, Aziz (1993) 'Reaping the harvest', *Eurobusiness*, October 72–6.

Prahalad, C. K. and Doz, Yves, L. (1987) *The Multinational Mission: Balancing Local Demands and Global Vision*. New York: The Free Press.

Reideknecht, Peter (ed.) (1966), trans. Kenneth M. Evans, *75 Years Brown Boveri 1891–1966*, Baden: Brown Boveri & Co. Ltd, 1966, 30.

Skaria, George (1995) 'Interview with Percy Barnevik', *Business Today* (India), 22 February–6 March, 100–5.

Svenska Dagbladet (1987) 'Mr Thage Peterson, the Swedish Industry Minister, has spoken publicly for the first time on ASEA's planned merger with Brown Boveri of Switzerland', summary of original article dated 18 August, 1.

Swiss Business (1987) 'ASEA–BBC: United they stand', *Swiss Business*, October, 20–1.

Taylor, William (1991) 'The logic of global business: an interview with ABB's Percy Barnevik', *Harvard Business Review*, March–April, 91–105.

Tully, Shawn (1985) 'Europe's king of robots' *Fortune*, 16 September 42–5.

The Wall Street Journal (1987) 'ASEA Brown Boveri union born of necessity', 12 August.

2

The merger that rewrote the rules

We violated every page in the takeover manual.
Percy Barnevik

Percy Barnevik had identified a likely partner, but what would the response to his overtures of courtship be? Despite its problems, BBC was a proud Swiss company and a national institution. ASEA and BBC had been fighting neck and neck for years. How could he win the company over to the radical proposition that they should work together? What was it going to take to make a partnership work?

The courtship – the Swedes go a-wooing

Although they were fiercely strong competitors, both ASEA and BBC had, for some years, considered themselves to be natural merger partners. There had been discussions and also some licence agreements between the two companies. They had actually been cooperating increasingly frequently between 1986 and 1987. Percy Barnevik may well have preferred a direct takeover of BBC, but realized that he could not afford to acquire control of enough BBC shares. In 1985–86 ASEA made some secret investigations into whether BBC Germany could be bought out from BBC in much the same way as most of BBC France had been divested some years earlier. But this led to nothing. He was not from the beginning thinking of a full merger when he put feelers out about deepening cooperation to BBC's chairman in spring 1987. He was probably not sure what the response would be and may have been surprised to get a positive answer.

It seems that Leutwiler needed little convincing. BBC was at the same stage of development ASEA had been at during the early 1980s and still had a long way to go to get back on course. Barnevik's turnaround skills were just what it needed. His track record with the successful acquisition and integration of

Strömberg of Finland, which had left the company's national pride intact, also helped. Union with a younger, more dynamic leadership was very attractive. BBC may also have hoped that joining with ASEA would help the company in its relations with its German subsidiary and that the Swedes, with no vested interest, could act as a catalyst for change. From a business point of view, Leutwiler also recognized that a merger would allow the two entities to broaden their R&D efforts and achieve synergies that could substantially improve profitability. BBC companies would have the opportunity to supply ASEA companies worldwide, particularly in the USA. This would add significant value to both companies. Like Barnevik, Leutwiler realized that the timing was right and that a merger offered a once-in-a-century window of opportunity.

The original proposal was to strengthen cooperation between the two firms. Bengt Skantze, who was then responsible for corporate development at ASEA and who was closely involved in the merger process, remembers:

> *We had a meeting where we presented ideas and suggested we should cooperate in power generation (where BBC was much bigger and stronger). Everyone said this was interesting and we put a working group together. Percy came home and everyone was sceptical. The two companies were competing in other areas, they said, how can we cooperate? Percy said 'Yes, but you have to start somewhere'.*

The initial investigation suggested that, indeed, cooperation between the two companies as they stood would be difficult so the more radical idea of a merger emerged very quickly. Barnevik's proposal for a full merger first met with a suggestion from Leutwiler to start with a joint venture for Transmission and Distribution, where the synergies were the biggest, and then continue with other areas if it went well. However, Leutwiler was soon convinced that it was impossible to have one joint operation and then compete in all other fields. Barnevik talked to the owners on the ASEA side, the Wallenbergs, and Stefan Schmidheiny on the BBC side to sound them out. They quickly agreed that the two sides should look at the ideas more closely. The need for secrecy presented challenges for those responsible for the early strategic analyses. 'It was extremely confidential,' says Bengt Skantze. 'Very few people were involved and we didn't visit each other. We analyzed what we could get our hands on and looked at the potential synergies – it is surprising how much you can dig out.' It was probably not possible to keep things totally secret within both companies. Where managers in ASEA or BBC who were not in the know were asked to provide information about the other company, it may have sparked some speculation in their minds. But, if so, it did not spread too far.

The idea was mooted officially in June 1987 under the auspices of the bank Crédit Suisse, and agreed in principle. Thereafter, the negotiations were conducted with amazing speed and stealth. As Bengt Skantze says:

It was driven by Percy's absolute determination to grow internationally. Leutwiler of BBC saw very early on that he could not turn around BBC in a reasonably short time. He was a very intelligent and straightforward person and there was no nonsense about it; he saw very clearly what had to be done. With Percy on our side and Leutwiler on the other, it made it happen very fast.

Other factors also helped to push the process along rapidly. Swedish managers have a reputation for their impatience to get contracts signed, but Barnevik had particularly good reasons on this occasion. He had learned a lesson from his previous acquisition attempt in Germany and insisted on absolute secrecy. A public bid for BBC would have been stopped for political reasons. Both Boards were, in any case, highly conscious of the political risks and the need to maintain confidentiality. Each was a mainstay of the business community in its own country and the proposed merger posed fundamental questions. Where would control lie now? Would decisions be made without regard to vital national interests? Secrecy and speed were also essential to avoid confusion and stop competitors stealing market share. Internally, the aim was to inject dynamism into the organization right from the start, and to persuade managers to 'focus on the future, not on their own security'.

Negotiating the marriage

BBC approached the negotiations in an equally positive and proactive manner. Beat Hess, then head of BBC's Legal Department, and now ABB's General Counsel, had first been told of discussions with ASEA about a possible merger by Fritz Leutwiler and Thomas Gasser, BBC's chief executive, in spring 1987. Now, in June, they told him to look at it seriously and prepare a full merger agreement in preparation for further discussions with ASEA. 'This was not so easy to write for two huge companies if you can't talk to anybody about it – but it was a clear instruction that it was top secret.' Hess was about to take his family for a week's holiday to Italy. 'Thomas Gasser said to me "Go by all means, but we need the merger agreement by the first week in July".'

Only three other people in BBC were informed. These were the head of corporate staff for taxes, the corporate controller and the chief financial officer. With Beat Hess, they would make up BBC's negotiating team. They barely had time to put their heads together before people disappeared to go on holiday. As Hess remembers, 'I used the whole week to write the merger agreement in the hotel. I came back with a handwritten full proposal for a merger agreement – we had no laptop computers then. The top page had suntan lotion marks on it!'

The agreement was to be BBC's proposal for the first meeting with ASEA in

Stockholm. To ensure secrecy, the BBC negotiators had to sign confidentiality agreements and buy their plane tickets for the trip outside the company. They were not allowed to talk to their wives about the negotiations. Nor were they allowed to tell their secretaries where they were going, and they went to the bank personally to collect their foreign currency. Beat Hess remembers arriving in Stockholm and being impressed at the empty streets – he had not realized that July is the holiday month in Sweden. The holiday season also contributed to the secrecy of the merger talks. The next day (remembered by participants on both sides for its beautiful summer weather), Bengt Skantze, as another security precaution, personally came to the BBC team's hotel and took them to ASEA's office for the meeting.

The four BBC negotiators now met the ASEA negotiating team of five people – the chief financial officer, the head of corporate control, the head of taxes and the company's chief counsel and his deputy. The small size of the negotiating teams is striking. Beat Hess says:

> We still work in the same way today in large transactions. It is one of the benefits brought in by Percy Barnevik. It is always the same people in relatively small teams. It means that at a high level you can call the CEO easily. Other companies create steering committees, task forces, sounding boards, etc. We don't. We have a maximum of three to four people who at least initiate transactions, nail down the core issues, and can then enlarge the group. This is to Barnevik's credit.

The Stockholm meeting was to be highly significant in setting a collaborative tone for the future of the partnership. Lars Thunell, ASEA's chief financial officer and leader of the ASEA team (and now Chief Executive of Sweden's leading bank S-E Banken), opened the meeting by saying that they were there to do a good job and Jean-Pierre Dürig, BBC's corporate controller and leader of the BBC team, replied in a similar tone that the BBC side was also there to make the meeting a full success and that they would do everything to make that happen. After brief introductions, the BBC team took their ASEA counterparts by surprise by presenting Beat Hess's draft proposal. 'They hadn't thought that we would come up with an agreement,' says Hess. 'But it gives you an advantage in negotiations if you have the chance to write the basic agreement!'

The ASEA team had also prepared an agreement with the help of two American lawyers from one of the top US law firms. The two sides agreed to look at the ASEA proposal and the lawyers, who were sitting in an adjacent office, were called in.

The meeting started to consider the ASEA document, which was over 100 pages long and emphasized the need for warranties and indemnities. There was discomfort on both sides about the document and its emphasis on warranties. Beat Hess took his legal counterpart on the ASEA team aside and said, 'This is not a US affair. This is a merger between two European firms. Why do we need warranties? We are merging entirely. If it doesn't work, there won't be anybody left to merit warranties.' ASEA's chief counsel was relieved to hear this and it was quickly agreed to dispense with the services of the American lawyers. Instead, over the course of two days, the two sides worked to take the language of both sides' proposals with the aim of extracting the best from the two documents.

The result was that, from a US-inspired document of over 100 pages, the discussions produced a final draft merger agreement of just 15 pages. The section on warranties was cut down to just one sentence, which stated that there would be no warranties. As Bengt Skantze says, 'You couldn't include guarantees. There was no one to blame, we were all in it together. There were no parents standing behind us. It was a Catholic marriage – you could not undo it.' Jean-Pierre Dürig agrees, 'There was no blaming each other for what skeletons each had in the cupboard. Due diligence would have killed it. If we had tried to analyze each other to find weaknesses, it would have ruined the deal.' He also likened the deal to matrimony. 'We had decided to go together like in a marriage. You don't question each other's lovers and liaisons in the past. You have to say we have fallen in love and that's it.'

Was it difficult to achieve the final draft? Hess says:

No, it was a question of attitude. Whether you want to be productive, be pragmatic and produce something that is down-to-earth. Whether you can see what the key issues are and not get lost in endless debates and negotiations. The amazing thing was that, despite the magnitude of the transaction and the fact that it was a cross-border merger, and that we had to transfer all of ASEA into a new company based in Zürich, we both recognized that we would have to limit ourselves to the key elements and get agreement on them so that the project would not be held up by details later.

Having hammered out the basic aspects in Stockholm, a second meeting was held in an airport hotel in Zürich to clear up the remaining issues where the two sides still had differences of opinion. This time, the negotiating teams were joined by the two chief executives – Percy Barnevik and Thomas Gasser. Barnevik was determined to push the agreement through, even if it meant making concessions to Swiss sensitivities. Beat Hess remembers:

We thought we would negotiate the final open issues that we were not able to sort out in Stockholm. Instead, Percy Barnevik came in and sat at the top of the table. On the left were the BBC team of four people and on the right were the ASEA team of five people. Barnevik had a copy of the draft agreement. He asked the two company legal heads to sit beside him. It was my first encounter with Barnevik. I couldn't believe my ears and eyes. He took the agreement and said 'I will now read it sentence by sentence. Anyone who has a comment to make will raise his voice and we will decide immediately on the issue.'

Barnevik proceeded to read the agreement from the first sentence to the last. ASEA's counsel, Hans Enhoerning, and Beat Hess raised their voices several times. Barnevik impatiently asked both lawyers to state their positions. 'What is your proposal? Not the concepts, but the actual language, immediately.' The lawyers dictated their proposals into Barnevik's pen. Barnevik immediately decided which proposal to go with. Hess was very impressed that on some really key issues, he decided on the spot to take the Swiss as well as Swedish proposals. By late that night the whole paper was decided and agreed.

For Jean-Pierre Dürig of BBC, the meeting with Barnevik was also a revelation:

This was new for us, to see the top man going into the details of what we had done, trying to follow our train of thought, asking constructive questions, putting forward respectful criticisms, listening to us, extracting our ideas and accepting our views. He is very hardworking, simple and straightforward in his approach.

A key issue in the negotiations had concerned how to evaluate the two companies. As Bengt Skantze says, 'We had decided very quickly that it must be 50/50 – it must be a totally equal partnership. We were both listed companies so we had to work backwards from there and adjust it by taking some things out of the merger so that we could justify 50/50'. It was decided on a mixture of stock market evaluation and the values of assets to be contributed to the new company. When the stock market values of the two companies were compared, however, there were substantial differences. To achieve equal values, it was agreed that BBC would raise $300 million from shareholders, but this was still not enough and ASEA kept substantial assets out of the merger such as a big hydro power utility in Sweden, stock in Electrolux and other companies.

Another issue concerned the way in which the two companies were to be merged. Questions that arose in the discussions concerned the role of the parent companies. Would they have equal voting rights? The Boards of both companies still saw themselves as the guardians of the interests of their particular shareholders (although this was probably less so in the case of ASEA's Board than that of BBC). For this and other legal and tax reasons, it was felt that, rather than a full merger, it would be more appropriate to enter into a shareholders' agreement whereby each company was a 50 per cent shareholder in the new company. As Beat Hess says, 'You could say it was a joint venture with two parties, but our goal was to reduce the role of the two parents because it was a *de facto* merger and we didn't want two entities with different interests.'

Negotiations about the structure of the shareholder agreement also concerned whether or not it should have mechanisms in case of profound disagreements between ASEA and BBC, such as a divorce agreement and defence clauses. Other issues involved how to treat intangible assets, such as patents and trade names, how to merge research, and how to organize international sales networks.

On the issue of evaluating assets and deciding what was to be included or excluded in the merger, a significant footnote to the story concerns a small Swiss company – Sicommerce, a distributor of cosmetics and healthcare products owned by BBC. There were lengthy and, at one point, heated discussions as to whether or not BBC should be able to keep this company out of the agreement.

Sicommerce was a distributor of the original Ladyshave ladies' electrical shaver, which had been a great market success and, at that time, made the company highly profitable. The ASEA team became very suspicious when one member of the BBC team tried to divert attention from its profitability and exclude Sicommerce from the agreement 'for technical reasons'. Unlike his colleagues who had quickly considered the ASEA team as future colleagues, it became clear that he felt that the ASEA team were the 'other party' and that his role was to defend Swiss and BBC interests against them rather than working to merge BBC with them. He raised a lot of issues that led to confrontation. Interestingly, although he succeeded in keeping Sicommerce out of the agreement, when the merger took place he was not chosen for a job in the new company.

Fortunately, the other members of the BBC team saw the long-term opportunities for both partner companies. Beat Hess says:

> We were convinced that neither side would have survived if they hadn't taken this opportunity to create a large company, I was personally convinced it was an excellent move. I put my national feeling aside. It was never an issue for me whether this was Swiss or Swedish. I thought it would give a tremendous push to shareholders and to employees. From day one, I was a supporter.

Barnevik once told a journalist that in the 1987 merger negotiations he had 'violated every page in the takeover manual' that he had developed during the last few years to help guide ASEA through its acquisitions. He said later of the negotiation process:

> When we decided on the merger between ASEA and Brown Boveri, we had no choice but to do it secretly and to do it quickly, with our eyes open about discovering skeletons in the closet. There were no lawyers, no auditors, no environmental investigations and no due diligence. Sure, we tried to value assets as best we could. But then we had to make the move, with an extremely thin legal document, because we were absolutely convinced of the strategic merits (Panni, 1993).

Once more, Barnevik applied the formula of 'better quick and approximate than slow and precise'; he felt that the potential gains outweighed the risks. He was also convinced of the need for integrity on both sides:

We had to be fast; there could be no leakage; we could not have lawyers around; we had to trust each other. If we had begun to look at bad debts, the health of invento-ries, their order books and pension reserves and so on, we would have ended up in guerrilla warfare for the next ten years. We had to take it on trust. If an American lawyer looked at our agreement, he would faint, saying 'My God, where are the pre-cautions?' (Financial Times, 1987).

Following the airport hotel meeting, there were further discussions and tele-phone conversations to clear up remaining issues and discuss implementation. The two sides completed the whole process in just six weeks. The rapid closure of the deal was facilitated by the fact that Barnevik had the support of the dominant shareholders of the two companies – the Wallenbergs of ASEA and Stephan Schmidheiny of BBC. Another factor that may have facilitated the process is that both Swedes and Swiss are 'low context communicators' – that is, unlike managers from some other cultures, they can get straight to business without a lot of small talk.

Everything was still in total secrecy. Not a word leaked out and nobody out-side knew anything about the merger. Barnevik later explained this need for secrecy:

Think of Sweden. Its industrial jewel ASEA – a 100–year-old company that had built much of the country's infrastructure – was moving its headquarters out of Sweden. The unions were angry: 'Decisions will be made in Zürich, we have no influence in Zürich, there is no codetermination in Switzerland' . . . Strict confidentiality was our only choice (Taylor, 1991).

In fact, the top management of both sides felt the merger to be so politically sensitive that they subsequently locked away the documents about the merger negotiations in a Swiss bank for 20 years. While much has been written about the merger process since the full merger was agreed on and announced, little is known about the process leading up to that consensus in June. However, that exciting story is also documented and will be released from the Swiss bank safe in the year 2007. Barnevik secured a promise from a few people involved not to comment on that pre-negotiation period in public, and instead to leave their account to the documentation for anyone interested in economic history in later years.

'Looking back', says Beat Hess, 'with some of the decisions we really took a risk that we would run into problems in implementation, but we were deeply convinced that it was the right approach for a large cross-border transaction of this kind.' One of the risks was that the European Commission might question the merger. The EU merger control regulations were not in force at that time, but it could have been possible for the Commission to raise concerns. In the event, ABB received clearance from the Commission three years later, when the company received a letter from the Commission saying that, after due consideration, it had no objection to the merger!

On 4 August 1987, the final merger agreement was signed at the Four Seasons Hotel in Hamburg at a meeting attended by owners Peter Wallenberg (who had succeeded his father Marcus in 1982) and Stephan Schmidheiny, top executives Curt Nicolin, Thomas Gasser and Percy Barnevik, and the members of the two negotiating teams. The agreement had been negotiated, but there was still a slight possibility that Wallenberg or Schmidheiny or one of the executives might ask for changes. Indeed, Curt Nicolin caused a little alarm by asking for a change just before the signature of the agreement. In the event, this turned out to concern a minor amendment to the wording of the sentence stipulating that the corporate language of the company would be English. Then the agreement was signed, followed by what one participant described as 'a nice dinner and a nice discussion'.

The terms of the marriage contract

Despite ASEA's superior performance, Barnevik and his Swedish colleagues believed that the deal had to be an agreed merger rather than an acquisition. Making a successful acquisition and implementing it is hard enough in any circumstances, but a hostile bid across borders is much harder. 'A takeover would have destroyed a lot, psychologically, politically and commercially', said Barnevik. If the merger demanded a spirit of equality to save management sensitivities, ASEA's superior profitability and its original role as senior partner were nevertheless reflected in certain aspects of the deal. The terms were as follows.

- ASEA and BBC would set up a new joint holding company with 50/50 ownership to be known as ABB – ASEA Brown Boveri Limited. Both firms would retain their stock listings in their own home countries, but the new firm would not be listed. Initially, at least, ABB would have two quoted entities.
- ASEA and BBC would keep their current boards and 'national profiles' and would contribute virtually all their assets and liabilities to the new company in exchange for equal voting rights and an equal split of the profits. Each would contribute 50 per cent of the capital.
- The deal left the two companies' non-power operations and interests unmerged. ASEA agreed to contribute its Fläkt air-treatment subsidiary to the group, but retained control of its key minority holdings in other Swedish companies, including its 10 per cent stake in Electrolux.
- As part of its dowry, and because ASEA's profitability and capitalization were higher, BBC agreed to contribute $508 million, in addition to its main assets, to the venture. It would raise this extra capital by means of a rights issue.

- The new company would be controlled by a 12-member executive committee, the members of which would be drawn equally from each company. Barnevik was to be chief executive while Thomas Gasser, former CEO of BBC, would be deputy CEO.

The deal, which was to go ahead at the start of 1988, created an organization that, in terms of size, stood 'heads and shoulders above the competition'. With a combined total of over 700 companies and 2500 factories spread across 20–30 countries, ABB emerged as an $18bn a year corporation with a workforce of over 160,000 (including 65,000 in the EU), and combined sales that were about the same as industry leaders such as GE and Siemens. The new merged entity resulting from the first large-scale restructuring of the industry in decades would be almost 50 per cent larger in heavy electrical engineering than its main rivals – Siemens, Hitachi and GE. The electrical and power business of GEC was only one fifth the size of the new company.

Merging ASEA's and BBC's research activities would produce a combined spending on R&D of Skr6 billion a year. The new company was cash rich, enabling it to make new acquisitions to strengthen its position, and it would have the resources to survive the current downcycle for heavy capital goods. Barnevik expected that $4 billion could be released from the business over the next 2 years by means of inventory control, cleaning up inefficient multiple-product factories, combining distribution channels, etc. The combined company would also have the power to procure the government financial support necessary to compete for contracts in developing countries.

Announcing the advent of such a formidable new competitor was clearly going to drop 'a bomb in the industry', as Arne Olsson, ABB's Head of Corporate Management Resources, puts it. The communications plan needed extremely careful thought. Olsson was one of the people Barnevik asked to give him some ideas about communicating the merger, including who to talk to and how to do it. 'I put together a two- to three-page paper which I thought was quite good and gave it to him. But then out from Percy came an 11–page memo which was a masterpiece of a communication campaign.' As Olsson says, the announcement was quite controversial, to say the least: 'It involved the trade unions and political issues – putting the head office in Switzerland, which the Swedish unions didn't like. But he produced a very well-planned and detailed communications plan – who to talk to, how to present it, who to talk to face-to-face, what to delegate and who to contact by phone or by fax.' Olsson says of Barnevik, 'He is a very skilled communicator, very convincing. There is a Swedish saying: "He could sell cold porridge to his own mother and make money on it"'.

The final step before a merger could be announced was that of securing the agreement of the two parent company Boards. On 10 August, simultaneous

Board meetings were held in Västerås and Oerlikon. Board members – most of whom still knew nothing about the merger – arrived at 9.00 am and were given an hour to study the papers. The aim was to secure agreement from both sides by midday. The meeting at BBC was likely to be the most critical. However, Leutwiler asked Schmidheiny to speak first, and his enthusiasm for the deal set the tone for the meeting. At 12 o'clock, Leutwiler and Barnevik could confirm on the telephone that each had agreement for the merger to go ahead.

This was just as well as the public announcement of the deal was set for 3 o'clock that afternoon.

Announcing the nuptials – the bomb in the industry

With the public announcement of the merger on 10 August 1987, Barnevik achieved a strategic surprise that any military genius would be proud of. At the press conference that he gave that afternoon in Stockholm, the financial and business journalists attending assumed it was a relatively routine affair. Many did not even bother to turn up. Little had happened in the industry for 40 years, after all. Some thought it was nothing more important than an announcement about a new plant in Norway or something similar. As Barnevik says, 'Then came the shock, the *fait accompli*'. Those attending were stunned to hear that ASEA, one of Sweden's national institutions, was merging with BBC, one of Switzerland's national institutions. In one decisive stroke, Barnevik caught his competitors totally unawares and broke the industry mould for good. 'Speed has been the hallmark of this merger', he told his startled audience. 'It is the merger of the century. It changes the industrial map of Europe irrevocably.'

Barnevik went on to describe the new company's plans for the future: 'The strategy is one of a two-stage rocket: restructuring, then growth. We must stretch out West and East from Europe'. The merged companies would first cut costs by eliminating uneconomic duplicate manufacturing and distribution operations and by combining research and development efforts. At least 100 factories would be closed and another 200 merged.

These actions would make ABB, with a likely turnover of $20 billion in 1988, the lowest-cost supplier of power generation and transmission equipment, electrical machinery, electric trains and transport equipment – its core businesses. Lower costs would enable the new company to invest more in research and improving distribution. 'We aim to achieve prominence as the company that utilities and others rely on in the long term', said Barnevik. The combined R&D spend would allow them to focus on the development of industrial processes and control systems for power plants. The partners would also undertake joint sales efforts in opening markets and developing a range of complementary services. Of the new firm's sales, 65 per cent would come from Europe, 15 per cent from Asia and Australia and 10 per cent from North America. It would keep up a rapid pace of restructuring to clear the way for expansion in North America and Asia. ABB planned to spend $2000 million on acquisitions, and $1300 million on R&D (7 per cent of turnover). Tight control of finances meant that another $4000 million could be released for investment, but that would take several years and would depend on cutting inventories and debtors and the success of the rationalization plans.

Although the spotlight was on Percy Barnevik, other top figures were also active in presenting the new company to the world. Peter Wallenberg, in his capacity as head of the Swedish Industry Confederation, said he was delighted with the deal, which 'clearly shows what Swedish companies need to do if they are to remain competitive internationally'. The merger was seen by some commentators as his crowning achievement. Curt Nicolin and Fritz Leutwiler, in a joint statement, said that the deal was an important contribution to strengthening European industry. It was a 'signal to European industry' of what it must do to counter Japanese and American competition. Arne Bennborn, deputy CEO of ASEA, and originator of the multidomestic concept, said that 'in future, Europe, rather than just the Scandinavian countries, would be ASEA's home market. ASEA Brown Boveri will actually have several home markets.'

A period of turmoil followed the announcement of the merger as governments, trade unions, competitors, and industry observers and analysts tried to assess its implications. Barnevik described it as a 'communications war of a few weeks where we had to win over shareholders, the public, governments and unions.' The shareholders needed little convincing, particularly as Peter Wallenberg and Stephan Schmidheiny, the principal investors were so strongly in favour. The stock markets responded favourably, with ASEA's shares rising 15 per cent in Stockholm and BBC's by 10 per cent in Zürich. Government reaction was less predictable. At first, ABB declined to give details of the impact of the restructuring on job cuts. Barnevik said, 'No government has asked for, nor got, any guarantee of employment.' In the event, the Swiss government and trade unions were relatively quick to approve the merger, but the Swedish government was more cautious. The merger reflected a very big break in tradition for them. Barnevik warned them in a public statement that delay in approving the merger would allow ABB's competitors in other countries to turn it to their advantage.

The Swedish government's main concerns were ASEA's future as a Swedish company and how much of the new group's R&D would be carried out in Sweden. It would have preferred to see ASEA take a 51 per cent stake in ABB. Curt Nicolin, one of the new company's two co-chairmen, said in an interview that ASEA had no intention of moving out of Sweden and also pointed out that the name of the new company would be ASEA Brown Boveri, not Brown Boveri ASEA! In a statement, the Swedish industry minister recognized that the merger would lead to a greater internationalization of Swedish industry, and that this was desirable for the survival of Swedish companies. He said that, if Sweden wanted to be part of the international economy, it would have to give and take, even if people were unhappy that the HQ would not be in Sweden. The mixed feelings in Swedish official circles were evident, however, when he remarked that he did not believe the merger would last: 'Our experiences with other joint ventures suggest that the two groups will eventually split up', he said.

The Swedish trade unions showed equally mixed feelings in their reactions to the merger. Although local unions in Sweden agreed to accept the terms of the merger, six central Swedish trade union organizations wrote to the government to protest against the merger plans. One union spokesman said that his main reservation was that 'the unions will never be sure who they are dealing with in the new organization, but I believe the merger is essential if ASEA is to remain competitive.' Trade unions in other countries where the two companies operated were also uneasy about the merger and its implications. Some spokesmen called for the formation of international unions. The following year, 70 trade union representatives from 20 countries would meet in Switzerland to discuss a united approach to ABB.

Other companies in the industry were shocked. 'It was a real bang in the industry,' says Bengt Skantze. 'It was the first time that this extremely conservative business had changed more fundamentally.' Competitors tried to play it cool in their public statements, although their remarks probably belied their true feelings. UK players, such as Babcock International and GEC, were reported to be 'intrigued rather than concerned by the move' (*Financial Weekly*, 1987). The chief executive of Babcock International agreed that the merger was 'the sort of thing one can expect in the longer term', but said 'I am not dismayed. Agglomeration is not bad but it is not absolutely necessary either'. A senior GEC manager declared, 'Major mergers are no surprise' but admitted that the company would be 'reviewing our strategies in the light of this development . . . There has been speculation about every combination of electrical engineering companies imaginable'. If this was true, the success of Barnevik and his ASEA and BBC collaborators in catching the competition off guard was even more remarkable. Barnevik remembers his courtesy call about the merger to the CEO of Siemens, Dr Kaske, who was on vacation in Greece: 'There was absolute silence on the telephone. I had to ask, "Karl-Heinz, are you there?" This biggest European competitor never thought we would be able to succeed with the merger.'

Competitive intelligence is vital for global companies

How would you feel if you woke up one morning to find your two closest competitors had declared that they were merging to form a new powerful alliance? The ASEA and BBC merger has to be seen as a failure of competitive intelligence on the part of their competitors. Douglas Bernhardt, one of Europe's leading competitive intelligence experts, says:

> *A firm which does not rigorously monitor and analyze key competitors is ill equipped to formulate or implement sound competitive strategy . . . Unfortunately managers at all levels in industry – many with ostensibly 'perfect' knowledge of their industry, their products and their strategic objectives – with great commitment and enthusiasm march forward onto the competitive battlefield with no understanding whatsoever of what their competitors can and will do'* (Bernhardt, 1993).

Do you know what your competitors are up to? What competitive intelligence systems do you have in place to identify their strategic intent?

Reference
Bernhardt, Douglas (1993) *Perfectly Legal Competitor Intelligence: How to Get It, Use It and Profit From It.* London: Financial Times Pitman Publishing, 6, 9.

How was such a surprise achieved. Essentially, says Arne Olsson, because ABB managed it as a project: 'These things are like projects and the success of a project is most often related very much to the competency and the skills of the project manager. Percy Barnevik himself is a very strong project manager. You must work with a very small team of people. Don't let it draw out in time because the risk increases. There is a bigger risk of a leak the longer it drags out and the more people who get involved.'

Inside the company, too, the merger announcement came as a total surprise. Inevitably, the news was met with very mixed sentiments in BBC in Switzerland. These ranged from those who were totally enthusiastic about the merger (some managers knew of Barnevik and admired him) and those who were opposed to it. Many people were naturally anxious for their jobs as they knew that Barnevik had drastically reduced central staffs and administration and had changed many people at ASEA.

Abroad, the news of the merger also came as a bolt out of the blue for both ASEA and BBC employees. Local ASEA and BBC operations that were formerly arch competitors were now expected to collaborate. Some local executives would be managing former rivals. This demanded a huge change of outlook. A. K. Thiagarajan, former Managing Director of ABB India and then a long-time manager for ASEA in India, recollects, 'It was a shock. I said, "It cannot be true!" I wondered what would happen. What would happen to the company, what would happen to me?' His colleague, H. K. Mohanty, now Vice-President, Corporate Personnel at ABB India, was then on the other side of the fence working for Hindustan Brown Boveri. He also recalls the initial reaction: 'There was a feeling of apprehension. It was excitement about coming together, but also fear of one another.'

It would take some months for everything to become clear. The merger negotiations had not agreed every point of detail and left various anomalies between the two companies to be settled, especially in the other countries. ASEA, for example, was involved in a consortium that was competing for a major power station project in India. BBC was one of its main rivals for the contract. As Swedish companies were forbidden by law to invest in South Africa, ASEA had withdrawn from its investments there, but BBC had four subsidiaries there. Such issues were not allowed to hold up the merger, but would need to be quickly resolved afterwards.

Although industry observers were well aware of the need for a shakeout in the power engineering industry, given the fierce competition and high capacity, the merger took them completely by surprise. In the months that followed, a stream of speculative comment appeared in the business press: 'This merger is a major all-European joint venture in the same category as the Anglo-Dutch Unilever and Royal Dutch Shell Groups,' said one observer (*Swiss Business*, 1987). Another predicted that 'the merger portends a formidable cocktail of talent mixed with an expansive multinational network spanning three continents; the fizz provided by ABB's stated market strategy that bigger is best' (*Euromoney*, 1988). Another noted that it was ironic that 'the company that most embodies the spirit of 1992 and pan-Europeanism should be a merger between two companies that come from outside the European community' (Hindle, 1989).

The reaction of business analysts, including investment researchers and stockbrokers, was somewhat mixed. 'A marriage made in heaven, with short-term benefits for BBC's shareholders and long-term benefits for ASEA's', said one stockbroker. 'An analyst's nightmare', said another, pointing to the problem of evaluating performance in three currencies – BBC's in Swiss francs, ASEA's in Swedish krona, and ABB's in US dollars (Arbose, 1988). Some analysts were pessimistic: 'Political realities may make synergies difficult to achieve', said one. 'Our major worry is that needed plant closings will not be undertaken because of political and organizational constraints.' This observer should have looked more closely at Barnevik's track record with ASEA.

Observers also speculated about the location of the new company's head office. ASEA's top management was thought, in deference to the Swedish trade unions, to prefer a neutral location, possibly in the Netherlands where ASEA's own finance company was already registered. It was known, however, that Zürich's municipal authorities had suggested to ABB the advantages that the Swiss city would offer as a conveniently located financial centre close to an international airport. They also suggested that Zürich would have tax advantages over other locations and promised to obtain sufficient work permits for foreign employees at the head office (a real sign of their keenness to attract ABB, given the usual difficulties that even large multinationals have in obtaining work permits for their people in Switzerland). In the end, Barnevik and his colleagues chose Zürich as head office with Baden, Västerås and Mannheim as regional HQs. Barnevik said, 'I felt if we were in Switzerland, it would be more balanced, and not look Swedish-dominated' (Kennedy, 1992). The decision to locate the new head office in Zürich was certainly a culturally-sensitive move intended to reassure the Swiss that ASEA was not taking over, but it was probably reinforced by other factors – notably tax considerations.

Much speculation centred on whether or not ABB would really work as a merged entity. As the *Financial Times* said on the day after the merger was announced:

> *Previous transnational merger attempts in Europe have rarely achieved the benefits expected of them, and Mr Barnevik will be faced with a serious test of his management skills in bringing together two dissimilar marketing organizations. After all the hype has died down, the new company will be battling it out in some of the most intensely competitive markets in the world* (Garnett, Dodsworth, Done and Wordsworth, 1987).

Barnevik was unruffled. When asked about the low success rate of transnational mergers in Europe, he said, 'I don't know about the failures, but Shell and Unilever are examples of successful mergers. We don't talk about failing. Our merger is irrevocable, because BBC and ASEA have nowhere else to turn' (Arbose, 1988).

In the light of such arguments, the Swedish government finally gave its approval for the merger in October 1987, clearing the way for the deal to go ahead. The last obstacle was overcome in December when the West German federal cartel office gave its consent. This was needed because of BBC's substantial presence in Germany, where it held 30 per cent of the heavy electrical machinery market. The cartel office decided that it would not create a monopoly because ABB's competitors – Siemens and AEG – each also held a 30 per cent share.

What was then the biggest cross-border merger of all time pushed ABB into the same class as its global competitors General Electric, Siemens, Hitachi, Toshiba and Mitsubishi. Many experts, however, still gave Barnevik and his colleagues less than a 50 per cent chance of success. A few observers were more prescient. The year following the merger, in an internal publication of one of those global competitors, Paolo Fresco, then GE's senior vice-president for international operations, predicted:

The lights are going out all over Europe, and the buccaneers have been turned loose. Among them is Percy Barnevik – this Swede with the beard, who swings from country to country, like the actor Errol Flynn, cutting deals and forming alliances. In six weeks, he put together the ASEA-Brown Boveri deal and formed a $15 billion power systems company. This product of Socialist Sweden is calling for a reduction of 50,000 jobs in Europe, for delayering, downsizing and rationalizing – all alien terms in the Socialist lexicon. A self-described enemy of incrementalism, his announced intention is to strengthen his US position. A convalescing GE power systems may find him the most formidable adversary it has ever faced.

How right he was.

The ABB merger as strategic disruption

Edwin Rühli, a Swiss professor at the Institut für betriebswirtschaftliche Forschung in Zürich, has suggested that ABB's strategic reorientation can be understood by using American strategy guru Richard d'Aveni's concept of 'Hypercompetition' (Rühli, 1995). D'Aveni points out that markets are increasingly dynamic as globalization, accelerated technological change, deregulation and changes in customer behaviour, lead to ever shorter product life and design cycles, new technologies, frequent entries by unexpected outsiders, repositioning by incumbents, and radical definitions of market boundaries (D'Aveni, 1994). Stable periods are rare and competition consists of a sequence of discontinuities. Competitive advantages erode ever faster and competition is characterized by intense, rapid and unexpected strategic moves of competing firms. Sustainable corporate success will no longer be achieved by attempts to sustain competitive advantage. Strategy in hypercompetitive environments is about developing a series of temporary, relative competitive advantages. A hypercompetitive firm not only has to constantly destroy the competitive advantages of competitors, but also keep on destroying its own competitive advantages. The disruption of existing competitive advantages and market structures is crucial in hypercompetitive environments.

Rühli suggests that, by the 1980s, the electrical engineering industry was about to become just such a hypercompetitive environment. And it was ABB's strategic reorientation through the ASEA and BBC merger that was a disruption of the worldwide electrical engineering industry. ABB's attack on the status quo, especially in the power area, stirred up competitors and changed the implicitly accepted international rules of the game.

Speed and surprise are the crucial capabilities for disruption, as ABB vividly demonstrates. As major shareholder Stephan Schmidheiny later described it, 'Nobody really expected this merger, because it was unthinkable. But this is precisely it: to think the unthinkable and then act' (Catrina, 1991).

What lessons came out of the merger?

Percy Barnevik once said that the ABB merger in 1987 was the 'biggest, most exciting' moment of his life (Taneja, 1996). The merger is a fascinating piece of corporate history in its own right, but it also holds some important points for other companies considering cross-border mergers. With the continuing trend towards globalization, more and more firms will be looking for such opportunities to create global critical mass or to disrupt their competitors. The advent of the single European currency, in particular, will mean that such mergers are not restricted to large firms, but will also encourage more cross-border mergers between small- and medium-sized firms. What can they learn from the ABB experience?

- **Keep it secret**. Limit the people involved to only those who absolutely need to know. Can strategic surprise of this kind be achieved some ten years later when firms have become more attuned to the need to maintain competitive intelligence efforts? Apparently the answer is 'Yes'. As this book was being completed, car manufacturers Daimler-Benz of Germany and Chrysler of the US were reported to have 'stunned' the global auto industry by announcing a trans-Atlantic alliance (Schmid, 1998). If you ask senior ABB managers today whether or not secrecy and surprise can still be achieved, they will also usually tell you that ABB always tries to avoid leaks on major initiatives and is usually successful.
- **Approach a merger as a project**. Make sure it is led by strong 'project managers'.
- **Keep the negotiating teams as small as possible**. ABB still operates with very small negotiating teams on major projects. This increases the chances of keeping it secret and means that team members make decisions more quickly and can communicate rapidly with the chief executive when the CEO's decision is needed.
- **Ensure the negotiators have a positive attitude**. Members of the negotiating team need to see each other as future partners rather than adversaries or protectors of old interests and ways of doing things. This is important for the success of the negotiations themselves and for the longer-term message it gives people in the two organizations about the need to collaborate. This may have implications for the people selected for the negotiating team.
- **Act quickly**. This is essential to achieving surprise. Don't let the process get drawn out. Concentrate on the essentials. Don't get bogged down in unimportant details.
- **Prepare a carefully considered communications plan**. Who should be communicated with, when and in what order, and how should they be communicated with? Who is it essential to speak to directly?

References

Quotes without references originate from the authors' personal communications – see page xviii for details.

Arbose, Jules (1988) 'ABB: The new energy powerhouse', *International Management*, June, 24–30.

Brege, Staffan and Brandes, Ove (1993). 'The successful double turnaround of ASEA and ABB – twenty lessons', *Journal of Strategic Change*, August 2, 185–205.

Carnegy, Hugh and Brown-Humes, Christopher (1994) 'The family firm fights back', *Financial Times*, 1 September, 23.

Catrina, Werner (1991) *BBC: Glanz, Krise, Fusion.* Zürich: Orel Füssli Verlag.

D'Aveni, Richard (1994) *Hypercompetition: Managing the dynamics of strategic maneuvering.* New York: The Free Press.

Dullforce, William and Garnett, Nick (1989) 'When the ketchup starts to flow', *Financial Times*, 15 November.

Euromoney (1988) 'Review of 1987 – Preview of 1988', 2, 25.

Financial Decisions (1988) 'Swimming against the stream', May, 45–9.

Financial Times (1987) 'The *Financial Times* has published a profile of Mr Percy Barnevik, the 46-year-old chief executive of the Swedish engineering group ASEA', summary of original article dated 15 August, 6.

Financial Times (1988) 'The *Financial Times* takes a brief look at the Wallenberg family, which controls one of the most powerful industrial spheres in Sweden', summary of original article dated 11 March, 18.

Financial Times (1988) 'Sweden: The *FT* talks to Peter Wallenberg, head of Sweden's leading industrial dynasty', summary of original article dated 21 November, 52.

Financial Weekly, 13 August 1987, 7.

Garnett, Nick, Dodsworth, Terry, Done, Kevin and Wordsworth, William (1987) 'The ASEA-Brown Boveri deal: joining up in the battle to beat the blues', *Financial Times*, 11 August, 12.

Hindle, Tim (1989) 'ASEA Brown Boveri: full of contradictions', *Eurobusiness*, July, 24–7.

Kapstein, Jonathan and Reed, Stanley, *et al.*, (1990) 'Preaching the Euro-gospel', *Business Week*, 23 July, 34–8.

Kennedy, Carol (1992) 'ABB: model merger for the new Europe', *Long Range Planning*, 25 (5) October, 10–17.

Kets de Vries, Manfred (1994) 'Making a giant dance', *Across the Board*, October 31 (9) 27–32.

Kets de Vries, F. R. Manfred, de Vitry d'Avaucourt, Raoul and Morcos, Raafat (1994) *Percy Barnevik and ABB*, INSEAD case study. Fontainebleau, France: INSEAD.

Klebnikov, Paul (1991) 'The powerhouse', *Forbes*, 2 September, 46–50.

Management Today (1988) 'Inside management', February, 16.

Miles, Gregory L. (1990) 'A lacklustre US business is ABB's diamond in the rough', *Business Week*, 23 July, 37.

Moss Kanter, Rosabeth (1994) 'Collaborative advantage: the art of alliances', *Harvard Business Review*, July–August.

Panni, Aziz (1993) 'Reaping the harvest', *Eurobusiness*, October.

Rühli, Prof. Dr Edwin (1995) *Applying D'Aveni's Concept of Hypercompetition to Analyze and Explain the Strategic Reorientation of ABB in 1988.* Zürich: paper presented to the 15th Annual International Conference of the Strategic Management Society, Mexico City, 1995, Diskussionsbeitrag Nr. 23, Institut für Betriebswirtschaftliche Forschung.

Schmid, John (1998) 'A jolt for auto industry', *International Herald Tribune*, 7 May, 1 and 4.

Svenska Dagbladet (1987) 'Mr Thage Peterson, the Swedish Industry Minister, has spoken publicly for the first time on ASEA's planned merger with Brown Boveri of Switzerland', summary of original article dated 18 August, 1.

Swiss Business (1987) 'ASEA-BBC: united they stand', *Swiss Business*, October, 20–1.

Taneja, Narendra (1996) 'Managing a vision', *Tycoon* (India), August, 24–31.

Taylor, William (1991) 'The logic of global business: an interview with ABB's Percy Barnevik', *Harvard Business Review*, March–April, 91–105.

The Wall Street Journal (1987) 'ASEA Brown Boveri union born of necessity', 12 August.

3

Barnevik's master plan

I tell my people that if we make 100 decisions and 70 turn out to be right, that's good enough. I'd rather be roughly right and fast than exactly right and slow.
Percy Barnevik

The merger was agreed in principle. The bomb had exploded in the industry. The biggest cross-border merger in history had been completed on paper. However, this was only the start of the process. A vast amount of work now had to be done to make the merger work. Percy Barnevik had engineered a major turnaround at ASEA, but ABB was five times as large as the ASEA of 1980, in terms of both numbers of employees and turnover.

The two-stage rocket

Very early on, Barnevik had described the strategy as a two-stage rocket: restructuring, then growth. However, many questions remained about what this meant in practice. In what sectors would the new merged entity compete? What was the best way to rationalize and restructure the two companies and to integrate them in practice? How would this boost the group's financial performance? What should the new organization look like? How could the company overcome the inevitable resistance to new ways of doing things, especially in the old BBC bastion in Germany? How could ABB motivate its thousands of managers and inject dynamism into the giant organization created by the merger? How and where should ABB expand internationally? How should the huge company be controlled and coordinated? What kind of leaders would be needed to implement the strategy and how should they be developed?

What, in short, was Barnevik's master plan for going global? In outline, it took the following shape.

Stage 1: restructuring

- **Focus on power, swim against the stream** Stay with the electrotechnical industry and prepare for the upturn in the power equipment market when emerging markets start to grow substantially.
- **Keep up the momentum for change** Make sure people know this is not just a change of ownership, it is a fundamentally new way of working.
- **Decentralize within a global matrix** Reorganize from top to bottom; build a structure that simultaneously encourages local entrepreneurial initiative and promotes global synergies.
- **Find and appoint the key people** Quickly identify the managerial 'superstars' who will have the competence and motivation needed to make this new organization work.
- **Create a centralized, transparent control system** Decentralization requires greater accountability and control and a common financial language.
- **Make English the corporate language** Simplify communication among the key decision makers around the world.
- **Create a new corporate identity** Give people around the world some new symbols that they can rally round and stimulate pride in the new entity.
- **Communicate the strategy and the supporting policies intensively** Make sure everybody knows where the company is driving and what must be done to get there – communicate, communicate, communicate!
- **Streamline operations** Get rid of the fat in the organization to cut costs, minimize overheads and allowed costs, and boost profit margins to provide a platform for longer-term growth.
- **Generate a new entrepreneurial spirit at BBC** Apply the ASEA turnaround formula to open up Brown Boveri to individual responsibility and initiative.
- **Align Germany with the new strategy** The success of the merger depends on Germany buying in to the new scenario.
- **Walk the talk** Top management must be persistent and tough, despite arguments, but take time to talk to people to make sure they buy into the vision.

Stage 2: growth

- **Reach out for the Americas and Asia** After expanding and consolidating in Europe, create an insider presence in the other major economic regions of the world. Dominate global markets by acquiring local competitors prepared to enter ABB's matrix. Build a truly global company with a multidomestic culture that holds the company together across borders and gives it global reach and combined strength to become the world's leading electrical engineering company. Forge a global network of rationalized, focused plants that will make ABB the world's fastest and lowest-cost producer.

In this chapter, we look in more detail at Stage 1 of the master plan and how ABB started to restructure itself. Then, in the next chapter, we will look at Stage 2 and the way that ABB started to implement its plan for global growth.

Stage 1: restructuring

Focus on power, swim against the stream

The first necessity was to take a view of the future and commit to it. A vital foundation for Barnevik's vision of the future was his belief that, while the power market was still a troubled sector in the late 1980s, demand would recover in the mid 1990s. He believed that power represented a unique opportunity to achieve both world leadership and profitability. He argued that a company does not have to be in a high-growth business to make money (indeed, there is sometimes a reverse correlation), and that it is possible to achieve good or high growth in a worldwide mature business by exploiting product and country niches and the exiting of competitors. He also contended that to go against the mainstream is often profitable and that, with the right strategy, properly implemented, a lot of money could be made in the electrotechnical industry. He used Sandvik and ASEA in the 1980s as examples of how superior growth in profits could be achieved also in mature markets.

Unlike some players, ABB therefore determined to stay in the business and prepare to meet demand when it picked up some six or seven years in the future. Other companies in the heavy electrical sector had responded by trying to pull out of the unprofitable power business or diversifying into more profitable areas, such as consumer and medical electronics. In contrast, ABB would swim against the stream of competition, aiming to achieve world dominance. In the meantime, it would exploit new high-growth niches, such as clean coal technologies, industry automation, environmental control, electrical drives and industrial robotics. It would attain competitiveness by aiming to be closest to the customer, manufacturing products with the highest quality and leading technology, and producing at a low cost.

Some observers worried about the company's dependency on the power sector, however. 'Much of Barnevik's strategy rests on rosy forecasts of booming demand for power equipment. Half of ABB's business is power sales – that dependency could backfire if growth sizzles and a lot of Barnevik's big bets might wind up looking foolish' (Dullforce, 1989). Only time would tell on this vital aspect of ABB's master plan. Certainly growth would not come from the power sector in the short term with demand in Europe and North America still slowing down. It was expected that the main impetus behind growth in the next two years would be from reorganization of the group and not from organic growth.

Keep up the momentum for change

A major priority in the reorganization was to keep up the pace of change. Speed had been a vital factor during the merger negotiations, but was even more important afterwards. Barnevik wasted no time in setting the restructuring process in motion. He followed the policy he had pursued at ASEA, which was to make all the difficult decisions as early as possible in the change process.

Legally, ABB was due to start on 4 January 1988. After the announcement in August 1987, there were five months to go, but, as Bengt Skantze says, 'You can't wait. Anyone with experience knows that you have to act because people start to talk. And Percy has an extreme sense of urgency. You have to push the button.' Apart from his desire to get difficult decisions over and done with as early as possible, Barnevik's sense of urgency came from his realization that he had to complete the integration process as fast as possible to avoid confusion and loss of market share. He believed it was 'better to move swiftly and correct an error here and there afterwards, rather than leave people hanging in the air, uncertain about their future' (Arbose, 1988).

> To make real change in cross-border mergers, you have to be factual, quick, and neutral. And you have to move boldly. You can't postpone tough decisions by studying them to death. You can't permit a honeymoon of small changes over a year or two. A long series of small changes just prolongs the pain. I tell my people that if we make 100 decisions and 70 turn out to be right, that's good enough. I'd rather be roughly right and fast than exactly right and slow (Taylor, 1991).

A first act was to select the new company's top managers. Barnevik and Thomas Gasser, the former CEO of BBC, together chose ten 'internal consultants' from ASEA's and BBC's existing management – 'superstars, the best and brightest'. They were given six weeks to design the restructuring of the merged entity – a task dubbed the 'Manhattan project'. Within six weeks, the ten had reported and were then appointed, each with clearly defined responsibilities, to form an executive Board – the 'Executive Committee' or 'Konzernleitung' – together with Barnevik and Gasser. The Committee, chaired by Barnevik, would set strategy and review the performance of the organization as a whole. It would consist of six executives from each company. Göran Lindahl, later Percy Barnevik's successor as ABB's chief executive in 1997, was one of the members from ASEA. The German arm of BBC, which generated 40 per cent of BBC's turnover, provided two of the BBC representatives.

In another early move, Barnevik initiated three major task forces that started work immediately in August 1987.

- **Organization** This task force had to answer the questions 'What should the organization look like? What business structure is needed? How should the countries be organized?'
- **Management** The job of this task force was to select the company's senior managers from throughout the world, from Group management down to who should run individual countries.
- **Finance and control** This task force worked on all things financial regarding the merger – how to control the business, and tax and accounting aspects.

Decentralize within a global matrix

ABB's global organization has attracted much attention and comment from business academics and observers and in Chapter 7 we will look at some of the leading analyses of its strengths and weaknesses. Since the merger, the company's structure has seen important changes in 1993 and 1998, but here we give a broad overview of the major organizational principles with which the company started in 1988. Bengt Skantze was responsible for the organization project that would determine ABB's global structure: 'To give you a flavour of the speed at which we worked, we said we should be ready in the first week of October 1987. The BBC people laughed and thought it was a gimmick. But it was no gimmick and we were ready on time.'

The challenge set by Barnevik was to create – out of a group of over 700 companies employing 160,000 people in 30 countries – a streamlined, entrepreneurial organization with as few management layers as possible. How, though, could a worldwide organization be built with as few as five people between the chief executive and the factory floor?

They were not starting from scratch, of course. We asked Barnevik if he had a master plan for the merger. He says:

The basic ideas of how to organize and manage a global organization were basically developed and tried out before the ABB merger in 1987 in:

- *Sandvik in 1969–79 (a $5 billion tool and specialty steel company active in 100 countries with 95 per cent of its business outside Sweden);*
- *the ASEA build up in 1980–87 from $2 billion to $9 billion orders and simultaneous internationalization;*
- *the Strömberg 'rehearsal' in 1986 with the merging of a 9000-people Finnish company with ASEA [see ABB Strömberg – a rehearsal for building a global organization, page 82].*

It helped of course that one of the two merging partners had the organizational structure in place and that it had been finetuned over the eight years 1980–87. We had it already proven. It also helped in convincing new managers that ASEA was considered a success story in 1980–87 with an annual increase of shareholder value, including dividends, of about 43 per cent per year in these years.

So, it is clear that Barnevik had a good idea of what he wanted. He sums up the organizational paradoxes that ABB needed to address: 'ABB is an organization with three internal contradictions. We want to be global and local, big and small, radically decentralized with centralized reporting and control. If we resolve those contradictions, we create real organizational advantage.' Barnevik's organizational innovations at ASEA provided the organizational blueprint for trying to resolve the contradictions. Eberhard von Koerber, who became one of Barnevik's close aides, describes the thrust of ABB's strategy:

From the very beginning, we strived to build a company that was fast, flexible, customer-focused and present as a local partner for customers around the world. We wanted to combine the economies of scale and scope enjoyed by a large company with the entrepreneurial drive and customer orientation of a small business (von Koerber,1996).

Göran Lindahl – now ABB's future chief executive, then head of ABB's power transmission business – called the organizational design 'decentralization under central conditions'. On the one hand, ABB would carry out a far-reaching decentralization to profit centres close to the customers. The aim, once again, was to reduce overhead, stimulate entrepreneurship, increase speed and flexibility and lay the foundation for a truly customer-driven company. At the same time, ABB would introduce the global matrix (see Figure 3.1) already used at ASEA through which it would seek to exploit its global size and presence with common technologies and economies of scales in engineering, manufacturing and procurement. The decentralization did not just apply to BBC. In 1987, the matrix in ASEA was only four or five years old and both ASEA and BBC needed more decentralization than before.

At the local level, ABB's 210,000 employees would be structured in a federation of some 1300 companies divided into 5000 profit centres located in almost 150 countries around the world. At the global level, worldwide business activities would be grouped into eight business segments, which included power plants, power transmission, power distribution, industry (such as metallurgy, process automation), transportation, environmental control, financial services and various activities (such as robotics, superchargers). The segments would, in turn, oversee 50 business areas (BAs) into which the company's products and services were further divided.

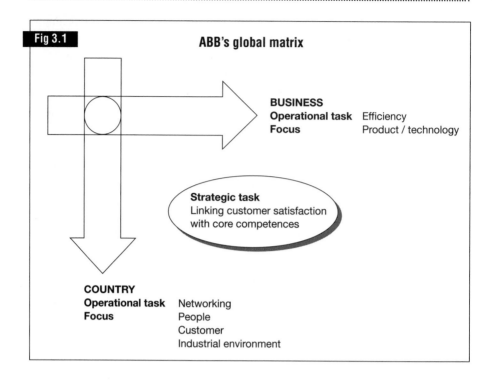

Fig 3.1   ABB's global matrix

BUSINESS
Operational task   Efficiency
Focus   Product / technology

Strategic task
Linking customer satisfaction
with core competences

COUNTRY
Operational task   Networking
Focus   People
    Customer
    Industrial environment

Table 3.1 Three kinds of business within ABB

Local	Regional	Global
Distribution transformers	Power transformers	Power plants
Low-voltage systems	District heating	High-voltage switchgear
Distribution plants	Low-voltage apparatus	Network control
Service	Motors	Power systems
Financial services	Electric metering	Relays
Installation	Cables	Power lines
Electrical wholesaling	Installation materials	Medium-voltage equipment
		Process automation
		Drives
		Metallurgy
		Process engineering
		Robotics
		Marine, oil and gas
		Superchargers
		Transportation

ABB's businesses ranged from 'superlocal' to 'superglobal'. Table 3.1 shows how different activities were classified by the company as 'local', 'regional' or 'global'. Some would be designated 'centres of excellence' for particular products or services within their particular business areas.

The four critical pieces in this organizational jigsaw would be the:

- Executive Committee
- business areas
- companies and divisional profit centres
- country organizations.

Executive Committee

At the top of the company, the Executive Committee, meeting every three weeks, would decide global strategy and performance. Their role would be to negotiate broad targets (defined in terms of growth, profit and return on capital employed) for each business and geographic area. Each executive committee member could be responsible for both a business segment and a geographic region or major country.

Business areas

Reporting to the Executive Committee were the leaders of the 50 business areas responsible for particular products, such as transformers or electrical motors. These were responsible for optimizing the business globally. The 'global result responsibilities' of the BA leaders would be to develop and champion a worldwide strategy for their businesses and capitalize on 'economies of scale' in research and development, supply management, production technology, financing and so on. Their responsibilities would include market allocation, coordinating and approving R&D and product development, transfer pricing, know-how transfer and risk management. The BA leaders and their very small staffs would hold factories around the world to agreed budgets and cost and quality standards, decide which factory would produce which products and allocate export markets to each factory. They would also be responsible for directing R&D. The strategy was to have a common technology in each product that their local companies could adapt to local or regional needs and specifications.

In agreement with country managements (see below), the BAs would also evaluate and approve acquisitions, joint ventures and large investments. They would be expected to act as coaches to their local teams, encourage the sharing of expertise by rotating people across borders, create mixed nationality teams to solve problems and build a culture of trust and communication across their global businesses. Each business area, typically with factories in different countries around the world and employing some thousands of employees worldwide, was, in effect, a multinational business in its own right.

At the outset, the idea was to locate the BA leaders and their small staff with the country operations that were strongest in their particular product or service area. For example, the BA leader for power transformers, a Swede, worked out of Mannheim in Germany. The BA leader for drives was a Finn who initially worked in Finland and eventually moved to Milan when ABB acquired companies in Italy. Later on there was a tendency to locate BA managers at the global headquarters in Zürich where they could be closer to other BAs and to segment managers (see Chapter 10).

As Percy Barnevik later described the rationale of the BAs:

Each [business area] has a management team with a global overview, deciding if we should put a motor plant in Shanghai or not, who will produce and develop what, who should export to what market. Each business area sets the world charter for that particular product. Otherwise, local businesses would run into each other and there would be chaos out in the market (Barnevik, 1996).

Companies and divisional profit centres

Reporting to the BAs would be the operating units, the companies and their profit centres. In the belief that bureaucracy only slows a company down and insulates managers from customer needs and market realities, profit centres would be kept deliberately small with as few as 50 people. The average profit centre would be led by a management team of around five people – a leader and four colleagues. These managers would have a lot of freedom and responsibility in making trade-offs to meet budgets and plans. It was also intended that the profit centres' individual identity should encourage a sense of employee belonging and ownership. ABB defined a profit centre as 'any self-contained unit that is responsible for its own product development, production and sales as well as for its own results and asset/liability management. A profit centre must be able to measure performance.'

The ultimate aim was to create a small business atmosphere. If you can do that, said Barnevik, 'you don't have to push or entice managers every day. It becomes a self-motivated force' (*Business Week*, 1993). He explained:

We are fervent believers in decentralization. When we structure local operations, we always push to create separate legal entities. Separate companies allow you to create real balance sheets, with real responsibility for cash flow and dividends. With real balance sheets, managers inherit results from year to year through changes in equity. Separate companies also create more effective tools to recruit and motivate managers. People can aspire to meaningful career ladders in companies small enough to understand and be committed to (Taylor, 1991).

The profit centres would be the operational junction or crossing points of the matrix. Few of them would be entirely viable as stand-alone businesses, but they are linked together in various ways. On the one hand, on the global business dimension, they would be part of a business area that focused on a particular group of products or services throughout the world. On the geographical dimension, each profit centre would also be part of a national or regional company.

Country organizations

Last, but by no means least, would be ABB's country structure. ABB's operations in the developed world would be organized as national companies (such as Asea Brown Boveri Aktiengesellschaft in Germany) with their own presidents, balance sheets, income statements and career ladders. The 'local result responsibilities' of these companies would be to articulate customer-based regional strategies and capitalize on 'economy of scope' with respect to customer focus, labour relations, people development, government contacts and so on. Their main function would be to keep ABB units in their country in line with their agreed budgets and manage local relationships to the company's advantage.

The country organization emphasized its regional or national identity and could exploit its integrated local presence. This meant, for example, that it could attract local talent by offering career development across different ABB units in the same country. It could also build and strengthen higher-level contacts with customers, governments, communities, trade unions and the media more than could individual companies and profit centres. When the various activities of ABB in a particular country were added together, it would make them a significant local operation, which could expect to receive government support and preference, especially in areas of national sensitivity or pride. Many ABB country presidents would therefore be significant players in their own right. This strong identity of the country manager and organization was particularly important in the early years of ABB when it was important to be recognized and accepted as a domestic player in each country. Over the years the global dimension in the matrix has been gradually reinforced for the global BAs. For example, in the reorganization in 1993, the four country managers in the Executive Committee were replaced by three regional managers in order to strengthen regional cooperation.

Percy Barnevik summed up how ABB's 1300 or so companies fitted into the country structure:

Along with the global structure, we also have country-level management teams, each overseeing a number of companies in their countries. Different companies belong to different business areas and each works within the global charter set by

67

their business areas. At the same time, each company operates inside its country as a local domestic citizen. We see ourselves as a federation of national companies with all of these local plants tied together under a country holding company (Barnevik, 1996).

A feature of the design was the way in which the organization would trade off internal coordination and competition via:

the creation of multiple internal markets for the transfer of intermediate inputs/factors. ABB's basic competitive logic is market performance and a focus on core businesses. Mainly for tax reasons there is no central coordination of transfer prices, but these are, however, required to be 'arm's-length market-driven prices', negotiated on a case-by-case basis. In large projects, in which several companies are involved, parties begin from the 'open book' principle and from a total price which is then usually negotiated down into a derived market price (Leppänen, 1994).

As at ASEA, a major purpose of decentralizing ABB's operations was to make the organization highly customer-driven (ABB's customers are both governments and private clients). This was no empty slogan. Barnevik's master plan emphasized the importance of mutual understanding and complementary working relationships with clients. The key question was how could ABB provide the most cost-effective solution for clients in each specific competitive situation? This demanded an all-embracing knowledge of the businesses in which it operated. The best way to build such insight was to forge close, long-term relationships with customers and invest much time and effort in those relationships, listening to them and learning from them. Without such effort, major investments in R&D would not be successful. To offer cost-effective solutions demanded an ongoing and deep knowledge of clients' real plans and priorities. What were those priorities?

First, a major priority for power utilities was, and continues to be, reliability. ABB saw this as the key to safeguarding the profitability of companies supplying power. Power suppliers – themselves increasingly competing in a highly competitive environment – need maximum availability, which means maximum reliability. Planned maintenance costs time and money, but unplanned downtime can be a financial disaster. To give an idea of the possibilities here, in a 400MW baseload power station in the US, just 1 per cent more availability per year means an additional $2 million in revenues. Suppliers of power equipment thus have to commit to technological development to help power companies lower the cost of each kilowatt by minimizing their maintenance expenditures. Power companies count on the commitment of ABB to reliability to support their own commitment to customers.

Another priority for clients was fuel efficiency – achieving maximum results with a minimum of effort. Competition to boost efficiency while maintaining reliability is still one of the major issues driving manufacturers of power-generation technology. When ASEA and BBC were founded in the late nineteenth century, the first coal-fired power plant achieved efficiency rates of 3 per cent. Then, 4 kg (9 lbs) of coal yielded 1 kilowatt hour of electricity. Today, 360 grams (14 oz) is enough to generate the same power. (Since 1980, the efficiency of some types of gas turbine power plants has risen from 46 per cent to 54 per cent, and ABB claims that one of its sequential combustion gas turbines leads the industry with an efficiency of 58.5 per cent.)

One priority that would become increasingly important for power companies was cycle time – the critical factor in a power producer's fitness to compete. Utilities and independent power producers would look for faster delivery of products and services at lower prices. Their concern was how long it would take to complete their power projects; how long before they could generate their first kilowatt hour? Shortening lead times would make power companies' predictions more accurate and lower capital costs – reducing overall time by 20 per cent could save as much as 24 per cent interest during construction. The sooner they generated electricity, the faster they would generate revenue.

Once equipment is installed, it needs to be serviced. For a power company, every lost production hour is gone for ever. In power generation, this can mean a huge cost penalty and is the last thing any power producer can afford. Every time a customer contacts an equipment manufacturer about a problem, as ABB realized, it can be a real 'moment of truth'. So, service is a vital business process for both the supplier and the customer. The profitability of ABB's customers' installations depends on continuous, smooth and reliable operation of their plants. Maximum availability is an absolute necessity. With 20 per cent of the world's power generation facilities being more than 30 years old and aging fast – 33 per cent by 2005 – service becomes absolutely critical. Repowering measures and retrofits can also extend the effective operating life of plant and the return on investment it generates.

However, another fundamental change in an era of globalization is that customers, although local, are not parochial in their perspective. Their vision is worldwide. Therefore, suppliers' vision must also be worldwide. As ABB said, 'In our hands, global trends receive local solutions'. Percy Barnevik summed up the aim of ABB's global–local structure in the following much-quoted way:

> *You want to be able to optimize a business globally – to specialize in the production of components, to drive economies of scale as far as you can, to rotate managers and technologies around the world to share expertise and solve problems. But you also want to have deep local roots everywhere you operate – building products in the countries where you sell them, recruiting the best local talent from the universities, working with the local government to increase exports. If you build such an organization, you create a business advantage that's damn difficult to copy* (Taylor, 1991).

Find and appoint the key people

Although the task force on organization had a blueprint to work from, moulding such an organization from the two pre-existing companies was no easy task. 'One of the problems was that the two businesses were very similar,' says Bengt Skantze. 'We created 50 business areas and had to make sure that there were no overlaps between them. Of course, with the countries there was 100 per cent overlap. It came out well in the end, however, and there were not too many difficult cases during the first years.'

A major challenge was to find people to fill the key leadership jobs around the world. What kind of people were needed to carry through the changes? Barnevik sought out 'people capable of becoming superstars – tough-skinned individuals, who were fast on their feet, had good technical and commercial backgrounds, and had demonstrated the ability to lead others' (Arbose, 1988). Such leaders had to be 'resilient, smart and truly global in their outlook'.

Determining the skills needed was one thing. The process for identifying individuals with those skills was another. Bengt Skantze says:

Given the business portfolio of the two companies, there were two managers for every product area or country. It scared us a bit – would there be a blood slaughter, especially out in the countries? Percy organized it through line management and the personnel people. There was tremendous interviewing on both sides. The top people interviewed each other and talked about their own managers. Percy interviewed hundreds of people, it was incredible. Then we discussed who should be where. Both sides had a pretty good picture of the people. There were very few casualties in the process. There was a slot for almost everybody. We changed a few people later on. Some didn't make it, but all got a chance.

Barnevik, his top management team and human resource specialists from both companies interviewed people around the clock. Barnevik showed immense stamina in this intensive process, during which he personally conducted some 500 interviews. Arne Olsson, ABB's Head of Management Resources, says, 'I thought he was running at top speed before the merger and that he had no more gears left. I thought he was in overdrive. But when the merger took place, he moved up another gear and accelerated.' Olsson was himself heavily involved in the management selection process, which would also pay off when selecting people in future:

I met and interviewed 60 to 70 people over the months. It was a good investment in time, not just then but 5 or 6 years ahead. Engineering is a male society; it is good to spend a couple of hours getting to know someone and forming a relationship. You can then come back to people later. Part of my philosophy is to invest time in meeting people. You learn about the business and expand your network. You build a network that you can use years ahead and which is very good for communication – that's a very useful side-effect next to the basic purpose of the interview as such.

Percy Barnevik later described the intense management selection process:

> During that period I personally interviewed 500 people. I didn't know 250 of them. We had three months to do it. It was a very stressful time. What complicated the matter was that the Brown Boveri managers did not necessarily have the same values that we had. We had at least three people interview each person. I lived for almost two months in a hotel in Baden, Switzerland. I would interview 7 days a week, sometimes 12–14 hours per day, one person after another. It was a crazy period . . .

> To make the merger fly, we needed a reasonably good batting average with the first people we selected. A mistake could really hurt the company. So I said to myself: If ever in my life I have to work like a madman, it should be now. I knew the ASEA people well, but I didn't know the Brown Boveri ones. Often, it would have been easier to pick an ASEA person because I knew he would perform. But that, of course, was not acceptable. I really had to take chances on people, although I couldn't be certain of how they would perform (Kets de Vries, 1994).

Not surprisingly, Barnevik hoped he would never have to go through such a process again.

By October, it was already known who the 'winners and losers' were. The 300 top jobs were spelled out, including all country managers, all business area heads, heads of central staffs and one layer below. Interestingly, whereas only one head was appointed for most functions, in the case of the control function, Barnevik asked the two former ASEA and BBC controllers – Tomas Ericsson and Jean-Pierre Dürig – to work together as joint controllers of the new ABB because he did not want to lose the deep knowledge of each company that they held between them. He also had a new task for them: in August, he asked them to start work on a new accounting and control system for ABB.

Create a centralized, transparent control system

Barnevik believed that the only way in which his plan for radical decentralization would work was to underpin it with a centralized, transparent reporting and accounting system that would allow all levels of management to monitor and review performance of the units around the world and give higher-level managers the opportunity to react in good time. He said, 'In the working of the company, I try to decentralize. But, at the same time, one of the contradictions is that the more you decentralize, the more control you need to have. Because I can never say to my Board, if something goes wrong, that it was not me, but him. You can never abdicate your responsibilities' (Skaria, 1995).

Accordingly, Barnevik asked his controllers to design a new global computerized system built on a system that ASEA had already introduced. When told it could take three to five years to have such a system up and running, Barnevik insisted it should start trial runs by August 1988. He later recounted, 'I said, "I give you ten months. I don't care what it costs, how many people it takes, or how we go about it. I'm an old computer man myself – don't fool me. And one more thing: it must be perfect at the beginning." They thought I was crazy' (Karlgaard, 1994).

In contrast with his close involvement in the selection of senior managers, Barnevik gave Ericsson and Dürig carte blanche to produce the new system. 'He didn't ask once how we were proceeding. He trusted us as professionals and as his experts to get on with it,' remembers Dürig. 'At the end of June the following year we brought him five binders with the new accounting procedures.'

The new system was called ABACUS, which stood for ABB Accounting and Communication System. Using PC software, every month, control staff specialists at each ABB operating company would send performance data via company-owned and Infonet international lines to ABB's main data processing centre at Västerås in Sweden. This linked to ABB's Zürich head office, which would produce accounts based on the data stored in Västerås. Every month, ABACUS would track some 32 performance measures on ABB's 5000 profit centres and compare actual performance with budgets and forecasts. The data would be collected in local currencies, but translated into US dollars to allow for analysis across borders. The greater simplicity that this afforded was much appreciated by BBC's group controllers who previously had worked with three major currencies. The system also allowed the data to be consolidated or broken down by business segments and worldwide product lines, countries and companies within countries. Managers were also required to comment in English on the progress of the business and explain deviations from what had been budgeted and forecast.

The system would give Barnevik and the executive committee monthly updates on such key areas as sales, orders received (regarded as even more important than revenue) and backlog, financial results and margins, by business area, region and country. Each month, Barnevik himself would receive detailed information on 500 different operations within the group, including all the BAs, the main countries in which ABB operates and national companies within them. This would enable him to look not only for the usual measurements, such as orders, cash flow and margins, but emerging trends in performance, both globally and by country.

ABACUS, however, was not only to be a tool for top management. The figures would be given simultaneously to managers at all levels in the company. ABB profit centre managers were now expected to be business controllers and the system was designed to give them the detailed performance data they needed to control their own operations. This would allow business area leaders to devolve much of the monitoring and controlling to the profit centres. Instead, they would select key measures in order to create and distribute 'performance league tables' that compared the performance of their profit centres. The aim was to encourage the profit centres to vie with each other to improve their performance.

A key element in ABB's accounting approach was to define profit on a full cost rather than a direct basis. ABB's full cost calculation system includes all direct costs; all overheads, including administration, engineering and applied R&D; calculated interest; calculated depreciation; and provisions for currency, country and other risks. All corporate costs, including business area administration, are allocated to operating units. This means that the profit centres have the accumulation of total costs for full absorption in cost rates. This approach has three important results. First, with all costs allocated, people understand what it means to operate on very thin margins. It was now ABB policy not to accept loss orders whatever the circumstances – that is, no loss on a full cost basis. Second, it means that the accuracy of allocations is crucial and managers have to spend a lot of time analyzing the drivers of cost and using activity-based cost (ABC) systems to make allocations as accurately as possible. Third, staff units have to be able to show that they are adding real value at a competitive cost. While full costing and direct costing produce the same net figure at the corporate level, ABB's controllers believed that direct costing is very risky in a decentralized organization and that the full allocation principle changes the behaviour of profit centre managers. For example, managers have to calculate the profit potential of each order during negotiations with customers. Whereas direct costing may produce a profit margin of 40 per cent, a full cost approach may give a margin of 5 per cent – managers are therefore less likely to concede crucial small percentages of margin during hard bargaining.

Putting the ABACUS system together was eased by the fact that the Swedes and the Swiss had similar accounting principles based on the 'German school of accounting'. There was little argument between them, for example, about accounting definitions. 'We spent nine months making our ideas understandable for our new colleagues around the world rather than haggling over whether we should do it this way or that way,' says Jean-Pierre Dürig. Certainly implementing the system worldwide and educating managers in its use demanded a big initial effort. In the period July–August 1988, four instruction teams working in parallel ran 13 international seminars on the system around the world for 700 controllers and accountants.

The big challenge was to instil discipline. Jean-Pierre Dürig explains, 'The system depended on consistency and people using the same definitions. There was no time to waste in discussing the underlying calculations.' A major change for those not used to ASEA's way of doing things were the tight reporting deadlines imposed by the new system. This greatly eased the year end accounting process. Dürig explains the difference between ABB and his experience at BBC:

> *Barnevik brought in a very tight reporting cycle. I had always had problems in BBC getting annual reports from some countries. I would go to the chairman but he couldn't do anything about it. So we could only close the books in April and then have the Annual General Meeting in June. Now in ABB, the last date for reporting was 25 January. Now, I could say, if you don't do it, I can find somebody else who will. You couldn't do that in BBC.*

Another subtle but important change that arose from the adoption of ABACUS came from the signal it sent out about the need for a new way of thinking in a global group. Essentially, ABACUS demanded that performance data be coded in two ways according to the two business and geographic reporting 'legs' (see Figure 3.2). The 'business leg' provided information about business segments, business areas and business units (profit centres). The 'geographic leg' reported on regions, subregions/countries and companies. Jean-Pierre Dürig recalls:

> *For Percy Barnevik, the business leg was more important, he looked at it first. This was a remarkable change from BBC where the primary and secondary reporting was the other way round. At BBC countries and regions came first. This gave more importance to rivalry and conflict between the countries. Barnevik was more interested in the products and businesses. After he had looked at those, then he looked at the countries. This was a very important way to promote a global approach.*

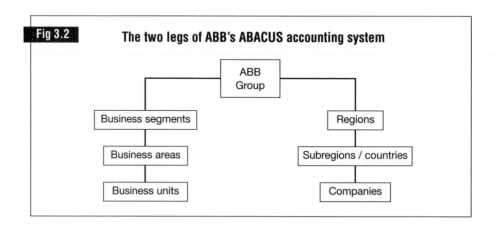

Fig 3.2 **The two legs of ABB's ABACUS accounting system**

Make English the corporate language

In the same way that ABACUS provided global corporate glue and a common financial language for the group, the new corporate language for communication between countries was to be English. ABB would insist that all senior managers, particularly those involved in international dealings, used English when writing and speaking to each other. Barnevik maintained that English was the 'world language' and that its use was essential to creating a truly global company. This may have eased the transition as Swedes and Swiss had to communicate with each other in a 'neutral' language, but it was a problem for some other countries. English was the language of only 20 per cent of ABB's people at the time of the merger. German was the most widely spoken language, followed by Swedish.

Some managers in the old BBC German operations resisted at first. Jean-Pierre Dürig, himself a German speaker, remembers having to send back memos that managers in Mannheim had written in German, requesting them to return them to him in English. Dürig welcomed the change: 'Instead of different currencies and languages, we had one currency and one language. This was much simpler.' However, many middle-aged German managers did not speak English and, as a result, did not survive the merger. As Barnevik said later:

> I write everything in English, even to Swedes. Sometimes we will sit and speak English to each other, forgetting that we are both Swedes. If people don't want to learn English, they can't work for us in senior management. Of course, you don't demand that all employees in Germany be fluent in English, but the top 200 who deal internationally must be. We are adamant about it (Kennedy, 1992).

As any ABB manager will tell you, the standing joke these days in ABB – given the huge number of cultures and mother tongues that the company encompasses across the globe – is that the international language of the Group is *Broken* English. No matter: ABB implicitly recognized that language, as an all-pervasive factor in its business activities, is not a peripheral concern but a strategic issue in managing a global firm.

Create a new corporate identity

ABB was pulling together two disparate corporate cultures. Barnevik was wise to realize that there was no point in trying to impose the ASEA corporate identity on BBC. This would not have worked, especially given the independence of BBC's German operations. Not that either company had given a great deal of attention to corporate image before. Indeed, one observer went so far as to describe both companies as heretofore 'inward-looking and rather provincial', and suggested that BBC's philosophy was *'zu leisten, aber nicht von der Leistung reden'* – perform, but don't brag about it (Catrina, 1991). However, here was an opportunity to create a totally new corporate identity around which former ASEA and BBC people could rally and that would appeal to those new companies ABB would go on to acquire. The most evident public symbol of that identity would be a new corporate logo.

Creating the new logo was another speedy project. Pentagram, the London-based international design consultancy that was chosen to design the logo, was used to having several months for such a project. Instead, they were given only weeks in which to do it. The distinctive new logo, with 'ABB' in red on a white background – now a familiar sight on ABB office buildings and advertisements throughout the world, reportedly cost £25,000 to design. This was a mere 'bagatelle', as one observer put it, given the many ways in which it could be exploited for communications purposes[1] (Catrina, 1991). ABB says that the ABB name and logo are its signature and project the strength of the Group. They are to be used in all the company's communication, thereby increasing Group unity and awareness of the range of products, systems and services that the firm can provide to its customers.

Communicate the strategy and the supporting policies intensively

The new logo was to be presented at a 'cornerstone' event to mark the beginning of the company. Having identified his senior team, Barnevik believed it important to share his vision of the company with them and give them a framework within which to do business. One of his main objectives was to make managers across the organization more responsible for performance. However, he realized that one of the biggest problems of the merger was to get the message of what the new company was all about down through all the layers in the organization. He believed that open communication was the best way to do this. At the beginning of January 1988, he invited the 250 senior managers to Cannes in the South of France for a three-day seminar, during which he laid out his way of looking at the new company and told them about ABB's objectives and strategies for the future. 'We did the whole thing full blast,' remembers Barnevik. He talked participants through 198 slides that explained, in detail, the principles on which the merged company would operate and the way in which people should act in the company. Participants were also told about the financial targets for the new group – 10 per cent for the result margin, and 25 per cent for return on capital employed.

One of the biggest surprises for participants from the former BBC was Barnevik's announcement that ABB would focus on the power and electrotechnical industry and that no major, unrelated diversification was intended. BBC had been heavily criticized for its own focus on its core power businesses. Barnevik presented ten questions to the audience about whether or not it was the right strategy to stay with power.

1 Have we or are we developing technologies for the future?
2 Are we able to use merger opportunities, cut capacity and costs to be a low-cost producer?

3   Can we exploit opportunities in niches and services?
4   Do we keep up quality, reliability and services?
5   Do we have domestic markets with entrenched positions?
6   Can we exploit export financing opportunities?
7   Can we use competitors' decline and exit ambitions?
8   Do we have staying power for the 1990s?
9   Can we project ourselves worldwide as the company in power, someone for utilities to rely on in the long term?
10   Do we have the flexibility and strategic ability to position ourselves in this turbulent and mixed scenario?

Barnevik's summation: 'Yes on 8 to 10 out of 10. Power is a sure winner and will propel ABB into high profitability.' Indeed, profitability was the first priority. Volume increases would not solve cost problems. ABB needed to become competitive and profitable before it could expand. Loss orders would no longer be accepted.

To back up his presentation, Barnevik introduced a 21–page corporate policy bible explaining the principles. This would be the foundation of what Barnevik later called ABB's 'global umbrella culture' or its 'global corporate glue'. Bengt Skantze remembers the policy bible. 'It was not an abstract document, it was a handbook of management in real life.'

Looking back ten years later at the slides and the policy handbook that were presented during the conference, he says, 'The policies that we made at the time of the merger were very important. Every company today has its statement of mission, policies, and values. ABB has one and, in a sense, it could belong to any company. But when we produced it the first time, it was new. It was a very handsome thing about how to manage a merger.'

Barnevik deployed his communication skills to the full. Bengt Skantze explains:

> One of the tricks was that Percy put tremendous effort into the cultural aspects of the merger and the way people's minds work and the way we think. People do not really react to written words. So we tried to put in slogans that people would remember. For example, we wanted to keep the organization flat. But people do not remember expressions like we want a 'flatter organization'. Instead, we said we do not want any 'sandwich men' [that is, unnecessary layers of management]. People would then say 'Oh, I don't want to be a sandwich man'. They would remember an expression like that.

Barnevik's presentation was rich in colourful metaphors that put the message across vividly. Bengt Skantze gives another example: 'There was, at least, earlier, a tendency for Continental managers to become detached from operations when they were promoted. This is unacceptable. We said that high-level managers must have a "finger in the pie".' Another key skill was

Barnevik's ability to back up his points with practical examples. 'Percy is a master of communication,' says Skantze. 'He has hundreds of real examples behind everything. He doesn't just talk principles, he has lots of examples to illustrate them. He'll say, "Look at that motor factory there . . ."'

Two central messages were emphasized at Cannes – the necessity for speed and the need for mutual confidence to avoid the 'we/they syndrome' between the merger partners. Participants were also warned about the dangers of looking inwards during a merger. Skantze says, 'We had lots of problems with customers during the merger because their suppliers were changed. We told people to not forget the customers. In the midst of a merger, it is very important to spend time with customers.'

Another message emphasized in Barnevik's slides was the need to build on the combined strengths of the two companies and 'negate the negatives. A true merger does not come automatically or naturally – it is unnatural. Managers who can understand the policies, including the policies for change, *and* live up to the special merger challenges will be the ABB "superstars"'.

At the end of the conference, the assembled ABB superstars were asked to transmit all of what Barnevik had told them to the next layer of management – 30,000 of them worldwide – within the following 60 days. That meant more than just sending out the policy bible. The document had to be translated into the local languages. The 50 business area management teams whose task forces were to execute the strategy were expected to hold their own conferences and sit with their people for a full day to hash it out. Similar meetings were to take place at regional level, so most middle managers would attend two sessions. The Cannes conference was also videotaped and made available to local managers. Barnevik's adage was 'Don't inform, *overinform*'.

Barnevik's performance at the Cannes conference and his evident commitment to the new company made a very big impact. His record at ASEA and the Strömberg acquisition also created a sense of trust in the plans. As Volker Leichsering, ABB's former head of corporate communications, says, 'ABB's new vision was to be a viable global competitor. There was a clear vision, mission, and corporate communications were installed straight away. There were clear targets and everyone knew where to go.'

However, as Barnevik admitted, 'Catchwords are only 5 per cent, 95 per cent is in the execution.' The initial conferences had to be followed up with a massive communication programme to reach everybody in the company. Also, Barnevik and the other Executive Committee members realized that they had to take the message directly to people. 'You cannot hide up there in an ivory tower,' he said. 'You have to be out there. I meet several thousand people each year and my colleagues do the same.' Barnevik would himself pursue a grinding schedule in the next few years, travelling and spending as much time with middle managers as he could. He was realistic about how fast he could move things. He would say in 1989, 'If we have mobilized half of them, that is fantastic. If we have managed 30 per cent, that's not so bad.'

Putting across the message of change right through the Group was an immense task. During the early period, ABB would run 14 three-day middle manager seminars each year held roughly every three weeks. Barnevik and his Executive Committee colleagues would use these as an opportunity to explain policies and strategies first hand. In real, active working sessions, they described how to work in the matrix, how to develop people, and about ABB's programmes to cut production cycle times and raise quality. Barnevik would say later:

> People think I am some kind of giant who is everywhere. Not so. It is a question of making values known and accepted by hundreds of managers who ultimately reach down to 25,000 more managers. The question is how to make 25,000 managers move like an army? It doesn't matter so much if you move in exactly the right direction or not, so long as you move. I tell people that if we make 100 decisions and 70 turn out right, that's good enough (Kennedy, 1992).

Streamline operations

One of the messages that Barnevik had given the managers assembled at the Cannes conference was the need to drastically cut costs and reduce overheads to boost profit margins. As at ASEA, Barnevik's major initial concern was cost-cutting by means of closing excess capacity. The merged companies would also cut costs by eliminating overlapping manufacturing and distribution operations and by pooling research and development efforts. At the beginning of 1988, ABB announced that the merger would lead to the closure of 100 plants and that another 200 would be merged. Some of the cuts would fall hard on the heartlands of the former BBC. Out of 17,000 jobs in Switzerland 2,500 would be cut. The company's German workforce of 36,000 would be cut by over 10 per cent over 3 years, some the result of natural wastage and early retirement, but some dismissals would also be necessary.

As at ASEA, some of the most drastic cuts fell on BBC's corporate headquarters. Barnevik set out to reduce the headcount at corporate head office using the 30 per cent rule, which means that 30 per cent retire or are made redundant, 30 per cent transfer into new service companies, 30 per cent are absorbed by operating units, and the remaining 10 per cent form the new head office. ABB's head office would employ only 150 people. Further attrition would occur. After three years, half of those who stayed on or transferred to the operating units had gone. Bengt Skantze says, 'We have a hatred of overhead. The 30 per cent rule has since been much quoted. People didn't believe it could be done, but we did it and we actually did it twice as we later halved it again.'

One example of the speed and determination with which things were now moving was the move of top management and the corporate staffs into the new head office building in Affolternstrasse by the railway station in the Oerlikon suburb of Zürich in 1988. This had previously belonged to the transmission and distribution segment of BBC, which was now summarily moved out and the building quickly renovated. As Beat Hess says, 'This would not have been possible before – it would have taken two years – but in no time, we moved into a refurbished office and started the new group.'

To carry out the rationalizations in the wider group, task forces were established, the aim of which was to turn ABB, within the first two years, into the lowest-cost producer worldwide. Under the direction of the business areas, the task forces would push through exchanges of products and components among factories to achieve economies of scale and streamline manufacturing, marketing and financial operations. The role of the business area management was to compare the manufacturing costs for a given product at all its plants and select the best one as a model for the others.

One example of streamlining was the proposal to exchange areas of power-generating equipment production between Germany and Switzerland. Turbine and generator production would be divided so that Birr, a BBC company in Switzerland, concentrated on the rotating parts and Mannheim on the stationary parts for the complete range. Although proposed in the first half of 1988, this exchange did not take place until later in the year due to resistance from employees and managers.

The disinvestments allowed by the restructuring would, of course, generate useful capital gains – some $600 million in the first year. A major real estate operation was set up under a manager at the Zürich head office to exploit the space – both factory and land – released by the rationalization of production. ABB established real estate companies in six major countries to take over the ownership of all ABB property. The industrial operations then became tenants, paying a market price, giving the real estate companies an incentive to ensure that the property was exploited in the most effective way.

Barnevik knew from his previous experience at ASEA that, inevitably, he would meet resistance to his plans. His relations with the company's Board, Executive Committee and the new top management team were relatively straightforward compared with the situation he had faced at ASEA in 1980. However, the radical redeployment of people and resources, and the cuts in the workforce, were bound to be opposed by some of the workforce and those who were to lose their jobs. The trade unions in those countries where change was to strike hardest would also resist the plans. Comparing the ABB merger with the ASEA turnaround, a Swedish top manager said at the time, 'It's like comparing a quiet jog with the New York marathon' (Brege and Brandes, 1993).

ABB Power Transformers – building a global business area

Swedish researcher Christian Berggren's study of the restructuring and change processes in ABB's Power Transformers business area demonstrates the differing impacts on the BA's existing plants and on its new acquisitions (Berggren, 1996). ASEA's transformer centre in Ludvika in Sweden, a world leader in transformer technology (known as the 'Mecca of transformers'), and its German factory at Bad Honnef, played an important role as teachers for the acquired businesses. The aim of the first 'catch-up' phase was to integrate the businesses within the discipline of the overall international business structure and improve the performance of the acquired plants to an internationally competitive level. This involved modernizing plants, reducing staff numbers (sometimes by half) and instilling a new sense of urgency and awareness of world standards and competition. Initially, the creation of the transformer BA meant less internal change for the core plants than the acquired plants. It did, however, imply some loss of independence for Bad Honnef and Ludvika as decision making about market allocations, exports, capacity and future products and technology were now transferred to the BA headquarters in Mannheim. However, compared to the plants acquired in the USA and other countries such as Canada, Spain, Australia and Poland, the core companies kept a large degree of autonomy, 'reflected in local management's detached attitude toward the BA-wide rationalization programmes' (Berggren, 1996). New internal benchmarking exercises and the emphasis on cross-border learning led to big improvements in the acquired plants but had less impact within the core group.

In 1993–94, the transformer business area started the 'convergence' phase aimed at establishing coordination and standardization across all the plants, involving a new quality drive, the development of common products and processes, and consolidation of production operations into an international two-tiered structure whereby assembly, test and service were dispersed locally and the production of core components was increasingly consolidated in each main region. BA policies and programmes would now affect the whole business area much more deeply than before, including the core, as well as the acquired, plants. The ultimate aim of the BA was to make the plants interchangeable by completely standardizing products, processes and management systems, thereby keeping a distributed structure but optimizing production globally. This would make it possible for excess orders from an overloaded plant to be smoothly transferred to another plant, and reductions to be made in global capacity without affecting production volume or local presence. It would also facilitate the adoption of best practice from the different plants worldwide, whereby the best approach to each step in manufacturing could be identified and adopted as the global standard.

While Christian Berggren observed that the first phase led to impressive improvements in manufacturing efficiency, quality and delivery times, he felt that the second phase was more difficult to anticipate. 'The business area must be understood as a dynamic and complex web of central initiatives on the one hand, implementation, adaptation and local initiatives on the other. The matrix structure of ABB tends to stimulate a complex interplay of initiatives; the emphasis on strong external relations, with suppliers and customers, increases the potential for diverse initiatives. This makes the structure of the business area dynamic, and outcomes open-ended' (Berggren, 1996).

Reference

Berggren, Christian (1996) 'Building a truly global organization? ABB and the problems of integrating a multi-domestic enterprise', *Scandinavian Journal of Management*, **12** (2), 123–37.

ABB Strömberg – a rehearsal for building a global organization

The purchase and turnaround in 1986 of its arch-rival in the Nordic region, the Finnish company Strömberg, was a major step in ASEA's Nordic strategy. Percy Barnevik describes it as a 'dress rehearsal' for ABB's later approach to acquiring companies and building a global organization.

Strömberg was ASEA's first major foreign acquisition. Rolf Leppänen, who for seven years was a senior manager in ABB's drives business area, Strömberg's core competence area, sees it as,

> a kind of exercise for the global future . . . it was also an important learning experience for ASEA which still remembered what happened in 1962, the last time it tried to buy Strömberg . . . [and it was], on a small scale, something that ASEA had to 'clone' in its later international acquisitions (Leppänen, 1994).

Gottfrid Strömberg founded the company named after him in 1889 and it had since become virtually a national institution in Finland. That a small national champion survived in the face of foreign competition, especially German and US firms, is a tribute to the company and its products. By the 1980s, however, Strömberg was manufacturing a very large range of products but operating out of a restricted domestic market. Percy Barnevik once described the situation:

> The company made an unbelievable assortment of products, probably half of what ABB makes today. It built generators, transformers, drives, circuit breakers – all of them for the Finnish market, many of them for export. It was a classic example of a big company in a small country that survived because of a protected market. Not surprisingly, much of what it made was not up to world-class standards, and the company was not very profitable. How can you expect a country with half the population of New Jersey to be profitable in everything from hydropower to circuit breakers? (Taylor, 1991).

In 1986 Strömberg had 9000 employees and was running at a loss of over 100 million Finnish marks (FIM) on a turnover of 2.5 billion FIM (Leppänen, 1994). It was attractive to ASEA for a number of reasons. Finland itself was a world leader in papermaking machinery technology and was, in particular, one of the world's leading suppliers of electrical drive systems to the global pulp and paper industry. ASEA had known Finland and Strömberg for a long time and continued to value the latter's drive technology.

This time, when ASEA made its bid, it prepared the ground very carefully. Confidential negotiations were carried out with key government representatives. One story has it that Percy Barnevik hired a helicopter on midsummer's eve to reach the Finnish Minister of Industry at his summer cottage in the East of Finland. According to one report, 'the trip was so successful that ASEA never had to furnish any real guarantees, for example, on employment' (Leppänen, 1994). ASEA's top managers also gave reassuring interviews to the Finnish media emphasizing the new international opportunities that would open up for Strömberg. Finnish businessmen who expressed doubts about the acquisition were invited to become members of Strömberg's Board.

ASEA gave Strömberg's existing management the task of turning the company, now known as ABB Strömberg[1], around. This involved three main themes (Leppänen, 1994):

- mutual exchange of product development and manufacture between Finnish and Swedish units;
- cost and capital rationalization within each Strömberg division;
- rationalization of central staff functions.

ASEA wanted right from the start to give the Finns a feeling that they had a special responsibility – a 'win-win' situation with ASEA, to use one of Percy Barnevik's favourite expressions. The solution was to focus on Strömberg's world class core technology of electric drives. At the end of July 1986, a team of three people, two from ASEA and one from Strömberg, was appointed to plan the merger and restructuring. One member had the special task of identifying and reorganizing the electric drives business, the most valuable part of Strömberg.

The team reported in September 1986 and key managers in Sweden and Finland were then asked to make joint recommendations on the next steps and to prepare the implementation of the merger plan in more detail. ASEA's top management demanded that all the changes be carried out very quickly. This resulted, during 1987, in the restructuring of Strömberg's independent divisions so that they had their own management teams, budget and balance sheet. The divisions took over most of the work previously performed by the central functions and separate support units were set up as profit centres to look after such areas as training, security, transportation, and so on. Out of 880 people in Strömberg's headquarters, 240 left the company, mainly taking early retirement. Rolf Leppänen notes that the main effect of the reorganization of central staff was not an immediate rationalization benefit but, rather, the psychological effect of encouraging a stronger profit orientation in the company.

Most of the organizational changes were discussed and prepared in cross-company task forces during the annual management workshop process started in

1989 after the ABB merger. During 1988–92, the divisions would become legally independent companies. On the initiative of ABB's head office, a group-wide communication programme on ABB's mission, values and policies was started as part of the strengthening of ABB's global culture. This was supported by ABB's Customer Focus initiative to improve the market and process orientation of ABB companies.

In 1991, Barnevik could say:

Strömberg is no longer a stand-alone company. It is part of ABB's global matrix. The company still exists – there is a president of ABB Strömberg – but its charter is different. It is no longer the centre of the world for every product it sells. It still manufactures and services many products for the Finnish market. It also sells certain products to allocated markets outside Finland. And it is ABB's worldwide centre of excellence for one important group of products, electric drives, in which it had a long history of technological leadership and effective manufacturing. Strömberg is a hell of a lot stronger because of this. Its total exports from Finland increased more than 50 per cent in 3 years. ABB Strömberg has become one of the most profitable companies in the whole of the ABB group, with a return on capital employed of around 30 per cent . . . In four years, Strömberg's exports to Germany and France increased ten times (Taylor, 1991).

'Why was it successful?', asks Barnevik. Because, he says, the company had access to a distribution network it could never have built itself.

We had our own insight into the impact of the changes when in the early 1990s, in the course of our research into the development of international managers, we talked with one of Strömberg's Finnish senior managers in the drives business in Helsinki. He told us:

The most important thing was that the management culture changed. Before ASEA bought Strömberg, it was decentralized on paper, but in practice it was a very centralized organization. All the important – and also many not so important decisions – were made by a very few people. In our company, we have six divisions and those division managers have a lot of power to do things within the whole range of the normal business. They can make all the decisions within their division. In most cases, those divisions have been divided into profit centres and power has been distributed to the profit centre managers. That's the most radical change. The other thing is that both the quality and quantity of reporting was increased. Before, as a manager, you received a monthly report which wasn't very reliable and there were a lot of centralized costs which were divided using certain rules. The result was that the people who were responsible for costs didn't feel as though they were responsible. The result of the change of culture was that the whole organization right down to the factory floor was very motivated. People were informed of past performance, they were told about the targets – which were very demanding but, on the other hand, were very fair – and the managers who really needed the power got the power to do the job.

Rolf Leppänen says that the importance of the Strömberg acquisition was that it was 'the final test for the Barnevik turnaround management before it would move to the European mainland'.

The Strömberg case shows two familiar factors:

Speed of implementation and the internal small business approach. All of the difficult decisions were made early in the process. These included the appointment of top management and the new company structure. Barnevik himself took charge of communications both with external groups as well as Strömberg personnel. He presented a clear vision for the future and a lot of facts in his persuasive manner. People became convinced of this 'global opportunity' (Leppänen, 1994).

As Rolf Leppänen points out, all of the national institutional factors favoured ASEA in its acquisition of Strömberg: 'Finland shares strong historical links with Sweden. Through emigration Finland has provided workers and management to Sweden and a significant part [of Finnish business is] dominated by Swedish language-speaking Finns' (Leppänen, 1994). Sweden and Finland share similar 'educational systems, knowledge-base of the people, worldview, religion and even product standards' (Leppänen, 1994).

The real test of ABB's master plan, however, would come in countries where these supportive factors did not exist.

Note
1 ABB Strömberg later changed its name to ABB Oy.

References

Taylor, William (1991) 'The logic of global business: an interview with ABB's Percy Barnevik', *Harvard Business Review*, March–April, 91–105.

Leppänen, Rolf (1994) *ABB Action Recipe: Strategic Management in the Growth and Restructuring of a European Enterprise*. Helsinki: International Networking Publishing INP Oy.

Generate a new entrepreneurial spirit at BBC

ASEA's people (including Strömberg – see above) had already experienced the Barnevik medicine, although there was still scope for further decentralization. However, for the old BBC, the change to the international matrix, with the breaking down of the functional organization and its formal hierarchies, the widespread rationalizations, coordination of production, and cuts in head office staff, were going to be particularly difficult. That the changes would meet with resistance from managers was hardly surprising, but the changes also started to encourage a new spirit of entrepreneurialism. Beat Hess, ABB's corporate counsel, remembers that:

BBC was one large organization in Baden. Now people there had the opportunity to create their own profit centres. People came to me and said 'I hear I can create my own company – but how do I do it?' We could help them with this. They always asked 'What will my title be?' We drew up a list of ten possible titles, starting with President and Chief Executive. People chose President and Chief Executive! So we said 'Here's what you do to create a company and you can be President and Chief Executive'. It gave a tremendous push to people to increase their profits. Things suddenly became transparent.

BBC had some large central staff units, such as BBI – Brown Boveri International – an organization of several hundred people administering BBC's export organization, mostly in developing countries. Says Hess:

There was no more big pot that you could get money from. You were either a profit centre or you had to sell your services. With one move, there were hundreds of people who asked 'Who will take my services?' and hundreds of people who replied 'We don't need you now'! If you were unable to turn your unit into a profit centre or sell your services, you were out. It was an excellent way to separate the services that had been built up over dozens of years in a big administrative organization from those that were really necessary. Services were reduced to the bare minimum necessary because suddenly profit centres could pick what services they needed. In the extreme case, they could say to the Legal Department 'We don't need you any more'. Or, they could say to the Marketing Department 'We will do our own marketing in Italy or India'. BBC had lots of marketing people who didn't know where their salaries came from.

Beat Hess is adamant about the need for change:

It was an abrupt end to all that. We turned a number of BBC units into profit-making companies. From year one to today, the Swiss ABB has been one of the biggest profit contributors to the group. This change of attitude was the motivating and driving factor for profit generation. Many complained and lamented about the changes, but they were so strongly implemented that those who didn't stop complaining just went. 'You can complain three times but, for heaven's sake, then stop or you go.' You can't have people sitting around complaining. You need people who are convinced it is the right thing to do. Everyone here is convinced of this.

What was the difference in working for ABB after BBC? 'Speed of action. Working late hours. It was much more demanding,' says Jean-Pierre Dürig. 'We were flying frequently to New York on Concorde and had to be back next day in the office at 8.00 am. That was not the way we worked in BBC.' Dürig also remembers the change in decision making:

After the merger, Percy Barnevik spelled out a few things. He said, 'If, out of ten decisions, seven are right, and three are wrong, I'm satisfied.' In BBC, you had to make ten decisions and get them all right. But it was preferable to make no decisions because that would have involved top management who, before Leutwiler, kept things static with no innovation. We couldn't make a decision because it was always questioned. It avoided a lot of trouble if we kept quiet. This caused a lot of frustration. Now we had much shorter ways to make decisions. More freedom of action and responsibility was given to lower levels with the opportunity to make errors without being shot on the spot. This encouraged people.

In addition to working long hours in the office, senior managers now had to be flexible. Dürig installed a telephone by his bedside:

If Percy called with a question at 1 o'clock in the morning from New York where it was 7 in the evening, I had my papers and I had to wake up and talk and explain. He was away during the week so we had to work on the weekends when he was in the office. Those not able to keep up the pace had to go. But Percy was also very generous. If I needed to go to the US or Singapore, he said 'OK, when are you back? Where can I reach you?'

Barnevik was aware of the need for a climate of open communication and responsiveness in forging a global organization. He had clearly already achieved this at ASEA. Dürig remembers calling a Swedish finance manager for some information. 'When I phoned, they said he wasn't there but that he would call back in two hours. Two hours later, he called me from Singapore. I thought he was still in Västerås. In BBC, you almost needed approval to phone the US.' The Swedes' heavy use of the telephone for international communication was another contrast for Dürig: 'They spent six hours a day on the phone. I used to say that in five years they will have grown a phone instead of their right arm!'

It was not only senior and middle managers who felt the impact of a new way of doing things at BBC. To force administrative staff to solve problems faster at one factory, for example, ABB moved an entire floor of administrators out of their separate office building into the noisy factory. Angry at first, they gradually came to see the benefit in being close to the shop floor. Factory workers no longer had to walk over to the office building to report problems such as machine breakdowns. The factory manager said, 'It was my idea to have the office in the factory 15 years ago. Back then, I was told it couldn't be done. Workers should work, not talk' (Schares, 1993).

Align Germany with the new strategy

The restructuring called for some tough decisions. Percy Barnevik explains the challenges in dealing with the human and organizational issues involved in a cross-border merger:

It's hard to tell a competent country manager in Athens or Amsterdam, 'You've done a good job for 15 years, but unfortunately this other manager has done a better job and our only choice is to appoint your colleague to run the operation.' If you have two plants in the same country running well but you only need one after the merger, it's tough to explain that to employees in the plant to be closed. Restructuring creates lots of pain and heartache, so many companies choose not to begin the process, to avoid the pain (Taylor, 1991).

Because of its traditionally independent role in BBC, ABB's $2 billion operation in Germany was a special challenge to win over. One of the main reasons for the merger was Barnevik's desire to obtain a stronger foothold within the EU and BBC had its largest business in Germany, which it considered, along with Italy and Austria, to be its home market. Germany would continue to be ABB's largest operation, but was a technology-driven, low-profit operation – 'a real underperformer' in Barnevik's words (Taylor, 1991). What happened here would be a signal to the rest of the organization and to other ABB stakeholders about the future. It was very important to get things right here.

In 1988, Barnevik installed one of his closest aides, former BMW executive Eberhard von Koerber, as head of ABB's operations in West Germany. His instructions were to reduce the centralized and functional HQ bureaucracy in Mannheim, introduce greater accountability, cut costs by 20 per cent, rationalize production overlaps, especially between Switzerland and Germany, reduce manufacturing time by a third, cut 10 per cent of the 36,500 jobs and take a big slice out of Siemens' European market share. ABB experienced six months of intense union resistance, including strikes, demonstrations, barricades and sit-ins, plus strident criticism in the press and passive resistance by German managers. Workers burned von Koerber in effigy and politicians and religious leaders demanded his sacking over the proposed personnel cuts.

Eberhard von Koerber was clear about the need to stand firm: 'You have to be sure you do the things the law entitles you to do, and never give in. And you have to endure the public onslaught' (Rapoport, 1992). It was only by issuing an ultimatum, by telling the unions that factories would be closed and work moved elsewhere in Europe that Barnevik and von Koerber achieved the cuts they wanted. Barnevik wanted to win the unions over: 'After a while, once the unions understood the game plan, the loud protest disappeared and our relationship became very constructive . . . Once the unions got on board, they became allies in our effort to reform management and rationalize operations' (Taylor, 1991).

As at head office in Switzerland, von Koerber reduced central Mannheim staff from 1600 to 100 in 2 years and moved resources away from the central HQ towards production facilities. Whereas the German subsidiary of BBC was a single company before the merger, and there had been few clear managerial responsibilities or accountability, von Koerber created 30 German companies, each with its own president and chief executive (this increased to 54 ABB companies in Germany 4 years later). The outstanding performers could now be identified and their talents could be used elsewhere in the group. During that time, von Koerber also trimmed factory capacity by over half. The results were dramatic and showed what could be done. ABB Germany's profit margins rose from a mere 1.4 per cent in 1987 to 2.9 per cent. ABB also gained market share on Siemens, with orders 18 per cent up in a European market that grew only 5 per cent in 1989. Sales per employee in Germany leaped from $55,000 in 1987 to $94,000 in 1990 and ABB Germany was seen to be catching up its arch-rival Siemens on its own home ground.

Barnevik said, 'I don't buy these excuses that you can't change Europe. People are not dumb. They know that if their company is not competitive, there is no job security' (Rapoport, 1992). Barnevik had stood his ground and acted tough in Germany, but he also believed that this had to be accompanied by positive direct communication. He said:

> Take one of the 600 middle-level managers in Germany. He may be 50 years old and have worked in a stable environment for the past 25 years. He may have to work some extra hours, change his methods, perhaps switch to another job inside the company and he asks why the hell should he. You tell him it is to increase low profitability. He says we have had a nice life on a 2 per cent margin for the past 25 years, so why do you want 5 per cent or even 7 per cent? Well, you talk of job security, long-term expansion, the threat from the Community's single market and that a strong company is good for him and his family. But somebody has to talk to Mr Müller and motivate him (Dullforce, 1989).

Barnevik also believed in the power of example in persuading people to change their ways of doing things:

> One of the real keys to success in this business is having the good examples to be able to convince people. When you talk to a guy in Germany who has 17 staff working to him, you cannot intellectually convince him that he could do the job with a third of the number. But if you put him on a plane to, say, Finland where they make the same volume but have a third of the staff, that is a different matter. Then he can't just shake his head and say, this Barnevik does not know what he is talking about (Brown, 1994).

Walk the talk

Germany showed what the Barnevik turnaround formula could achieve, but the early days of the change process were difficult, even for battle-hardened Barnevik. He felt it was worth it, however. He believed that, in the end, the company came through the early restructuring process better, leaner and more ready to compete in world markets. As one industry observer commented,

'From an outside perspective, ABB is still in a colossal ferment of merging, expanding, and cost-cutting. But the ferment does have direction and, as his colleagues freely testify, that direction comes from Barnevik himself, who is unsparing in the intellectual and physical resources he devotes to his job' (Dullforce, 1989). One of those colleagues, Beat Hess, pays tribute to Barnevik's role:

> *I can't say enough that the one key figure was Percy Barnevik, the person who knit-ted everything together. It was not only a merger of those two companies. It was first a merger and then a complete reorganization of the entire Group. I am convinced we could not have succeeded without a complete turnaround from top to bottom. Barnevik was a relentless driving force and was right behind it and made sure our objectives were effectively implemented, always with the reliable support of his secretary, Lena Lundgren.*

Barnevik admits that the reorganization was tough: 'The cross-border restruc-turing of companies at the beginning of the merger – the closing down of plants – is a particularly painful example [of tough decision making]. While the process is necessary, it wears you down. The decisions are highly visible; it becomes a very emotional matter' (Kets de Vries, 1994). Barnevik remembers closing a Swedish plant when a Swedish company was merged with a Swiss one and relocated to Switzerland. He received letters from senior ASEA man-agers pleading with him not to 'destroy' ASEA Sweden, not just because they had lost their jobs but because they felt Sweden had lost out. There were torch-lit demonstrations and marches to the mayor's office and Barnevik was met by demonstrators at the airport.

He remembers similar events in Switzerland and Germany:

> *What is difficult here is to combine empathy with decisiveness. You have to go on living. Limit sleepless nights, remorsefulness, and all that. Now I had a hell of a rep-utation in Sweden and in Germany. I was called a sort of raider . . . I was described as the sort of ruthless person who gets satisfaction out of getting rid of people. The newspapers called it 'Percy's reign of terror.' When you do these kinds of things, people think that you are a terrible character, that you really don't give a damn. But it is a job you have to do. I think good managers do that job well. Napoleon used to say that the best generals are the generals of retreat. The offensive generals are the ones who become famous, but to be able to handle a retreat is something that is often underestimated . . . If a person is a ruthless, unemotional character I don't think he's suitable for the task of firing people* (Kets de Vries, 1994).

Barnevik believes that, despite the necessity to achieve change quickly, it is also vital to take time to talk to people:

> *It is easy to write a letter to 5000 people saying that's it, we don't need you any more, or we are not hiring any more people, and just give an order. To sit down for hours*

and talk about it and listen to their problems and fears is more difficult. But if you don't take the time to go through that, to convince people, but instead push it because you lack time, that is a problem (Brown, 1994).

Although Barnevik certainly drove his vision relentlessly through the organization, he emphasizes the need for an open style at the top:

I appreciate that at times I can overwhelm people. I'm aware of the risk, sitting in my position, of not getting enough feedback and having a sufficiently open attitude. It is comfortable having people agree with you. The temptation is always there . . . In this organization, for people who know me well, there is absolutely no problem with saying, 'You are wrong. I disagree.' But, of course, in an organization of this size there are many people who don't know me that well. In the Latin countries especially, and maybe in Germany, there is a tendency to be a little cautious, not to offend the top guy. It is a challenge to make people really speak their minds and tell you things openly, particularly unpleasant things. I can only say that I am aware of the problem, that I work at it. With new people whom I don't know well, I go out of my way to try to build their confidence so that they don't worry about that aspect of the conversation (Kets de Vries, 1994).

Bengt Skantze recalls his experiences of both the ASEA and the ABB change processes:

In a large group, especially after a merger and the increased complexity that goes with that, you must have a top management that is extremely persistent and tough, that never stops, despite arguments, that keeps the idea and can see your vision. But then you have to say, 'yes, we are going to do it.' You have to build up, and talk to hundreds of people below so they understand the problem. The strength of ASEA and ABB is that we communicated a strategy and followed it. That gives credibility to management. We are not coming up with a lot of ideas. Our strength is producing a straightforward, simple strategy and then implementing it.

One of the most important factors in making the restructuring work was a widespread determination in the company to prove the doubters wrong. Percy Barnevik says:

Many people were stunned by the merger. Never in their wildest dreams had they thought that this would happen. Many of them said to themselves, this is going to hell, this is not going to work. At Brown Boveri there had been infighting for 100 years between Germany, Switzerland, France and Italy. Other critics of the merger said that the Scandinavians would not fit in continental Europe at all. It was going to be a complete disaster. We were going to prove them wrong; we were going to show them that restructuring across borders could work. The desire among so many of us to prove that the merger would work was an important glue during those first few years (Kets de Vries, 1994).

Lessons from a successful double turnaround

Staffan Brege and Ove Brandes have suggested (from the perspective of 1993) some important lessons from the 'successful double turnaround' of ASEA and ABB (Brege and Brandes, 1993), including the following:

- A Board that wants a radical turnaround orientation should replace the incumbent CEO with an externally recruited one, preferably with executive experience of similar strategic and structural changes.
- The Board should give the newly appointed CEO full support and *carte blanche*, at the same time presenting challenging goals and demands for reasonably fast improvements.
- Viable core competence and core businesses are important requisites for turnaround success.
- An important prerequisite for a successful turnaround is the initial crisis consciousness and the climate for change within the organization.
- The new CEO and the top management team need a 'helicopter view' and the capacity to draw consistent conclusions from large amounts of information to solve short-term emergencies, develop strategic visions, determine business portfolio priorities and reorganizations, introduce new control systems and appoint managers.
- Core business and core competence strategies present the best opportunities for turnaround success – a phase of retrenchment is necessary before expansion can begin.
- Competitive strategic business unit (SBU) strategies are the basis for corporate strategy success – each business must survive on its own qualifications. Don't allow arguments about synergies to be used as an excuse for neglecting retrenchment programmes for weak businesses.
- Divisionalization and decentralization are important instruments to vitalize the organization and increase the profit- and market-orientation.
- Critical points in the restructuring are:
  – to define the SBUs clearly enough so they can have their own profit and loss account and balance sheet;
  – the follow-up, with adequate control and reporting systems;
  – the appointment of SBU managers who can take full responsibility for their unit.
- Cultural change in the depths of a large organization is a slow process – the most obvious change in attitudes will be seen in the case of profit centre managers. Widespread crisis awareness will make change happen faster because the basic values have been questioned.
- The new CEO should immediately take charge and establish the change process at a high pace. It is important to show early improvements.
- The new CEO should give the organization a sense of long-term direction, but at the same time strengthen the crisis consciousness in the organization by emphasizing the seriousness of the prevailing situation. (The CEO's initial

position of power is that designated by the Board, but they also need to establish other power positions.)

- The new CEO should make use of the 'Bennborn effect' to involve current members of top management in contributing well-articulated ideas towards formulating a new strategic orientation (thereby facilitating its implementation).
- The CEO and top management team must establish a productive dialogue with SBU managers and gradually delegate the strategic initiative to the SBU managers. The dialogue is a part of the learning process that leads to SBU managers gradually taking over the strategic initiative.
- The new strategy must be durable with gradual adjustments and step-wise implementation (if necessary, hold back information on the next steps to keep the organization focused on the current activities).
- Maintain a high pace of change, but, at the same time, show feeling for the timing of important actions and the limits of management capacity.
- The CEO and top management team can never abdicate – they must stay strong and deeply involved.

Reference

Brege, Staffan and Brandes, Ove (1993) 'The successful double turnaround of ASEA and ABB – twenty-one lessons', *Journal of Strategic Change*, August, **2**, 185–205.

Stage 2: growth

Reach out for the Americas and Asia

Growth was the second stage of the master plan. Barnevik's global strategy was to consolidate and expand in Europe and reach out from there to the Americas and Asia. His overall aim was to have manufacturing plants in domestic markets that remained closed to companies that did not have production capacity there. ABB could then use its global network of rationalized, focused plants to become the world's lowest-cost producer and a complete supplier of all relevant products and technologies.

The fruits of the restructuring and rationalization would take time to realize. Barnevik said it was like turning a ketchup bottle upside down. First, none comes out and then everything happens. What would happen when the ketchup really started to flow?

Note

1 Even at 1987 prices, this seems a good bargain. A study by Washington State University in the USA shows that developing a new corporate logo can cost anywhere from $100,000 to $1 million to develop. (Beatty, Sally (1998) 'Brand logos receive the academic treatment', *The Wall Street Journal Europe*, 18 May, 9).

References

Quotes without references originate from the authors' personal communications – see page xviii for details.

Arbose, Jules (1988) 'ABB: the new energy powerhouse', *International Management*, June, 24–30.

Barnevik, Percy (1996) *Percy Barnevik on Globalization*. St Gallen, Switzerland: presentation to the International Management Symposium, University of St Gallen, 20 May.

Brege, Staffan and Brandes, Ove (1993) 'The successful double turnaround of ASEA and ABB – twenty-one lessons', *Journal of Strategic Change*, August, 2 185–205.

Brown, Andrew (1994) 'Top of the bosses', *International Management*, April, **49** (3).

Business Week (1993) 6 December, 56–9.

Catrina, Werner (1991) *BBC: Glanz, Krise, Fusion*. Zürich: Orel Füssli Verlag, 248, 249.

Dullforce, William (1989) 'Where "paradise" is to be found in acting quickly', *Financial Times*, 5 April, 26.

Karlgaard, Rich (1994) 'Interview with Percy Barnevik, *Forbes*, 5 December, 65–8.

Kennedy, Carol (1992) 'ABB: model merger for the new Europe', *Long Range Planning*, October, **25** (5), 10–17.

Kets de Vries, Manfred (1994) 'Making a giant dance', *Across the Board*, October, **31** (9) 27–32.

Leppänen, Rolf (1994) *ABB Action Recipe: Strategic Management in the Growth and Restructuring of a European Enterprise*, Helsinki: International Networking Publishing INP Oy.

Rapoport, C. (1992) 'A tough Swede invades the US', *Fortune*, 29 June, 76–9.

Schares, Gail E. (1993) 'Percy Barnevik's global crusade', *Business Week*, 6 December, 56–9.

Skaria, George (1995) 'Interview with Percy Barnevik', *Business Today* (India), 22 February–6 March, 100–5.

Taylor, William (1991) 'The logic of global business: an interview with ABB's Percy Barnevik', *Harvard Business Review*, March–April, 91–105.

von Koerber, Eberhard (1996) *Improved Performance: What Distinguishes the High Achievers?* Vienna: presentation to the European Petrochemicals Association, 1 October.

PART

GIANT STEPS TO THE GLOBALLY CONNECTED CORPORATION

Sowing the seeds of the triad

*We wanted to be where the customers of tomorrow are, active in
these new markets as a partner in their economic development and
their move to greater competitiveness and independence.*

Eberhard von Koerber
Senior Adviser to the CEO and Corporate Management
and former President, ABB Europe

In 1985, Kenichi Ohmae, Managing Director of consultants McKinsey's Tokyo office and a renowned strategy guru, wrote a book called *Triad Power: The Coming Shape of Global Competition* (Ohmae, 1985). In it, he argued that corporations hoping to compete in the global arena must become 'insiders' in what he called 'the triad' of Europe, Japan and the United States. This means nothing less than full membership of the local business communities at each corner of the triad. Why? Because the rapid pace of product innovation and development no longer allowed firms the luxury of testing the home market before taking them abroad. Moreover, because consumer preferences varied subtly by culture and were in constant flux, companies must intimately understand local tastes and be able to react instantly to changing market trends and prices. Political considerations were also important – insiders should possess greater immunity to protectionism than outsiders. Finally, capturing markets in all three parts of the triad was often the only way to achieve the economies of scale world-class automated plants demand in order to pay for themselves. 'Instead of an opportunistic approach to generating business worldwide, you really have to commit your firm to the building of a global corporate infrastructure from the beginning', said Ohmae (Ohmae, 1985). This was essentially the strategy that Barnevik was to pursue for the second stage of his master plan – growth.[1]

By 1990, the reshaping of the new merged entity was well underway. ABB had shed some 40,000 jobs, although it would soon start to add new jobs. The restructuring was an enormous task, but Percy Barnevik and his fellow top change agents had some luck at this time in that the new ABB was well placed to take advantage of some technological developments. Nuclear power accidents and environmental considerations were giving a big encouragement to sales of gas turbine power plants and, in particular, to combined cycle (CCGT) plants. By utilizing the hot waste gasses from gas turbines to generate steam for conventional steam turbines, these CCGT plants generated power relatively efficiently and with less harmful emissions than coal-burning plants. Another advantage was that they could also be built more cheaply and quickly. Although they represented only a relatively small part of ABB's business, the combined ASEA/BBC technology and ABB's increasing competitiveness dramatically increased sales of related equipment. This helped to ease the pressure on the restructuring.

Timetable for an 'acquisition frenzy'

Barnevik's triad strategy was to consolidate and expand in Europe and reach out from there to the Americas and Asia. The overall aim was to have manufacturing plants in domestic markets that remained closed to companies not having production capacity there. ABB could then use its global network of rationalized, focused plants to become the world's lowest-cost producer and a complete supplier of all relevant products and technologies.

The merger had produced a $4 billion pile of cash, half of which was immediately available for building global muscle. The first step was to consolidate existing holdings. As Barnevik preferred to own 100 per cent of a new company when he made an acquisition, he would spend $1.5 billion over the next 4 years buying minority positions left over from joint ventures formed by ASEA and BBC before the merger. 'If you are going to run a global group and you have to consider national interests all the time, it doesn't work', he said. If ABB wanted to integrate companies into the group, with a free flow of trade and technology, a minority stake would make it difficult for ABB to allow its proprietary technology to flow in.

Most attention would focus on new acquisitions. With the restructuring in full swing, Barnevik now launched what one article called no less than an 'acquisition frenzy' (Kapstein and Reed, 1990). The aim was to expand both the geographic scope of ABB's operations and build market share in countries where it was already present. The objective, as one former ABB executive put it, was 'domination of global markets by the local acquisition of competitors who are prepared and willing to enter [ABB's] matrix structure' (Leppänen, 1994). Let's look at the timetable of the first five years:

- **October 1988** in (former) West Germany, ABB buys the steam turbine business of AEG and signs a nuclear reactor joint venture with its rival, Siemens;

- **November 1988** ABB buys Italian electrical engineering group Franco Tosi;
- **In the first year** ABB makes some 15 acquisitions worth $544 million; total employment at the end of 1988 was 169,500;
- **January 1989** ABB plans to take effective control of the Italian heavy electrical industry by agreeing with the Finmeccanica/Ansaldo group of Italy to form four joint venture companies in power generators, boilers, turbines and transformers with sales of $1.2 billion; ABB will inject its technology into a grouping of some 32,000 people (including 10,000 outside Italy) and plans a massive restructuring; Italy becomes ABB's largest home base after West Germany and Sweden and gives it a major presence in two of the then four big EU countries; in the UK, ABB also takes a 40 per cent stake in BREL, railway operator British Rail's engineering subsidiary, together with Trafalgar House (40 per cent) and a management buyout group (20 per cent), adding $450 million in annual turnover;
- **February 1989** ABB establishes a joint venture in North and South America with Westinghouse in electrical transmission and distribution equipment; in October, it announces it will exercize its option to take complete control at the end of the year, an investment of $750 million;
- **March 1989** ABB sets up a joint venture with Jeumont Schneider of France in industrial drives; in the following months, it buys shares in a Danish railway coachbuilder and takes over a Swedish State-owned railway coach-building concern; it also reaches agreements with the Swedish and Finnish goverments for the acquisition of freight wagon-building and maintenance units, and buys Ericsson Signals System which has a European spread of business; ABB also forms part of the German-based consortium building high-speed trains in competition with the French; Percy Barnevik talks of the 'nice smorgasbord of opportunities' that ABB has acquired (Dullforce, 1989);
- **November 1989** ABB announces an offer worth $1.6 billion for a major US firm, Combustion Engineering, a Stamford, Connecticut-based boiler and nuclear plant builder which also had a position in automation and instrumentation; in 1989, ABB buys about 40 companies amounting to $3.09 billion; the number of employees now rises to 189,500;
- **By 1990** ABB is three times larger than its closest competitor in several of its core businesses and is demonstrating good profitability considering the rapid growth and large-scale internal restructuring; by mid 1990, ABB has bought 60 companies worth some $4.5 billion;
- **In 1990** ABB begins expansion in Eastern Europe and prepares for expansion into Asia; the rate of acquisition slows in Western Europe and the USA and a period of consolidation and restructuring begins in these regions; acquisitions amount to $700 million while divestitures total $1.1 billion; employment increases to 215,150;

- **January 1990** ABB completes the takeover of Combustion Engineering, boosting its North American sales to $7 billion; it takes a majority share in Polish turbine manufacturer Zamech and buys the loss-making Spanish power plant and transmission company Cenemesa, Conelec, Cademesa (CCC), with sales of $200 million;
- **June 1990** ABB links with Bergmann-Borsig, a major East German electrical equipment supplier;
- **In 1991** against a background of recession in the West, ABB continues to invest in Eastern Germany, and concludes joint ventures or cooperation agreements in Czechoslovakia and Poland; by the end of 1991, ABB employs some 10,000 people in Central and Eastern Europe; acquisitions and divestitures each amounted to just over $600 million in 1991; employment falls slightly to 214,400;
- **In 1992** ABB accelerates recession management; employment in Central and Eastern Europe rises to 20,000 people in 30 companies; ABB creates more than 20 new manufacturing and service units in the Asia-Pacific region by means of joint ventures, acquisitions and greenfield investments; acquisitions fall to $253 million and employment drops to 213,400;
- **In 1993** ABB continues to expand in Europe, including the former Soviet Union, the Americas and Asia-Pacific regions; business is boosted by the introduction of new advanced cycle system gas turbines which deliver up to 58 per cent gross efficiency; acquisitions amount to $211 million and employment falls again to 206,000;
- **In 1994** as ABB experiences strong earnings growth in all its industrial segments, fuelled by recovery of demand, especially in Western Europe and North America, strategic acquisitions continue in Asia, including China, India, Vietnam and Malaysia, and in Central and Eastern Europe; acquisitions amount to $196 million and employment rises slightly to 208,000.

The marketing strategy, called 'PPH', behind this acquisition drive was based on market presence, full product-line coverage and hit ratio. The rationale was that host governments often required that a company maintain a manufacturing presence and full product-line coverage in order to compete with local firms. By acquiring market presence, expanding and using the national holding company to achieve product-line coverage, ABB aimed to maintain a high hit ratio. ABB based its strategic expansion decisions on market-related data. Countries and regions were classified according to installed electric capacity per capita to indicate the relative size and potential of the power generation, transmission and distribution markets. This 'map' served as an indicator of which markets ABB might examine for entry, expansion of production capacity or exit.

Consolidating the European leg

Much of the early part of the acquisition schedule was concerned with expanding and consolidating ABB's European base as the foundation for global expansion. The goal was to give ABB a strong competitive edge inside the European single market. In 1988, ABB had made 64 per cent of its sales in Western Europe and, though ABB's two founding companies both had operations outside the EU, the then West Germany provided its largest domestic market. The European electrical engineering industry was still a high-cost one and was very fragmented. ABB set about getting its new acquisitions in shape for the single market with a programme of cross-border rationalization and sharp cuts in costs and capital.

Eberhard von Koerber explains the new climate that ABB was trying to instil in Europe:

[We were] focusing not only on winning economies of scale by eliminating overlapping production, but also on building a new corporate culture in which continuous productivity, quality and cycle time improvements, and the ability to foresee changes in the business environment and then react quickly, became part of our everyday business practice (von Koerber, 1997).

The restructuring and integration of the new firms involved enormous activity. ABB worked fast to close or merge plants, move in new machinery where necessary – as in Italy and Spain – and shrink working capital. As had happened with BBC's operations, every time ABB acquired a new company, its business area managers would send in teams – usually of two or three specialists – to cut overheads, streamline inventories, cut out some operations and outsource parts to subcontractors. They would swap products and components between factories to get economies of scale. ABB's strategy and systems, including the ABACUS information and communication system, were plugged into the company. An experienced ABB manager would often take over day-to-day management, while the former management would be sent to ABB operating units to learn the ABB way of doing things. The business units that emerged from this process would then start to specialize in one aspect of their specific product group and, at the same time, customize ABB products to suit their local markets.

For those who had known the BBC approach to acquisitions, that introduced by the Swedes was a huge change. The decision to make an acquisition, for example, was usually made much faster. Previously, at BBC, all the central staffs (planning, control, marketing and so on) were each asked for an opinion on the potential purchase and how it fitted with the group. As one former BBC manager said, 'By the time they had come up with one overall opinion, the opportunity was lost!'

Speed was a major feature of all the early restructuring in ABB. A business area manager we interviewed back in 1991 told us that the speed with which changes were carried out was the crucial factor:

Decisions taken early are normally the good decisions. Things that drag on are normally not so good. We have lots of examples of things that have gone well and not so well and the difference is mainly to do with time and speed, where good intentions have not materialized in actions taken. We were very quick in reorganizing after the merger. We got people together from around the world and explained what we had decided, who should be manufacturing and selling what, and the technology we should use in future. That was a good example of speed. But, if decisions about which factory should specialize in certain products are not followed up quickly enough and things are allowed to slide, then you are not able to take full advantage of the scale effect.

T50 – another cultural revolution for ABB

In 1990, The Boston Consulting Group (BCG) introduced the world to the notion of 'time-based competition'. In its influential study, *Competing Against Time* (Stalk and Hart, 1990), BCG said, 'Demanding executives at aggressive companies are altering their measures of performance from competitive costs and quality to competitive costs, quality *and* responsiveness. Give customers what they want when they want it. This refocusing of attention is enabling early innovators to become time-based competitors.' BCG showed how focusing on responsiveness in this way could raise productivity, increase prices, reduce risks and improve market share.

Time-based competition perfectly fitted Percy Barnevik's aims of speeding up ABB and instilling a culture of constant change. A task force had already been set up in Zürich in 1989 to study the reduction of cycle times and Bert-Olof Svanholm, President of ABB Sweden (where ASEA's former operations were well ahead with restructuring) had decided to implement a programme in his country.

Percy Barnevik had learned early in his career that it is possible to improve product payback 'even when your absolute development costs go up 50 per cent if you cut the time in half, because you earn money at a higher rate and over a longer period after the earlier product launch' (Barnevik, 1997). The BCG study confirmed what he already knew about the need to slash lead times and he made his senior managers read and digest it. Together, the BCG study and the initiative in Sweden would lead to the introduction of 'a new industrial revolution' in ABB's plants around the world. Known as T50 (T − 50 = time minus 50 per cent) in Sweden, where it started in June 1992, the objective was to halve all lead times in the firm's activities by the end of 1993. This was to be achieved by decentralizing work responsibilities and widening individual worker skills within teams. The main result would be to put the notion of customer satisfaction right at the heart of ABB's priorities.

Bert-Olof Svanhom (who also later became Chairman of Swedish auto manufacturer Volvo) pointed to the power of the concept: 'Time at work is a concept everybody can understand' (Taylor, 1993). In addition, its value as 'a universal change method' is that it is indisputable and uniform at all organizational levels (Hart and Berger, 1994). Up to then, most companies had given the highest priority to reforming direct production methods. By now, manufacturing was so efficient that it accounted for a relatively small fraction of total sales-to-delivery time. According to Svanholm, 'For too long, the direct production area alone has been the *autostrada* of manufacturing and little attention was being given to what happened before and after it' (Taylor, 1993).

Reduction of total cycle time was now the goal. The definition of 'cycle time' encompassed the time from the decision to develop a new product to launching the product, from initial customer enquiry to confirmed quotation, from customer order to delivery and payment, as well as response times for information and service.

The restructuring and rationalization at ABB made it well-suited to the new approach. Svanholm said, 'We have become a very decentralized organization over the past ten years. If we had tried this in the old days of stratified management hierarchies, there would have been so much resistance, and it would have been abandoned within a fortnight'.

The original inspiration for the T50 programme in Sweden had come from the so-called 'push-button project'. The push-button department was known for causing work-related injuries, including severe neck and shoulder problems. The main causes were highly repetitive and specialized tasks. High absenteeism and personnel turnover rates resulted in poor delivery performance. Management reorganized the department so that employees' tasks were enlarged and enriched in a multi-functional team responsible for the entire product assembly, production scheduling and materials supply. This was supported by process engineering, a new pay system and extensive training for team members to learn the different manual tasks of the team, including traditional supervisory duties such as time reporting. The results were a dramatic improvement in delivery performance. So much so that ABB used the experience of the push-button project to promote the T50 concept.

T50 – a 'programme with a beginning but no end' – depended on four important themes. The first was decentralization, which fitted with one of the underlying thrusts of ABB. This decentralization of authority was from the corporate to the company level and decentralization within the company to multifunctional target-oriented high-performance teams of 10–15 workers responsible for the entire customer order process from order reception to shipment and invoicing. The executive in charge of T50 in Sweden said, 'The old system handed down orders from above through different, fragmented departments and it was very time-consuming. Now we organize around the flow of production through the team approach' (Taylor, 1993).

Second, the new approach demanded a big effort in competence development to heighten the skills of team members, including on-the-job training and education in such areas as scheduling, order processing and quality control.

Third, T50 depended on a focus on 'cycle times as the primary generator to mobilize energy and commitment – to give a more holistic perspective where internal or preferably external customers could be identified for each process' (Hart and Berger, 1994).

Fourth, T50 relied on a communication system to spread success stories and disseminate and apply the lessons learned in one ABB company or team to another. In ABB Sweden, this worked through a central T50 corporate resource responsible for a network of T50 liaison managers in each ABB company in Sweden that organized seminars and conferences to exchange experience and ideas.

One success factor was the support of the trade unions. These had come to appreciate Percy Barnevik's changes as the positive results of the restructurings were starting to show. The unions established their own committees to monitor the T50 programme and make sure that it worked with the full involvement of their members. T50 meant a smaller workforce and fewer jobs, but, as a Swedish union leader said, 'If we can increase sales in the longer term, then employment opportunities will go up as well. We know ABB must stay ahead of its competitors' (Taylor, 1993).

For employees, T50 meant better working conditions, increased job interest with ongoing skill improvement and, eventually, a better pay rate linked more closely to individual effort. For ABB as a whole, it meant the prospect of bigger profits, better productivity and higher-quality products as well as lower absenteeism and labour turnover. T50 achieved some early and remarkable cuts in cycle times in Sweden. The time for making high-voltage DC transmission equipment was cut from three to two years, for example. The components division cut cycle times from 86 to 35 days. This was just the start. Other positive effects included the reduction of barriers between white- and blue-collar workers. It also resulted in a flatter organization with fewer managers and more workers taking on responsibilities. This meant a significant change in the role of the manager: 'They have many more demanding jobs to do now. Before they were a combination of policeman and errand boy. Now they act as a support for workers' (Taylor, 1993).

Percy Barnevik said of T50's results:

I would say that we in the Western industrialized companies are still 'prisoners of Taylorism'. Workers are regarded as a commodity, still seen as some sort of machine specialized in certain functions – maybe using 10 per cent of their brain capacity. The way they are rewarded is through collective bargaining. When these people go home after work, they build a summer house, raise a family and manage a family budget. It is a disgrace that much of this competence is not used in our factories. Within ABB we have gained good experience with so-called 'high-performance teams', particularly in Sweden. The idea is that teams of production workers take over new tasks from the white-collar people. They handle supply, customer complaints, quality supervision, etc. Individual workers get a chance to advance. They are trained in handling a PC, basic statistics, etc. We have had an extremely positive result from this far-reaching delegation of responsibility to the shop floor. Continuous training is not just a catchword, it has become an integral part of our organization with real substance. We have increased worker training by a factor of three or four in recent years' (Schares, 1993).

By the late 1990s, ABB had drastically reduced cycle times by means of its time-based strategies. In 1988, it took three years to build a medium-sized combined cycle power plant. Having reduced that to two years, by the late 1990s ABB was quoting ten months for completion. 'These are improvements you could not dream of 10 years ago', says Percy Barnevik (Dauphinais and Price, 1998). However, ABB's top management believes that there is no end to the improvements that can be achieved. 'You reduce 50 per cent, then you aim for another 50 per cent reduction,' Barnevik asserts. 'We must continue on the route toward ever-decreasing cycle times while aiming for zero defects' (Dauphinais and Price, 1998).

References

Barnevik, Percy (1997) *Global Forces of Change: Remarks to the 1997 International Industrial Conference, 'Inventing the Future'*, San Francisco, 29 September.

Dauphinais, William and Price, Colin (Price Waterhouse) (1998), interview with Percy Barnevik, 'Creating a federation of national cultures: reflections of Percy Barnevik', in *Straight from the CEO: The World's Top Business Leaders Reveal Ideas that Every Manager Can Use*. London: Nicholas Brealey Publishing, 42.

Hart, H. and Berger, A. 'Using time to generate corporate renewal', *International Journal of Operations and Production Management*, **13** (3), 12, 24–45.

Schares, Gail E. (1993) 'Percy Barnevik's global crusade', *Business Week*, 22 October.

Stalk, Jr., George and M. Hout, Thomas (1990) *Competing Against Time: How Time-Based Competition is Reshaping Global Markets*. New York: The Free Press, 1.

Taylor, Robert (1993) 'Resetting the clock', *Financial Times*, 10 February, 14.

Creating the American leg

The ABB restructuring in Europe was not complete when Barnevik turned to North America. The region accounted for 30 per cent of the world market for electrical engineering equipment, but only 10 per cent of the new ABB's sales. Barnevik's aim was to get 25 per cent of revenues from North America within 5 years.

His reasoning was simple. As Bengt Skantze, who was in charge of corporate development for ABB at this time, explains:

Internationalization in ASEA came about with the Nordic strategy. With the merger, we suddenly had an axis through Europe and we were now very strong in the Nordic countries, Germany and Italy. Our strategy was to become number one in the business, but you can't become number one without being big in the US because the US is one third of the world business. Our market share there was only 5–10 per cent. On the other hand, the Nordic countries represented 3 per cent of world potential and our market share was 50 per cent. We dominated certain areas, but they weren't very big. You don't have to be a mastermind, therefore, to see the strategy. This is typical of ABB. Percy says that strategy is 5 per cent analysis and 95 per cent implementation and this is true.

Breaking into North America demanded another bold move. Senior ABB executives had gone straight from the Cannes conference in January 1988 to start talks with no less a company than Westinghouse, once one of the great names of the American power engineering business. By the late 1980s, Westinghouse's electricity distribution subsidiary had become what one business magazine called a 'one billion dollar dinosaur'. Its 6 per cent profit margins in a slow-moving market were far behind the margins of other Westinghouse businesses. Barnevik saw a chance to buy a leading US power company.

ABB's representatives negotiated two proposals with Westinghouse. First, they negotiated to take over the whole of the American company's power transmission and distribution business. Second, the two sides proposed to set up a joint venture in the power-generation business. The talks were more prolonged than the ASEA-BBC merger discussions, however. They lasted one year in fact. In February 1989, ABB bought 50 per cent of the Westinghouse power and distribution business (and later bought the other half) with its 10,000 people for $700 million. The power-generation joint venture, however, was stopped by American anti-trust legislation. This was a decided setback: 'We had thought we could handle it, especially with Westinghouse supporting us, but it didn't happen', says one of the senior ABB executives involved. ABB later estimated that this inability to put the whole power sector together in one shot set the company back two to three years in America. Percy Barnevik once said that this was one of his biggest disappointments ever.

However, ABB now gave the same turnaround medicine that it was applying in Europe to its new American ABB Power Transmission and Distribution company, which was to make equipment ranging from house meters to transformers for big power utilities. The formula, as in Europe, was slash production time, improve quality and enhance customer service. For example, to reduce costly work-in-process at the St Louis transformer plant, ABB boosted the number of workers per transformer from two to six and cut the number of units in simultaneous production from 50 to 17. Short-term results were impressive. Inventory costs were cut by nearly $4 million and production time per transformer was cut by one third, to 50 days. Quality soared and delivery on time rose from 80 per cent to 94 per cent. Several big customers such as the Tennessee Valley Authority returned. Profits rose 38 per cent in two years to $65 million.

ABB's approach involved more than just cuts in expenditure. Under the new regime, spending on research and development was sharply increased to introduce a new line of 'global' transformer products. These combined the best designs of ASEA with technologies acquired from Westinghouse and BBC. Because the models' core technology was easier to build, quality would be higher and costs lower. The global design could be customized to local markets. The ability to combine technologies from around the world was to become a hallmark of ABB's approach. To achieve this synergy, and to give American managers the know-how they lacked, ABB sent European production teams to the US, while American managers visited ABB plants around the world. It took time for former Westinghouse managers to adjust to ABB's decentralization, however. At Westinghouse, head office and the electricity distribution unit had made most of the strategy and purchasing decisions. Under ABB, authority was pushed down to hourly workers. Many shop floor supervisors were reluctant to let them join in decision making. By the same token, workers hesitated to take initiatives. ABB wanted its American workers to be bold and take initiatives, but such a culture would take time to take root.

Catching an American giant

The Westinghouse power businesses would add significant strength to ABB, but it needed more weight to establish a strong North American base. While the deal with Westinghouse was being completed, ABB came across the US power and process automation group Combustion Engineering (CE). The bid for CE showed Barnevik's determination to secure world leadership in the power industry and his characteristic speed of action, although it would be one of the most controversial of his moves. When Barnevik heard that rival power firm Alsthom of France was negotiating to buy CE, he quickly countered with a $1.6 billion offer, 57 per cent above the current stock price. CE immediately accepted the offer.

CE was once one of the great names of the American power business, but had gone astray as a result of misguided diversification. The negotiations were a different story from Westinghouse as it was the acquisition of a listed company. As a stock deal, it could go through faster and the talks took only six weeks before the agreed takeover. Like the ASEA and BBC merger, this was a phenomenally rapid deal for such a large undertaking (CE had $3.5 billion in sales).

The CE deal was widely seen as an opportunistic thrust by Barnevik. In fact, although carried out very quickly, the process was more deliberate than some reports suggested and there was some strong strategic sense behind it. The impression given by many journalistic accounts of ABB's actions, and in particular of acquisitions like CE, is that Barnevik decided on them alone and carried them out single-handedly. In fact, although he was determined to move fast and avoid the kind of 'paralysis through analysis' that had hampered BBC, he was careful to sound out the opinion of his ABB 'speaking partners' among the company's senior management and staffers, who were called in to ask for the implications of the CE purchase on ABB and its balance sheet. Obviously the Executive Committee was also involved, particularly the segment managers concerned.

The original starting point for talks with CE had been a more limited venture. To start with, the discussions had focused on some form of cooperation in the power generation business. ABB was completing the purchase of Westinghouse's transmission and distribution operations and cooperation with CE in power generation would compensate for the block put by the US anti-trust authorities on the proposed power generation joint venture with Westinghouse. The match between ABB's turbine manufacturing operations in the US and CE's steam-generating boilers and coal- and oil-burning technology offered a better chance of avoiding anti-trust action. But the talks soon went further as the two sides found synergy in both geography and products. CE had process engineering skills in chemicals, petrochemicals and paper-making that fitted with those of ABB in metallurgy and cement-making. CE's expertise in automation and measurement control was close to ABB's drives and automation manufacture and both companies had environmental technologies.

Another advantage to the deal was that the US was then a low-cost country between very low-cost countries such as Greece and Portugal and very high-cost countries such as Germany and Switzerland. In addition to the big US market, therefore, it also provided ABB with relatively low labour costs. There was another, more fundamental attraction. In the late 1980s, most power stations in the USA were aging – many were 30 years old. A vast body of corroding, polluting and inefficient plants urgently needed to be replaced or refitted. With the recent enactment of Clean Air legislation in the US, it was expected that substantial business would result in the near future. Some estimates put the market for new power plants at $12 billion a year, plus another several billion for supplying transmission and distribution equipment, so the potential was huge. Many utilities had bought equipment from CE so it was likely that any utility modernizing its power stations would turn to CE for boilers. ABB would then be able to sell on its turbines, transformers, switchgear and other equipment. Finally, CE had an impressive global network of licensees around the world, including Japan and large parts of Asia.

CE would not only give ABB an American presence, it could also help it achieve another strategic objective – to expand in Eastern Europe, as CE had joint ventures in the former Soviet Union, including a big petrochemical project in Tobolsk, and in Asia, where CE also already had some operations.

In 1990, CE was not losing money at the operating level and was expected to be able to reach an acceptable level of return in another two years. Its $3.5 billion in annual sales would increase ABB's worldwide turnover to $25 billion, of which some $5 billion was in North America, thereby giving ABB a significant presence in the world's largest economy. Barnevik recognized that the addition of the Westinghouse operations and CE to the group represented a fundamental change for ABB. It would no longer be a European-based international operation, but a business standing on two legs – one in Europe, the other in the US. 'We are buying a US corporate structure. We are now Americans in America with a $7 billion business there, of which $1.5 billion is exports' (Dullforce and Garnett, 1989). With the integration of CE and the transmission and distribution business that it took over from Westinghouse, ABB had become 'an American producer and exporter with a unique breadth' in the power field, said Barnevik. 'The US power utilities like having a competitor in the field that really believes in power' (Dullforce, 1991). Much would depend, however, on whether or not and when predictions about the forthcoming demand for new power equipment were fulfilled.

Reshaping the American operations

ABB had arrived on the North American scene in force. As Bengt Skantze says, 'Suddenly we had 25,000 people in the USA. Twenty per cent of our business was in the US, almost overnight – well, in this business two years is almost overnight! It was a dramatic change for us.' Unfortunately, the deal with CE was complicated by some early surprises. As a public bid for a listed company in the US, ABB had only had access to information available to the public. The surprises included some large losses that had not been revealed in the purchase negotiations. CE also turned out to be much more diversified than ABB had thought. Ironically, its oil and gas businesses, which did not interest ABB at that time, would turn out to be an important asset in the future. Within months, Barnevik purged CE's chief executive and most of its top managers. Barnevik supported the acquisition: 'You cannot become the first new entrant in a century into the US power field smoothly and nicely. You are bound to pay for that strategic value.' Gerhard Schulmeyer, the CEO of ABB's combined US operations, also justified it: 'We wanted an absolute, solid presence in the power market in this country, and we needed a quantum step' (Klebnikov, 1991).

Barnevik and Schulmeyer quickly set about rationalizing CE. This included immediately selling off the company's three aircraft and the lavish headquarters building with its collection of artwork and cutting head office staff from 600 to 90 people. When Barnevik told the Americans that they had to reduce head office numbers, they did not believe it was possible. Barnevik told them to go and look at Strömberg in Finland and Mannheim in Germany where it had already been done successfully. Schulmeyer sold unwanted CE businesses and brought in new, aggressive technician-managers to improve productivity. 'Barnevik and the Vikings are extremely results – and performance – oriented,' said a former CE executive who stayed on with ABB. 'They're not sloppy in their thinking. They don't dwell on small talk. We all work enormously greater hours than we did before we were acquired. We all have fax machines in our homes' (Klebnikov, 1991).

Some observers worried that, with the purchase of CE, ABB was biting off more than it could chew after all the other acquisitions and restructuring that it was carrying out in so many disparate cultures. In defence, Barnevik said that taking over CE was different from merging ASEA with BBC. The CE acquisition involved taking over a self-contained company with a similar decentralized structure, unlike BBC where there was much overlapping and costs and capital to be squeezed out. Rationalization was needed but the biggest impact would be on the market side. The two companies could run side-by-side. ABB would need to encourage a new global perspective in its US acquisitions. 'The companies that we have bought in the US are so focused on the American market that we have to help them think about the rest of the world. We add the global dimension they lack' (Rapoport, 1992).

Global or otherwise, ABB faced strong competitive struggles ahead in the US. In addition to the reshaping and integration of its acquisitions, Barnevik also hoped that new power technology would give it an edge. One of the fiercest battles was to be for the gas turbine business, the fastest-growing sector of the power market, which was expected to take off in the next seven years and was forecast to be a $3–billion-a-year market in the US in the 1990s. General Electric was then the world leader in gas turbines, due to its large installed base and to development cooperation with GE's own jet engine division. ABB aimed to narrow the gap.

ABB was weak in the big machines of the gas turbine sector, but, in 1989, it formed an alliance with the jet engine subsidiary of Rolls-Royce to get its own access to advanced jet engine technology. Would ABB be able to take on GE on its home ground? One US utility top executive said, 'Once ABB's turbines get out into the market and demonstrate a reliability and service record that's equal to or better than GE, we [utilities] will be indifferent to whose turbines we buy' (Klebnikov, 1991). ABB's efforts in gas turbines would lead to one of its most important technological developments in 20 years when, in 1993, it announced the manufacture of a turbine that produced 240 MW working at 58.5 per cent efficiency. In an industry that was working on 53–56 per cent efficiencies and predicted changes to the end of the decade in fractions, this was a remarkable figure. ABB claimed that higher efficiency was achieved without significantly increasing temperatures in the turbine.

The CE purchase produced one other surprise. In 1990, ABB had to resolve a crisis in relations with the Finmeccanica/Ansaldo Group in Italy, with which it had concluded joint venture deals the year before. Problems arose after ABB's acquisition of CE's boiler business, which, the Italians believed, threatened their own production of boilers. The deal agreed in 1988 was rearranged to leave ABB with the transformer business and 10,000 people. Finmeccanica and Ansaldo retained the boiler and turbine business and licenced ABB turbines. ABB nevertheless retained a substantial business in Italy, but it was a lesson in the need to pay attention to the feelings of local partners in a global grouping.

ABB's action recipe in different markets

Among the materials supplied to us by ABB was a paper written by Rolf Leppänen, a former ABB manager from Finland who worked in the company's drives business area for seven years. He describes ABB's approach to business and managerial reform as an 'action recipe', the core of which is time consciousness and a small business approach. As applied to ABB's acquisitions, the recipe involves four core principles:
1. immediately reorganize operations into profit centres with well-defined budgets, strict performance targets and clear lines of authority and accountability;
2. identify a core group of change agents from local management, give small teams responsibility for championing high-priority programmes – and monitor results closely;
3. transfer ABB expertise from around the world to support the change process without interfering in it or running it directly;
4. maintain high standards and demand quick results.

Leppänan analyzes how ABB's action recipe for business and managerial reform worked in different settings and suggests that the key to success lies in how well the recipe responds to or interacts with the local 'business environmental factors'. In the case of Strömberg, Finland as a test ground for the action recipe outside Sweden was a familiar market – and therefore a very sensible and logical place to try it first. Zamech in Poland was an unfamiliar market but the external conditions were favourable. The arrival of ABB in Poland was 'a godsend to the Polish economy and Polish worker' (Leppänen, 1994). The story in Italy, where BBC had been deeply rooted in the North Italian electrotechnical industry but ASEA only had a small presence, was somewhat different. In Italy, the State still played a very strong role in the economy and State-owned companies had a dominant position. In 1988–89, ABB tried to make a joint venture agreement with State-owned Ansaldo. ABB had thought that Ansaldo would eventually be privatized but underestimated how long this would take. As the top people in all State-owned companies, including Ansaldo, were political appointees, they were not free to operate in strictly economic or industrial terms. Says Leppänen:

It was difficult to find a common framework or even language in the discussions. ABB's rational accounting and control-oriented argumentation . . . was the wrong approach in this case . . . ABB should have realized that the possibility of getting a State-owned company such as Ansaldo into their global business matrix was doomed to failure from the beginning (Leppänen, 1994).

As one ABB senior manager, a Swiss-Italian who had formerly worked for BBC, said: 'In my opinion, the major issue is very simple: whatever you try to do, you have to understand the way your partner operates and carefully analyze the boundary conditions of the country you are in' (Leppänen, 1994).

Reference
Leppänen, Rolf (1994) *ABB Action Recipe: Strategic Management in the Growth and Restructuring of a European Enterprise.* Helsinki: International Networking Publishing INP Oy, 5, 120, 131, 132 and 133–4.

Barnevik described the challenge of managing local sensitivities:

> *It does require a huge mental change, especially for country managers. Remember, we've built ABB through acquisitions and restructurings. Thirty of the companies we've bought have been around for more than 100 years. Many of them were industry leaders in their countries, national monuments. Now they've got BA managers playing a big role in the direction of their operations. We have to convince country managers that they benefit by being part of this federation, that they gain more than they lose when they give up some autonomy'* (Taylor, 1991).

It was not only in the West that ABB would have to tread sensitively.

ABB moves East

A drastic restructuring was underway in ABB in Europe and the US with dozens of unwanted, duplicated or obsolete factories being closed down. The prospect of a single market in Western Europe had been one of the original drivers of the ABB merger, but the political events in Central and Eastern Europe at this time opened up new challenges and opportunities. If most of what was taking place in ABB conformed to a master plan, this surely was 'emergent strategy'. At the time of the ABB merger in 1987–88, few people could have imagined the huge economic opportunities and the attendant access to cost-competitive labour and manufacturing resources that were about to appear in the East. With the fall of the Iron Curtain a year later, Barnevik saw a one-off chance to enlarge ABB.

Eberhard von Koerber, later President of ABB's European regional management, describes the background to the decision:

> *In 1988, this new company with a new vision and new leadership could see the cracks in the Communist wall surrounding Eastern Europe. But even we were surprised by the speed of change and in 1989, literally overnight, we were handed an unprecedented opportunity. The need for basic infrastructure – literally everything from telephones and electrical sockets to decent roads, airports, industrial plants and safe and efficient power supply – matched many of ABB's core businesses* (von Koerber, 1997).

Barnevik argued that 'now is the time to do it because nobody else is doing it.'

Bengt Skantze, who was closely associated with ABB's acquisition drive, says:

There was a lot of scepticism about investing in Eastern Europe in the early 1990s, there was no legal framework, lots of risk. But we have a simple strategy – forget the noise; it may take time, but if we are not there, we will lose out.

David Hunter, later Head of Central and Eastern Europe within ABB's European regional management, and who was to be the company's first country manager in the region in Poland, believes that the resolve to go into Eastern Europe in 1990 was 'a unique strategic decision'. It was certainly visionary, although ABB, as an early mover, could manage its risk by acquiring good companies on favourable terms. Its aim was to get its technology and management practices established while restricting its exposure. It would rarely spend more than $20 million on a single acquisition. Spreading investment over many different ventures was also seen as less risky than spending the $500 million needed for a single acquisition in the West. Eric Elzvik, later in charge of corporate development at ABB and who was closely involved in ABB's acquisitions, puts it into perspective:

It meant putting money on the table and some exposure for the company but it was not that big. It was more dangerous to go into the USA, paying a large amount of money with all sorts of exposures. It was very foresightful but it was not brave from an economic point of view – it was brave from a publicity point of view. Failing in the investment would not have imperilled ABB.

One estimate puts ABB's investment in creating its Central and East European network at $300 million in the first 5 years, but declares this sum 'peanuts considering all the assets it acquired' (Hofheinz, 1994).

Eberhard von Koerber shows how the Central and Eastern Europe acquisitions fitted into ABB's scheme:

While speed was essential, this was not a move made recklessly. Rather, it followed our strategy of having a deep local presence in all our markets. We wanted to become an insider, not an invader. We wanted to be where the customers of tomorrow are, active in these new markets as a partner in their economic development and their move to greater competitiveness and independence. There was no question that we were taking a risk. The economic and political landscapes were changing on an almost daily basis. Governments were forming and dissolving just as fast. But the fundamentals were there: a large potential market, a well-trained labour force and, perhaps most importantly, an incredible will to change (von Koerber, 1997).

Bengt Skantze explains the challenges:

It is a very industrialized part of total Europe. They have existing major industrial units and manufacturing. Technical skills are available but they were not able to follow the latest technology. They have a technical background but no financial background and did not understand how a free market works. There are 400 million people there and with living standards improving there must be big potential. It may take 10 or 20 years but ultimately it will be a very important market. Having concluded that, therefore, the strategy is simple and logical and again you don't have to be a mastermind to understand it. You identify a market logically, although timewise nobody knows exactly when it will pay off, and you invest significant resources there. The implications are that you have to be there very early to identify good players, and to make joint ventures, etc.

In addition to selling its power plants, switching systems, locomotives and robots, the other opportunity seen by ABB was that low-cost production in the East could give a competitive edge to many of its global products and services.

Establishing a beachhead in Poland

Other companies were still coming to terms with the collapse of the Berlin Wall when ABB made its first deals in Eastern Europe. Ever since the days at the end of the nineteenth century when Walter Boveri had worked on projects in Russia, BBC and ASEA had both been active in Eastern Europe, and had a network of licencees already in existence. In Poland, for example, BBC opened its first representative office in Warsaw in 1907, and ASEA established a representative there in 1919. ABB was therefore already acquainted with some of its potential acquisitions.

The countries were at different stages of development. Following economic reforms in the late 1960s, Hungary had become the most open and market-oriented economy within the Communist bloc and would be the first investment choice for many Western firms (including General Electric, which bought a Hungarian lighting manufacturer in 1990). ABB, however, took a hard look at demographics and market size. While Hungary had 10 million people, Poland had 38 million, and a substantial power engineering industry, so ABB started its expansion drive in Poland.

ABB's involvement in the East had begun when the head of the power generation segment created a small special group in Zürich to spot acquisitions and joint ventures in the region. This group negotiated the first power-generation joint venture in Poland with Zamech, the country's only turbine maker, based in Elblag near Gdańsk in north-eastern Poland.[2] ABB took a 76 per cent share, with the then Polish government retaining 19 per cent and the employees holding 5 per cent. Two more joint ventures followed with Dolmel, the country's largest generator manufacturer based in Wrocław.

At the end of 1990, ABB had 4000 workers in Poland. The company realized that it had to establish a local organization of business units with profit and loss responsibility in the country as it had with its businesses elsewhere. David Hunter, an American who had formerly worked for Westinghouse for 20 years, had joined ABB in 1990. Having worked for six years in Switzerland and Sweden, he had come to know and admire both ASEA and BBC. He was appointed country manager for Poland in 1991:

When I arrived in Poland, there had been a representation office of eight or nine people which had been selling products for some years. Now I was country manager, responsible for the market and customer relations. My task when I arrived was to create a local management team, to manage the joint ventures and acquire some new activities, and create an impression among the Polish government and community that ABB was a local organization. And not least, with a lot of support from the business areas in carrying out improvements, I had to make the whole organization profitable.

Hunter's first problem was image. ABB was seen as a company that had come in and stolen valuable State assets under the last Communist regime. A new privatization law was introduced in 1991, but ABB's first joint ventures had been agreed under the old joint venture law. There was a delay in convincing the new government that its intentions were honourable.

Hunter remembers:

For the first year, we were engaged almost daily in defending ABB's presence from some heavy criticism. We had to get the message across. I consciously decided that our operations in Poland would be run by local management. The one lesson that is valuable to anyone trying to do business in emerging markets is that the risk of taking inexperienced local management into responsible jobs is less than taking an experienced expatriate who doesn't know the local situation.

Hunter, as President of ABB Polska, saw himself as a coach to the Polish managers. 'I had to be the cheerleader for local management. My role was to defend them from criticisms from inside ABB. I had to encourage them but not micro-manage them. But in the end, it was local management who defended ABB from local politicians.'

ABB's new Polish partners had a strong tradition of engineering excellence, but had fallen on hard times, especially once their markets in the former Soviet Union collapsed. Previously operating within a centrally planned economy, they had concentrated on production rather than marketing. Their functional organizations, multilayered management hierarchies, confused product-line profitability and resulting slow decision-making processes were inappropriate for the new business environment in which they found themselves. One observer sums up the challenges as follows:

The change in Poland, as in other Central and Eastern European countries, was a clash of two cultures: the old one driven by production orientation and the new, Western one by marketing and finance. In the old system people had no feel for money, but the system produced a proud tradition of engineering. For these reasons, people are very eager to learn Western-style management, but in matters of technology they are less ready to be pushed around (Leppänen, 1994).

ABB's revitalization strategy rested on a number of principles derived from the same turnaround philosophy that it had applied in Europe and North America, and which it believed could bring a typical East European company to profitability within two years:

- do not buy whole companies, but buy potentially profitable divisions and refuse to take a minority position;
- begin devising a business plan while talks are still taking place;
- once the acquisition is concluded, immediately reorganize by dividing operations into profit centres with well-defined budgets, performance targets and clear lines of authority and accountability;
- reduce administrative staff using the 30 per cent rule;
- identify a core group of change agents within local management and make small teams responsible for championing high-priority programmes – look for 'hungry wolves' (smart, ambitious young talent) and train them intensively in ABB's way of doing things;
- bring in ABB expertise and technology from around the world to support the change process, but do not interfere or run it directly; if appropriate, appoint an experienced Western restructuring manager to stand alongside and support local management;
- install the ABACUS accounting system;
- start English lessons for middle managers so they can communicate with head office and other parts of ABB;
- put in new testing approaches to raise quality to Western levels;
- set high standards, demand quick results and monitor performance closely.

The goal was to make ABB's Polish operations as productive and profitable as possible. ABB would not make special allowances for Eastern Europe and was not prepared for the change process to continue indefinitely. It would provide more technical and managerial support than it might do for an operation in Europe or the US, but it would be just as demanding where results were concerned. A major change for the new acquisitions was the introduction of ABB's accounting and finance systems. Previously, 80 per cent of total costs had been allocated by central staff accountants rather than tracked to specific products and services. This meant that managers did not know how much their products cost to manufacture or which ones were profitable.

Other important changes took place in leadership. As David Hunter had decided, Polish managers from the former company would generally hold all positions from the chief executive down. In only one or two exceptions, Western managers might be appointed as restructuring managers to assist the Polish management or as finance officers if such expertise was lacking. These appointments would be made regardless of previous rank or seniority. Indeed, ABB was keen to promote smart, young talent and most of the senior appointments came from middle management. Pawel Olechnowicz, a 44–year-old who had previously run the steel castings department and been elected general manager by employees just before the creation of ABB Zamech, was given the top job to oversee the transformation there.

The first task of the new management was to develop a detailed agenda for change. At Zamech, for example, the management team identified 11 priorities, ranging from reorganizing and retraining the salesforce, to cutting total cycle times and redesigning the factory layout. 'Everything has changed', said Olechnowicz. 'We did it through controlled chaos' (Wagstyl, 1996).

ABB brought in new technology, including computers, to aid design, and new products, such as gas turbines. Although Zamech's engineers had only worked on less sophisticated steam turbines before, they were able to sell their first gas turbine in 1991. ABB also took two other initiatives to support the change process. First, it created a team of high-level ABB experts from around the world in such areas as finance and control, quality management, technology and corporate restructuring. Members would visit the site frequently to advise on problems. Second, to educate the new leaders in the basic business concepts that they lacked, ABB set up a 'mini MBA programme' in Warsaw to teach business strategy, marketing, finance, manufacturing and human resources.

At Zamech, the changes were producing results within a year. It had started issuing monthly financial reports that conformed with ABB standards, cycle times for production of steam turbines had been cut in half to meet the ABB world average and streamlining of the factory was underway. Production costs were slashed as the new accounting procedures showed how the factory had previously wasted resources such as manpower, raw materials and factory space. The workforce was reduced from 4300 to 3200 by 1993 by means of retirements and outsourcing support activities, such as cleaning. The company was eventually able, however, to start recruiting again as its performance improved.

One of Zamech's managers described the change in climate at Zamech: 'People are ready to train and learn because they feel a new sense of involvement. That didn't exist before' (Wagstyl, 1996). A senior ABB executive involved in the turnaround process at Zamech told the *Harvard Business Review* in 1991:

You can *change these companies. You* can *make them more competitive and profitable. I can't believe the quality of the reports and presentations these people do today; how at ease they are discussing their strategy and targets. I have worked with many corporate restructurings, but never have I seen so much change so quickly. The energy is incredible. These people really want to learn; they are very ambitious. Basically, ABB Zamech is their business now* (Taylor, 1991).

ABB's early deals in Poland brought first-mover benefits. Over five years, ABB acquired more companies and made some greenfield investments so that by 1994 it had grown to 12 legal entities active in all ABB's core business areas. Part of David Hunter's strategy was to involve Poland in all ABB activities, not just power generation. ABB was able to bring its great experience to bear on Poland and its other East European ventures, but senior managers admit that Eastern Europe was a huge learning experience for them, too. Not everything could be expected to go smoothly in such a vast undertaking. As ABB was simultaneously cutting headcount in Western Europe, for instance, some Western staff were reluctant to cooperate with the new ABB affiliates in the East. German staff did not trust the Poles to reach quality standards. Some Swedish technicians at first refused to send technical drawings and later sent plans written only in Swedish. Such attitudes threatened the global transfer of technology and expertise that ABB saw as a key strength of its matrix and would be a concern for David Hunter and ABB's top management for some time.

Hunter's efforts to improve the company's image and turn round the other Polish acquisitions began to bear fruit early on:

By the beginning of 1993 we started to get good press in Poland. People could see the new investment, the software, the new washrooms, etc. They were enthused. And the companies were profitable. This was due to local management. The Poles can work hard and they can manage. It also didn't hurt that we had a dominant position in power generation. Besides the fact that we could show that the companies were profitable, they could also produce quality that was up to Western standards.

Leapfrogging eastwards

Poland would continue to be ABB's biggest and fastest development programme in the region and to be the biggest market outside the Commonwealth of Independent States (CIS), the successor countries to the Soviet Union. ABB was also concerned to build a presence in other parts of the region, even in some seemingly remote outposts. In 5 or 6 years, ABB built a network of some 60 companies in the region, establishing the largest manufacturing operation of any Western company. Unlike some of its competitors, ABB was not deterred by the chaos of the newly emerging market economies, the great distances or poor communication links. While other companies saw competition from Eastern Europe (and Asia) as a big threat, Percy Barnevik saw it as 'a heaven-sent opportunity' to sell as well as manufacture ABB's main products cheaply. In the words of one observer, 'As early investors burnt their fingers in Eastern Europe, ABB negotiators cherry-picked their way round the region.' By 1996, the line-up of ABB operations in the former socialist bloc included:

- **Poland** turbines, power and rail engineering, switchgear – 7000 employees;
- **Czech Republic** process and power engineering – 7000 employees;
- **Russia** power engineering, including turbines, pollution control, service – 3000 employees;
- **Romania** electronic meters and service – 2000 employees;
- **Ukraine** power plant control systems, switchgear and pollution control – 1500 employees;
- **Hungary** power engineering and service – 600 employees;
- **Croatia** turbines – 500 employees;
- **Slovakia** electrical installation and service – 500 employees;
- **Latvia** service – 400 employees;
- **Bulgaria** low-voltage apparatus – 100 employees;
- **Estonia** switchgear and service – 100 employees;
- **Kazakhstan** oil and gas well equipment – 50 employees;
- **Lithuania** electrical engineering – 25 employees.

As an example of its concern to achieve wide local presence, no matter how small the country, ABB also opened a sales office in Albania. Running operations in these markets has its hazards. In Karlovac in Croatia, ABB's turbine factory came under shellfire when fighting broke out between rival Yugoslav irregular armies.

Changing attitudes among its new employees was one of the major tasks facing ABB. Percy Barnevik, says:

> *It used to be a society where you were supposed to watch your back, not take initiatives. You say 'It's up to you now', but they are often afraid of making a decision on their own. In that old, top-down Communist system, they developed a certain way of behaving, which doesn't fit into a market economy. So you have to tell them that they're allowed to make mistakes, that we like them to take initiatives* (Hofheinz, 1996).

Some issues demanded a complete reversal of thinking by local management. ABB, for instance, often found high inventory levels in its new acquisitions: 'You might meet a guy there, and he is very proud of his huge copper inventory!' recounted Percy Barnevik. As he said, this is a pile of financing waiting to be put into circulation (Hofheinz, 1996).

The concept of marketing also demanded a major reorientation for the new members of the ABB group. In the early days, ABB found that East European engineers regarded marketing as something almost humiliating. If they made a good turbine, they felt, why should they have to persuade anybody to buy it? They had to be persuaded that sales was not an inferior job but a professional task concerned with learning about the customer's problems and working with them to enhance their operations. Barnevik pointed to this 'tremendous change of thinking' and how imperative it was not to 'underestimate the amount of effort [needed] to really penetrate their minds and bring these ideas through' (Hofheinz, 1996).

As in Poland, ABB tried, wherever possible, to use local managers rather than send in expatriates, believing that they had much better knowledge of local conditions and needs, and that it was important not to wound their pride in their own traditions. In each country, ABB applied its turnaround principles of decentralization and profit responsibility, while at the same time supplying support by means of the global matrix. For example, managers at newly acquired enterprises were paired individually with Western counterparts who acted as coaches. This was so successful, that ABB later used its Polish and Czech managers as coaches to its Russian and Ukrainian managers. This was part of ABB's leapfrog strategy for further expansion eastwards, whereby it used its Polish and Czech operations as springboards or staging posts for more risky undertakings further east.

ABB also used teams of roving managers who ranged across the region coaching new employees in the new skills and practices required. Eberhard von Koerber described these 'rapid deployment forces' as 'skinny, sporty, long-distance runner types, mid-thirties, resistant to the temptations of loneliness and wilderness, go-getters who like the smell of powder; a special breed whom you also need in armies' (Kennedy, 1996). To make up for the poor communications infrastructure in the region, ABB also set up a satellite communications network to enable fast decision making.

Percy Barnevik says that ABB's biggest investment in Central and Eastern Europe has not been so much the money paid for these companies, but the amount of management time that ABB puts into revamping previously State-owned enterprises (*Fortune*, 1994). He himself was devoting one fifth of his time to the region in the early years. Eberhard von Koerber, in his later capacity as President of ABB's European region (after having run Germany), also had to give it a great deal of attention. He said, 'I am allowed to count my time there as knowledge transfer. I'm passing on knowledge, motivating them, giving them targets, switching on their energy, making them equal members of our family.' Like Barnevik, he is clear about the virtue of developing the wealth of hungry business talent in Eastern Europe: 'It's the soft investment that makes us competitive. It's making use of brains that are 90 per cent underutilized. People who don't understand this have no access to the solution of our poor competitiveness in Western Europe' (Kennedy, 1996). It is not only a question of what ABB can teach Eastern Europe – Barnevik believes that Western economies should learn from these young, hard-driving, hard-working competitors before it is too late.

Bengt Skantze also believes that a long-term vision is needed when investing in emerging economies:

> *You may ask is it irresponsible to put so much effort into a market where the payback may take 20 years? What about shareholders? For all the investments, we made very detailed business plans. The newly acquired businesses all either got export opportunities or the opportunity to supply back to our units in the West. We had a platform of work for them. So, even if their market had dried up, they could still survive until the market took off. So it was not such a 'cowboy' strategy. In the majority of cases, the home market turned out much more positive than expected. The export problems were greater. Colleagues in Western Europe were sometimes not so keen to give them markets or to give up markets in their favour.*

This initial reluctance on the part of some Western managers to welcome their new partners in the East may have been one of the biggest surprises for ABB's top management. Much of the drive behind ABB's activity in Central and Eastern Europe comes from a commitment to tackling environmental problems in the old Communist bloc and a genuine belief on the part of Barnevik and managers of the likes of Eberhard von Koerber and David Hunter that they are making a vital contribution to the economic transformation of Eastern Europe – in their view, the most important challenge facing Western Europe. Investment in the East is a win–win strategy as it will benefit both East and West. Says Barnevik, 'We will have a new Asia-Pacific right on our doorstep. You don't have to invest out of fear or charity. You can do it out of self-interest' (Wagstyl, 1996).

ABB's rivals have not been as forthright in their approach to Eastern Europe. Says David Hunter, 'We find that ABB is more aggressive in going after companies that involve serving the home market. Our traditional competitors are much less willing to invest in people locally. They prefer to outsource and put in people to ensure quality and schedule. They don't "buy the cow".' But ABB's success intrigued other companies. Hunter smiles:

> *Percy Barnevik communicated some rules for investments in emerging markets. For example, once you decide to move, move fast. Double your estimate of what it will cost. Get close to the unions. Empower local management. Insist on Western quality from the beginning – no transition period. Concentrate on investing in people first – new machines can come later. I showed overhead slides several times to the business community. Other investors always wanted copies!*

Percy Barnevik has been described as the kind of higher-level managerial thinker or 'humanizer' who seeks not only to increase profit and growth but also to develop positive human potential, and who inspires people by communicating both human and economic goals wider than the corporation itself. This is in contrast to the pure 'analyzer' who seeks only to motivate people by satisfying needs for money and promotion. This is due, in particular, to his 'pragmatic understanding that [his] business depends on developing material and social infrastructures and [to] his belief that business opportunity in Eastern Europe requires investment in those countries' (Maccoby, 1994). Whether or not Barnevik would agree with this interpretation, ABB's contribution to the improvement of living standards in emerging economies is certainly a source of pride for many ABB managers.

ABB Elta: creating a partnership in Eastern Europe

ABB was prepared to be flexible in the way that it applied its turnaround formula in Eastern Europe, as demonstrated by the case of ABB Elta, a Polish transformer factory that ABB acquired in the town of Łodz[1]. While smaller than Zamech, ABB Elta is in many ways a microcosm of the challenges that ABB – and, indeed, other Western investors – have faced in Eastern Europe.

Elta was founded in 1925 as a private factory. It was nationalized in 1945 when the Communists took power and then worked within a centrally planned economic system over the next decades. In addition to selling its products to the Soviet Union, it was able, as a low-cost producer, to export them to other countries, such as India, Pakistan, Nigeria, Libya and Turkey.

The company prospered until the start of the 1980s when Poland's deteriorating economic situation led to the collapse of Elta's domestic market. Elta's senior managers increasingly realized that the company was not flexible enough to meet the challenges of a more competitive environment and was also badly in need of new investment. They increasingly felt the need for a strategic partner to help them reshape and reinvest for the future. Through previous contacts and the sale of licences, ABB was aware of Elta's technological competence and potential. In 1992, after two and a half years of negotiations, the Polish government sold 51 per cent of the shares to ABB. (ABB later increased its shareholding to 70 per cent in 1993. Significantly, Elta's managers tended to refer to the new arrangement as a 'merger').

The first step at Elta, taken in June 1992, was to restructure the functionally organized company into six profit centres to push responsibility down and involve more people in decision making. The workforce was reduced (from 2000 people to under 1300). To upgrade Elta's technology and production processes and achieve shorter production cycles, ABB experts and consultants were brought in from Sweden and Germany to help with technical issues and to advise on a new factory layout. Another early action was to start intensive management training for all managers. The biggest surprises for many managers here were the new market philosophy and the need to calculate not just material costs, but all costs including maintenance and quality.

A Swedish manager was appointed Chief Finance Officer to introduce new financial disciplines. A Franco-Swiss manager, Ernest Meier, former general manager of one of ABB's high-performing transformer plants in Switzerland, was appointed in August 1992 as a temporary Restructuring Manager to work with Elta's general manager in reorganizing the company. An urgent task was to introduce a long-term common strategy and business plan that everybody at all levels could understand and commit to. ABB Elta's 'Vision 2000' set out a plan to generate profits for long-term growth. However, time was short and the company faced many challenges in achieving its goals.

The market situation

In Poland, its main market, ABB Elta had a strong position with, for example, over 90 per cent of the market for power transformers. Elta's home customers, however, were short of money and the company faced competition from its lower-price domestic competitors.

Customer and service orientation

Much depended on Elta's ability to instil a customer focus in the organization. Because of Elta's virtual monopoly in Poland, service had not been important before. Elta made strong efforts to improve its marketing. It introduced a central marketing function and aimed to provide 24-hour customer service to give it an advantage over foreign competitors. (This was difficult because people were reluctant to work antisocial hours, despite special pay.)

Competing internationally

Although its main market was domestic, Elta had a good position in 'traditional' Polish export markets. Its lower salaries and cheaper materials gave Elta a 25–30 per cent price advantage over Western firms on international markets, including other ABB companies. As Polish factories were not previously allowed to handle their own foreign trade, however, Elta had no in-house experience in such vital areas as tendering, insurance and transport and tried to solve this through intensive training and hiring new people with appropriate experience.

Relationships with suppliers

Elta's international cost advantage partly depended on its access to lower-cost Polish suppliers whose performance it also had to improve, through training, to achieve better prices and improve quality (which was vital as Elta was now aiming for ISO 9000 quality certification). As a member of a global corporation seeking to greatly reduce lead times, it now insisted that a specific week be agreed for delivery, rather than a particular quarter as previously.

Changing the 'old' mentality

Elta's biggest internal challenge was to change the mentality of its employees to be more 'results-oriented'. Under the previous reward system, salaries did not depend on performance but Elta now rewarded higher performers. Old ways persisted at first, though. The biggest barrier to change remained a deep-seated fear of taking responsibility. According to a senior manager, 'People are afraid of making mistakes and of being punished or losing their jobs'. Elta's top management expected to gradually bring in and train younger people without the heritage of the past. In the meantime, it was important to keep emphasizing the goals. A top manager explained, 'If you take the pressure off people for one week or one month it is normal that they will forget about the goals. Without a push, change is not possible.'

Training, training, training

Elta's Vision 2000 depended greatly on continuing intensive training to reinforce the required changes in attitude. One manager said, 'I worked as a manager for 20 years in a completely different situation with different goals, not profit. We knew it was not very good but we didn't know why or how to change. It was not easy for me to change.' A major training priority was for Elta's key people to learn English, ABB's international language.

Communication

Elta's top management also aimed to improve communication in the company. As Ernest Meier said, 'The instinct to inform and to ask themselves who is interested does not exist. A lot of information goes to Polish managers but they do not pass it on. Nor do they give information back to you. This is not a cultural problem – the Poles are actually very open people – but an educational problem stemming from what happened after 1945.'

Quality management

Elta aimed to introduce a 'zero failure' philosophy and its operations now had to achieve ISO 9000 quality certification. This was difficult, as one manager explained, 'With ISO you need to follow the rules, but you can't get people to do this. The old mentality was not to follow regulations. It is part of the Polish mentality. To survive two wars and the Communists, people learned the need to be flexible.'

Leadership and responsibility

Another area of concern for Elta was leadership. Ernest Meier told the Polish top team, 'You must be locomotives, not the wagons following behind. You are in front – you say when we go, in what direction, and how quickly. They must learn to do it themselves. Sometimes they are surprised they can do it.' The profit centre organization meant a big change for the responsible managers. As one explained, 'I now have to think of myself as an owner of Elta. Before I was only responsible for technical issues. Now I am responsible for everything, including business issues and people too'.

Integration into the ABB group

Integration into the ABB group presented both challenges and opportunities. To prevent its 26 power transformer companies from competing with each other, ABB allocated different markets between them. Elta was responsible for the Polish market and could also export components to ABB companies in other countries. The allocation of markets initially frustrated Elta's managers when they saw other ABB companies tendering for foreign contracts which Elta felt it had a better chance of winning because of its competitive prices. On the whole, however, managers were happy about cooperation with other parts of ABB. Ernest Meier brought in former ABB colleagues from Switzerland to help upgrade Elta's operations. Elta managers were also able to visit other ABB companies to learn about different approaches. Meier worried, however, that Western colleagues in ABB were afraid that more activities would be transferred to the lower-cost East and that they might become less willing to share their ideas.

Some managers appreciated the contact with a global group and the resulting change in outlook. One said:

> Multinationalization has a big impact on the Polish mentality which was not service-oriented before. ABB is not a company from just one country, it is not just Swedish/Swiss, it has a global perspective. You meet with people from all over the world and you start to think in another dimension. This is the way the world will be in future as barriers come down.

Another manager enthused about the new skills that she had acquired, 'I never learned so much in such a short time. It has been hard but so interesting.'

Elta's top managers also took part in the twice-yearly meetings of their ABB business area to discuss the strategic and technological direction of the global business. One manager said, 'Sometimes there is very heated discussion but the atmosphere is very good. The first meeting that I went to had a very open discussion and people were saying "I don't agree!" I was very surprised, we had lived for such a long time in a closed system.'

Ernest Meier, the restructuring manager, admitted that he had come to Poland intending to implement action plans in typical 'Western' style. He came to understand, however, that this would not always work. A major problem was a lack of understanding about basic management among some managers. Meier could see that often people did not understand what he was talking about, despite the early training they had received. When he asked one manager about his orders backlog he was met with the response, 'What's that?' He came to realize that he was speaking in a vocabulary that was unknown to them, 'like people speaking Russian to me!'

During his first months at Elta, Meier worked with the old general manager who had been in the post for 18 years. This manager found it very difficult to accept Meier's recommendations. Educated in the old system, he did not understand general management and finance and was eventually replaced by another senior Polish manager who understood the imperative for change. Meier decided that he had to begin by educating Elta's people at a basic level with 'very simple things'. He introduced, for example, regular management meetings and weekly reports on quality activities by each profit centre.

Ernest Meier's contribution was much appreciated by Elta's managers. As one said:

He has been the most important person in our restructuring. He created a new mentality and gave people new knowledge about everything. He taught us that it is necessary to build a new house from the bottom up not from the roof down. He spends many hours teaching people.

Another manager said:

He understood quickly that it is not always possible to change a Polish company with Swedish or Swiss approaches. We are a Polish company with Polish people and problems. Meier understood that the process of change must be adapted to local conditions. I always ask him why we should change and he always explains why.

Elta's Polish general manager was convinced that 'without the joint venture with ABB in 1992 this company would not exist today.' Of managing change in an East European company, Ernest Meier said, 'What you must do is show people the *results* of a new approach like customer focus or good supply management. It cannot be too theoretical, they have had too much doctrine in the past.'

Meier believed that Western companies making acquisitions in Eastern Europe must be clear about the qualities needed by managers who are brought in to act as change agents there:

We must be careful about who we send here. Sometimes people who are successful in the West can be a disaster here. People who come with 'imperialistic' thinking will not succeed, especially in Poland. The Poles are very individualistic. The Russians after all could never completely dominate them during the last 45 years. In Poland, you must go slowly. You must be a teacher and you must respect people. You must be humble and not play the messiah or the superman from a Western country. You must be with the people here and work together with them.

You must stand in the team, not outside. Then you have a much greater chance to see what the problem really is. You also have to give an example. You can't arrive late and go early and then ask people to work hard.

Now a successful ABB affiliate, Elta has since won important orders from Poland's national power grid company, and exports to important ABB markets such as China and Malaysia.

Note

1 In 1994, on behalf of Germany's Europa-Akademie, we prepared a case study on ABB Elta, to illustrate the issues involved in managing change in economies undergoing transition (*ABB Elta, Creating a Partnership in Eastern Europe*, Europa-Akademie für Führungskräfte Ruhr, 1994).

Building the third leg of the triad in Asia

By the early 1990s, ABB had consolidated and restructured Western Europe, it had established a major presence almost overnight in the USA and had started developing its network in Central and Eastern Europe. Now it was time to build the third leg of its global triad – Asia. At the beginning of the 1990s, this was the fastest-growing region in the world and 'where the big battle is', according to Percy Barnevik.

ABB's objective in Asia was to raise sales from 13 per cent of total revenues to at least 20 per cent. Expansion in Asia rested less on big acquisitions than in building up ABB's own potential in countries such as India, China, Indonesia and Malaysia. As Bengt Skantze says:

In this region you have to grow mainly from within because suitable acquisition opportunities are rare. We have a somewhat standard model for how to build up our business in these countries. It starts with a sales office which sells the products from our European and American centres. From that base we gradually build up local activities, starting with service and maybe installation and erection work. Then we establish local engineering and finally even manufacturing. In that way you finally have quite some local value added.

ABB's Asian expansion has been another huge undertaking. Skantze explains:

A major issue is how to build the local organization, find people and train them. It's an enormous task. Our human resources people exemplify it like this. If you want to build up an organization of 50 people in Malaysia, you have to look at 100 candidates for each job and select 10 for interview. Therefore you are dealing with 5000 applicants. Multiply this all over Asia and you can see it is an enormous task to build it up in a reasonable time. Once on board you have to train them and couple them back to the technical centres. It is the biggest challenge of them all and takes time.

ABB has put a lot of emphasis on building a presence in India and China, which it expects will account for $6 billion sales between them in the early years of the next millennium, nearly half its forecast $15 billion total for Asia. The company already had some small activities in India on which to build. ASEA had been in India since the 1920s. Its Fläkt subsidiary opened up there in the 1960s, as did BBC, which established some factories in the subcontinent. By the time of the merger, these had become medium-sized operations (ASEA with 1000 people, BBC 4000 people and Fläkt 1000 people). They were still, however, in relative terms, small and unknown in India. A. K. Thiagarajan, former Managing Director of ABB India[3], remembers:

> At that time, we were not one of the big multinational companies like Philips. We were in niche markets, Fläkt was in pollution control, and ASEA was in industrial engineering. India was not on the priority list of the company. We were far away, considered to be a difficult country, relatively ignored and unimportant. Today we are one of the top one to five multinationals in the country. This was a big change for us.

H. K. Mohanty, Vice-President Corporate Personnel for ABB India, describes the pre-merger companies:

> We were not one of the top companies here (today we are three times the size of GEC). We had existed for many years, although the quality was poor and efficiency was low. Demands on quality and competitiveness were not high. ASEA had been here since 1928, trading opportunistically and was very much a bureaucratic Indian company. At the time I joined BBC, nine years before the merger, there was no global vision in the company. Most multinationals operated like that. The government gave out manufacturing licences and decided what capacity was allowed and where factories could be built. It was very difficult to operate with a vision in this country. Since deregulation, however, it is possible to have a vision. It was a very good coincidence when Percy Barnevik came with his vision.

After the initial surprise of the merger announcement in 1987, the three former Indian subsidiary companies started to work together to build a new organization. The regeneration process was assisted by the advent of economic reforms in India and the move from a socialistic, government-driven economy to a more open market economy. Restrictions on foreign shareholdings were loosened, import duties were reduced and the local market started to grow rapidly.

After the merger, the strategy was to, likewise, grow very rapidly and become a full-range ABB company by 2000, adding 2–3 products each year. Growth was to be achieved by both acquiring existing businesses and through greenfield sites. Mohanty explains the problems: 'It is very difficult to acquire publicly owned, small Indian companies. They are expensive, the ones that are for sale are often badly managed, and they are often grossly overmanned. It takes two years for an acquisition to be fully integrated so the greenfield approach is quicker.' ABB's Indian top management also concentrated on building a large marketing organization to get close to customers across the subcontinent. This eventually consisted of 500 people in the field and 26 offices, one in every important industrial city in India.

Internally, the strategy demanded a drive to raise management competence in technology and develop a strong cadre of Indian managers. ABB also introduced new management concepts, such as cycle time reduction. Thiagarajan says, 'This was about a vast change in productivity outlook, working smarter rather than working harder, fewer people rather than more people. We communicated the benefits to people so that they could accept it. This caused ripples initially.' As in other ABB acquisitions, the new strategy demanded a reduction in headcount. This was distinctly countercultural in a 'protected, conservative country where it was traditional to have overmanned, low-productivity, high-bureaucracy companies and where there are many difficulties with trade unions and labour relations are very strong.'

The Indian top managers felt a dilemma that called for a more gradual approach to reducing the workforce. H. K. Mohanty says, 'ABB was downsizing globally. Here we saw that it was a need, but there were many unexpressed fears. People worried about their employment. We decided not to go for it like a bull in a china shop.' Asked today, however, what they would have done differently after the merger, they believe they should not have delayed difficult decisions but instead pushed downsizing through harder and merged with Fläkt very early on (instead of leaving it until 1994). Says Thiagarajan, 'We should have downsized more than we did. It was the strength of both organizations ASEA and BBC that carried us through'. Change in ABB's Indian subsidiaries was also supported by change in the wider economic environment. With the economy opening up to the world, more and more Indian firms have been exposed to global forces and so delayering and restructuring have become more common.

India would become a key market (with, eventually, 10,000 employees out of ABB's 40,000 people in Asia). The head office would be moved from Bangalore to New Delhi to be close to central government, although ABB still has significant operations in Bangalore, including 600 software engineers producing applications software for ABB and other companies.

Just as ABB used Polish and Czech managers to leapfrog to other countries in Eastern Europe, so ABB India sends people out to other Asian countries to help in quality and customer focus programmes and sometimes to take up managerial positions. Thiagarajan says, 'We are very proud of this merger. We tried consciously to create a new organization. Our motto was to take the best of the old organization to create a new one. It was not taking over. There was no feeling of drowning.'

What added value and competitive advantage does ABB India believe it derives from its parent company? Thiagarajan recounts the benefits of being part of a global group:

Finance and access to ABB technology are very important. The very size of the Group gives us economies of scale and scope. We are a project business and being part of this Group makes us large enough to go into the projects we want to. We can supply so much more because we have more resources than any other contender. We are nowhere near technological self-sufficiency, but we have access to the most modern technology worldwide. We also have access to export markets for sourcing and access to modern management practices and systems. We have modern computer systems, help during reorganizations, and with quality and TQM, ERP solutions and personnel systems. There are people constantly floating in and out of here. There is also the importance of the name and the recognition received by big companies. We have the brand image, a very strong brand image in industrial products. Percy Barnevik is well known and pushed the name with large customers. He was written about in the business magazines and this rippled through to India. So there is clear added value from the parent.

One impact of ABB's reputation and strong brand image is the help it provides in managing relationships with its 'partner' organizations. H. K. Mohanty explains, 'ABB does not shoot for 100 per cent equity on its companies here, that is too expensive. Every new company is owned at 51 per cent equity, never less. We have joint venture partners in all our companies, but all think of themselves as ABB. Everyone identifies with ABB as an organization.'

That ABB states and demonstrates its commitment to local development wherever it operates has also been an important advantage. Thiagarajan says:

ABB has always been known and perceived by the government as committed to India. Percy Barnevik has always said that India is a country of the future and Göran Lindahl is doing the same. It shows in the investments – the buildings, new factories and acquisitions. We are committed partners in the large-scale India Power programmes. We have contributed 1000 megawatts per year and $400 million in India already.

How does the high-achieving culture of ABB work in India? What have the Indian affiliates inherited from the Swedish-Swiss parent company? Says Thiagarajan:

The influence from ABB is only positive. Any competitive company in the West tends to be more figures-driven and short term. In India we look a little more longer-term. Our human relations are normally better. Cultures are different. We tried to keep ours and to still come a long way. Perhaps we have learned from the Swedish informality, and the ability it gives you to cut through a large organization. ABB is generally a democratic organization and by and large we are a more open organization. It is one of our strengths. We appreciate having other people come and show us things. Maybe sometimes there is a tyranny of the lack of direction!

H. K. Mohanty agrees:

There is freedom here. Yes, in India we value the respect towards the father and this is the behaviour of people here. But the values on the inside of the company work differently. We can disagree professionally with the boss here. It is not held against us. You have to say it in a particular way. We have many knowledge workers here at the centre and the young people have a different outlook. There is a sense of fair play.

ABB India's managers have clearly enjoyed being part of a successful merger process. Says A. K. Thiagarajan, 'I have been able to secure my company. We have grown from a small unknown company to one of the best-known organizations in India.' We'll come back to ABB India in Chapter 9 to look at some of their current and future challenges.

Preparing for the Dragon Century

China – with its vast potential markets of over 1 billion people and rapid economic growth, its increasing demand for advanced technology, and with the twenty-first century already labelled as 'China's century' (or, as futurist John Naisbitt calls it, 'the Dragon Century' [Naisbitt, 1994]), it is clear that this huge country would be a magnet for ABB and other Western companies. Infrastructure development is a prime objective of China's economic planners, who are striving to maintain the country's economic growth while dealing with the growing gap in living standards between rich and poor and that between coastal areas and the inland regions. It has huge ambitions in power generation. In 1979–96, China built 87 power projects, using $13 billion worth of foreign capital. In future, ABB expects that China will order a new nuclear power plant from foreign suppliers every year on average.

ABB's own Chinese business started to take off in 1992. Göran Lindahl was heavily involved in building ABB's presence in China, as well as in Asia at large, as the segment manager for the region during these important start-up years. His personal experience of Asia should turn out to be useful later on since he has taken over as CEO of ABB. Percy Barnevik also gave a lot of personal attention to promoting ABB in this vital country. During a visit to China, he publicly said ABB was inspired by China's remarkable economic achievements. He also took part in 1996 in a two-day conference on developing China's power industry, of which ABB China, the group's local holding company, was a joint sponsor. The Vice-chairman of China's State Planning Commission, Ye Qing, told the conference that strengthening international cooperation is pivotal to China's reform of its electric power industry and that China's recently enacted first Electricity Law stressed that the power industry should expand faster than others. In return, Barnevik said, 'To boost the industry, China should employ technology as well as management systems and training, and attract foreign investments and financing through increased global cooperation.' Ye noted that China would set up a number of large thermal power plants, hydro-power plants, nuclear power plants, superhigh-voltage transmission and distribution projects, and clean coal technology model projects during the next few years. 'We have reason to believe,' he said, 'that we'll have a lot of opportunities to cooperate with ABB, which enjoys the advantages of leading technology and quality in these fields.'

However, the question that ABB has asked itself is, while recognizing its long-term attractiveness, how best do you serve such a market? In the event, ABB has selected a joint venture approach. The key factor is transfer of technology, but it has to make sure that it retains control over it to avoid an outflow of technology. Some of ABB's competitors have been prepared to go into China with minority shareholdings, but ABB is determined to keep control of its technology.

Erik Elzvik explains the difference between the challenges in China and Eastern Europe:

> In China we have had to go for smaller joint ventures because that is the only way to get in there. In Eastern Europe, we were more fortunate because we were able to get in early and get good existing companies and could upgrade them to our way of working. But in China and Asia, we have to take a longer way of developing. Sales and market operations take a long time to develop. In centralized economies like Eastern Europe used to be, there were also no sales or market. They have good engineers and production but it takes time to develop the other side. It takes even more time in China.

ABB's workforce in China would grow to some 5000 people by the late 1990s in 19 joint ventures, making it ABB's third largest operation in the Asia-Pacific region after India and Australia. The company planned to have 40,000 employees in China by the year 2010. One effect of ABB's expansion in Asia has been its increasing involvement in large-scale projects. In China, it is involved in the Three Gorges dam project, to improve irrigation and navigation along the Yangzi river and because it will generate huge amounts of hydro-electric power. This is a dramatic project. Totalling over $24 billion, this is the world's largest hydro-electric venture, described as the most ambitious construction project since China built the Great Wall, and it attracted fierce competition among foreign suppliers (Tomlinson, 1997). The dam, 185 metres high and 2 kilometres long, is the world's largest and will create a lake twice as large as Lac Léman, Europe's largest lake. When completed, it will deliver

18,200 megawatts of power, well above the 12,600 megawatts produced by Brazil's Itaipu, previously the world's largest hydro-electric dam. In a $250 million deal, ABB was selected in August 1997 to supply 8 of the first 14 generators, which are to be installed in 2002, with power deliveries starting in 2003.

However, not all of the Western companies participating expect to make big money from the project. In negotiating contracts, the Chinese have driven a hard bargain and awards for power-generating equipment were given at prices lower than bidders had originally hoped. So why do it? Because, according to *Fortune* magazine, doing business in China is all about establishing relationships (Tomlinson, 1997). Even if these relationships do not pay off immediately, companies are gambling that profits will materialize in the future as the market continues to grow. Companies are also betting that China will eventually unlock more of its market to foreigners, and they want to be there first. This certainly fits ABB's strategy of being an early mover to forestall competition.

In Malaysia, a consortium led by ABB was awarded the Bakun hydro-electric project – another astonishing project, the largest ever undertaken by ABB, and an engineering challenge that would have stirred Charles Brown's imagination. Malaysia is also undergoing fast economic development. As originally planned, the project would utilize the vast hydro potential of Sarawak to cope with the increasing electricity demand in Peninsula Malaysia and Sarawak. The Bakun dam in Sarawak state would generate 2400 megawatts of electric power and transmit 70 per cent of its output by high-voltage direct current (HVDC) cable across Sarawak and the South China Sea to Peninsula Malaysia via a 670-kilometre underseas cable, the world's longest. The project was worth $5 billion, most of which was to go to ABB. The project would exceed world power and voltage records for HVDC cables and the total cable length of more than 2000 kilometres would far exceed that of any previous project. ABB and its main consortium partner, Companhia Brasileira de Projetas e Obras (CBPO) of Brazil, a large civil engineering company, were to supply the hydro-electric generating plant with the dam and powerhouse and the power transmission with HVDC converters, overhead transmission lines and three submarine cables. Completion was planned for 2002–03, although at the time of writing, the project was postponed indefinitely because of the late 1990s Asian economic crisis.

Percy Barnevik said of the project, 'Malaysia's energy requirements are growing rapidly as the country's manufacturing sector takes off and purchasing power increases. ABB is committed to supporting this positive development with the most advanced technology available for an important renewable energy source.' If one of ABB's goals in Eastern Europe is to put right some of the environmental damage caused by industry under the former regime, its

133

concern to contribute to development in Asia has brought it under fire from environmentalists. Percy Barnevik puts ABB's case forcefully:

> *We in the rich world have a responsibility to change our own lifestyle when it comes to economizing on the consumption of resources and to eco-cycle concepts. We also have a responsibility towards the developing countries by transferring to them the experiences of our own industrialization as well as efficient and clean technology, which can help them along the road to so-called sustainable development. They must avoid the mistakes we made during our industrialization. The warning here is the ruthless exploitation of the environment during the industrialization of the former Soviet Union.*
>
> *Billions of deprived people in the East and South have started to move. It is no longer a question of small developing islands like Singapore or Taiwan, but 700–800 million people in countries like China and India are now experiencing a rapid economic growth. In ten years perhaps twice as many will be able to share in this growth. The increased strain on the global environment resulting from the accelerating growth will overshadow all previous experience.*
>
> *Certain people in the rich world paint doomsday scenarios and assert that our common environment will not be able to cope with this industrialization and increased consumption of energy, ultimately an improved standard of living of the globe's impoverished people. With what right can we stop this development towards a higher standard of living in the poor nations, which we ourselves have experienced over the last 100 years? This question should be posed loudly and clearly. The answer is that we do not have this right, but instead the obligation to lessen our own impact on the environment and to help the poor nations on the road to sustainable development. The supply of energy and in particular electrical energy represents here an important motor in the development, irrespective of whether we talk about rural areas, cities, industry or transportation . . . I am glad not only that the ABB consortium has won [the Bakun project] on the basis of better technology and economy, but also that ABB is committed to developments within this part of the world through both the transfer of the best possible technology and the establishment of local businesses and industry* (Barnevik, 1996).

The post-multinational company of the future?

In 1990, ABB was described as 'the company standing by with the Rennies', to soothe its corporate indigestion (Dullforce, 1990). ABB's creation of its worldwide presence certainly demanded enormous effort and energy. Some observers worried that the acquisitions were straining ABB's finances and management's capacity and that service would deteriorate. ABB, it was said, had tried to acquire too much and manage too many disparate cultures and had grown faster than the ability of all its far-flung parts to communicate with each other. The acquisition of Combustion Engineering in the US, in particular, was seen as a big test of the strategy of decentralization. The turnaround put large demands on managers' ability and many were replaced. ABB was not helped by the onset of recession in the early 1990s in Europe and North America. By 1991, 60 per cent of the company's geographical spread of business was in recession, which made it all the more important to speed up the company's global growth.

Percy Barnevik himself described how 'horrified, depressed, almost desperate' top management could become when he found that, three or four months after a worldwide programme started in 1990 to squeeze accounts receivable and free up working capital, he visited an accounts receivable office that had not even heard of the programme when it was supposed to be their priority (Taylor, 1991). His solution? Don't inform, *overinform* – even if it means breaking taboos among some European managers about sharing information.

Some observers looked beyond the short-term problems that ABB faced as it reshaped itself. According to *Business Week* magazine, Barnevik had confounded the sceptics and was described as having built 'Europe's most dynamic manufacturing giant' (Kapstein, 1990). 'With the foundation of his global company in place, . . . Barnevik is now attempting a corporate makeover that has never been tried anywhere. Barnevik is determined to shape ABB into what he believes is the model European company of the future. ABB, he says, is on its way to becoming an entirely new breed of corporation, breaking ground for the post-multinational company of the 1990s' (Kapstein, 1990).

Notes

1 By the late 1980s, it was widely recognized that Asia as a whole, and not just Japan, was a major region for the future. When Percy Barnevik talked of the third leg of the Triad he generally meant Asia, including Japan. ABB executives sometimes talk of the third leg as Asia *and* Eastern Europe. Similarly, proponents of the Triad concept would now see the American leg as including all the Americas, north and south, and not just the USA.

2 When we talked with Percy Barnevik in 1998, he reminded us that Zamech was an example of one of the companies ABB acquired that had their own proud histories – Zamech had established a subsidiary in Hamburg in Germany in 1840, long before ASEA or BBC were created.

3 The companies that were eventually consolidated under the ABB India holding company in 1995 included ABB ABL Limited, Universal ABB Power Cables Limited., ASEA Brown Boveri Limited, Birla Kent Taylor Limited and ABB Alfa Stal Refrigeration Limited.

References

Quotes without references originate from the authors' personal communications – see page xviii for details.

Barnevik, Percy (1996) *The Bakun Project: A Good Strategy for Sustainable Development.* ABB Power Systems' Home Page on the World Wide Web.

Dullforce, William (1991) 'ABB ASEA Brown Boveri: First the creation – but the fruits have still to be fully realized', *Financial Times*, 5 April.

Dullforce, William (1989) 'Where "paradise" is to be found in acting quickly', *Financial Times*, 5 April, 26.

Dullforce, William (1990) 'Risking corporate indigestion', *Financial Times*, 21 March, 27.

Dullforce, William and Garnett, Nick (1989) 'When the ketchup starts to flow', *Financial Times*, 15 November.

Gibson, Marcus (1995) 'How ABB became Europe's best', *The European*, 5–11 October, 19.

Hofheinz, Paul (1994) 'ABB's big bet in Eastern Europe', *Fortune*, 2 May, 24–30.

Hofheinz, Paul (1994) 'Yes, you can win in Eastern Europe', *Fortune*, 16 May, 110 (3).

Hofheinz, Paul (1996) 'Inside ABB', *Russia Review*, 17 June, 8–13.

Kapstein, Jonathan, and Reed, Stanley, *et al.* (1990) 'Preaching the Euro-gospel', *Business Week*, 23 July, 34–8.

Kennedy, Carol (1996) 'ABB's sun rises in the east', *Director* , September, 40–44.

Klebnikov, Paul (1991) 'The powerhouse', *Forbes*, 2 September, 46–50.

Leppänen, Rolf (1994) *ABB Action Recipe: Strategic Management in the Growth and Restructuring of a European Enterprise.* Helsinki: International Networking Publishing INP Oy.

Maccoby, Michael (1994) 'From analyzer to humanizer: raising the level of management thinking', *Research Technology Management*, September–October, **37** (5), 57–9.

Naisbitt, John (1994) *Global Paradox.* London: Nicholas Brealey Publishing, 179.

Ohmae, Kenichi (1985) *Triad Power: The Coming Shape of Global Competition.* New York: The Free Press.

Rapoport, Carla (1992) 'A tough Swede invades the US', *Fortune*, 29 June, 76–9.

Taylor, William (1991) 'The logic of global business: an interview with ABB's Percy Barnevik', *Harvard Business Review*, March–April, 91–105.

Tomlinson, Richard (1997) 'Dam! America misses out on the world's biggest construction project', *Fortune*, 10 November, 98–102.

von Koerber, Eberhard (1997) *Enlargement to the East: The Decisive Moment for Europe's Future.* Zürich: Churchill Symposium, 18 September.

Wagstyl, Stefan (1996) 'Woven into the fabric', *Financial Times*, 10 January, 15.

The globally connected corporation

*Our identity is out there in the companies at the same time as we
are a global company.*

Eric Elzvik
Vice-President, Corporate Development, ABB

So far, we have looked at ABB's early two-stage strategy of restructuring
followed by growth. Before we go on to consider how ABB has been reaping
the harvest of that strategy and its plans for the future, let's step back for a
moment and in the next two chapters think about ABB as a 'post-
multinational' company.

How do we make sense of what ABB has achieved? ABB's success, in one of
the most fiercely competitive, tight-margin industries in the world, is all the
more remarkable in that the company has been pioneering a new form of
global organization to meet the new challenges. Percy Barnevik described the
paradoxes that ABB has tried to resolve as the simultaneous attempt to be
'global and local, big and small, and radically decentralized with central reporting and control.' In essence, Barnevik and his senior colleagues at ABB have
tried to resolve these contradictions by creating what we call a 'globally connected corporation', a loose–tight network of processes, projects and partners
that can only be held together by highly committed people and strongly held
principles. This is an organization that aims to foster sharing and collaboration
between its operations in different parts of the world and to develop continuous cross-border feedback for organizational learning. It is 'connected', not
only in the way that it links its people and operating units across the world, but
also in the way that it aims to work closely with clients and suppliers, and be
deeply embedded in the countries where it is present. This 'spider's web', as one
ABB executive describes it, is a unique response to the 'think global, act local'
slogan. Being a globally connected corporation involves:

- deep-rooted local presence
- global vision

- globally distributed strategy
- cross-border understanding
- global values and principles for managing creative tension
- global connection at the top
- global ethics.

Deep-rooted local presence

First, there has to be something globally substantial to connect. The first requirement of a globally connected corporation is quite simply to be there globally in all the important regions and countries, but to be there in a way that goes way beyond merely selling there. ABB's concern to add value locally, manufacture locally wherever possible and be seen to be committed to supporting economic development has certainly given it deep presence. Its goal has always been to become an insider, a domestic player and, thus, secure an improved local market position, as well as access to the local talent pool. It has gone further than most companies in this respect. It is, indeed, deeply connected to the countries and communities in which it operates. A survey in 1997 by *The Economist* found that, 'Few companies, even the most familiar household names, are truly global. The average multinational produces more than two-thirds of its output and locates two-thirds of its employees in its home country. Although both operate worldwide, the culture of General Motors is distinctively American, that of Volkswagen identifiably German' (*The Economist*, 1997). *The Economist*'s survey showed that, out of the top 15 'transnational corporations' (as defined by UNCTAD) by foreign assets in 1995, ABB ranked as follows.

- **Foreign assets as percentage of total** ABB was fourth at 84.7 per cent, only just behind Volkswagen (84.8 per cent), Nestlé (86.9 per cent) and Bayer (89.8 per cent). (General Electric had 30.4 per cent.)
- **Foreign sales as percentage of total** ABB was second at 87.2 per cent, behind Nestlé (98.2 per cent). (General Electric had 24.4 per cent.)
- **Foreign employment as percentage of total** ABB was second at 93.9 per cent, behind Nestlé (97.0 per cent). (General Electric had 32.4 per cent.)

Bengt Skantze says, 'The thing that really distinguishes us is our local presence. This includes a lot of small offices. It has given us advantages in many markets. We are the most internationally present group in our business.'

Although the balance of influence in ABB's global matrix has shifted over time towards the global dimension (as we describe in Chapter 10), ABB's local presence remains vital. Göran Lindahl, who took over as CEO in 1997 (and who engineered a major shift towards control by the business areas in 1998), believes that ABB's local presence will shield it from many future instabilities around the globe, especially in emerging economies. 'We will be part of those societies and their development', he says.

Global vision

ABB certainly has a global vision – again, one that goes beyond merely being in as many countries as possible. It thinks of the world as one place, as opposed to a collection of markets. At one level, this is about people's perceptions and feelings. ABB's people around the world see and feel the whole rather than just their local pieces of the organization. They are told that they are part of something bigger than their local operation and they are told that they are an important part of that bigger whole.

At another level, ABB's vision is about the organization as a whole and how its far-flung pieces might work to make it bigger than the sum of the parts. Right from the start, ABB's vision was to be a global player with a widely coordinated network of production units in many markets, combined with international sales and service organizations. In this respect, it differed from its main competitors, who typically manufactured in their home market and exported to other markets. On the one hand, ABB's local presence and insider identity meant that it could grow domestic sales in the countries where it was present. On the other hand, its global network meant that it could source products from the quickest and cheapest site in the group. In addition to its ambitious cost-reduction programmes, competition between the various production units within the same business segment can reduce costs by 25 per cent.

The ability to gain access to cost-competitive labour and production in Eastern Europe was a fortuitous boost for this strategy. When ABB competes on large projects in Asia, for example, it goes in as a team of high-tech system suppliers from Western Europe and the USA, plus low-cost equipment suppliers from Poland, Romania, Thailand or China. In that region, its major competition is Japanese firms in partnerships with their own low-cost suppliers in China, Malaysia, Vietnam and other countries. It sees this combination of leading-edge technology and low-cost production as the only way it can compete and be profitable in these competitive markets.

That Percy Barnevik held this vision at a very early stage is shown by the interview he gave to the *Harvard Business Review* in 1991. Using transportation as an example, he said:

> *First, we know what core technologies we have to master, and we draw on research from labs across Europe and the world. Being a technology leader in locomotives means being a leader in power electronics, mechanical design, even communications*

software . . . Second, we structure our operations to push cross-border economies of scale. This is an especially big advantage in Europe, where the locomotive industry is hopelessly fragmented . . . There are European companies still making only 10 or 20 locomotives a year! How can they compete with us, when we have factories doing ten times their volume and specializing in components for locomotives across the Continent? . . . That specialization creates huge cost and quality advantages. We work to rationalize and specialize as much as we can across borders.

Barnevik's vision recognized the limits to specialization. ABB could not ignore borders altogether. If it expected to win orders for locomotives in Switzerland, it had *better* be 'a Swiss company', he said. That meant understanding Swiss environmental concerns and the need for locomotives that could handle the particular demands of Alpine operating. Barnevik pointed to other advantages of having a multidomestic presence:

India needs locomotives – thousands of locomotives – and the government expects its suppliers to manufacture most of them inside India. But the Indians also need soft credit to pay for what is imported. Who has more soft credit [in 1991] than the Germans and the Italians? So we have to be a German and an Italian company, we have to build locomotive components there as well as in Switzerland, Sweden and Austria, since our presence may persuade Bonn and Rome to assist with our financing . . . We test the borderlines all the time. How far can we push cross-border specialization and scale economies? How effectively can we translate our multidomestic presence into competitive advantage in third markets? (Taylor, 1991).

Barnevik expanded on the advantages of multidomesticity in an interview with *Forbes*, the American business magazine. Here he showed how a domestic identity helps win not only domestic orders but export orders as well: 'When I was living in America in the mid 1970s, I was running a steel company. I was building a tube plant and a welding and wire plant – expanding like hell. And when I was in Washington, talking about steel quotas, there I was: a Swede asking for protection [for steel products] in the US.' That experience strongly influenced Barnevik's global vision for ABB: 'The nuclear power plants that we are building in Korea are from ABB Combustion Engineering in the US. When I go to Seoul, you know who I visit? Not the Swedish ambassador, not the Swiss ambassador – I go to the US ambassador, because I represent a US company' (Klebnikov, 1991). As the owner of major US manufacturing assets, ABB enjoys the marketing support of the US government, even though the corporate parent was originally a European company. Barnevik says, 'That is what "multidomestic" means' (Klebnikov, 1991).

Eric Elzvik, in charge of ABB's corporate development, says multidomesticity makes:

ABB a special type of environment. Maybe we are not unique but we are different. We drive down responsibility. Our multidomestic presence plus global coordination is a winning combination. Our identity is out there in the companies at the same time as we are a global company. Some companies have matrix organizations and some have got rid of them. It can suit other organizations in different time periods. What distinguishes us is our structure and organization, and the way we want to approach customers. The competitors still have a key core centre and export from there. Maybe they have an edge sometimes in certain situations. But for ABB, there is no other organization that could suit it better. We have a complicated product strategy. Our difference is in the way that we cover markets, locally and globally. Others are not able to do both. This is a key reason for the company's success.

Globally distributed strategy

The globally connected corporation has a vision that calls for global coordination and cooperation. It does not, however, have a strong corporate centre running a centrally imposed global strategy. ABB's strategy, as one manager put it, is 'out there' in the operating units. David Hunter, who previously coordinated Central and Eastern Europe, says that global strategy is 'the distillation of thousands and thousands of local decisions made each day'.

ABB's growth pattern has partly determined its nature. It has, in the course of time, acquired some very substantial international businesses with a long history of independence, including ASEA, BBC and its German operations, Strömberg and Combustion Engineering. Bengt Skantze, who has been closely concerned with ABB's organizational design, talks about the difference between an 'international' group and a 'global' company:

There are international groups like General Electric of the US and Electrolux of Sweden. In international groups, most or much of the business is carried out abroad, and managers travel the world all the time. But everyone knows that all important decisions are taken by the group of people back in the parent country. This was true even in ASEA with the matrix. But in a global company like ABB it is different. Suddenly the companies abroad are not subsidiaries to head office. They are very 'heavy' and important in their own right. So it is not just Swedes and Swiss taking all the important decisions – although some decisions are taken in Zürich, of course. It is a huge difference from before. The corporate centre is small and the companies out there also run global businesses in their own right. We have to take account of that when we manage and discuss things.

In such a multicentred organization, the corporate centre becomes one of many global focal points in the organization (see Figure 5.1). Its role is much more about communicating a vision and treating colleagues in the other

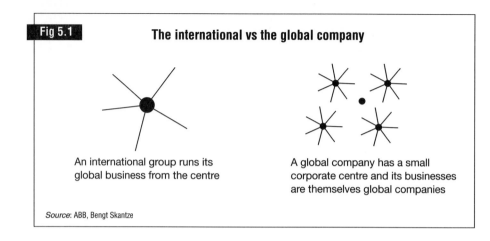

Fig 5.1

The international vs the global company

An international group runs its
global business from the centre

A global company has a small
corporate centre and its businesses
are themselves global companies

Source: ABB, Bengt Skantze

centres as peers rather than subordinates, working in collaboration with them
and supporting their initiatives in achieving the vision.

The challenge is to encourage collaboration with and between people from
an enormous diversity of countries and cultures. Skantze says, 'Things are
changing somewhat, but if we look around the world in so-called international
groups, there is usually a high percentage of one national group. In ABB there
are many nationalities – this needs a very different management style. We
have to learn to work closely with many nationalities.'

Cross-border understanding

How does ABB work with many different nationalities? Skantze attributes
some of its approach to its Swedish inheritance:

*Swedes have a very personal management style. People know each other very well,
they meet privately, talk on the phone, it is very informal. People at the top don't only
know people at the top but know people all over the organization. To combat bureaucracy it is important to have this private touch. You still have rules and decisions
must be made in a certain way, but there is a human touch which can cross many
organizational lines. When Percy Barnevik goes around the Group, people will say 'I
have met Percy', even the junior sales guy. This reflects the Swedish style.*

Skantze admits that managing a group with many nationalities is very difficult:

*It takes a lot of effort to build up a natural relationship. I thought I was interna-
tional, having worked all my life in international groups before ABB, but then found
out that we must understand and respect others' ways of doing things. This takes
effort from both sides. There have been some problems with some people – people*

who were insensitive and said, 'I know how to do this', etc. They may have been very brilliant but it does not work with people like that. The extra thing needed here is that we must have this international understanding – a real genuine interest in working with other nationalities, not just on paper, in how to get trust, how to get people from other countries in the team, and organize people across borderlines.

However, it is easy, even for managers with no national axe to grind, to fall back on their national comfort zone when, for example, making decisions such as where to locate activities. As Skantze says:

There are so many pitfalls. If you, as a Swedish manager, put things in Sweden a couple of times because you know the environment, you can have problems. You have to create confidence that you are a genuine international manager, not looking at your passport. The countries fight for their country – and that's OK, although we tell them to be global.

Global values and principles for managing creative tension

To recap ABB's organization, the company consists of some 5000 highly decentralized operating units (profit centres). These are structured as a matrix organization with global and regional/local result responsibilities. The global result responsibilities of the executives in charge of the global business segments and BAs are to develop a worldwide strategy for their operations and capitalize on economies of scale in R&D, supply management, production technology, and so on.

The regional dimension consisted until recently of three regions (Europe, the Americas, and Asia and Africa) divided into 100 or more country organizations. The three regional managers with small regional staffs were established in the reorganization in 1993. The purpose in Europe and in the Americas was to strengthen the regional cooperation across country borders. This was particularly important in Europe with the emerging Single Market and European financing of infrastructure projects involving several countries. In Asia the main purpose was to give regional support to emerging markets with new ABB establishments. Five years later the regional centres had served their purpose and were eliminated in an effort to streamline. The local result responsibilities are to formulate customer-based strategies and capitalize on economies of scope with respect to customer focus, labour relations, human resource development, government contacts and so on. As the company itself describes it, 'We are a collection of local businesses with intense global coordination'.

Eberhard von Koerber, formerly in charge of ABB's European region says, 'Of course, it's one thing to describe this approach to business and quite

143

another to manage it. While it brings us great advantages, it is a management challenge to make it work. This success does not come easy' (von Koerber, 1996). The real achievement has been delivered by people who sometimes have to pay a big price in juggling many different interests. The fundamental challenge in managing a globally connected organization is how to manage the tensions between two conflicting internal imperatives (see Figure 5.2):

- competition
- cooperation.

Competition

To drive efficiency and responsiveness, ABB promotes strong internal competition. Every operating unit is expected to build its business independently. Even central functions such as corporate communications are expected to generate revenue by selling their services to the operating units, which are free to buy services outside ABB if the price is not competitive. While the company has, over time, drastically rationalized its production to cut costs and reduce the duplication of products and components, it also keeps enough factories going in parallel to keep managers on their toes. ABACUS, the company's computerized central information system makes timely information on details of every operation's performance widely available within the organization. Business area leaders are always seeking efficiencies and may decide to move production to more efficient plants.

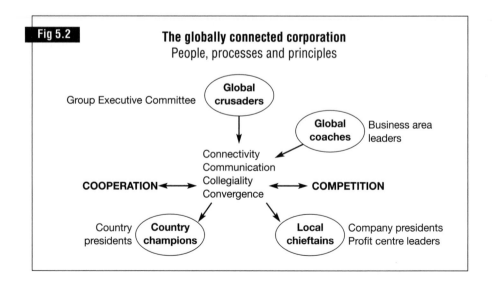

Fig 5.2

The globally connected corporation
People, processes and principles

144

There is no doubt that ABB is a very demanding organization to work for. Furthermore, as ABB has expanded into the emerging economies in Eastern Europe, Asia and elsewhere and has started to hire and develop local managers hungry for success and ambitious to show their ability to compete, some Western managers are having to run faster to keep up.

Cooperation

Competition must be constructive, however, if it is not to block the cross-border feedback and flow of ideas that is vital for a global learning organization. ABB is often the largest competitor in a business segment, but that size often derives from a combination of relatively small operations. ABB's far-flung operating units are often relatively small and need to be able to tap into the company's global network of expertise and resources. ABB managers around the world need to see themselves as complementing each other. Each business area has factories around the world, each with its own president, design manager, marketing manager and production manager. They are all working on the same problems and challenges and learning a tremendous amount in the process. ABB has tried to create a process of continuous expertise transfer as a unique source of competitive advantage.

From the perspective of ABB's (often small) acquired companies, the corporate parent represents huge added value in terms of the access to technology, expertise, global sourcing or finance it provides. As we saw in the case of ABB India, in developing countries, the company's name provides local managers with a stamp of quality that creates additional local leverage by virtue of a perceived greater status. It also brings them prestige in the group to begin to send out their own people to other parts of the world to share expertise they have developed.

Creating the 'culture of trust and exchange' necessary for the global transfer of expertise demands a big change in mindset for many managers. The required outlook is described by one Swedish manager who says, 'I am paid to run my own local operation in ABB in Sweden but I think I also have a mission to contribute knowledge so that we can improve the overall activity of ABB in my business area. There is not very much payback in my pocket for that. In fact, it probably takes money out of my pocket.' The challenge is to demonstrate that sharing brings benefits for both sides and that contributing one idea can bring half a dozen in return. Conflict cannot always be avoided in the matrix, with its multidimensional reporting lines, however. One Italian manager in ABB says:

We are all in the same boat and have to find a way to row in the same direction. We must solve our internal problems inside and not transfer them outside the company.

We must sit down together and fight it out and then go to the customer with a very well-defined strategy. If we do not, our customers and competitors will take advantage of us.

Eric Elzvik talks of the importance of being 'ABB-minded'. How does he define such an outlook?

This is to understand our basic policies, how we work with decentralization but also with very clear policies. It is having a mind for cooperation and seeing that we can cooperate across borders despite decentralization. This is a change in thinking. Before they became part of ABB, people were very independent – 'ABB was my competitor – I was Mr. Strömberg, etc.' It is about working with the contradictions – big and small, centralized and decentralized, etc. People are willing to accept complexity in the matrix.

ABB must hold and constantly work with the tensions between competition and cooperation. Its approach is not about resolving the tensions. Rather, it is based on having the tensions there all the time. It lets both things coexist, but puts the focus of attention of its managers on a number of key points to help align people within the complexity:

- customer focus
- connectivity
- communication
- collegiality
- convergence.

Customer focus

One of the major reasons for the radical decentralization of ABB's operating units is that it puts the business very close to its customers. Barnevik says that 'everything changes when there's a real customer yelling at you from the other end of the phone connection'. Direct links to customers turn a small unit into a 'real business'. As another manager says, 'You have to accept that the customer is in charge and sacrifice everything for him. This idea has to be embedded in your mission'.

Decentralization and Barnevik's relentless insistence on the importance of customers means customer focus is now well-understood in ABB and the company puts a lot of effort into monitoring its performance. As one senior ABB manager says, 'Everything you do should start with the customer. The best way to assess how you are doing is to measure customer satisfaction, to assess whether the customer is more satisfied with your performance and delivery times than with your main competitor's performance.'

Customer focus at ABB

ABB says that its approach to business can be summed up in a simple sentence: 'Satisfied customers and motivated employees are the keys to competitive success.' A simple idea, but how does ABB make it work in the real world?

In 1990, ABB introduced what has become a continuing programme of radical change called 'Customer Focus'. This is based on the belief that the customers' needs are central to the company. By means of the programme, ABB aims to learn directly from its customers what products or performance characteristics are needed. It consists of a collection of initiatives built around three major elements – Total Quality Management, supply management and cycle time management.

There are customer focus teams and groups set up across the business segments and their component functions. They issue and implement the Customer Focus programmes. Each individual company also has a customer focus manager whose responsibility is to implement Customer Focus programmes.

An example of a Customer Focus initiative is the T50 programme that started in ABB Sweden (see T50 – another cultural revolution for ABB, page 102). This aimed to halve total cycle time from taking the order, through design, engineering, and manufacture to shipment for all products. As part of the programme, ABB Sweden changed its structure from specialist departments to 'horizontal' product divisions of 30 to 100 people each. It then further reduced these into ten-person 'high performance teams'.

Initially, the Customer Focus programme concentrated on the continual improvement of internal operational performance as a necessary step to meeting customer demands. The next stage was to 'move the customer into the centre of the company', basing operational and strategic decisions on what the customer needs. The aim was to put employees and ABB's suppliers in closer touch with customers and improve the way information is shared. ABB describes it as follows:

There are a lot of challenges. Our customers, facing their own tough markets, demand continuously higher-quality products and systems. They want them faster and at lower prices. And they want more reliable service. If we can't meet those demands for continuous improvement, there is a world full of competitors who will.

That's why ABB launched Customer Focus in 1990 as a guiding principle to the way we do business. It is an attitude about everything we do that prompts us to constantly ask ourselves, 'How can I add value for the customer?'

It's a big challenge, but ABB has a big advantage. Unlike other global companies, ABB puts a top priority on building deep local roots in the communities in which it operates. ABB hires and trains local managers who know their local markets. ABB works in small entrepreneurial units, where employees can see and hear every day what their customers need. And they make the decisions locally on how best to meet those needs.

Then ABB supports them with a global organization and information network, equipped with advanced technological know-how, economies of scale in supplying

> *parts and products, financial muscle to get large projects up and running, and the accumulated operational and management expertise of more than 200,000 employees in over 100 countries worldwide*
>
> *Our commitment to Customer Focus has been reinforced by the measurable impacts it has had on employee morale and the bottom line. Workers and managers are taking greater responsibility for ABB's business success and, in the process, developing new ways of working that tap much more of their creative and problem-solving talents. In some cases, Customer Focus has also contributed directly to higher market share and higher revenues. Savings have also been significant in lower costs for inventory, repair and rework, floorspace, and materials, as well as much higher labour productivity.*
>
> *ABB intends to keep its customers competitive, taking advantage along the way of the rapidly changing global business environment to find opportunities for further growth.*
>
> (From ABB's home page on the World Wide Web)

Connectivity

Few of ABB's 5000 profit centres (with 40 employees each on average) are totally viable as stand-alone units. They depend on each other for ideas, information and resources. Whether these flow across country borders and organizational boundaries depends in turn on the promotion of a feeling of connectivity. This is a frame of mind that encourages people to take independent action yet feel part of and responsible to a bigger whole from which they derive important competitive benefits and to which, in return, they must add value.

ABB has many ways in which it fosters connectivity. In addition to the reporting linkages that connect operating units at the global and local levels, there are 'forums for exchange' that foster learning. Business area management Boards meet four to six times a year to formulate global strategies. BA staff with special responsibility for areas such as R&D and purchasing travel constantly to confer with local management and promote coordination. Functional coordination teams, made up of functional experts from different operations, meet twice a year to discuss production, quality, marketing and other issues. Apart from formal mechanisms for connecting people, the informality of the Swedish style may also help people to link across organizational boundaries. Over time, this informality may rub off on other national cultures within ABB, making them more open to connection.

Connectivity in ABB is also about top management making the time and effort to reach out directly to a wider population than just their immediate reports. Percy Barnevik, the ultimate global connector, said:

I personally meet 4000 to 5000 people every year and my colleagues in the Executive Committee do the same. When I stop in India, Brazil or Finland, I do not want to talk to 5 managers but to 100 or 200. We also bring people together along global business area lines, in the regions and in functional areas. Once every 18–24 months, we gather together 400 to 500 managers for a week and some 100 key managers come together twice a year (Price, 1997).

The way in which ABB connects top and middle management, people and teams, customers and suppliers, countries and continents, industrialized world and developing world, and ideas and opportunities makes it a microcosm of the new, emerging digital economy. Indeed, a key element in promoting connectivity in future will be the exploitation of new information and communications technology. Barnevik believes that every company with global aspirations must be an IT company:

IT changes everything in your life, whether it's manufacturing, distribution, or retailing. Soon, there will be no non-IT companies. The writing is on the wall: globalization of business demands global organization. You can't begin to do that without IT. Nor can you think about efficiency improvements, product development or service. Speeding up IT competence is the key for competitiveness today. If you don't have an understanding of speed in the world and the impact of IT on business, you are going to be a loser. Today and tomorrow, the customer is king. Competition is getting global. Prices are falling. Low-cost countries are moving in. If you don't use IT to connect to your customers, it's like moving in the wrong direction on the escalator.

The degree of connectivity will, of course, vary according to whether or not a particular ABB business is 'superglobal' or 'superlocal'. It will be higher in global businesses like power plants and oil and gas, for instance. An example of connectivity in practice in ABB is the design of a refinery in Thailand that was carried out with collaboration between designers working in Brno in the Czech Republic, the Hague in the Netherlands, and Houston in Texas, all linked via electronic 'workbenches'. In another project drawing on resources from around the world, a coal-fired power plant in the Philippines is being put together by an ABB consortium with factories in the US, Germany, Poland, India and Malaysia.

One way in which ABB has shown its connectivity to the local economies in which it operates is to help local small companies. In Ireland, for example, it has participated in a scheme where it is one of a number of large companies, including Gallagher, Hallmark and Nestlé, that are mentoring smaller companies to help them develop more open minds and think strategically.

Communication

ABB has seen very fast growth and the acquisition of many disparate companies and cultures. Its ability to create a sense of connectivity between its widely dispersed operations depends greatly on effective communication. A hallmark of Barnevik's leadership style has been clear, evocative communication (he is famous for the battery of slides that he carries with him). This is based on an understanding that what top management says has to resonate with what they do and with what others in the organization feel, value and do. ABB puts great effort into evolving and communicating its values (one of which, indeed, is the need to overcommunicate if necessary to make sure that people understand an issue). Ever since the Cannes conference in 1988, ABB has given enormous attention to internal communication. The ABB values – meeting customer needs, decentralization, taking action, respecting an ethic and cooperating – are spelt out in booklets translated into the local languages of ABB's units. They are reinforced by means of intensive in-house management education programmes in which the CEO and other top managers actively participate.

Cross-border feedback and learning depend on communication also flowing from the constituent parts of the network to the centre and between the parts themselves. David Hunter, ABB's former Head of Central and Eastern Europe, says:

> We must communicate better. Global strategy is the distillation of thousands and thousands of local decisions made each day. If you don't listen and pick up the tell-tale signs of these, you can't make global strategy. It is cause and effect – like the butterfly in chaos theory that flaps its wings in Bangladesh and causes a hurricane in the Atlantic. We're operating in chaos and must learn to be better at chaos management. ABB should be better at it because we have so many listening posts. The question is how do we communicate better?

Collegiality

Collegiality – the feeling of being a member of the global corporate club – is vital to support cooperation and worldwide learning. Continuous information exchange occurs when managers in one country or unit feel compelled to contact managers in other countries or units with a problem or an idea. As one senior ABB manager says:

> Sharing of expertise does not happen automatically. People need to spend time together, to get to know and understand each other. They must also see a payoff for themselves. All sides must get real benefits. We have to demonstrate that sharing pays – that contributing one idea gets you 24 in return.

An excellent example of the way that collegiality works in practice in ABB's global network is the restructuring of ABB Elta, the power transformer factory in Łodz in Poland that ABB acquired in 1991 (see Chapter 4). To support the reshaping of the company, ABB appointed as Restructuring Manager a Swiss former manager of one of ABB's most successful transformer factories in Switzerland. His job was to work with and advise the Polish President of the company and coach its senior managers. One of the ways in which he tried to help the company rethink its strategy and operations was to invite former colleagues from Switzerland to visit Elta for two to three days to suggest new or alternative ways of doing things to the Poles. When this kind of exchange is multiplied throughout ABB's worldwide network, the potential for global learning is enormous.

The Elta example also shows the tension between cooperation and competition. As in ABB's other East European companies, the quality of Elta's products, with the help of its parent, has improved to ABB corporate standards. With lower costs, the Polish products are increasingly competitive. Elta's restructuring manager was dismayed to find that some colleagues back at his former factory felt threatened by what he was doing in Poland. At the same time, some Polish managers initially felt restricted by being allocated less lucrative markets than other ABB transformer companies. Collegiality does not come easily in a company that has gone global through a rapid spate of mergers and acquisitions. ABB has worried that cultural arrogance on the part of some Western managers might inhibit their willingness to share their ideas and expertise with ABB companies in Eastern Europe and Asia.

Convergence

Ultimately, ABB's success will depend on the degree to which the organizational culture and management style of its different units worldwide are able to converge. This is not to say that total standardization is necessary, although ABB has achieved an amazing degree of consistency across a wide range of countries and cultures already.

The story is told that a group of ABB managers were gathered from throughout the world for a seminar. None had met before. Yet, they all presented astonishingly similar pictures of the corporation. In other companies, managers would still have been arguing at the end of the week. At ABB there is unparalleled consensus of purpose and culture. And this is despite the fact that ABB expects its local companies to operate very much as local concerns. Despite the complexity, the organization manages to send and echo clear and consistent messages.

Not that you can necessarily recognize an 'ABB person' in the same way that you could once identify an 'IBM person'. Yet, when talking to ABB managers across the globe, they are clear on what their company stands for and recognize what are essential ABB ways of working and what they can do differently locally. It takes the sweat of people to make the ABB concept work. What do they look like? What is asked of them?

Globally minded leaders

A globally connected corporation needs globally minded leaders to make it work. Barnevik saw this as a crucial bottleneck and that ABB needed to develop more of them. On the other hand, he also believed that ABB did not need thousands of global managers – only 500 out of a total of about 15,000 managers:

> *I have no interest in making managers more 'global' than they have to be. We can't have people abdicating their nationalities, saying, 'I am no longer German, I am international.' The world doesn't work like that. If you are selling products and services in Germany, you better be German!* (Taylor, 1991).

ABB is held together by four types of leader:

- global crusaders
- global coaches
- regional and country champions
- local chieftains.

Global crusaders

A German business magazine once called Barnevik '*Ritter Percyfal*', an allusion to Sir Perceval, the knight who set out on the quest for the Holy Grail. Certainly, Barnevik has at times seemed like a missionary in his fervour to promote his vision for ABB. He and his top management colleagues have been relentless travellers, taking the corporate message around the ABB world. Has Barnevik helped to create sufficient numbers of global crusaders who carry the message? Is this a message of the company now or is it still that of one individual? Excellence guru Tom Peters said in his book *Liberation Management* (1992), 'I'm not confident that an ABB without Barnevik wouldn't deteriorate – his abiding hatred of bureaucracy is critical to making the ABB structure work.' (We look at this question in Chapter 9.)

Barnevik once described the ABB global manager:

> *How are they different? Global managers have exceptionally open minds. They respect how different countries do things, and they have the imagination to appreciate why they do things that way. But they are also incisive, they push the limits of the culture. Global managers don't passively accept it when someone says, 'You can't do that in Italy or Spain because of the unions,' or 'You can't do that in Japan*

because of the Ministry of Finance.' They sort through the debris of cultural excuses and find opportunities to innovate (Taylor, 1991).

Global coaches

The global coaches are another type of global leader. These are the BA heads who have responsibility for the overall, global strategy of their businesses. Theirs is a particularly challenging role. They may have to bring about shifts in resources from country to country and this may sometimes involve closing factories. They have to encourage product specialization and allocate export markets to each unit. All of this can be threatening to the management of countries and operating units. However, their ability to get things done (certainly up to 1998) has depended more on influence and persuasion than formal line authority. Like the global crusaders at the top, they travel constantly. Ultimately, their influence depends on the extent to which they are seen to add value to the local operations. They also know that they are expected to resolve conflicts themselves, rather than take them to top management.

One BA manager describes the role:

You have demands on yourself from all sorts of people. In a matrix you don't have the hiring and firing line management tools. You have to persuade people with other means. You have to make them understand and talk sense and be practical and down to earth. You have an advantage because you have a wider outlook, you know what is happening in the world and corresponding businesses in other places, so you have a yardstick. It is important to know what kind of people you are talking to and to try to adjust your way of talking to them. Otherwise you can sit and argue for days. Building up relationships helps when you get down to the practical level.

David Hunter, former Head of Central and Eastern Europe, believes:

the global manager is someone who can put the whole group picture and priority equal with and even ahead of his own company's interest. A business area leader shouldn't have that problem – they are supposed to be global and most are. But big country presidents are also supposed to be global – sometimes when the interests of the customer don't coincide with their own.

Country champions

Up to 1998, ABB's country managers (and the three major regional offices in Europe, the Americas and Asia that ABB set up in 1993) had the full array of ABB businesses under their local control. Their job was to keep those units in line with their agreed budgets. They did not have to understand specific technologies or cross-border cost tradeoffs in all the businesses, but had to ensure that short-term financial performance met agreed expectations. They had to ensure also that local relationships (with governments and trade unions, for example) were managed to the company's advantage. (The 1998 restructuring of ABB, described more fully in Chapter 10, modified the budgeting and control roles of country managements which were now expected to negotiate responsibilities with the business areas.)

Barnevik once explained the huge mental shift required by country managers and the need to convince country managers that they benefit by being part of the ABB federation, that they gain more than they lose when they give up some autonomy. As Bengt Skantze says, 'A difficult job is that of country manager. If you are not used to the matrix, you think to yourself, "I have this country, it is mine." But you must work in the matrix or you will die. You must build your network.' This is particularly difficult in Europe, given, as we shall see, a shift to the East in employment within ABB. Managers in Europe must suffer considerable pain when they have to dismantle operations, pass on their know-how to others, sometimes lose their jobs *and* smile.

Before ABB removed its regional structure in 1998, a country manager could shift to a regional management role, responsible for a number of countries. This, too, demanded a change of outlook. David Hunter, who was country manager for Poland before taking charge of Central and Eastern Europe, says:

I was out in the trenches [in Poland]. Now I am back here in Zürich responsible for operations in Central and Eastern Europe. I have a different perspective here. I see functions along the matrix when setting priorities for developing markets. I saw it in Warsaw but then I was an advocate for local development and ignored anyone who didn't agree. But now I am part of the Group and try to find a balance between things.

The balance of power between the countries and global management has probably varied over time. Some larger or more successful countries in ABB's global network may in the past have maintained some degree of independence, even to the extent that they were able to resist the introduction of corporate initiatives such as the customer focus programme. The structural changes in 1998 that shifted relative influence towards ABB's global business areas might have altered this picture, but the country manager's influence over an individual business unit may still depend to some extent on whether the latter's business is local or more global in nature.

Local chieftains

The local chieftains (we hope they don't mind us calling them that) are the 1200 company presidents and the 5000 profit centre leaders, the front-line entrepreneurs. Their job is to have their face to the local market and to be seen as a local company – as 'German in Germany', as Barnevik put it. They are under considerable pressure to stay close to customers and produce results –

and, yet again, are expected when necessary to share ideas and resources with other units elsewhere. They are the 'eyes and ears' of the company. Although Barnevik said that he was not interested in making managers more 'global' than they had to be, some degree of global vision or international outlook is desirable if they are expected to contribute outside their own operations. As one senior ABB manager in the USA points out, 'Conducting business on a global scale requires the dedicated attention of management at all levels. Even the plant floor supervisor and his or her workers must focus on operations from a worldwide perspective, if for no other reason than to understand the forces that influence the markets for their products and the security of their jobs' (Agthe, 1990). If operating unit leaders are not global managers in themselves, though, they do need to accept and manage a dual reporting responsibility to their BA leaders and to their country or regional managements.

How is ABB to develop the managers it needs to manage these different tasks? Moving between the different levels involves greater managerial transitions than traditional notions of promotion from junior manager to middle manager to general manager to top manager. Are the jobs of the different types of ABB manager such strong profiles in themselves that it is hard to shift between them? Can one make a good global crusader or coach if one has come from being a local chieftain before? Such questions about management development become pressing in view of the continuing changes in ABB's environment, and we look at what ABB is doing in this critical area in Chapter 11.

Global connection at the top

A crucial aspect of the globally connected corporation concerns the composition of its top management. The other dimensions of global connection may not work effectively if there is a discrepancy between the message that top managers propagate about global cooperation and sharing and if that top management group is itself seen to be globally unrepresentative. The globally connected corporation must be globally connected at its highest reaches. Having such representation at the top of the organization is perhaps the most powerful way to give credibility to the group's global vision.

An international top team is a role model for the rest of the organization. This is more than symbolic. Previous research that we have carried out into international top teams in other organizations (Barham and Heimer, 1997) shows that internationally mixed top teams implicitly or explicitly contribute more to the development of an international company than single-nationality teams. Variety at the top of the corporate centre means that the organization is more able to match and process the diversity in the environment it operates in. Top teams must be acutely aware of how their visible behaviour has an impact on their organization. They can use this knowledge to develop the ability of people in the organization to think across national borders, deal with their differences, benefit from different ideas and perspectives and find ways to resolve conflicts. Overall, mixed-nationality top teams demonstrate a greater propensity to engage in and develop communication processes that bring out and benefit from different national perspectives than one-nationality teams. They involve more people across the organization in decision and strategy making. They demonstrate a sense of deep curiosity for each other's ways of doing things.

Creating an internationally mixed top team at ABB may have been a greater challenge than at first appears. Percy Barnevik's concern to ensure that restructuring and growth took place according to the principles that he had tested at ASEA meant that it would have been natural to give most top jobs to Swedes. As it happened, he was also concerned to push the merger through and get the partnership off the ground in a positive way so BBC managers were given equal representation. Although, within a year, many of the latter had been replaced by Swedes, ABB has since increasingly internationalized the composition of its top management bodies. Percy Barnevik recognizes that 'when cleaning a house, you start at the top of the staircase and set the tone up there.' He says that a challenge for global companies:

is to create a truly multicultural environment. For companies that build added value in many countries, it's not unusual any more to appoint national managers for local subsidiaries – many companies do that today. However, you are into another league of globalization and multiculturalism when you have several nationalities on the Supervisory Board and in the Executive Committee. Not only does it broaden the perspectives in these bodies, it also sends a powerful signal from the top to the whole organization (Barnevik, 1997).

If Percy Barnevik says that any multinational approach to management has to start from the top, how has ABB done in this respect by the late 1990s? On ABB's supervisory board, there are 11 members of 8 different nationalities. On the Group's Executive Committee, there were until very recently 8 members of 4 nationalities, including Swedish, Swiss, American and Danish. This does not mean that international representation can remain constant in terms of numbers. After the organizational changes announced in August 1998, the Executive Committee actually had fewer international members. We asked CEO Göran Lindahl what this meant. 'You have to build on the people you have available,' he says. 'We do not go on passports. We go on skill and competence. We have a cadre of Asians who are moving up and some of whom may be at the top in 10 years' time. But it takes time to develop people.' At the next level down, the 35 or so business area managers come from countries such as Brazil, Canada, Denmark, Finland, Germany, Italy, Sweden,

Switzerland, the UK and the US, while among ABB's head office staff, there are about 140 people of 17 different nationalities.

Global ethics

Finally, but crucially, a global presence brings benefits, but also brings responsibilities towards global constituencies – customers, employees, and communities in different countries, as well as the environment. ABB is clear that it defines its stakeholders, as its employees, customers and shareholders but it believes that it can create value for them by working 'with society'. Most ABB managers we have met genuinely believe that ABB is a deeply ethical company. Managers are proud of its contribution to local economic development in emerging economies and its concern to promote environmentally friendly power technology.

Global ethics confront managers with dilemmas, and one of the most difficult ABB faces by the very nature of its business is the impact on the environment as it tries to promote economic development. Volker Leichsering, ABB's former head of corporate communications, presents ABB's case succinctly:

> *The key factor is that, if we look at it in a rational way, it boils down to one question: 'Should we help the developing world to enhance and increase their standards of living or shouldn't we?' Do we have the right to have all the electricity and energy we need in the West, and deny it to the emerging world? We believe we don't have the right to do that. If we don't help them, then we become an environmental sinner because they will try to obtain their electricity with basic technology. And if they do that, they could pollute the environment to a degree that would really make the world suffer.*

ABB and sustainable development

ABB has been giving increasing attention to 'ecoefficiency' – 'a continuously improving process of producing more with less'. ABB started its own environmental management programme in 1992. The company's efforts toward sustainable development comprise three main elements:

1 Developing and supplying ecoefficient products and systems.
2 Transferring state-of-the-art technology to developing countries.
3 Continuously improving its own environmental performance.

At the end of 1997, at a top management forum attended by 400 senior ABB managers, CEO Göran Lindahl launched the second generation of environmental objectives for the ABB Group to be achieved by 2000. These focus on the full integration of environmental policies into strategic planning in the company's global business areas. A key element is the introduction of lifecycle assessment for the company's core products. This means that ABB will be concerned not only with the effects of its own manufacturing but also with what suppliers do with a product, transportation impacts, and, not least, the impact on the environment during the product's operational life.

One of the 'technological leapfrogs' that Göran Lindahl has promised was introduced in 1998. ABB claims that the Powerformer, a revolutionary generator which supplies power directly to the high-voltage network, provides a wide range of benefits to the environment.

The globally connected corporation is strongly linked within itself and with the countries and communities in which it operates. This poses both management and moral issues. ABB does not claim to have all the answers to either side of the conundrum, but it believes that, on balance, it is verging to the right side. It certainly is not afraid to state its position.

Global transitions and change

One of the most important dynamics of the globally connected corporation is the shifting balance of influence between local and global management. In ABB's case, there has been a marked shift in influence away from its country managers to its business area managers. In the next chapter we look at the challenges of overcoming psychological obstacles to change as companies move through this kind of global transition.

References

Quotes without references originate from the authors' personal communications – see page xviii for details.

Agthe, Klaus E. (1990) 'Managing the mixed marriage', *Business Horizons*, January–February, 37–43.

Barnevik, Percy (1997) *Global Forces of Change: Remarks to the 1997 International Industrial Conference, 'Inventing the Future'*. San Francisco: 1997 International Industrial Conference, 'Inventing the Future', 29 September, 27–8.

Heimer, Claudia and Barham, Kevin (1997) *International Top Teams: Putting Them Together and Making Them Work*. Berkhamsted: unpublished discussion paper, Ashridge Centre for Management and Organization Learning, 1997.

Klebnikov, Paul (1991) 'The powerhouse', *Forbes*, 2 September, 46–50.

Peters, Tom (1992) *Liberation Management: Necessary Disorganization for the Nanosecond Nineties*. London: Pan Books.

Price, Colin (1997) 'Creating a federation of national cultures: reflections of Percy Barnevik',

Lessons from the CEO. Davos, Switzerland: World Economic Forum, Price Waterhouse, February, 1–11.

The Economist (1997) 'Worldbeater, Inc.', *The Economist,* 22 November, 132–3.

Taylor, William (1991) 'The logic of global business: an interview with ABB's Percy Barnevik', *Harvard Business Review,* March-April, 91–105.

von Koerber, Eberhard (1996) *Improved Performance: What Distinguishes the High Achievers?* Vienna: presentation to the European Petrochemicals Association, 1 October.

Managing global transitions

The challenge that proved most difficult and the one that affects all companies embarking on change was the emotional response of people. We had to change not only how people viewed their jobs, but how they viewed themselves.

Bonnie J. Keith
ABB Inc.

By pushing the boundaries of what was formerly thought possible, or even desirable, ABB has helped us to formulate a model for understanding the challenges that companies face as they evolve internationally. Some business academics have suggested that firms evolve through a number of different stages as they grow internationally. The commonly recurring stages that are described are:

- domestic – when the firm operates exclusively in its home country;
- international – when a company conducts business with other countries, generally through exports – that is, sales offices abroad;
- multinational – the company is present in many countries around the globe and adds production facilities to its sales and distribution activities;
- global or transnational – there are many definitions of these, but they generally refer to a stage in which there are connections between countries that make the company more than the sum of its parts.

Stage models of internationalization, which dominated much of the writing on international management up until the early 1990s, are certainly useful in discussing what has happened to some companies, yet perhaps less helpful when trying to predict how they will develop. Too many companies have evolved in an unusual way, seemingly jumping stages. The models also often focus managers' minds too much on the question 'Where are we?', as if these stages were static, fixed and well-defined, rather than 'What is changing, where do we need to go and what is stopping us from getting there?'

Another danger is that stage models give the impression that internationalization is an unavoidable, incremental path. Companies are known to have retracted back to a national or international orientation or to have been stuck in a multinational mode, never making it to the transnational company – a future made desirable for many by the example of ABB. For some of them, globalization would not have been the right strategy to go for. Of course, in some instances, companies retract to earlier states in their development, or get stuck in others, for the wrong reasons. They give up too early and make the wrong conclusions about what is possible.

There is one more problem with stage models. In effect, they mask the change processes and the emotional reactions that internationalization can unleash in organizations – reactions that can complicate or undermine the international strategy if they are not addressed. Just as at a macro level, globalization on the wider stage brings fears about loss of economic sovereignty and unemployment, inside organizations, similar anxieties about power and jobs are to be found. And if internationalization brings demands for new skills on the part of managers and employees, some individuals will fear that they are not equipped. 'Will *I* still be competitive?' is a natural reaction on the part of employees who see their organization moving in new directions.

In the 1990s, we saw a shift away from stage models to the frameworks proposed by gurus such as Bartlett and Ghoshal. Instead of stages, they invited us to look for *characteristics* of global companies, which is helpful in overcoming the problems that the normative progression stage models imply. While these ideas moved our thinking along, we were still far away from being able to understand what could help companies be successful in finding their own ways to internationalize.

In our work, we have many times seen managers and consultants struggle to come up with any other credible example than ABB for the often excessively glorified transnational company. Clearly a very disheartening experience when one's company is miles away from ABB's ability to focus and deliver, and miles away from having charismatic leaders such as Percy Barnevik and Göran Lindahl. It was out of this frustration that we began to think about the irrational nature of the processes that occur when, for example, an international German holding company decides to abandon its international operations because it is just too hard to shift the mindset of its managers away from the centre of the universe – which is an industrial town in northern Germany, of course.

We felt inspired by ideas about personal transitions that come from individual psychology and which have helped us work successfully with groups and companies undergoing change. Our understanding of the dynamics of organizational change has led to our observation that globalization (as is the case with any other organizational vision) is often achieved at great personal cost to the individuals involved, and that people will only be genuinely engaged if they buy into the need for change, find value in it for themselves and can agree on first steps. We do not believe that globalization can be achieved without a good understanding of how to mobilize people. We have noted, too, Stephen Rhinesmith's challenge that, in the field of international management, business strategists do not talk to psychologists, and vice versa. Hence, a collection of strengths – and their respective blind spots – accumulate on either side of the fence (Rhinesmith, 1996). We were therefore intrigued by the possibility of proposing some ideas that might help to integrate the strengths of both camps and, more importantly, be useful to companies trying to work through what globalization means for them, and what they can and cannot do. We have tried to combine an understanding of the strategic drivers for globalization with an appreciation of the human side of change.

We believe that when companies get stuck or retract on their own path to globalization, they are expressing specific ways of dealing with fundamental transitions that are inherent in the globalization process and lead to significant mindshifts in the managers running these companies. We therefore prefer to think about transitions rather than about the stages of internationalization *per se*. To understand the challenges that Barnevik and his team were trying to address, let's consider ABB in the context of the transitions that we see companies facing as they evolve internationally. These are (see Figure 6.1):

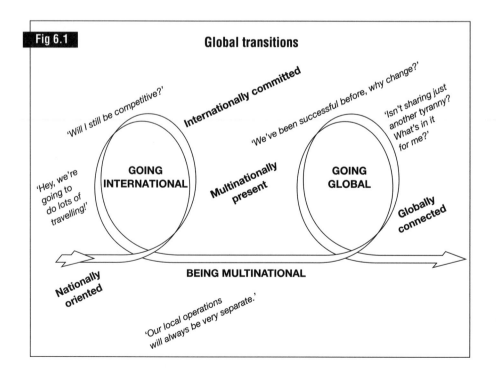

Fig 6.1 **Global transitions**

- going international
- being multinational
- going global.

Going international

In this transition, firms move from being *nationally oriented* and towards being *internationally committed*. Even where firms are internationally active, that activity can be very much an add-on in the minds of its managers. Becoming internationally committed means that managers no longer regard international activities as peripheral but as strategically vital. Both ASEA and BBC, because of their small home markets, became internationally committed at an early stage in their evolution. BBC's decision to go over to the production of steam turbines at the expense of losing its home market is a classic example of becoming internationally committed.

Many of ABB's client power companies in Europe are themselves today in this transition. Having been State-owned, protected industries, the advent of the European single market and deregulation, privatization and open capital markets mean that more and more utilities are looking for opportunities outside their own home markets. As one of the big regional German power companies said to us:

> The opening of the energy market will leave only the fittest national companies playing against the international giants. Even if we did not have significant international ambitions, we still need to understand the perspective of the international players. We need to be more active internationally and to learn how to act in open markets. How do we attack new markets and enter new countries?

For such large and well-established companies, going international brings the need to develop international pioneering skills. Internationalization also means culture change as its managers have to overcome their traditional outlook and adapt to new ways of doing things. As this company said, 'Our biggest challenge is to identify those people in the organization who need to be developed internationally in order to act as agents of change in introducing a market orientation.' For those managers selected or hired to implement the international strategy, the new international role will often be exciting and self-fulfilling, if demanding. But for those who are not selected or who fear resources will be diverted away from their own operations and projects, these can be threatening times. When BBC committed itself to international markets in the early 1900s, there must have been people in the organization who resented the new direction, perhaps feared for their livelihoods or predicted doom for the company. The challenge is not only to find the international pioneers, but to secure the support and buy-in of a wider range of people in the organization.

To complete a transition successfully, people have to let go of some aspect of their way of operating. Here, they often find it painful to let go of the assumption that their national perspective is valid internationally, but it is necessary to do so.

Being multinational

Between the two critical transitions of 'going international' and 'going global', companies experiment more boldly with their presence outside their home market. They move towards becoming *multinationally present*, having sales offices and eventually perhaps manufacturing operations abroad. This was essentially the state of exploration that ASEA and BBC were in during the first part of this century, even right up to the 1980s. The key challenge for firms here is how far control of their international operations should be centralized or decentralized. At one end of the spectrum, some firms are involved in arm's-length management of a scattered collection of subsidiaries. As we have seen, BBC tended towards this end of the spectrum in its dealings with its foreign subsidiaries. At the other end, some firms have tended to control their international operations quite tightly from the centre. ASEA may have tended more towards this end of the spectrum. In both cases, the essential common point is that what happens in one country has little impact on what happens elsewhere. The countries are treated quite separately and there is little need or attempt to encourage interaction between them. Even where the company has a worldwide presence, there is no global vision for the company. People in the countries have little incentive or reason to think about the organization as a global integrated entity.

In a slower-moving world, a multinationally present approach was appropriate for many firms, although it posed some difficult management issues, such as how to manage conflict between the centre and the subsidiaries. BBC had found this particularly difficult. The interaction of organizational and national culture means that cross-cultural skills and understanding are needed at the corporate centre, especially in firms at the more centralized end of the spectrum. Another challenge is to know when, and if, pressures for global integration are becoming as important as pressures for global responsiveness. It is part of Barnevik's genius that he recognized these pressures earlier than his competitors.

While the success of ABB helps us to conclude that ASEA and BBC really needed to change, this might not be right for other firms. We believe that any diagnosis aimed at resolving whether or not a company needs to globalize has to look at the following four dimensions.

- **Opportunity** – How are the markets developing, what opportunities are there to be spotted and seized?
- **Intent** – What strategic intent is there in the company for globalization, and what is the gap between what is espoused and what is actually pursued?
- **Readiness** – What is the organization's readiness to embrace globalization?
- **Capability** – Has the organization the skills, resources and culture of change to help it move through another critical transition successfully?

Going global

For many firms today, being multinationally present may be an increasingly untenable stance. Things are happening much faster now. Globalization is driven by, and is driving, new technologies that allow global action. Everything is more closely interrelated, everything is connected to everything else. Instantaneous communication means that, increasingly, things happen at the same time in different parts of the world rather than with a time lag from country to country. Barriers to trade between many countries are falling away, and capital and ideas flow more freely than before. The power-generation business in particular has seen international frontiers disappear.

Whereas, for many firms, being multinational was a slow transition, allowing the luxury of a slow learning process over years, going global in today's fast-paced international environment means that learning must be accelerated. Organizations do not have the time to go on reinventing the wheel all over the world. They must be able to take ideas and innovations from one part of the world and adapt and improve them for application elsewhere. As Jack Welch, CEO of ABB's competitor GE says, 'The aim in a global business is to get the best ideas from everywhere' (Welch, 1997). Managers must be ever faster in recognizing opportunities, destroying unnecessary bureaucracy and cooperating across organizational units.

For a firm that recognizes this imperative, it means a move towards becoming a *globally connected* corporation – one that is both centralized to reap economies of scale *and* decentralized for local responsiveness. The challenges are to maintain the local responsiveness of the multinationally present approach, while at the same time achieving swiftness, agility and cross-cultural ease across the organization. The aim is for the firm to deliver the highest-quality products and services from the lowest-cost base to the most favourable markets or countries with the most appropriate management and technical resources. And to do this without worrying about the location of resources and people. Unlike the multinationally present corporation, which has one head office and where the main source of innovation is often the corporate centre, the globally connected corporation may have many centres, each pursuing global strategies and innovation within the overall corporate framework.

This is a company that depends on developing a mindset among its managers that encourages them to take independent action, yet feel part of and responsible to a bigger whole from which they derive important competitive benefits, and to which they in turn must add value. Such a frame of mind fosters sharing and collaboration between its operations in different parts of the world and helps to develop continuous cross-border feedback for organizational learning. Such an organization must also encourage high energy and continuous change, but without leading to 'burnout' among its people. It is an organization that not only keeps its people around the world connected with each other, but also stays closely connected with its customers, suppliers and other stakeholders.

Connecting up the organization to achieve the advantages of scale and coordination is a major aim of a global strategy. However, as we noted above, it can also be a threat to the power base of some senior managers, especially the country 'barons' who are used to running their own independent fiefdoms. As the example of BBC shows, intellectual agreement between managers from different countries about the necessity for cross-border cooperation or integration does not necessarily lead to action. For some people, it may mean adapting to new ways of working and giving up seemingly well-tried approaches. The ability to move fully through personal transitions that initially involve emotional resistance before people are mobilized into action is critical here. A recent survey in 1997 of global companies concluded, 'Operating successfully on a global scale means rethinking every aspect of the company's activities. Sourcing, production, brand management, distribution, finance, governance, performance targets, excutive development – all must be recast' (Martin, 1997). As ABB clearly demonstrates, globalization, like other international transitions, is a process of culture change in an organization that will have a profound impact on many, if not most, of its people.

To give one example from ABB. In 1993, ABB Inc., ABB's US country management, initiated a strategy to 'shop the globe' for the manufacturing needs of its businesses. As Bonnie J. Keith, the company's Director of Supply Management, recounted, this presented many challenges, ranging from the complicated logistics of coordinating supply purchases among hundreds of businesses for thousands of technically complicated products to analyzing commodity markets and understanding foreign exchange movements (Keith, 1995). But, says Keith, 'the challenge that proved most difficult and the one that affects all companies embarking on change was the emotional response of people. We had to change not only how people viewed their jobs, but how they viewed themselves.'

ABB's purchasing managers were at first in denial about the need for change.

The company tried first to confront their resistance with compelling data. ABB's expenditure on supplies in the US amounted to 50 per cent of its cost of doing business, but the worldwide restructuring offered an unusual advantage in reducing those costs – precisely part of Percy Barnevik's strategy to become the lowest-cost supplier. With its presence in 140 countries (in 1993), half of them in soft currency markets, it could use its local contacts to buy more where the dollar was strong. Although the data was clear, however, it was not enough to persuade people: 'How were we going to reorient hundreds of purchasing managers, training them to be as comfortable purchasing components from Finland as from Fort Wayne? We had to craft a process to deal directly with their emotional reactions and basic responses to change.'

Early meetings about the new procedures during the 'rejection stage' met resistance, with participants asking 'What about buying American?' or 'We're making money, so why change?', and claiming that language barriers prevented quality products, time zones prohibited efficiency or that different countries had different rules. The purchasing managers were resisting two major changes in their jobs. First, they had to 'reconfigure' their jobs in the US and then, secondly, identify supply sources from around the world. Their greatest discomfort and 'sense of loss' was the realization that they had to learn their jobs from scratch again. The company therefore introduced the changes in stages, simultaneously providing training and a personal support network.

The network set up by ABB is an excellent example of the way in which personal connectivity can promote change processes. First, it created an information network for purchasers to communicate among themselves about supply management issues and the problems of adjusting to change. This not only reduced individual discomfort, but produced a new camaraderie – 'No one was in it alone.' The support helped some managers to move on to the acceptance stage. Positive results started to show as new contacts through the network enabled people, for example, to identify other ABB companies in the US using the same components and work together as a team with them to purchase from a single supplier instead of many different suppliers. Such success stories were widely communicated and helped to move to the next phase – the global market.

To address the many complexities of international purchasing, ABB aimed to develop a network of 2000 supply managers worldwide who could 'learn from each other, communicate successes, facilitate the use of suppliers in their local markets, and develop teams relevant to specific projects.' Within the network it developed a process to help managers purchase in soft currency countries, including procedures for supplier selection and quality assessment. ABB supply managers in every soft currency country were seen as providing 'eyes, ears and support to peers who are buying materials several time zones away.' Connectivity at work again.

ABB Inc.'s supply managers were now expected to have 'the expertise of a commodities broker and the experience of a foreign currency trader.' The network and internal education enabled buyers to analyze data from the commodities and currency markets, to bypass outmoded purchasing patterns and select other ABB companies in the global network or an ABB-recommended supplier in a soft currency country. One of the most important factors was the way in which success breeds success. As people in the network communicated about significant results, perceptions of what was attainable, both for themselves and for their companies, also altered. 'Without the learning process – people to people, peer to peer,' said ABB Inc.'s Supply Director, 'our strategy could not have been launched . . . It is clear that, even in an engineering company, it is people who drive and sustain fundamental change more than numbers ever will.'

When companies successfully go through the global transition and the accompanying fundamental change, an important dimension of maturity is the position of responsibility they now occupy as a global player. As a global presence brings benefits, it also brings responsibilities towards global stakeholders – customers, employees, communities in different countries, as well as the environment. Actions in one corner of the world lead to ripples in another. How will the company notice these effects and find a way to contribute constructively across the globe?

We believe that ABB has indeed set a world standard for organizing on a global scale. Yet, how can other companies move through these transitions? Commentators sometimes say that ABB is a young company. We do not totally accept this judgement. The company would not have been able to achieve as much as it did, had there not been all the accumulated experiences on either side of ASEA and BBC. Still today, some managers in ABB tell the story of the company with an almost seamless transition from ASEA to ABB, or BBC to ABB. When they talk to us about 'We started doing this 19 years ago . . .', they are clearly referring to a collective memory reaching far behind even the announcement of the merger. When the negotiation team from ASEA met the team from BBC, they came together as one in a very short space of time because they could both see that the merger would be a natural progression for both of them. The lucid and pragmatic stance taken by people on both sides speaks of insights and mindsets that had in them the seeds of globalization. People who treated the negotiation as adversarial did not make it in the end. ABB merged with its feet running, and this was not only due to Percy Barnevik's sense of urgency and his charismatic and directive leadership. The company made the transition well because it had been prepared for that for many years.

Other companies wishing to make progress towards globalization will need to acknowledge the transitions they face, and understand the limits and possibilities of what they are doing. What are the critical elements of each transition, and how can companies help themselves to move on?

Engaging organizations via global transitions

The development of companies by means of global transitions depends on the power constellations and emotions involved (Heimer and Vince, 1998). Some important questions arise. Who has something to lose? Who stands to gain from the change? How much is the change a departure from the previous status quo? Is moving through a transition really progress for the organization? How do key players deal with the anxiety that the transition creates? Do they accept the uncertainty and risk associated with it, and are they willing to struggle for clarity until they achieve insight? Or do they, indeed, deny or avoid the change?

Each of the transitions follows the dynamics of any change process, where people move from a state of contentment, and possibly even complacency, through to anger and denial, until they begin to struggle and engage with the change and finally reach a state of mobilization and insight. Companies and groups of companies move through these change cycles at different speeds.

As the battle for competitiveness in an increasingly global landscape intensified during the 1990s, we observed companies struggling through these transitions, and sometimes reverting back to their earlier state after some painful experiments. These experiments were often not reflected on, leading to 'superstitious learning' that reinforces their original world view because they do not explore the various factors that impinge on a situation, and they draw conclusions without being challenged (Levitt and March, 1988). Leaders judge their timing right or they may be advocates of an overly challenging vision for their company. Of course, one can never predict accurately. And yet we have learned that there are several things that international leaders can do to help their organizations engage positively with the transitions and move through them.

How do you know where your company is in relation to the transitions? We have looked at how you can recognize where a company is, and what you might do to help mobilize people to make progress or else conclude that a transition is not for you. We don't see this model as a norm that everyone needs to follow. What is important for the international development of a company is to be rigorous about what it can and cannot do, and be clear about where the organization really is or can go.

Going international

Do you recognize any of the following?

- 'People in Indiana are not going to like this!' Around 80 per cent of your people are nationally based, and the centre of gravity is your home country.
- The CEO's vision of internationalization is not really shared by others. They don't see the benefits.
- 'It is really hard to find the right people to do this international job.' They are either too inexperienced, or their families don't want to move countries!
- 'Let's get this very international guy in to do the job.' That way, nothing needs to change for you.
- 'Let's just try out a couple of things and see how this might work for us.' Random behaviour, no focus, or no clarity about what your working hypotheses really are.
- 'We don't really know what international means.' But your competitors seem to.
- 'We didn't realize it was going to take that much to build up an operation in Singapore.' You underestimated resources and timescales.

This transition touches on a variety of emotions. They can range from fear of the unknown ('What happens if we fall off the earth if we keep sailing west?') to people's excitement about the discovery of new horizons. They realize that they will never look at the world in quite the same way after they decide to go. Some managers only realize what profound changes are needed after they have set off.

If, as a leader of the organization, you believe that internationalization is the way forward, what might you do to engage your organization and help it progress through the transition?

How to engage your organization in 'going international'

- **Organize mind openers.** Take people to different places and let them experience a different country with its smells, tastes and people.
- **Go out there.** Take as many people from different hierarchical levels with you as you can. Meet local expatriates.
- **Hire people with international experience.** But think about how you will integrate them.
- **Protect your international pioneers.** If there is no critical mass, people are likely to reject what they have to say about the organization.
- **Go on benchmarking visits to other countries.**
- **Systematically debrief people.** Share their experiences when they go abroad, to avoid superstitious learning.
- **Find a way for people to see the benefits and discover what is involved for themselves.** Telling doesn't work.

- Send people on international projects.
- Give key people responsibility for important international accounts.
- Take trade union representatives with you on a trip abroad.

The emphasis of these interventions is on stimulating the contact with the outside, so that people inside the organization can experience the international possibilities for themselves. Bringing international people into the organization at this stage can lead to rejection or token foreigner behaviour rather than real learning.

Being multinational

During this state of exploration, different 'voices' can be heard, such as the following.

- **'I get really bored at the Board meetings, because what the others are up to has nothing to do with my country.'** Countries are run separately, there is no attempt to achieve business partnerships, there is no transfer of learning between countries.
- **There is no vision at the top of what the company could be.** It is just the sum of the parts – the different countries.
- **'What can I really do to add value here?'** Functional managers at the centre are nervous about their role.
- **Shareholders fear expansion of the company.**

This transition touches primarily on issues of power and contentment within the status quo. This is when there is much talk about potential 'synergies' and many people are quietly hiding in a large organization that doesn't really ask them to cooperate across borders. How, then, can we help move people on or be clear about whether or not they really want to move on to a different way of working internationally?

How to engage your organization in 'being multinational'
- Hold your meetings in different countries.
- Let local people run the local companies.
- Bring large numbers of international people into the head office.
- Make international experience a requirement for promotion.
- Consciously develop a breed of international managers.
- Make international assignments attractive.
- Make sure the country managers have something to gain from co-operating with other countries.
- Create greater cooperation and coherence by starting up regional head offices.

- **Bring people across the globe together to think about the strategy of the organization.**
- **Create functional best practice forums to engage people around the world in thinking about how to improve what they do.** Appreciate the way different cultures work. Then they will understand what benefits cooperation can bring.
- **Set up international teams** – they provide learning that helps stretch the organization into becoming global.

The outward-facing interventions of the first transition are still valuable here but, in addition, the idea is to create a greater dialogue between people inside the different parts of the organization.

Going global

As ABB has shown, speed is critical for this transition. How do you recognize whether or not it might be imminent?

- There is a strong push from your customers who require you to be present all around the globe.
- Your attempts to produce growth have reached a ceiling.
- Developments in certain regions of the globe are occurring, but there is no technical know-how available there.
- You worry that your Executive Board is composed of members from one single nationality (and the occasional token foreigner).
- You lack competences and resources to help open up markets and network across the globe.

During this transition, power is, again, a major issue that needs to be dealt with. Going global means challenging or even destroying power hubs and networks. People need to see the benefits for them. For the visionaries, the advantages of the globally connected corporation are obvious, but how do you move things forward?

How to engage your organization in 'going global'

- **Develop a vision of what the organization could be.** Communicate it, even by using the media.
- **Provide clear measures of performance globally.** Make people's performance transparent.
- **Break down country fiefdoms.** Create operational and knowledge-sharing networks across the globe.
- **Run global management development programmes.** These will ensure a rich pool of international talent.

- **Create a 'cultural whirlpool' for key people who need to be international.** Create geographically dispersed international teams that meet in different locations every time – this avoids their falling back into their national complacency.
- **Provide a global IT infrastructure for communication.**
- **Allow as much freedom to experiment as possible.** Global cooperation requires spontaneous opportunities for people to come together and ignite around ideas.
- **Make people responsible and accountable for global cooperation.**
- **Change the roles of the country managers.** Alternatively, link them up with people who look at the whole globe.

In the first transition of going international, leaders need to listen and let people experience things themselves before they can engage them. During the state of exploration of being multinational they need to talk – to help people understand the possibilities that lie ahead. People need to play with their ideas and possibilities. During the second transition of going global, leaders need to actively create and shape their organizations. The challenge, of course, is to maintain the sort of pace that ABB has now created as a global benchmark.

Going international	=>	Listen
Being multinational	=>	Talk
Going global	=>	Create

What does renewal and change mean for a global company such as ABB? Given that the company has accelerated the pace of globalization, what is its responsibility for what is now happening worldwide? How, for instance, will it look after the new losers? What is it doing to prepare for the 'global teenagers' from the developing world who will emerge as employees, customers and shareholders in the future?

The ideas put forward in this chapter are tentative and have only started to emerge in the process of researching and writing this book about ABB. We would be delighted if you would be interested in joining us in an enquiry to research these transitions more fully.

References

Quotes without references originate from the authors' personal communications – see page xviii for details.

Heimer, Claudia and Vince, Russ (1998) 'Sustainable learning and change in international teams: from imperceptible behaviour to rigorous practice', *Leadership and Organization Development Journal*, 19 February, 83–8.

Keith, Bonnie J. (1995) 'A system to support change', *The Wall Street Journal Europe*, 24 July.

Levitt, B., and March, J. G., (1988) 'Organizational learning', *Annual Review of Sociology*, **14**, 319–40.

Martin, Peter (1997) 'A future depending on choice', *Financial Times*, 7 November, 16.

Rhinesmith, Stephen H. (1996) *A Manager's Guide to Globalization: Six Skills for Success in a Changing World*. Chicago: Irwin Professional Publishing.

Welch, Jack (1997) 'Transfer of the best ideas from everyone, everywhere', *Financial Times*, 1 October, 16.

CHAPTER

7

....

Making sense of things with the management gurus

While ABB may not be a model *that every other company can adopt, it is an* example *of what most companies can achieve.*
Sumantra Ghoshal and **Christopher Bartlett**

Having created the biggest ever cross-border merger, announced a radical and innovative organizational reshaping and embarked on a massive programme of global growth, it was inevitable that ABB would attract the attention of the management gurus. Here we present the way in which four different gurus, or sets of gurus, view ABB. Two of the views come from what is an essentially North American perspective, two come from Europe. We offer these different perspectives as lenses that each highlight different aspects of the organization, with the hope that this will illuminate as much as possible about ABB.

ABB as the 'buckyball organization': Tom Peters on ABB
....

We start with Tom Peters, the American consultant, writer and co-author (with Bob Waterman) of *In Search of Excellence* (1982), one of the best-selling business books of all time. The book attacked what Peters and Waterman saw as the excesses of the 'rational model' and the 'business strategy paradigm' that had come to dominate Western management thinking. They advocated instead a return to 'first principles' – 'attention to customers ("close to the customer"), an abiding concern for people ("productivity through people") and the celebration of trial and error ("a bias for action").' *In Search of Excellence* was, in part, a reaction to the vogue for applauding Japanese management practices and the focus was entirely on (mostly large) US firms. However, five years after the book appeared, in his next blockbuster, *Thriving on Chaos* (1987), Peters was forced to declare that there were no excellent companies.

'Time, and quite a short time at that', he says, 'had not treated some of *In Search of Excellence*'s almost perfect instruments very well'. The era of sustainable excellence was over. The word 'excellence' needed to be redefined – excellent firms don't believe in excellence, he suggested, only in constant improvement and constant change. The excellent firms of the future would cherish impermanence and thrive on chaos.

ABB, of course, did not exist when Peters and Waterman were writing *In Search of Excellence*, and Barnevik's revolution at ASEA did not come within the remit of a book that was essentially about leading US firms – if, indeed, the excellence gurus were even aware of ASEA. Some of the general lessons about closeness to customers, productivity through people and bias for action did, however, fit very well with what we know of Percy Barnevik's aspirations for ASEA, and later for ABB. By the time of his second book, not only was Peters starting to rethink the definition of excellence, he was also looking further afield for his exemplars. One of the striking differences between the first book and *Thriving on Chaos* – evidence perhaps of how fast the world was starting to globalize – was the attention that Peters gave, just a few years later, to the international dimension of business. The global village had arrived, he said, you have to be an internationalist. Whether Americans like it or not, they are all participants in a single global market.

When *Thriving on Chaos* was published in 1987, the ABB merger was only just about to take place. By the time that Peters' next book *Liberation Management* first appeared, in 1992, ABB was well on the scene. Peters hoped that this new book would go much further than his previous books in extolling a management revolution. And the first example that he chose to give of the new revolution in his preface was ABB. Here Peters called Percy Barnevik a 'pathfinder' who was leading the way to 'liberation management' – a 'departure from the obvious comfort zone, not playing it safe, and reaching creatively'. What does Peters mean in practice by liberation management and how does ABB fit the profile?

Peters' first concern is organizational structure – it takes up over 50 per cent of the book. This is another big change from *In Search of Excellence* where customers came first and structural issues, which took up only 2 per cent, came second. Peters reaffirms the importance of the close-to-the-customer message, but says that it won't work unless you have demolished – as Barnevik did – the corporate superstructure that impedes close-to-the-customer culture change. His book, he says, is animated by a single word: fashion. This is, more than ever, fickle and ephemeral. Product lifecycles have shrunk from years to months. Customers have 'ever-shifting, ever narrower gauge needs.' All of which means that companies must engage much more closely with customers to the point of symbiosis. Fashion, says Peters, demands liberation, with 'everyone exhibiting flair and bravura, pursuing breathtaking failure as assiduously as success.' To be able to offer customized solutions to fleeting customer problems calls forth the 'pirate and gambler in us all' and cries out for the 'wholesale exercise of the human imagination' – 'as the service sector grows and the service component of manufacturing comes to dominate, everyone of us is in the "brainware business".'

In the introductory section of the book, entitled 'Necessary Disorganization', Peters describes how Percy Barnevik had begun 'to concoct what may be the most novel industrial firm structure since Alfred Sloan built "modern" GM in the 1920s'. No other manufacturing firm, he says, has been as bold as ABB in owning up to tomorrow's challenges. He cites the 95 per cent reduction of corporate staff overnight that happened as a prime example. Getting rid of central staff is an essential element of decentralization. You can't 'manage' at all from the centre in a fickle economy. Instead, to deal with a 'fashionized' environment, you have to unleash the power of subordinate units with distinct personalities of their own. Small-scale, independent units, such as the 5000 'feisty' profit centres into which ABB 'de-organized' itself, play the lead role in responding to a fickle marketplace. (Peters also pointed to the way in which the profit centres were beginning to reorganize into ten-person, multifunction high-performance teams, although this process had only started relatively recently.)

According to Peters, ABB is a 'buckyball organization' or a 'buckyborg'. What does he mean by this? Here, he likens ABB to the 'Buckminster fullerene' (the 'buckyball' molecule named for the American inventor and engineer), the atoms of which fit together so well that they make it seem like one giant 'superatom' and make it so resilient, it retains its integrity under a variety of conditions. ABB's profit centres are the atoms that make up ABB's buckyball and keep it resilient. They do that because those atoms consist of on average 50 people, which, Peters believes, is the magic number for making organizations most productive.

Barnevik is the most insistent enemy of bureaucracy that Peters says he has ever met, pointing to the fact that the 'gargantuan operation' has just three layers of management, with only two layers of management between the 'big chiefs' and the high-performance team members on the shop floor. Peters notes that, as often as not, ABB is the biggest competitor in a particular business segment, although that results from a combination of relatively small operations. To heighten the sense of ownership, each of the profit centres has its own profit and loss statement and balance sheet, and it owns assets. Most importantly, it serves external customers directly. Direct attachment to customers transforms the little unit into a real business. Noting Barnevik's description that the profit centres are run collectively by 5000 profit-responsible individuals with teams of 3 or 4, 'suddenly', Peters says, 'vast ABB seems a lot more "manageable".' On the other side of the matrix, Peters finds the role of the BA managers in holding ABB together particularly important. He describes the BA leaders and their staff as 'roving itinerant preachers – cajoling, comparing unit and competitor results, arranging job shifts for key people so as to transfer – and leverage – knowledge gained from here to there.' Indeed, for us, it is the BA concept that makes ABB seem more manageable.

Peters admits that he has always 'railed against' matrix organizations for their propensity to become 'hopelessly complex bureaucracies' that 'gut the emotional energy and "ownership" of those closest to the marketplace'. However, ABB's approach, he says, passes his 'high-energy/accountability test'. ABB's BA idea differs dramatically from the traditional matrix because:

- BA teams are purposely kept very small;
- local profit centre managers are accountable for meeting goals that are agreed – they 'are not beholden to numerous managers as in the traditional matrix';
- ABB wants to be an insider – BA staff, according to Peters, 'do not promiscuously move production workers around in pursuit of short-term advantage – in sharp contrast to the silly shenanigans of many 1970s-style headquarters-based matrix managers;'
- BA chiefs live by persuasion and being helpful – they are on the road away from the political centre all the time.

Another advantage of the BA concept, as seen by Peters, is that they 'live where it makes sense and move when it makes sense'. In the traditional matrix, BA equivalents are typically based at corporate headquarters and win debates by being close to top executives. Peters noted approvingly that there were no BA heads or teams based in Zürich. This, however, was to be one significant feature of the BA concept that ABB would modify in 1993. We'll come back to this in Chapter 10.

Peters also explains the seeming contradiction between ABB's drive for decentralization and its search for 'old-fashioned' scale economies. This was explained, he said, by the atomized structure of European industry. ABB's acquisition drive frequently gave it ten or more plants in one industry, each making the same low-volume, highly specialized component, and each generating low revenues. Instead of ten plants doing the same thing, ABB would aim to cut the number to two or three. Each plant would produce far fewer products than before rather than try to produce the whole range. On the other hand, Peters recognized that while ABB rationalized, it also encouraged 'superheated' internal competition by, for example, making performance information widely available via ABACUS. Peters also describes how, when ABB closed the 200-person power semiconductor plant in Sweden to concentrate production at its 150-person plant in Switzerland, it left the Swedish power semiconductor design group intact. This had some special skills and ABB did not want to lose its energy or independence. Keeping the two design groups encouraged vital 'brain competition', according to Barnevik.

Peters agrees that one of ABB's most important features is the potential of its global matrix for leveraging knowledge. ABB will rise or fall on its ability to turn its small units in any BA into a learning network. Liberation management depends on learning processes. In ABB's case, these derive, on the one hand, from the structure of profit centres, which forces high customer contact. On the other hand, the BA structure promotes learning and knowledge transfer. Most BA teams, says Peters, *are* pursuing economies of scale but these are mostly learning scale, not production scale. Peters says it is not the 'hard' advantages, such as being able to make efficient purchases, that are ABB's real power, but what he calls the 'soft stuff' that comes from effective global coordination. He cites Sune Karlsson, then leader of the power transformers BA, who wanted his local companies to think small, worry about their home market and a small number of export markets and learn to make money on smaller volumes. The challenge was to convince local managers that they could run small operations more efficiently, meet customer needs more flexibly and be profitable.

To be competitive, Karlsson, according to Peters, emphasized slashing delivery time, maximizing design and production flexibility, and focusing on domestic customers – rather than attempting to achieve volume efficiencies. Karlsson said that his operation's most important strength was that it had 25 factories around the world, each with its own president, design manager, marketing manager and production manager. These people were, said Karlsson, continuously working on the same problems and opportunities and learning a tremendous amount. Karlsson talked of creating a process of continuous expertise transfer as a source of advantage that none of ABB's rivals could match. To do this, competition must be constructive – the key task is creating 'a culture of trust and exchange.' While the formal gatherings are important, most progress derives from creating information exchange throughout the year. 'The system works when the quality manager in Sweden feels compelled to telephone or fax the quality manager in Brazil with a problem or an idea . . . Sharing of expertise does not happen automatically. People need to spend time together, to get to know and understand each other . . . People must also see a payoff for themselves. I never expect our operations to coordinate unless all sides get real benefits. We have to demonstrate that sharing pays – that contributing one idea gets you 24 in return.'

Peters saw ABB's T50 programme (described in Chapter 4) for cutting cycle times as 'the most dramatic learning spearhead of all' in the company. As he says, raw speed is only part of the issue. It begs the question 'Speed for what?' Fashion, says Peters, means getting new ideas out of the door faster, but it also means producing more clever products and 'intertwining with customers in ever more intimate ways.' Going much faster, and getting rid of functional and other organizational barriers are 'as much efforts to get dramatically closer to customers as they are to churn out orders or new products at a frantic pace.'

In *The Pursuit of Wow!* (1995), a follow-up to *Liberation Management*, Peters analyzes Percy Barnevik's style as a 'turnaround champ.' Many corporate leaders, he says, have faced 'monstrous change agendas in the past ten years, but only a few have made a genuine about-face'. Barnevik, along with Jack Welch of General Electric, is one of the few to do so. What do they have in common?

- **They are 'frighteningly smart'.** Most CEOs are very bright, but they are in a league of their own.
- **They have 'animal energy'.** 'It's exhausting just to watch these guys.'
- **They are 'irrational about action'.** They can't countenance, let alone understand, procrastination.
- **They use 'distilled vision'.** They've boiled down the message to a few critical principles that they ceaselessly communicate to front-line employees, senior executives, securities analysts – 'and, doubtless, their local fresh-veggie vendor'.
- **They 'cut to the chase'.** They realized they had one brief opportunity to stage a real revolution; they 'compressed years of work into months'.
- **They have a 'disgust for bureaucracy'.** They are 'genetically averse to all forms of bureaucracy'.
- **They are 'performance freaks'.** 'Lead, follow, or get the hell out of the way.'
- **They are 'straight shooters'.** Bad news or good news, they tell it to you straight.
- **They believe 'tomorrow is another day'.** They think and decide fast, and don't rehash yesterday's work; they can leave mistakes behind.
- **They are convinced that 'half a loaf is no loaf at all'.** They do not believe in half measures; 'it ain't done till it's done'.
- **They are 'driven individuals'.** They believe the impossible is possible and are determined to prove it, 'and then reprove it, day after day.'

If this is a true picture of Barnevik – and there are certainly some very strong echoes of what we know about his intense style in this profile (compare it with Manfred Kets de Vries' profile of Barnevik later in this chapter) – it is a pretty tall order for any successor to live up to. On the other hand, does ABB, as it approaches the millennium, need a different style of leadership now? We look at this issue later in the book.

ABB as the 'individualized corporation':
Sumantra Ghoshal and Christopher Bartlett on ABB

In 1989, just as ABB was getting under way, Sumantra Ghoshal and Christopher Bartlett, professors, respectively, at the London Business School and Harvard Business School, brought out their highly influential book *Managing Across Borders*. This has become a classic of the international management literature and analyzes the challenges facing companies operating in the new world business environment. They described how, in the postwar era, companies had traditionally pursued one of three overseas strategies:

- global strategies – typical of Japanese companies, exploiting global-scale efficiency;
- multinational strategies depending on local differentiation – as pursued by many Western firms;
- less commonly, international strategies – built on the ability to transfer and adapt innovative product and process technologies to international markets, of which Ericsson, the Swedish telecommunications firm – a sister company to ABB in the Wallenberg sphere – was a rare example.

Bartlett and Ghoshal showed how the nature of international competition was changing and that no single strategy was by itself sufficient any more. The new highly competitive, fast-moving global business environment required companies to simultaneously capture global-scale efficiency, be highly responsive to local needs, and develop a worldwide learning capability that promotes continuous innovation.

Very few firms have lived up to the challenge of managing the paradoxes inherent in what Bartlett and Ghoshal call the *transnational* organization. ABB was not one of the transnational firms that they described, although in many ways it has come the closest to the model. Now, they have taken their analysis further to explore the collapse of an outmoded corporate form, the divisionalized corporate bureaucracy, to reveal the emergence of what they believe is a fundamentally different management philosophy that focuses on the power of the individual as the driver of power in the company and on the importance of individuality in management. ABB, they find, is a major example of that new philosophy.

Some of Ghoshal and Bartlett's ideas, in many ways, bear strong resemblances to those of Tom Peters, although, as befits leading business scholars, they present their ideas in a less proselytizing and more academic manner. Like Tom Peters, they describe leaders such as Barnevik as today's Alfred Sloan, leaders who realize they are leading their companies through a unique period of history when environmental forces demand major organizational change. They echo Peters' notion of the 'brain-based company' when they too argue that, in today's dynamic global environment where competition is increasingly service-based and knowledge-intensive, corporate leaders must recognize that human creativity and individual initiative are far more important as sources of competitive advantage than homogeneity and conformity. The image of the 'organization man' as a cog in a corporate machine has become not only dated but dangerous. Rather than forcing employees into a corporate mould defined by policies, systems and constraints, they see the task as being exactly the opposite. For them, the challenge is to build an organization flexible enough to exploit the 'idiosyncratic knowledge and unique skills of each individual employee.' In their latest book, Ghoshal and Bartlett call this organization model 'the individualized corporation' (Ghoshal and Bartlett, 1998).

The three core capabilities of the individualized corporation are its ability to inspire individual creativity and initiative in all its people (such as ABB's policy of decentralization), link and leverage pockets of entrepreneurial activity and individual expertise by building an integrated process of organizational learning (such as ABB achieves by means of its BAs), and continuously renew itself. Where Bartlett and Ghoshal differ from Peters' formulation is that, whereas Peters refocused on structural change as the basis for a customer-based strategy, Ghoshal and Bartlett suggest that the new organizational philosophy must de-emphasize strategy, structure and system, and that managers must embrace a philosophy based on purpose, process and people. The new model sees organization as a 'portfolio of processes' rather than a 'hierarchy of tasks', and demands new roles, attitudes, knowledge and skills for front-line, middle and top managers. ABB in particular exemplifies this new view of building organizational capability.

An organization man is reborn

Ghoshal and Bartlett say that they became intrigued by ABB when they learned how the transformational changes that occurred during the restructuring of ABB's US acquisitions affected the activities, motivation and performance of one manager, Don Jans, general manager of ABB's US relays business. The latter, they say, had previously spent most of his 32–year career as 'a classic Organization Man' in Westinghouse. When ABB bought the Westinghouse business in 1989, Jans and his colleagues expected the 'occupying troops' of ABB to move in and evict them. Instead, to their surprise, they were asked to stay on.

Staying on involved more than just a move from one employer to another – it meant managing in a totally new type of environment. For example, at

Westinghouse, Jans had five levels of management between himself and the CEO. At ABB, there were only two. At Westinghouse, decisions were top-down and shaped by political negotiations, but at ABB front-line managers such as Jans were expected to take more initiatives, and decisions were more objective and made on the basis of analyzed data. From being an implementer of others' decisions in a huge corporate machine, Jans now had to be an 'entrepreneurial initiator' with full responsibility and accountability for developing his own company as a viable, enduring business. He was supported by a seven-person steering committee or 'sounding board', the members of which came from ABB's relays BA, the US power transmission and distribution headquarters, and colleagues running other related ABB companies. He was also expected to contribute outside his own company by sitting on the steering committees of ABB relays companies in other countries.

As a further inspiration, Jans and his American colleagues were highly impressed by the way in which Percy Barnevik and Göran Lindahl (then head of ABB's power transmission segment and now Barnevik's successor as CEO) 'walked the talk', treating them as colleagues rather than acting as superiors, continuing to be engaged in challenging and supporting them, clearly articulating their vision of the future of the power industry and conveying a strong sense of the company's core values. That included emphasis on the importance of individual initiative and constant urging of people 'to question assumptions, propose solutions, and take action.' For the first time in his career, say Ghoshal and Bartlett, Jans was fully involved in decisions that shaped the world in which he operated and felt that the wider goals to which he was contributing were linked to a set of values that were personally meaningful for him. They also cite Jans' boss, another Westinghouse veteran, as saying that it was the ABB culture of delegated responsibility and intensive communication that made the organization work – 'it was an amazing change. I felt like I had rediscovered management after 39 years.'

ABB as a 'portfolio of processes'

In a conventional hierarchical company, power and authority reside at the top according to Ghoshal and Bartlett. Corporate-level executives drive the company by virtue of their control over strategy. While this is true in part in ABB, it is not the complete truth about the way that its top management views its task. Top management is deeply involved in setting the company's 'strategic commitments', such as betting on the growth of emerging markets such as India and China, but the analysis and decision making involved in this is far less demanding than the huge time commitment that top managers make in promoting the broad corporate purpose and a set of values to guide behaviour.

Within the broad strategic vision, the actions of middle management are far from control-dominated. The steering committee of each front-line company that brings to bear perspectives and experience from other parts of the group turns the budgeting and strategic planning processes into constructive dialogues rather than imposed objectives. With the small numbers of staff, ABB managers are forced to create horizontal linkages to supplement traditional vertical linkages. These include supervisory forums, such as the BA Boards and the company steering committees.

The formal structure is 'given life' by the ABACUS information system and a management style that makes the 'process "X-ray" of ABB more like a CAT scan in which the internal functions can be seen in dynamic interaction.' Top-level management aims to offset top-down processes with bottom-up initiatives. Göran Lindahl describes the management style as 'fingers in the pie'. The information provided by ABACUS means that top-level managers can reach down to the front line if they sense a problem. The objective is to help rather than to interfere. Lindahl's three questions are 'What's the problem? What are you doing to fix it? How can we help you?'

ABB's approach, according to Ghoshal and Bartlett, transforms the hierarchical landscape of the traditional organization as the top-down bias of the hierarchy has been overlaid with a strong bottom-up drive and initiative. The vertical, financially dominated communications have been supplemented with horizontal knowledge-intensive interactions. Static tasks and responsibilities have been replaced by more flexible roles and relationships. However, say Ghoshal and Bartlett, we cannot understand these firms in terms of formal structures – we have to see them as a 'portfolio of processes'. At the heart of ABB are three processes.

- **The 'entrepreneurial process'** This supports the 'opportunity-seeking, externally-focused entrepreneurship of front-line managers'. It is based on front-line, middle managers and top managers playing very different roles than they used to. The front-line managers in the companies and profit centres are no longer just the implementers of top-down decisions, but are the main initiators of entrepreneurial activity, creating and seeking new opportunities for the firm. Middle managers – in ABB's case, its BA managers – are no longer preoccupied with their traditional control role, but become a resource to the front line, coaching and supporting. Top management, having radically decentralized resources and delegated responsibilities, concerns itself with pushing the entrepreneurial process by setting broad objectives and stretched performance standards that the front-line initiatives must attain. The entrepreneurial process depends on 'an abiding faith in people that allows for true empowerment.'
- **The 'integration process'** This 'overlays the advantages of bigness – of size, scale, and diversity – on the advantages of smallness – flexibility,

responsiveness, creativity – by linking the dispersed resources, competences and businesses of the company.' Here, the middle managers, the BA leaders, play the main role, although integration requires intensive involvement and support at all levels of the organization. It depends in particular on fostering collaboration – ABB's expectation that people must act with 'mutual confidence, respect and trust . . . and remain flexible, open and generous.' This in turn depends on top management appointing people who reflect such behaviours to key positions and modelling that behaviour themselves.

- **The 'renewal process'** This 'creates and sustains [the organizations] capacity to continuously challenge its own beliefs and practices, thereby revitalizing the strategies that drive the businesses'. The objective is to provide a mechanism – lacking in the traditional divisionalized structure – for challenging the company's strategies and the assumptions behind them. Top management must serve as the source of organizational disequilibrium by focusing the firm on a very stretched, future-oriented corporate mission that is communicated with conviction and intensity. It must also directly drive the change process, as when Barnevik 'jump-started massive change' by acquiring Combustion Engineering and Westinghouse's power businesses. It is front-line managers who have to manage the tension caused by the gap between current performance and future aspirations set by the stretch vision. This 'tension-filled' process demands a high level of credibility and trust. It is the role of the middle managers, the BA leaders, to ensure credibility and trust by creating a participative and transparent decision-making context in which strategy is defined by peers rather than imposed by top management.

Ghoshal and Bartlett emphasize that ABB is not 'an organization of front-line cowboys held together by senior management acting as a venture fund team. Instead, it has redefined roles and relationships at all levels of management, to drive the company's ability to constantly seek and exploit new opportunities. It is this companywide process that brings the large-company benefits to the front-line managers and distinguishes the Individualized Corporation from those companies that have tried to achieve the same results through faddish quick fixes like internal venturing and "intrapreneurship" programs' (Ghoshal and Bartlett, 1998).

As if this all sounds too good to be true, Ghoshal and Bartlett are quick to point out early on in their book that ABB is not a 'perfect company'. While it may not be a *model* for every other company, they say, it is an *example* of what most companies can achieve. As they indicate, however, one of the biggest challenges set by this new way of looking at organizations is the need to tear up old job descriptions and develop the new competences required for the new management roles and tasks. We will look at some of the ways in which ABB is developing its people and their competences in Chapter 11.

A parent that adds value: Goold, Campbell and Alexander on ABB

Writing in a refreshingly hype-free style, Michael Goold, Andrew Campbell and Marcus Alexander, authors of *Corporate-Level Strategy* (1994), analyze whether or not and how ABB might, as a parent, provide value to the organization at large. Goold, Campbell and Alexander are directors of the London-based Ashridge Strategic Management Centre, a centre dedicated to research and consulting with multibusiness companies. Goold and Campbell (Alexander joined them later) first came to prominence with their book *Strategies and Styles* (1987), in which they investigated the role of the corporate centre in 16 UK-headquartered leading multinational companies.

Parenting advantage for Goold, *et al.*, means that the corporate centre should aim to be the best possible parent for its businesses. Under its stewardship, they should perform not only better than they would as stand-alone entities, but also better than with any other parent. The central concept developed in their assessment of the company's parenting advantage is that of 'linkage influence', which is how the corporate parent encourages or requires its units to cooperate in order to gain more value for the whole. The underlying assumption here is that the parent helps to create opportunities that would otherwise be avoided or overlooked by the individual units.

It is easy to interest people in ABB because of its sharing of information, people and resources across boundaries. Goold, et al., remind us that there is no intrinsic value to sharing. What at first sight looks like a valuable corporate doctrine could potentially lead to either value creation or value destruction. In the case of ABB, it works. Considering primarily issues of organizational structure, the three authors put the way most analysts have looked at ABB's matrix organization on its head and make a helpful contribution to our understanding of the organization's success.

Mastering the breakdown of fiefdoms

Very few of ABB's operational units would survive if they were on their own. In an interesting reframing of the usual analysis of ABB's matrix organization, the authors suggest that while the outcome of its restructuring has been a flexible matrix that provides linkages between separate units, this might not have been its most significant achievement. The authors argue that ABB used its matrix concept to break down existing power bastions and hierarchies that developed in different countries over time by the atomization of the business into thousands of profit centres. What they term 'decentralization with a safety net' is a framework that provides a 'mechanism allowing the orderly separation and reformation of what was formerly grouped together'. In their eyes, 'the matrix has provided a framework to stop "atomization" becoming destructive and totally chaotic'. While this applied to existing businesses, the matrix structure made it equally possible for ABB to make acquisitions of complicated companies and integrate them rapidly by breaking them down within the overall framework, rather than by building them into something even bigger.

Goold, *et al.*, describe an organizational concept that relies on the interdependence of companies that are not viable as stand-alone ones. While they have full profit and loss responsibilities, these companies are linked together via:

- the BAs, focusing on groups of products and services offered worldwide;
- regional companies providing an integrated local presence across different BAs.

For the authors, atomization, global integration and regional identity create an ambiguity and complexity that, for many other companies, could be cumbersome. It works for ABB because it provides flexibility in a business with real pressure to globalize and where, at the same time, there is value in having a strong national presence. On the whole, the parent adds value and yet it has done so by exposing the company to enormous risk.

On the one hand, the matrix might have been liberating as an orderly way of breaking down hierarchy and creating a sense of more individual ownership, yet it also made each unit more fragile and dependent. The authors would argue that, as a way of linking together independent units, the ABB matrix is overly complicated. The gamble was on whether or not the linkages would work in holding the company together and, at the same time, provide greater value than before. If the environment the company operated in had been different and if there had been less value in linking multiple business dimensions together, a clearer but less flexible structure would have been more appropriate and easier to manage. (In 1998, ABB did indeed move to make decision-making lines clearer in the matrix – see Chapter 10.)

ABB's parenting advantage

Linkage influence, say Goold, *et al.*, 'can lead to value destruction. If the networking mechanisms become cumbersome, costly and bureaucratic, the end result may be to combine the worst of all worlds, rather than the best. Similarly, if certain dimensions of linkage are economically far more significant than others, seeking to network on multiple dimensions may prove less beneficial than a clear focus on one'.

What made ABB's high-risk strategy, with its extraordinary amounts of in-built tension, successful? The answer is that ABB's linkages made economic sense. As seen from the perspective of the early 1990s, the company did not develop an excessive internal focus, avoided low-value linkages and averted high overhead costs of the linkages. The company had three main areas of achievement (some of which are more clearly articulated by the authors than others).

- **ABB benefited from both scale and focus.** By means of its matrix concept, the company benefits from multiple dimensions of linkage at the same time. It does not have to make tradeoffs between centralization and decentralization, scale or focus. BAs helped to remove contracting difficulties to allow units to develop product specialization advantages.
- **Consolidation of ABB into global businesses, leading to cost reduction while creating 'global muscle'.** Advantages here include, for example, purchasing scale advantages provided by BA coordination and networking of functional experts rooting out needless duplication or divergence.
- **ABB developed a strong commercial focus.** As the authors highlight, many engineering businesses tend to focus on increasing sales volume and product range at the expense of margin. Groupwide customer focus programmes, initiatives for tighter cash management and the use of the ABACUS system helped achieve greater profitability, reduce timescales and simplify operations. Goold, *et al.*, also note that the BAs' drive to rationalize product lines and allocate export markets has consistently improved the profitability of ABB's acquisitions.

There were a number of key success criteria for ABB.

- **Visibility of the performance of individual units.** Spotting opportunities for linkages that create value requires companies to have a functioning performance measurement system. ABB's financial reporting system ABACUS enables people to spot these opportunities and act on them.
- **Shared and well-known critical success factors for the businesses.** For ABB, the parent has been able to add value because many of the synergies of multiple linkages are appropriate and the leaders know their business very well. ABB's businesses 'share a lot of critical success factors in common, with which most senior ABB managers have a long personal experience.' The leaders have exhibited a clear view on the criteria for their 'strategic heartland' (the authors' term for core competences) and applied these criteria to portfolio decisions.
- **Clear boundaries between parent and units.** To make 'linkage influence' work, the decentralization contract needs to be clearly established. Goold, *et al.*, point to the danger of parental involvement leading to loss of local accountability. In ABB, there are no fuzzy boundaries – there are clear terms of parental involvement and due observation of the process. Without these clear limits to people's responsibility, there would be lack of credibility and consistency of the parent's influence.
- **Facilitative parent.** ABB's centre acts as a facilitator, rather than a bureaucratic policy formulation and controlling agency. Any heavy-handed approach to the matrix would have swamped units with regulations and

cost. The parent at ABB demonstrated the ability to influence effectively without using the full weight of hierarchy.

- **Mental maps of the parent.** Goold, *et al.*, believe that ABB's parent organization has the right mental maps to unblock what stands in the way of creating value across units in the organization. The contribution of individuals, such as 'Percy Barnevik's ceaseless travelling and preaching of the need to network' has been key.

Issues for the future

The ABB parent has built its success on a network of linkages – a risky strategy that has paid off. The authors are careful to recommend that companies assessing whether or not they should emulate ABB's formula should exercise tremendous rigour – not only because of what has made ABB successful, but because of some of the unanswered questions the company leaves us with.

Focus more on the heartland

Goold, *et al.*, who use the notion of a 'heartland' when talking about strategic core competences, point out that, as a result of acquisitions, ABB has some businesses that lie outside its heartland. They quote a senior manager within the company: 'We have not taken a hard enough look at the acquisitions and pruned the portfolio. The main value added from Zürich should be to say: "I don't care if this business generates a ton of money – get rid of it. It won't always make money and we don't really understand it." It has been four years since some of the major acquisitions, but we haven't focused quickly enough on the core.' (One of Göran Lindahl's first actions on becoming CEO in 1997 was indeed to divest non-core businesses.)

Ensure the development of the right breed

Many people inside and outside ABB find the requirements for managers in the matrix daunting. To continue to make it work, the company will need to ensure that it can attract and develop the right kind of talent. Goold, *et al.*, quote a senior executive of the company: 'To manage this sort of organization you need very secure, mature people who are able to delegate as opposed to command. These are not easy to find among Western managers. ABB itself has a strong culture of hard-nosed, dictatorial people – they have been successful, and it is not easy to change.'

Sustain the performance

Again, Goold, *et al.*, give a voice to others to raise their concerns – this time to a competitor of ABB: 'They are very impressive. They have certainly shown they can take out costs. But there is quite a lot of strain in the system. The real test will be in the years to come. Can they continue to deliver in a steadier state?' Since the merger, ABB has certainly put itself constantly on the edge as a result of its unique combination of clear structures (clear roles, control mechanisms such as ABACUS) and the high degree of self-organization (ABB's reliance on people to make the matrix work). Chaos theory teaches us that, by accepting to stay on the edge, you can achieve constant innovation and creativity. While this is certainly desirable, is it also sustainable? If it is an uncomfortable place to stay in, could it be the only way to survive in such a complicated environment as ABB's?

Goold, *et al.*, are wise enough not to offer any answers, yet provoke in us a number of questions that heighten our curiosity about the future of ABB as a company, and as a pioneer in the area of global organizing.

A man who set world standards:
Manfred Kets de Vries on Percy Barnevik

In many years of prolific contribution with a focus on applied psychoanalysis and management policy, Manfred Kets de Vries, one of the grand masters of management thinking, has consistently challenged rational management theory for being unrealistic, if not downright wrong, about the reality of organizational life. In his best-known books, *The Irrational Executive* (1984) and *Organizations on the Couch* (1991), he uses applied psychoanalysis to propose bold and refreshing ways of looking at the 'darker side' of leaders and organizations. Interested in the profile of entrepreneurs and extraordinary leaders, Kets de Vries has not shied away from trying to talk about 'charisma', a term psychologists tend to avoid because they cannot explain or measure it. Clearly, Percy Barnevik was an interesting leader for Kets de Vries to look at.

Percy Barnevik has been famous for his willingness to talk about ABB and his organizational concepts. He has also been well known for shying away from talking about himself. In a rare opportunity, Kets de Vries of INSEAD helps us to catch a glimpse of the man who has hardly been 'behind' the scenes of ABB's success (*European Management Journal*, 1996). The person that emerges from Kets de Vries' writing is a soft-spoken, very intense and philosophical man, who is driven by a passionate belief in his organizational model as well as the wish to make a contribution to society. He is described as a rational yet humanistic showman who exudes contagious enthusiasm and radiates an irresistible self-confidence when talking about his vision.

By setting Percy Barnevik alongside Jack Welch and Richard Branson in his analysis of extraordinary leaders, Kets de Vries, writing at a time when Percy Barnevik was still the CEO of ABB, puts him in a category of people who have written management history. He refers to all three as men who have developed new organizational concepts, 'new prototypes' in line with our post-industrial age, able to discharge us from Alfred Sloan's model of the 'modern organization'. He elaborates his points by describing two key leadership roles – the architectural and the charismatic role.

The minimalist architect

How does Percy Barnevik design organizations, and what does this tell us about the person? ABB's loosely structured organization model follows a clear set of design principles.

The organization is conceived in terms of the employees and customers, rather than people in the head office. All units are kept small to give people a maximum sense of identity, involvement and ownership. Another design principle is a certain sense of control, meaning that employees throughout the organization are encouraged to take responsibility for their work and are given the space to make their own decisions. This operational autonomy is intended to avoid alienation and depersonalization, and minimize the potential for confusion in the decision chain. Everyone has as much close customer contact as possible, and everything is designed around processes rather than functions, so that the customer can receive excellent service.

This model is rounded out by a small central organization that provides minimalist control and reward systems, keeps the organization's values alive, and sets the pace for continuous change. These leading-edge systems hold the company together via information technology and rewards such as gain sharing, designed to create commitment. Constant indoctrination during workshops, seminars and meetings ensure that people internalize or are reminded of ABB's values. Through role modelling, Barnevik and his senior executives have created a fast-moving environment in which people make quick decisions (of which at least 80 per cent should be right) and continually seek to renew the way things are done in their organization.

According to Kets de Vries, these principles create the environment in which people can be committed to the organization and to delivering the best service to customers; where they can be creative, high-performing, innovative individuals and have fun.

What does this design tell us about the man behind it? Like Tom Peters, Kets de Vries describes a man who fights bureaucracy passionately and has a deep-seated aversion to complacency. This is also a man who treats employees as adults and looks to surround himself with people who are inner-driven and want involvement and responsibility. Kets de Vries paints the picture of a man who pushed authority, responsibility and accountability as far into the organization as he could; a person who has pushed the boundaries of traditional organizing.

The humanist visionary

Outlining the charismatic role of Percy Barnevik, Kets de Vries exhorts well-known leadership features with striking vigour. He writes, as if captured himself, of Barnevik's strong vision. Kets de Vries believes that, beyond creating commitment to his way of thinking, Barnevik tries to create pride in what ABB is trying to do. Clearly, Barnevik's goal to create the world's number one engineering group is part of that. Yet, he also highlights social concerns that have the potential to elevate the company's mission to almost charitable status for the people who believe in it: 'Barnevik has said that he is motivated by a desire to create a better world by creating employment (particularly in Eastern Europe where he is the largest employer), and to make the world more liveable by providing clean energy and transportation.' Kets de Vries notes, 'This vision of engaging in good works, of looking beyond the bottom line, is a very effective way of motivating and challenging people who work for him.'

To ensure that others share his vision, Barnevik relentlessly tries to get it across to people. As Kets de Vries points out, he is a master of impression management, fully able to excite people by his self-confidence and enthusiasm for what he is trying to do. His vision has a compelling strength because his personal beliefs and values are part of it – this gives him passion and conviction. While this is the outward-facing side of his leadership persona, a few more invisible features of his personality have played an equally important role in shaping his performance as one of the most remarkable contemporary leaders.

Kets de Vries suggests that, by communicating high performance expectations to his people and creating a minimalist structure to allow people to exercise power over their own areas of work, he has let go of his immediate need for control. He suggests that Barnevik is able to postpone the gratification of his more immediate power needs to reap the benefits of greater power in the long term by achieving increased productivity of his organization. This does not mean that people in ABB operate in complete freedom. Kets de Vries points out that Barnevik developed accountability by showing both compassion and setting a limit to excuses.

A rarely discussed yet vitally important aspect of organizational leadership relates to the shadow side of organizational life. Kets de Vries argues that Barnevik does not evade it, falling into conflict avoidance, micro management or abrasive behaviour. Instead of denying or denigrating negative feelings in the organization, he creates an environment able to 'hold' the affectionate as well as the aggressive energy of his people. He does this by going first – by listening to others, expressing affection and directing aggressions outwards to the competition: 'Percy Barnevik constantly reminds his people of enemies such as Siemens and General Electric.'

A role model for the new millennium?

Kets de Vries' account of this extraordinary leader is rich in insights into the person and certainly helps us to understand some of the reasons for Percy Barnevik's success (his charisma and his elegant organizational design concept). Kets de Vries concludes that Barnevik has set standards for the future that other leaders of organizations should follow. Yet, how could anyone follow Percy Barnevik's path? Stories of remarkable people can, in themselves, inspire us to be bold and believe in what we want to do. Yet, understanding what it is they do and applying the principles we learn from them is equally valuable. While Kets de Vries helps by providing inspiration and illuminating principles for organizational design and leadership, he leaves certain questions unanswered.

It is easy to get caught by the enthusiasm Kets de Vries' writing exudes, yet his account of the man behind ABB's success is one-sided, showing us only the strong and positive parts of the picture. In doing so, he elevates Barnevik to the Olympia of mythical leaders, to whom we attribute superhuman powers. While this might serve our childish fantasies and needs for dependency, it distances us from the real Barnevik and the possibility of relating to him as adults (a type of relationship Barnevik himself seems to value). It makes it more difficult to see Barnevik as someone who might know a lot more than us and who has done impressive things, but whose learning we can grasp. If we are to see him as a role model for the next millennium, we need to be able to see his human limits, understand his dilemmas and appreciate that he has no easy answers either. We need to see how he has been able to rise beyond his weaknesses.

While CEO of ABB, Barnevik seemed to be dealing with a number of dilemmas. From Kets de Vries, we derive a good sense for how Barnevik avoided choosing one side of each dilemma over the other and, rather, solved it by embracing both sides. These dilemmas are:

- control and empowerment
- centralization and decentralization
- speed and efficiency
- affection and aggression.

Control and empowerment

Rather than letting go of control, Barnevik has modernized it. Instead of achieving compliance by using the power of his position, he achieved commitment by using the power of conviction. Instead of acting as organizational controller, he provided people far down within the organization with data on how they and others perform, so that they could self-organize to achieve high performance levels.

Centralization and decentralization

Kets de Vries' describes a man who is comfortable with both centralization and decentralization, keeping a close watch on key performance indicators centrally, and for the rest relying on a network, which solves problems wherever they occur. Embracing both sides of the dilemma seems to have been possible through ABB's IT systems, Kets de Vries claims. Yet, Barnevik seems more interested and passionate about decentralization.

Speed and efficiency

Decisiveness emerges as one of the elements of Barnevik's management philosophy, as revealed by Kets de Vries. Speed of action does not mean that everyone always has to get things right at ABB. Barnevik expects people to make mistakes, yet they should be right at least 80 per cent of the time.

Affection and aggression

Barnevik is as able to express affection and compassion as he is to express tough rigour. He is careful to direct his own aggression, and that of other people in ABB, towards the outside to avoid in-fighting. Neither of these two extremes (which are often split and not fully owned in organizations) are dirty words in ABB.

Other dilemmas

It is not very clear to us how Barnevik dealt with two more dilemmas we see and which are not fully developed by Kets de Vries:

- renewal versus recharging
- social concerns versus ethical dilemmas.

Renewal versus recharging

Organizations that are constantly striving for improvement, change and renewal are usually bad at giving people a rest from time to time. Nowhere in Kets de Vries' writing (and in anyone else's we have come across, for that matter) do we hear about celebration and rest in ABB. 'Resting' and 'recharging batteries' seem to be unspeakable words in ABB – quickly mixed up with complacency and contentment. How long can people sustain this extraordinary pace? Do they have to? Does this pattern reflect a blind spot in Barnevik's thinking? When Percy Barnevik goes on holiday, he doesn't rest – he takes a fax and a phone. When he gave up the job of chief executive at ABB, his wife gave him a tie with a picture of a hammock on it – a token of the greater family time that he himself thought he would be taking. Instead, he went on to take up the top job at Investor, one of the world's great industrial power centres.

Social concerns versus ethical dilemmas

Barnevik expressed laudable aspirations about helping to create a better world for us all, yet one cannot avoid thinking that these ambitions must meet, in the day-to-day, with concrete needs for decision making on matters that are all too often in a grey zone between the ethical and the unethical. How does Barnevik deal with the fact that some of the products and services that ABB provides, on the one hand, create better living conditions for people in the short term and, on the other, in the mid to long term, might damage the environment? Why does this subject strike us as being an unspeakable one as we try to make contact with the organization to write respectfully yet critically about it?

Whatever the questions we are still left with, we cannot help but feel greatly impressed by the profile of an extraordinary leader. Barnevik emerges from Kets de Vries' accounts as a man with great psychological maturity, able to handle very complicated dilemmas. The fact that he might be overlooking important aspects of organizational health only serves to make him more human to us. He is most definitely a role model to inspire us well beyond the year 2000.

What the gurus reveal

The two 'North American' perspectives from Peters and Ghoshal and Bartlett may partly reflect a very American concern with what is new, changing and innovative in the world. Peters rightly applauded the way in which Percy Barnevik decentralized and 'liberated' ABB, opening it up to entrepreneurial behaviour in an increasingly dynamic business environment. If he were to re-examine ABB today, we wonder if he might put more emphasis on the challenges of holding a global organization of 5000 entrepreneurs together. He certainly described the BA concept, but we are left with the impression that what he was most impressed about was ABB as the 'bureaucracy buster'.

Ghoshal and Bartlett's elegant notion of the 'individualized corporation' also emphasizes ABB's entrepreneurial process, but gives equal weight to the integration process. Have they, however, overemphasized 'process' above 'strategy and structure'? A Swedish researcher, Christian Berggren, actually uses the example of ABB to take what he calls the 'process school of international management' to task (Berggren, 1996). In recent years, he says, so much of the discussion in international management research has focused on subtle forms of coordination and communication and there is a need for renewed attention to the hard core of strategy, structure and control.

Goold, Campbell and Alexander's analysis is, indeed, more concerned with such issues. It is less about business in a new management epoch and more about what constitutes effective corporate 'parenting' in any era. Their past research has focused to a greater extent on organizations structured as strategic business units and their analysis of ABB is perhaps not as deep as that of some other organizations they have looked at. It will be interesting to see what emerges from new work that they are undertaking on corporate parenting in more complicated organizational forms.

Finally, both Tom Peters and Manfred Kets de Vries have profiled Percy Barnevik as a global leader. Both have given us a picture of the high-energy, totally committed, driven nature of his management style. Kets de Vries also gives us insights into the humanist aspects of the man. Both profiles make us wonder. We suspect that all great leaders have their 'shadow side' with which their colleagues and subordinates have to cope, but we don't really find out about this aspect of Barnevik here. However, we know from our own discussions in ABB, that it is quite remarkable what a profound impact he seems to have on those who work with him. Jean-Pierre Dürig, now retired from ABB and a former long-time Brown Boveri manager, told us that he could not talk about Barnevik 'objectively' because of his deep respect for him.

Let's give the final word here to Bengt Skantze, who has known Barnevik since Sandvik days:

> *Percy has two very obvious skills – communication and motivation skills. He is a very skilled communicator and he is also very happy. He gives examples and makes it very down to earth when he talks to investors and press conferences. It is a personal talent. You don't appreciate it when you have it, it just comes naturally. But when you compare him with someone else talking about the same thing, there are huge differences. Inside the company, he can move around the organization and touch a guy on the arm and ask 'How's it going?' The guy is on a cloud for the rest of the day. Percy does it to hundreds of people every week. He makes telephone calls, systematically keeping in touch. He is always there for people. You could always get to him on the phone. This is true of the new management too. Nobody is isolated.*

Nobody is isolated – that is the essence of what we call the globally connected corporation.

References

Quotes without references originate from the authors' personal communications – see page xviii for details.

Bartlett, Christopher A., and Ghoshal, Sumantra (1989) *Managing Across Borders: The Transnational Solution*. London: Hutchinson Business Books.

Berggren, Christian (1996) 'Building a truly global organization? ABB and the problems of integrating a multi-domestic enterprise', *Scandinavian Journal of Management*, **12** (2), 123–37.

Ghoshal, Sumantra and Bartlett, Christopher A. (1998) *The Individualized Corporation: A Fundamentally New Approach to Management*. London: Heinemann, 192.

Goold, Michael and Campbell, Andrew (1987) *Strategies and Styles: The Role of the Centre in Managing Diversified Corporations*. Oxford: Basil Blackwell.

Goold, Michael, Campbell, Andrew and Alexander, Marcus (1994) *Corporate-level Strategy: Creating Value in the Multibusiness Company*. New York: John Wiley.

Kets de Vries, Manfred (ed.) (1984) *The Irrational Executive: Psychoanalytic Explorations in Management*. New York: International Executive Press.

Kets de Vries, Manfred (1991) *Organizations on the Couch: Clinical Perspectives on Organizational Behavior and Change*. San Francisco and Oxford: Jossey-Bass.

Kets de Vries, Manfred (1996) 'Leaders who make a difference', *European Management Journal*, October **14** (5), 486–93.

Peters, Tom (1987) *Thriving on Chaos: Handbook for a Management Revolution*. London: Macmillan.

Peters, Tom (1993) *Liberation Management: Necessary Disorganization for the Nanosecond Nineties*. London: Pan Books.

Peters, Tom (1995) *The Pursuit of Wow!: Everyone's Guide to Topsy-Turvy Times*. London: Macmillan.

Peters, Tom and Waterman Jr., Robert H. (1982) *In Search of Excellence: Lessons from America's Best-Run Companies*. New York: Harper & Row.

PART

REAPING
THE HARVEST

CHAPTER 8

The world's favourite case study

*Behind the catchwords of 'multidomestic', 'big–small',
'global–local', 'decentralized–centralized', is an enormous effort by
our people to transform the organization from the grass root level
upwards and make ABB a company of continuous change towards
ever-increasing goals.*
Percy Barnevik

In the previous chapters we have described the history of the two main partners in the ABB merger and the deep technological and international
experience that they brought to the partnership. We have tried to look
behind the scenes at the 1987 merger negotiations and how ABB created a
bombshell in the European power engineering industry. We have described
Percy Barnevik's two-stage master plan – first, for a dramatic restructuring
and streamlining of the new company, and then for its audacious global
expansion from Western Europe into the Americas, Central and Eastern
Europe, and Asia. In the process, we have seen how ABB's unique combination of a multidomestic presence and a global matrix structure caught the
imagination of business observers and academics. We have also tried to
make sense of ABB's experience by considering the views of leading management gurus and have introduced our own notion of the 'globally
connected' corporation.

We start this last part of the book by looking, first, at ABB a decade after the
merger, to find out how the master plan has worked out so far. The company
has had great reviews, but variable profitability has been noted by financial
analysts. The company has consistently been among the most admired
European companies in recent years, but what is it like to work for? Is the
famous matrix really working, what accounts for its success and how has it
been modified in the light of ABB's changing business environment? Why,
also, is ABB Europe's most respected company and why, indeed, has ABB
become the world's favourite case study?

In the process of answering these questions, we look at how some of the key players, including Percy Barnevik, reflect on what ABB has achieved in the past ten years. Let's start by looking at why ABB has become such a popular case study.

ABB – the world's favourite case study

One measure of ABB's success is the sheer acclaim that it has attracted from business peers and academics alike. In 1998, *The Wall Street Journal Europe* was moved to say, 'Among managers, only General Electric Co.'s Jack Welch enjoys as much worldwide praise as Percy Barnevik' (Latour and Steinmetz, 1998). This was just the latest in a long series of ovations.

Europe's most respected company

ABB has figured prominently in survey after survey. For example, in 1994, an international survey of senior executives in Europe's top 500 companies ranked Percy Barnevik as Europe's most admired chief executive. He was praised as 'professional, humane, determined, close to his employees and an excellent communicator' (Brown, 1994). In the same year, ABB was voted 'Europe's most respected company' (with UK retailer Marks & Spencer) in a survey carried out by the *Financial Times*. Top executives were asked to identify their most respected European companies, regardless of sector, on seven dimensions of excellence – customer focus, staff, products and services, business performance, leadership and management, strategy, and environmental issues. ABB won for its strategy, leadership and management qualities. (The survey gave some interesting insights into the international outlook of European businesses – Italian and French companies tended to vote for international companies, suggesting, said the *Financial Times*, a more pan-European focus; British and German executives were more inclined to vote for domestic companies.)

ABB would win this award for each of the four years running up to 1997. In these surveys ABB was rated very highly for business performance and maximizing employee potential, and Percy Barnevik was named Europe's most respected business leader, esteemed for strategic vision and focus. As an indicator of the values and priorities of European managers, the surveys showed that the most important corporate attributes were quality and implementation of corporate strategy, management of complexity and skill at balancing the interests of customers, employees and shareholders. Interestingly, when later FT surveys asked which company they respected most, regardless of country of origin, European managers voted for General Electric of the US, with ABB coming second (a position it shared with Microsoft). None the less, ABB was cited most frequently as the benchmark against which other European companies measured their performance. For a company that, less than ten years before, had sprung from the vision of the CEO of a middle-ranking firm headquartered in the Swedish provincial town of Västerås, on the edge of continental Europe, this was an outstanding achievement.

Why is ABB the world's favourite case study?

We asked Percy Barnevik himself why he thought ABB had become the world's favourite case study. His explanation is:

> *Because of timing. This case came at a time when the Americans had started to re-enter the world after the isolation period and were looking for solutions and saw the New Europe coming out, and then Asia. They saw the attractive reopening of Eastern Europe and were interested in how to organize and handle it. The Japanese like Sony were building up their second head office in America all of a sudden, and put a lot of their added value transplants in the UK. So we can say that the world started to confront these globalization issues and it was no longer enough to have something like an international division which was the way the Americans used to organize themselves. You had to find other ways to run a network in the world. People were also intrigued by how we tried to create a multi-culture organization with many nationalities from top to bottom.*

Barnevik also says that people were interested in the way that ABB has *'practically* handled being global (global business areas) and local (multidomestic), and being small (5000 profit centres) and big (global size).' It is a company with some compelling catchwords – 'global–local', 'big–small', 'decentralized–central control'. In addition, as the biggest cross-country merger so far in 1987, it attracted a lot of attention at the start because of its speed, mixed nationality teams, cultural sensitivity, a 'policy bible' as the global corporate glue, and so on:

> *This happened to take place when many companies were looking for new organizational solutions in an increasingly globalized world and when business schools and management institutes were looking for ideas and cases. In the universities they were still stuck in the old organizational thinking and theories, and were also looking for new ideas. So the timing was the reason why it had such a huge potential. Also the merger itself created immediate attention. 'Will they succeed, will they pull it off, can they resolve inevitable national clashes?' At that time these cross-border mergers were not so common. There were Shell and Unilever long ago at the turn of the century, but in recent times there had been few big cross-border mergers.*

Barnevik warns against idealizing the ABB case:

We should not make any retroactive nice painting of what happened. The merger was very burdensome and strenuous for some time for many people inside the company. It sounds easy when you talk about it afterwards but there were 500 managers appointed that autumn. There were a couple of hundred who could not make it to the top in Spain or Italy for example, so with all the overlap and duplication in factories, and to really reap the benefits, you had to close plants and move products. And if you, for example, moved AC technology from Sweden to Finland, and DC technology from Finland to Sweden, you could say, 'You exchanged and you became stronger and specialized'. But then the Finns felt like losers for the DC and the gain of AC was not obvious. That is how the human mind works. In that situation, to really turn people's minds in a positive way, away from the digging of trenches and internal fighting and suboptimizations, we had to say, 'We have to beat Siemens, we have to beat General Electric. [Barnevik slaps the table.] We have to show these guys that we can make it, we will surprise them.' And you had to work hard to create a sense of pride. Not that we were at war with anybody, but we had to create that idea that we would prove that we can make it: 'We will be the biggest in robots and now we are going to go to the customers and beat the competitors, build up in Asia and be the pioneer in Eastern Europe'. You had to create some of that sentiment to overcome these other difficulties. It is not a strange strategy, but the important thing was to make people feel part of it, engaging them, firing them up so that they feel that they have something burning inside them. Of course this is difficult to sustain decade after decade but those first few years were critical for us. And that might explain it a little.

Ten years on, Barnevik is also keen to demystify a number of things that have almost become part of the ABB trademark. For him, the original concept of the multidomestic enterprise bears a deceptively simple notion that can be glossed over when only the catchword is considered. For the visionary ex-CEO of ABB, multidomesticity initially meant capitalizing on existing home markets of the merged and acquired companies while adding global economies of scale – an eminently pragmatic consideration.

At the time of the merger it was important not to be regarded as a foreigner everywhere. We were not homeless but we had many homes and it was crucial to build on these national roots. We had some 30 home markets, and had to be Finnish in Finland, Swedish in Sweden. . . . In most countries we had a 100-year history. We have a Czech company from the time of Napoleon which is 200 years old. We have 150 companies more than 100 years old. We could say, 'we have grown up in this country, we are a citizen of your country, we are run by locals.'

Similarly, the legendary multinational mix in the company's culture had a simple driver supporting global cooperation and the formation of ABB's 'corporate glue'. ASEA had a head start in implementing Barnevik's holistic concepts. The dynamic in the newly created ABB could have been in-fighting about which country and company was best. Directing attention to the outside world (customers and competitors), valuing national companies and yet strongly encouraging cross-country cooperation was designed to bust the Swedish/Swiss/German power hubs. Says Barnevik:

Of course, when you had a success story behind you for eight years at ASEA in the same industry it helped a lot. But there is also a seed of destruction in that because we had to make the Swedes understand that this was really a merger and not a takeover. While we were faster on our feet and had a higher profit in Scandinavia, BBC had deeper knowledge and research capability and stronger market position in a number of markets where we were hardly present.

The openness of ABB's communication policies also helped to fuel interest in the ABB case. Barnevik says:

Some people criticized it and said that we were too open with the information – why not be more secretive? But you cannot be secretive if you have 200,000 people. There is no way that you can engage 25,000 managers in a secretive manner. You have to take the bad with the good. And I felt that the negative of a leaking out of how we intended to operate, our strategy and our plans, although a negative where direct competitors were concerned, was a small negative compared with the big negative of not making people inside the company enthusiastic and join the bandwagon.

Looking back on the ten years, Barnevik also sees a tendency towards an increasing role for the global BAs. For example, pricing used to be a local matter in many BAs but now they need global price policies as the environment and customers become more globalized. Customers are also less nationalistic now with, for example, privatization of earlier national monopolies. An organization is not carved in stone but must develop and adapt to a changing environment over time.

Why is ABB valued by those who use it as a case study? We asked Dr Stephen Tallman, Associate Professor in the David Eccles School of Business at the University of Utah and currently a visiting senior lecturer at Cranfield School of Management in the UK. Tallman has used the various cases written about ABB in teaching international strategic management for several years. He says:

In many ways, ABB (at least as presented in these materials) appears to be the exemplar of the 'new global' firm, the company concerned with intensively integrating activities around the globe – not just looking for a single world market. Their strategy of worldwide technological leadership combined with attentiveness to local market demands reflects the perceived need for global firms to transcend simple worldwide cost leadership strategies. Even more, the seeming success of ABB in creating a network organization of interacting but decentralized subsidiaries in a formal matrix structure has become the ideal of international management theorists. ABB vastly simplifies teaching MBA students about the future direction of the multinational organization, as it seems to already be waiting at the end of the path.

Does Barnevik think that the case studies fairly represent what ABB was trying to do and the reality of ABB's matrix and control systems? He replies:

The quality of the 40–50 case studies I have seen (some are more or less copies of others) varies considerably. However, most of them are of good quality and I find it amusing to find people all over the world who know a lot about ABB. Whether in the US, Germany, Malaysia or Japan, I run into people who feel like experts on ABB and put detailed questions to me on ABACUS, for example, which I cannot always answer precisely. I am sometimes intimidated by meeting people who know more about ABB than I do!

Barnevik approves in particular of the widely used case studies produced by Harvard Business School (covering ABB as a global corporation, the ABACUS accounting system and the change processes at ABB Deutschland), those by the French-based international business school INSEAD and those from Linköping University in Sweden. Barnevik re-emphasizes, however, the importance of implementation:

The interesting thing with ABB was not, of course, just certain concepts about the matrix or decentralization, all of which were fairly well-known things in themselves. It was how do you do it, how do you mobilize people, how do you make them rally round it? It is easy to write down a purpose and describe processes and organizational concepts. The huge challenge is to make thousands of people not only understand but 'buy in'. The challenge is 5 per cent intellectual work and 95 per cent hard work and excellence in execution. Difference in execution is what differentiates the successful companies from the less successful. You can succeed with different organizational models.

Barnevik also says that there is no single fantastic theory or secret to success. It depends on having a situation where a large number of details are right.

Does Barnevik recognize himself in the case studies that have been written about him? He says:

When it comes to me personally, I become inevitably a victim of myths, like sleeping four hours per night, meeting my children in a limousine on the way to the airport, etc. The truth is, of course, that I am much more of a normal person with a family, hobbies, etc. I have my strengths and weaknesses like most people. What is important is to be aware of your weaknesses, as in my case, being dominant or overly impatient, and work at that. At the same time, I feel that normally the management values that I stand for are generally correctly reported: 'Walk the talk', decentralization, empowerment, speed in action, mix nationalities, joint teams, 'change culture', 'hands-on' mentality, etc.

A successful cross-border merger?

Forbes magazine once described ABB as 'a company with no discernible identity' (Klebnikov, 1991). This was surely an exaggeration, particularly in 1991, only three years after the merger. Other observers took the opposite tack and worried that the original parent countries would continue to dominate the company. In 1988, one journalist wrote, for example, 'If ABB fails to work as a true European entity and functions merely as a Swiss, Swedish and German joint venture, that doesn't leave hope for the future of other alliances that are sure to follow [in the run up to the single market]' (Arbose, 1988). Ten years later, there are still outside observers who speculate whether or not the real power in the organization still resides in these three countries and indeed, whether or not 'the Swedes' are still in control.

How do ABB senior managers who have experienced the company's development over the last ten years see this issue? Beat Hess, ABB's Corporate Counsel and a former Brown Boveri employee, says:

> *It took years of hard work hammering the two cultures together. There was some discussion initially about 'Were the Swedes taking over?' Thanks to a small group of people and Percy Barnevik, we felt that this was not an issue [see Table 8.1]. We felt that we were doing something for the good of the shareholders and the employees. Even if there were more Swedes than Swiss, who cared if they were making a strong contribution? The difference disappeared over the years and eventually there was very little discussion of nationalities. It is now about performance and dedication and not your passport or the ASEA or BBC that you came from. It took ten years to create this group and we can be proud of the achievements that we have made.*

Table 8.1 No country dominates – major countries by numbers of employees, 1997

Countries	Number of employees	Percentages of total
Germany	29,138	14
Sweden	24,293	11
USA	21,433	10
Switzerland	12,483	6
India	9,630	5
Finland	9,241	4
UK	9,174	4
Italy	8,495	4
Poland	7,738	4
Norway	7,209	3
Czech Republic	5,759	3
Others	68,464	32
Total	213,057	100

Source: ABB Annual Report 1997

Jan Roxendal, President of ABB's Financial Services segment, who had joined ASEA in Sweden in 1984, says:

In ABB after the merger, the differences disappeared very fast – unlike the bank in which I had once worked where, seven years after it had merged with another bank, they were still very much two banks and you could tell which bank a person was from. It was quite different in ABB. The two companies were in the same industry. And there were so many acquisitions, it didn't matter if you came from Combustion Engineering or wherever. The old mentality disappeared very fast. People are now proud to be ABB. It's partly to do with positive publicity and an inspiring CEO. I believed very much in the Group from the beginning. I believed in the Group because of the individual. I believed in the leader and then believed in the concept. He was so convincing. I believed it could not be anything but a success. I had to leave a relatively safe unit in ASEA and come down here and start from scratch in a hostile environment in Zürich at a time when people were saying ABB would fail.

So, has ABB successfully handled that most difficult challenge of cross-border mergers: managing cultural differences between the partners to produce competitive advantage? Whatever success ABB has achieved here is due, many insiders acknowledge, to the role played by Percy Barnevik. How does he himself look back on the process? We asked him to reflect on ABB ten years after the merger. What were the key milestones on the way to making ABB a success? He points, first of all, to his experience before ABB at steel and tool company Sandvik, a $5 billion, 'very international' company with 93 per cent of sales outside Sweden today. It was smaller than ASEA and ABB but none the less had some 40,000 people:

There I introduced the matrix, country managers, and the responsibilities and policies that I believe in. I ran North America for five years, and I worked there centrally for ten years. In the 1970s I worked there with decentralization reducing headquarters and introducing the matrix. This company was far ahead of the electrical engineering industry in internationalization. I learned a lot, both in my central role at the headquarters for five years, and as head of the US operations for five years. It was useful to see how it worked from both ends. Later on, when we were firmly established in the big countries, we strengthened the role of the global BAs, just like ABB is doing now.

Then I had eight years in ASEA, which was a top-heavy headquarters and technology-driven, hundred-year-old Swedish giant. They had their share of trouble with reduced demand after the oil crisis. ASEA had half of its sales in Sweden itself, which is almost unbelievable today. With eight million people in Sweden, how can you sell half of your whole business there? It is like selling half of your whole business in New Jersey if you are an American. And that while selling infrastructure, trains and power plants, etc. In order to change this around and be a global player – first a Nordic player, then with ABB a European player, then a transatlantic player, and then a global player – we worked step by step. These were eight years during which we worked very hard to make these organizational and management ideas and policies a living reality. We went through the same things, decentralizing and cutting headquarters with young people moving up, hundreds of new profit centres being created, moving away from the functional thinking and creating the matrix, the local role and the global role. So when the merger came, ASEA was already working along these lines. Quite rightly, BBC at the time had already taken some decisions (but not yet implemented them) during their management meetings the year before. The ASEA experience gave a 'flying start' for the merger. The fact that ASEA had both grown substantially in size and increased share value by 43 per cent annually during those eight years helped to convince people at BBC. It was in a way more difficult when I came to ASEA in 1980, since the Sandvik case did not count much with the electrical engineers.

ASEA's track record gave him a certain credibility, says Barnevik:

There were Swiss Germans and Italians hesitating – 'Why split it up like that? You can't reduce central functions like that' – and so on. But, of course, when hesitant people could see how it worked in other places, it helped a lot. It was, for example, not a Procter & Gamble experience, where people could have said, 'But this doesn't work in our industry'. When the merger happened, it was a matter of getting away from a Besserwisser [know-all] attitude among these young pushy Swedes coming down to these 20 years older guys.

This was a difficult balance to achieve. If I had had two companies like ASEA 1980 and BBC 1987, it would have been difficult both to do the merger and to change the structure in both merger partners at the same time. A merger would not have succeeded.

I remember how some ASEA managers contacted Wallenberg in 1980 and said, 'This young guy from the steel industry – he is not even an engineer – is destroying the company!' There were people who honestly felt that destruction was on the way with all the organization, people and policy changes. But it was necessary to make the company market-oriented, internationally oriented and to free up the potential inside the big hierarchy. Even if the financial success was limited in the past decade, ASEA had been around for a hundred years and they had achieved a lot of 'first in the world' and technical leadership. Who was I to come in and turn it upside down? For myself, the Sandvik experience was absolutely necessary.

Barnevik points also to what he calls the 'Finnish rehearsal', when ASEA bought Strömberg in 1986:

We tried to run that as a merger too. There were 9000 people in Finland, so that was on a much smaller scale than the big merger the year after, but it gave us very valuable lessons – how can you speedily integrate, make decisions about who should do what, handle common subsidiaries abroad? We had a dress rehearsal on a small scale before we went into the big one.

That meant, says Barnevik:

> that when we merged and went out with that famous Cannes bible on 4 January 1988, we didn't do just a little part of it, or try it out. We did the whole thing full blast: 'Now it is a new company, called ABB nothing else. Here is how we want to operate.' We started up the merged ABB on 1 January 1988 with the whole concept and organization in place. Since then it has emerged over time and I believe it is good to change the organization about every five years to adapt to a changing environment. The decentralization, with closeness to customers and action orientation, is deeply rooted but increased globalization is a continuing process.

From a bilateral game to a 'multigame'

However, as Barnevik points out, the company did not have the luxury of focusing entirely on internal transformation:

> The electric engineering industry started restructuring after the ABB merger, and to position ourselves, we acquired about 150 companies with 130,000 people after the merger including Combustion Engineering and Westinghouse T&D in the USA, and a lot of other companies. A big task was to integrate all these newcomers into our organization, our management principles and culture. We also divested 80 companies with some 70,000 people in the first few years. Not much had happened in the structure of the electrical engineering industry since the war. But after our merger, Siemens moved, the French and British came together with a merger, GE was activated, Westinghouse and AEG went downhill towards oblivion and the two American boiler-makers, CE and B&W were up for grabs. In Europe almost all of the medium-sized vanished in two to three years. It was like a ketchup bottle – first comes nothing and then everything. Of course I could have said 'Let's wait for five years now, we have to consume and digest the merger'. But at the same time we couldn't sit by as an onlooker. We had to act. So we got another challenge on top of the merger, immediately after the merger, which was as big as the merger itself!'

Despite the immense challenges of integrating the huge number of acquisitions in different countries, it may actually have helped ABB to overcome potential cultural conflict among the original partners. As Barnevik says:

> In a way, this brought a big positive with it because rather than sitting with our ASEA and BBC origins, the Americans came in. So there were no longer two companies talking about 'Who is best here and who is best in that'. Now, all of a sudden, 30–40,000 Americans were in the picture. Then the Norwegians came in with 10,000 people, the Finns were also 10,000, and 10,000 Italians started to be activated. It became a 'multigame' that took it away from that bilateral focus that we had a little at the beginning.

None the less, Barnevik says that his greatest negative surprise during the merger process was the very strong national sentiments which made restructuring immediately after the merger difficult:

You just had to overcome it. In these modern times we are tribal people. If you look at gene theory, most of what we do today and how we behave is based upon the past 50,000 years. The primitive reactions that you stick to your tribe, to people you know and who speak the same language like your family and tribe, all that is strongly rooted. You can't be angry because of that and say, 'You are disloyal', it is like you are hungry or thirsty, it is built into you. You have to try and make it easy for people, to reach out to other cultures. You had to work at it and to reward people who were good role models – a Swede who was promoting Switzerland, or a German who brought Italians into his team in a global assignment. All those people who deliberately took a lead to build the ABB corporate glue. And you had to set examples from the top. We were proud of our policy bible (although that is papers, and even if you read them, you forget about them). It is 'walking the talk' that decides it. The national conflicts at the restructuring in the beginning were the biggest hurdle.

It is not only national feelings that have to be addressed. Barnevik remembers:

when you had three automation systems, all of them working, some more developed than others, and you had to go for one and standardize. Of course, for an engineer who has spent 5 years of his life, maybe 80 hours a week, this was not easy. He knew that his system was a good system. I had people in tears who felt that you destroyed their life. And I couldn't imagine really that a research and development man can have such enormously strong emotions about his system, his solution. That was tough to handle, and some couldn't handle it.

The positive surprise for Barnevik was the enormous loyalty from managers who were not immediate 'winners' at the time of the merger:

There were two Belgian country managers, both good, and you had to put one in charge, the other had to be sales manager or the lobbying manager in Brussels. We had to try to accommodate both. Both were good, with a track record. The surprise was loyalty among the losers who didn't go out in the media badmouthing the company, disappointed and revengeful. There were many disappointed, but the loyalty of putting the company first among so many of them – that was really positive. And out of these terrible fights and all that internal work to get it settled in the first year, very little leaked out. Of course, in Mannheim with the union action that was visible publicly. But overcoming these internal difficulties really reflected tremendous loyalty among people. It was also satisfying to see how, increasingly, people from different camps came together in joint teams and developed real friendship.

What is Barnevik's greatest satisfaction looking back at the merger? He says:

It is difficult to pinpoint one event. The overriding satisfaction is that the big merger worked, that we succeeded in creating an ABB culture with the new ABB name and a global glue holding together these many nationalities and companies which joined in, including integrating the big American acquisitions and the new companies in Asia and Eastern Europe. As a result of that, the shareholders, who believed in us, were well rewarded: ABB AB shares growing 30 per cent per year 1980–96 against the Stockholm index of 23.5 per cent and ABB AG shares growing 22 per cent per year 1988–96 against the Zürich index of 14 per cent (see page 314 (Note 5) for the change in the parent company names and pages 306 to 311 for a closer look at ABB's share price performance).

As Barnevik says, ABB's success was not a foregone conclusion:

There were many people who said that you cannot really combine these nationalities and cultures. In Brown Boveri, they had been fighting between themselves – the Swiss, the Germans, the Italians and the French. There were stock exchanges in all these countries, they had local shareholders in the different companies whose minority rights should be protected. And then if you had the guys in Zürich saying that we should move these turbines from Italy to Germany because that is cheaper and better competitively for the Group, in Italy they said, 'Who the hell are you to run over the Italian shareholders? Why should they carry the burden for Germany?' There was a German BBC, there was the Swiss BBC, etc. So all of a sudden Scandinavians and Americans came along, not to mention East Europeans and Asians later. It was a huge task to forge it together, to build a common identity and to create that common glue so that we pulled in the same direction.

Multiculturalism is a practical, not an ethical, issue

Of course, the concept of getting nationalities together sometimes comes across as a dogma. For Barnevik, however, it is a practical issue and not something to be encouraged for its own sake:

It is not at all any advantage in itself to force Germans to work with Italians. The more people trust each other, know each other and there are no misunderstandings in language, the better. Most of us speak broken English. So why bother people with all this mixing nationalities? This is true for 95 per cent of teams. But I talk about the 5 per cent global people – those in the BA team for transformers worldwide, setting the charter for all countries. If you had five Germans sitting there in that global team without Scandinavian connections, without anyone who lived in America, nor any Asian experience, they would be extremely handicapped. They would be looked upon with a certain distrust. People would say, 'These guys only comprehend their own German colleagues' rather than having a global approach. In such a team, you have a tremendous advantage in having some Continentals, some Americans, some Scandinavians, some Asians, so that you have coverage, a global outlook, with all these inputs and all these informal networks.

Multiculturalism also makes it easier to rationalize production and gain acceptance for transferring technology into Asia, as the firm globalizes. Barnevik points to the example of ABB's Swedish transformer factory in Ludvika being replaced by ABB's factory in Thailand as the supplier to South East Asia. The Swedes naturally resisted as they were worried that quality would suffer and that the company would lose customers in important markets such as Malaysia. If, however, the Swedes can be linked with the Thais and persuaded to send out some managers to help the Thai factory improve its quality (by, for example, giving the Swedes a bonus based on the Thais' results), it makes the opposing Swedish plant 'suddenly proud of Thailand, seeing Thailand as a smaller brother, and being financially rewarded for it'. Barnevik says:

I do not make propaganda for mixing as a moral thing. It is just practicality. The Board of ABB, the Executive Committee of ABB, the global management teams – that is where you really have to get in mixed nationality teams.

What would Barnevik have done differently? He reflects:

Since speed has been such an extremely important ingredient both in my Sandvik and ASEA history and now ABB history, a number of mistakes were inevitable, for example, in people appointments. You tend to make more wrong decisions than if you took more time and know people better before you make appointments. Our slogan was not to behave like the old accountant who was 'rather exactly wrong than roughly right' (you have to use short, effective slogans so that people remember). You can come up with the perfect solution but then you are late and you are then wrong. If you make a mistake, you can always correct it. You have the right to make a mistake. The only thing people don't forgive you for is if you don't correct the mistake afterwards. So our consolation was that, although we made some wrong appointments, we corrected them. And those times when we waited to get a better decision, it was usually better to decide immediately. So, although we are considered fast, in those cases, we would have been faster.

Barnevik says that, in the course of putting the merger together and the years thereafter, there were also business misjudgments:

None of us in the late 1980s could dream that the demand for power in North America would completely collapse in the 1990s, leaving us with a lot of overcapacity after the CE acquisition. As regards speed in execution, I must, however, generally say that those times we postponed decisions to investigate more, I usually regret that we did not move even faster.

Flexibility versus forecasts in the 'age of uncertainty'

Barnevik's remarks on speed of execution and ABB's early US experience lead us to one of the important lessons to be learned from ABB when taken as a case study. This concerns the ability of organizations to forecast the future in today's complicated and fast-moving global business environment. In Chapter 3, we suggested that the basis of the master plan for ABB was a belief that the power market would recover in the mid 1990s. This was the basis for staying in the business and preparing to meet demand when it picked up. It has to be said that this turned out to be an overly optimistic view of the future, although the company believes that the emerging markets are moving in the right direction.

In particular, ABB believed that the potential of the US power market was so huge that the company had to take some important measures to establish itself strongly there. This was bolstered by a belief that the power stations were long overdue for replacement or refitting and that reinvestment stimulated by a Clean Air Act would take place within two years. This, too, ABB managers admit, was a miscalculation. When the US power industry deregulated, all investment stopped. One of the reasons for this was that, in the late 1980s, the power grids in the US were unconnected. Deregulation of the power industry has led to the connection of grids across the USA. Cheaper power from night-time Boston, for example, can be used in California. The result is overcapacity, so, for the time being, US utilities can live with old or obsolete power stations. ABB admits that it has therefore struggled with the US and has been forced to carry out a lot of restructuring. It still believes that the long-awaited re-equipment will take place, especially as the stations that were 30 years old in the late 1980s are now 45 years old, although this may not happen for some years yet.

The Combustion Engineering deal was also seen by some observers as too expensive. ABB managers admit that, because it was a stock deal, the company had to spend a lot of money and that it found some 'incredible black holes' in the balance sheet, but, they say, the critics have missed one point. ABB immediately divested half the purchase price. Out of Combustion Engineering also came ABB's oil and gas activities, which are now a $2 billion business, plus 'pull power' for over $1 billion worth of products to the oil and gas industry from other ABB units. Without Combustion Engineering, this $3 billion plus operation would not have happened in this way. ABB believes that the oil and gas sector will be a very important business for it in future and will give the company big opportunities. So, they say, even if it cost a lot, it was not necessarily a mistake to acquire it. After-the-event rationalization, of course, but probably true.

ABB in North America

Despite early setbacks, ABB's position in North America recovered with sustained economic growth in the late 1990s. So, ABB's major power acquisitions in the late 1980s and the penetration of industrial markets there, including oil and gas, make it well-positioned for the future. In the USA, ABB employs 21,400 people (plus over 2000 in Canada), more than 10 per cent of its total worldwide workforce, at 50 manufacturing facilities and more than 300 sales and service centres. Revenues of $4.1 billion in the US in 1997 accounted for 13 per cent of ABB's total worldwide revenues of $31.3 billion. By the late 1990s, ABB supplied some 40 per cent of utility boilers in the US, was the foremost supplier of power-transmission and distribution equipment, and was a leading supplier of industrial automation systems for process industries, such as paper and pulp, chemicals, pharmaceuticals and metals. Over 40 per cent of its products and services there were dedicated to environmental technologies and solutions. Exports made up 20 per cent of ABB's US revenues.

ABB has become a favourite case study in North America too, not just because of its staus as a global organization, but because of the way in which it has turned troubled businesses into profitable ABB subsidiaries. For example, the ABB Industrial Systems plant in Columbus, Ohio, has been described as having 'become a model of performance by creating a small-company culture that fosters speed, flexibility and creativity among employees' (Teresko, 1996). In 1996, *Industry Week* magazine named the Columbus plant one of 'America's Best' in a competition involving 170 plants across America. Another case study, that of the Ford-ABB Oakville Paint-Finishing Project in Canada, demonstrates ABB's approach to building closer and more effective relationships with customers (Frey and Schlosser, 1993).

References

Frey, Jr., Sherwood C., and Schlosser, Michel M. (1993) 'ABB and Ford: creating value through cooperation, *Sloan Management Review*, Fall, 65–72.

Teresko, John (1996) 'ABB industrial systems (America's best plants)', *Industry Week*, 21 October, **245** (19), 32–6.

One senior manager points to an advantage of ABB's US presence:

There was a small victory for us recently. The Chinese premier went to Bill Clinton to discuss lifting the embargo on nuclear power exports to China. He pleaded successfully for an opening up of such exports. Which American companies would be involved? GE does not have the right technology. So it is Westinghouse and ABB. We are really now classified as an American company. Our competitors try to stop this all the time.

We asked Percy Barnevik whether or not the adverse developments in the US power market could have been foreseen. He says:

In America you have 800,000 megawatt in power capacity roughly and they have historically had a 25 per cent safety margin for peak load demands. In electricity you cannot say to a customer 'I am sorry, I have to shut you off tomorrow'. You have to be absolutely sure that you can deliver, for example, when it is 100 degrees Fahrenheit and ACs are going at top speed. And that was so for decades and decades.

Then the 25 per cent became 10–15 per cent, over 10 years, because they improved trading with electricity, and when the independent power products came along, they squeezed more out of it. Privatization and deregulation created a mentality that led people to behave differently. Then they gave incentives to customers – if you use power during the night rather than the day, you get an even bigger discount than you got before. That whole change in behaviour meant that, all of a sudden, you had got more than 100,000 surplus megawatt capacity. I simplify it a little now but it meant, all of a sudden, you didn't need any more capacity. While they used to buy 20,000 megawatts a year, they were now buying 3000 or 4000 megawatts per year. It is like eight million cars would have been half a million cars a year in the US. Think about Chrysler, General Motors and Ford, what would they have done? So, to excuse myself, I should say that our competitors and our customers were in the same boat. I was sitting with Hydro Quebec and Ontario Hydro when they showed me their plan for the next ten years. They were buying a lot from us and others, and then they didn't buy. They were even handing back equipment for a while.

So, says Barnevik, what you learn from this is that you cannot really forecast the future but have to study early signals and react fast:

I remember in 1988, when we had our first management meetings, we spent in 2 days maybe 20 minutes on Eastern Europe, and then came those Hungarian border guards who cut down the barbed wire and the first small stream of East German tourists started to come out and then the whole thing collapsed in one year. Who could have forecast in 1988 the collapse of the real estate speculation bubble? In the West, who saw the financial collapse in the early 1990s? All those ruined people. Who saw the Asian crisis coming? There were a few voices but they were not very strong. It was the same in earlier times and you can joke about Mr Daimler, who said that there would never be more than 5000 cars in Europe because there would not be enough chauffeurs around. Or, take a more recent example – the Chairman of DEC said as late as 1976 that he never could see any reason why anybody would need a computer at home!

This teaches you, says Barnevik, that in the 'age of uncertainty', the answer is not better long-range planning, more experts or 'think tanks':

You have to be fast on your feet, you have to be flexible, you have to live close to the market, you have to catch signals early and you have to see breaks in trend lines. The history of business and industry is the history of people who saw changes early. Enron saw the possibility of private power ownership in Asia all of a sudden with owner-operated schemes, and they were early out there and captured that market, two to three years before anybody else in America. That's how business history is written, you see discontinuities early, and then it is a matter of getting your organization to adjust to it. And then it comes down to how you are organized? Are you organized so that you can change direction? Can you throw in resources, and adapt fast to a changing environment? The only real safeguard you have is to build in that

*speed in response. This, in turn, depends on creating a 'culture of change' that sup-
ports these values and employees with responsibilities, motivation, advancement
opportunities and the willingness to raise their competence. And a proactive top management is vital.*

The chief executive has a particular responsibility in keeping the organization
tuned to a changing environment. Said Barnevik while still CEO, 'One of my
most important tasks today is to see how the world is changing; not to do
patch-up work, but be proactive and be early out there and face reality in the
eye' (Skaria, 1995).

Strategic disruption – the restructuring of the power equipment industry

Being there early and facing reality in the eye was certainly the key to the ABB
merger. ABB's strategy has been described as that of a 'hypercompetitive' firm
that seeks to continually change the basis of competition in its industry and,
in particular, to strategically disrupt the competition by means of speed and
surprise. If this is the case, then one measure of ABB's success must be the
degree to which the merger brought about a fundamental restructuring of the
power equipment industry. On this dimension, there can be no doubt about
the success of the merger so far.

The creation of ABB – the 'bomb in the industry' – really started the ketchup
flowing and led, within two years, to an unprecedented industry-wide
restructuring and transformation of the international, and particularly the
European, power equipment industry. This restructuring and consolidation
continued throughout the 1990s. When the merger took place, the power
engineering industry still consisted largely of highly independent manufacturers operating within impermeable national borders. This has changed
considerably. The forces driving the change included a severe drop in demand
for power-generation equipment. The US market in particular was dormant for
years (we described above the impact on ABB itself). Nuclear programmes
came to a halt in many countries. The cost of product development increased
enormously. Traditional products no longer sufficed and new technology,
such as gas turbine-powered plant, became increasingly important.

The major restructuring initially took place in Europe. The aim of the major
players here was to form power bases in continental Europe with manufacturing and joint venture presence in the US. The big companies bought out
smaller power firms and suppliers across Europe, including most of the power
equipment industries of such countries as Italy, Belgium and Spain. Four
major groups emerged in Europe and North America. These were ABB, GEC-

Alsthom, Siemens and General Electric. In Europe, ABB became the biggest company, with GEC-Alsthom second and Siemens, until then the dominant European company in the industry, in third position.

When the ABB merger took place in 1987, only General Electric Company (GEC) of the UK and Alcatel-Alsthom of France took it at all seriously. As Barnevik's acquisition drive proceeded, however, the previously dominant players woke up and started to strike back. GE began to compete much more vigorously internationally. Siemens was at first absorbed by German reunification, but then started to copy the time-based competition methods of ABB, using its enormous financial resources to start a war of attrition. The result was a marked decline in prices in ABB's key segments in the mid 1990s. Let's look briefly at some of the players who emerged – or did not emerge – from the restructuring.

GEC-Alsthom (Alstom)

One of the most dramatic changes in the industry triggered by the ABB merger occurred when GEC, the UK's biggest power engineering company, merged its energy and heavy equipment business with Alsthom of France to form Europe's second-largest power business. In 1989, the new group tried to obtain a major presence in the US by acquiring Combustion Engineering's Boiler division, with which Alsthom had had close contacts for many years. The owners demanded too high a price for GEC-Alsthom, however, and ABB stepped in (as described in Chapter 4). While GEC-Alsthom had announced earlier in 1989 a big joint venture with CE this collapsed as CE changed sides to ABB. GEC-Alsthom showed strong growth up to the mid 1990s when, like other players in the power industry, it was hit by the increasing price competition. In 1996, GEC-Alsthom acquired the power and distribution business of AEG to create a third European 'leg' in Germany in addition to the UK and France. This made GEC-Alsthom both a significant industrial player in Germany and the second world leader in power transmission and distribution after ABB. After the acquisition of that part of AEG Elektrotechnik, GEC-Alsthom, unlike ABB, made no attempts to integrate immediately the German culture, and kept the powerful AEG brand for its German operation – the slogan was to beat ABB and become the world's number one in transmission and distribution.

The organizational structures of the two companies are also very different. ABB's matrix contrasts with the divisionalized organization of GEC-Alsthom. Unlike ABB's T50 and Customer Focus programmes, GEC-Alsthom had no global programmes for streamlining and rationalization. Nor, as noted by Christian Berggren, did GEC-Alsthom have national organizations and presidents like ABB, although in some important countries it appointed a general delegate, a high-ranking local national who reports directly to the CEO, takes care of political and government contacts and coordinates social and financial issues. Latterly, there are signs that GEC-Alsthom has been giving more attention to the geographical dimension of its business, formalizing a worldwide 'corporate network' of country presidents or resident directors present in 60 countries to support the product divisions. Is this a nod in the direction of multidomesticity *à la* ABB?

GEC-Alsthom was floated on the stockmarket in June 1998 and renamed Alstom. Some industry experts expected this to lead to further consolidation as, after the initial year when the two parents undertook to retain a substantial minority stake, the company would be open to possible purchase.

Siemens

Siemens was the leading power equipment supplier in Europe in the 1970s, but is now the third largest company. It was one of Germany's oldest and largest conglomerates and made everything from lightbulbs to power plants. Its power-generation, distribution and transmission businesses were initially left out of the industry restructuring. However, in 1989, Siemens merged marketing, sales and development of PWR nuclear reactors with Framatome of France to form a new company – Nuclear Power International (NPI). It also started to build up a US presence by looking for joint ventures and formed one for steam and gas turbines in India. Its power-transmission and distribution business was regarded as an industry underachiever by business observers. ABB's ruthless cost-cutting and its shift of production and marketing abroad produced a strong contrast with Siemens. ABB margins were nearly twice those of Siemens.

One of Siemens' biggest weaknesses is that it still has two thirds of its capacity in high-cost Germany. It had also had trouble pursuing some of its high-tech ambitions. Siemens has tried to recast itself as a dynamic company open to change in pursuit of higher profitability and greater shareholder value, but its size – 386,000 employees generating $60 billion in sales – is said to have stifled entrepreneurial initiative. Siemens has therefore been criticized for its inability to react to changing markets or to turn round underperforming units. One observer called Siemens 'a slow-moving giant' and warned that time was running out for the company (Lowry Miller, 1996).

In 1997, Siemens bought a smaller UK engineering company – Parsons Power Engineering Systems – from its Rolls-Royce parent. Later that year, it acquired the non-nuclear power generation business of Westinghouse. At the same time, the company shed nearly $3 billion of activities, including its defence technology and dental technology units. It also invested heavily in reorganizing unprofitable units, including its transportation systems. In 1998, Siemens sold most of its personal computer business – Siemens-Nixdorf (SNI),

Europe's last remaining large-scale personal computer business – to Acer – the Taiwanese computer company seeking to tap Siemens' European knowledge. Some analysts questioned whether the deal was sufficient. Said one, 'Siemens has proved itself a slow player in comparison to other international companies such as an ABB or a Philips' (Crampton, 1998).

Westinghouse

ABB bought Westinghouse's power-transmission and distribution business in 1989. Despite excellent industrial technologies and a reputation for hiring and developing excellent people, the latter were bound by an authoritarian structure. By the early 1990s, Westinghouse had, said one observer, 'fallen victim to an insular organization and a befuddled senior management' (*The Economist*, 1997). A new CEO brought in during 1993 waged one of the most extensive restructuring campaigns in US corporate history, selling off businesses and investing heavily in its media subsidiary, acquiring various US broadcasting networks. Abandoning a plan to split the company into two, however, it announced that, at the end of 1997, it would become a media firm known only as CBS Corporation, the television network that the company bought in 1995. The rest of the firm's industrial business would be sold in pieces. The 111–year-old Westinghouse Electric Corporation would cease to exist.

General Electric

With CE taken over by ABB, and Westinghouse having pulled out of the industry, GE was the last bastion of independence in the US power-engineering industry.

ABB certainly regards GE as a very formidable competitor. It is the third most profitable company in the world after oil companies Royal Dutch/Shell and Exxon and was the world's most valuable in terms of market capitalization ($254 billion in 1998, up from $100 billion in 1995) until overtaken by Microsoft in 1998. GE also moved into Eastern Europe by buying Tungsram, a lighting manufacturer, from the Hungarian government in 1990, although its investments were not as extensive as those of ABB. In the early 1990s, GE took advantage of the recession in Europe, purchasing $17 billion of assets there. GE itself is much more diversified than ABB, with businesses in aircraft engines, major domestic appliances, information services, media, engineering plastics, lighting, rail transportation, medical systems and financial services in addition to its industrial and power systems business. In the late 1990s, a major contributor to GE's profits was its jet engine business, which was thriving on the boom in airlines' purchases of planes. GE's jet engine technology also enabled it to build a range of very successful smaller gas turbines, which were able to avoid some of the cost pressures in other parts of the power market.

Percy Barnevik is often compared to GE's CEO Jack Welch, who has been attempting a similar corporate makeover in the US firm, aiming to create a 'boundaryless' company by removing the vertical boundaries of the hierarchy and knocking down the internal walls that separate functions. Welch also tried to revitalize and animate GE by simplifying communications, stripping out excess bureaucracy and trying to free people up to be creative. Percy Barnevik says of GE:

> You will find a lot of similarities with what Jack Welch is doing and his philosophy of small groups and the globalization of the company. I think there are a lot of similarities between what is happening in ABB and General Electric in areas like small and big organizations, innovation, speed, entrepreneurship, and flexibility. Sometimes, if you compare Welch's speech with mine, one is not too sure who wrote which one (Skaria, 1995).

GE has also been expanding in Asia and has set up a regional headquarters there. CEO Jack Welch will retire in 2000 and there has been a lot of speculation about the impact his retirement will have on the company.

ABB's responses to its competitors

Against this competitive background, ABB has restructured the profile of its businesses, the most evident outward change in ABB. The business is now more focused with (until the 1998 reorganization) three core industrial business segments:

- power generation, constructing power plants and complementary systems;
- power transmission and distribution, dealing with problems connected to the distribution of power;
- industrial and building systems, producing a range of industrial products and systems, among them fast-growing process automation, instrumentation and robots.

Financial services, which provides financial support to the other segments and to external customers, formed a fourth segment. In the three power and industry segments, ABB reduced the number of BAs from 50 to less than 40. It also merged its transportation activities with those of Daimler-Benz to form a 50/50 joint venture called Adtranz.[1]

Another restructuring of the business segments in 1998 (described in more detail in Chapter 10) sought to make fast-growing non-power businesses such as automation and oil and gas more visible to investors.

Making direct financial comparisons between the different firms in the electrotechnical industry is not easy. In 1996, GE posted an operating return on sales of 13.9 per cent, including its huge financial services business. Siemens' pre-tax return on sales was 3.5 per cent. ABB's operating margin was 6.3 per cent. The electrotechnical industry has been getting even tougher for the survivors. While the cost of building a new power plant averaged $1,000 per kilowatt in the early 1990s, the cost had dropped by 1998 to only $400. This not only means cost-cutting, it also means further consolidation in an industry that is still suffering from huge overcapacity in power-generation and transmission equipment. Some observers suggested that only GE and ABB are actually making any money in power-generating equipment – and that on huge revenues and very small margins. GE itself announced late in 1997 that it would restructure some of its operations, including power systems. The price war in the industry was expected to lead to further dramatic industry consolidation in the late 1990s. How does ABB feel about this situation? One senior ABB executive told us, 'It will not be easy. We can't lean back on experience. There will be new constellations. We triggered the GEC-Alsthom merger and more will happen. GE and the Japanese are on the move.'

What might the new constellations be? ABB managers do not expect to see ABB make any big moves, but it has pulled off some other dramatic coups in the years since the merger – Combustion Engineering and Adtranz, for example. So watch this space.

We are racing ahead here. One of the reasons why ABB has become the world's favourite case study has been the attention attracted by its high degree of decentralization, its multidomestic strategy and its unique global matrix structure. Let's take a closer look at how ABB's strategy and structure have developed over the past ten years and how this has translated into financial performance.

Note

1 A significant change occurred in ABB's transportation business. At the time of the merger, railway equipment was a fragmented industry with countries able to support one or more national champions, some of which were State-owned. This changed when European rules demanded the opening of national markets and national railway companies also started to move responsibility for design and project management to the private sector. The resulting consolidation in the industry led to the emergence of three large European groups – ABB and competitors GEC-Alsthom and Siemens.

Percy Barnevik had always said that further consolidation in the European railway equipment industry was necessary. At the beginning of 1996, ABB merged its railway activities with the railway activities of Daimler-Benz's AEG subsidiary in Adtranz – ABB Daimler-Benz Transportation – to form the world's largest railway transportation company, with worldwide sales of $6 billion and total worldwide staff of 22,000 in 40 countries. This created a clear world leader with critical mass in the industry and effectively removed a large competitor. The merger made Adtranz some 40 per cent larger than the railway businesses of its two main rivals, Siemens and GEC-Alsthom.

Daimler-Benz had originally purchased AEG, a proud name in the German engineering industry, as part of a strategy of transforming itself into a diversified group covering aerospace, electrical engineering and information technology, as well as the core activity of cars. However, ever since Daimler-Benz had bought it, AEG had been a loss maker. Adtranz aimed to aggressively seek new markets by building a new generation of trains and locomotives. ABB no longer has any operational influence over the railway business. The company's headquarters are in Berlin with international group coordination centres in Brussels and Zürich. Adtranz is present in 60 countries and has 8 plants in Germany. It has been shifting jobs to lower-pay countries such as Poland and Hungary, where it had recently acquired operations.

Percy Barnevik said that he hoped the Adtranz merger would kick off a much-needed round of restructuring in the overcrowded railway equipment sector. For the German company, the move was an important step towards the internationalization of Daimler. Competition continues to be tough in the industry in general and the 1990s have seen major restructuring to reduce capacity and improve efficiency. While Adtranz posted a pre-tax profit of 40.5 million Deutschemarks, ($24.3 million) when it first released annual results in March 1997, at the end of that year, it announced that it, too, was to restructure to reduce costs and intended to cut 3600 jobs, most of them in its German operations, its largest single subsidiary employing 8000 people. The German operations had posted losses since the creation of Adtranz. 'We cannot guarantee any activity or any plant any more', said a company spokesman.

Adtranz has been affected by lower-than-expected earnings from cost-cutting, increasing price pressure, intense competition and overcapacity in its European operations. For 1997 as a whole, Adtranz recorded a $111 million loss, including its share of the restructuring charges. With the railway business predicted to move back into profit in 1998, it was expected that the merger and the major restructuring programme would start to bring the desired advantages from 1998 onwards. ABB has said that it is committed to the transportation business for the long term and believes in it.

References

Quotes without references originate from the authors' personal communications – see page xviii for details.

Arbose, Jules (1988) 'ABB: The new energy powerhouse', *International Management*, June, 24–30.
Berggren, Christian (1996) 'Building a truly global organization? ABB and the problems of integrating a multi-domestic enterprise', *Scandinavian Journal of Management*, **12** (2), 123–37.
Brown, Andrew (1994) 'Top of the bosses', *International Management*, April, **49** (3), 26–32.
Crampton, Thomas (1998) 'Acer to buy Siemens' PC plant', *International Herald Tribune*, 24 April, 13.
Klebnikov, Paul (1991) 'The powerhouse', *Forbes*, 2 September, 46–50.
Latour, Almar and Steinmetz, Greg (1998) 'Swedish massage', *Wall Street Journal Europe*, 18 May, 1 and 9.
Lowry Miller, Karen (1996) 'Siemens: Why there's still no payoff', *Business Week*, 30 December, 21.
Skaria, George (1995) 'Interview with Percy Barnevik', *Business Today* (India), 22 February–6 March, 100–5.
The Economist (1997) 'Westinghouse RIP', 29 November, 91–3.

C H A P T E R

The payback from multidomesticity

The key difference in future will be the pace of change. Things have changed in the world before, but what is fascinating now is that today's changes are happening so fast. By the year 2010, the biggest home markets for ABB will include China and India, right up there with Germany and the US. Russia, Indonesia and Brazil will also work their way up to the top rankings. These changes will happen so quickly and will be of such a large scale that they will dwarf the developments in Western Europe on which we focus so much of our attention today.

Percy Barnevik

Just look at the global spread of ABB's business shown below. What's the story behind this impressive global portfolio of contracts?

The global spread of ABB's business

A sample of ABB press releases.

4 March 1996   ABB forms joint venture to manufacture district heating systems in China.

13 March 1996   ABB wins orders to supply equipment for repowering Siberian plant.

23 April 1996   ABB wins clean-coal power plant order for Germany.

14 June 1996   ABB opens greenfield factory for power-generation equipment in Indonesia.

18 June 1996   ABB wins order to modernize cogeneration power plant in Poland.

27 June 1996	ABB wins order for turnkey thermal power plant in Colombia.
2 July 1996	ABB wins New Zealand order for advanced gas turbine.
16 July 1996	ABB awarded second boiler contract for Indonesian private power project.
6 August 1996	ABB wins turnkey order to develop natural gas resources and build power complex in Peru.
13 August 1996	ABB builds India's first operational private power plant.
22 August 1996	ABB acquires electrical manufacturing company in Bulgaria.
17 September 1996	ABB expands electrical equipment business in southern Africa.
3 October 1996	ABB consortium wins railway electrification contract in Greece.
7 February 1997	ABB consortium to build 775 megawatt combined cycle power plant in Argentina.
19 March 1997	ABB announces second joint venture in Vietnam to produce advanced switchgear and distribution transformers.
12 April 1997	ABB plans to invest $750 million in core industries in the Philippines over the next 4 years.
12 August 1997	ABB acquires major switchgear company, ZWAR, in Poland.
2 September 1997	ABB and consortium partner Foster Wheeler Pyropower of the USA are to refurbish coal-fired power plant in Poland.
12 September 1997	ABB begins construction of turnkey 700 megawatt private power pant in Morocco.
30 September 1997	ABB receives $500 million contract to build ethylene plant in Saudi Arabia.
7 October 1997	ABB receives $700 million order to build a 1500 megawatt power plant from National Power PLC of the UK.
21 January 1998	ABB wins a $660 million order to build a power plant in Taiwan.
21 January 1998	ABB consortium wins $190 million orders to design, build and operate Massachusetts power plant.
26 January 1998	ABB receives $170 million order to upgrade Michigan gas-fired power plant.

26 January 1998	ABB financial services and operating units team up on $63 million Mexican power-transmission and distribution project.
24 March 1998	ABB establishes major power transformer joint venture in China.
2 April 1998	ABB wins major order for power and desalination plant in Abu Dhabi.
2 April 1998	$3.2 million turnkey substation project in Key West, Florida won by US unit of ABB.
7 April 1998	Brazilian utility companies give contracts worth $170 million to ABB to link power grids in the northern and southern sections of the country.
22 April 1998	ABB awarded $160 million contract for North Sea subsea oil installations.
29 April 1998	ABB wins $250 million order for turnkey power plant in Mexico.
19 May 1998	ABB wins $280 million order for power link between Argentina and Brazil.
8 September 1998	ABB signs long-term cooperation agreement with Gazprom of Russia.
5 October 1998	ABB wins £350 million turnkey order for gas-fired power plant in the US.

Looking back over the decade since 1988, the development of ABB's strategy and structure can be divided into two phases:

- **1988–93** the multidomestic phase, when the emphasis was on decentralization and creating a local presence around the world;
- **1993 onwards** the global phase, when, while multidomesticity remains important and the company continues to expand into emerging economies, the emphasis has been on regional and global integration. From 1998, global integration becomes the dominant theme.

We look first at how the multidomestic dimension of ABB has worked out and at the benefits that the establishment of a strong local presence around the world has brought.

ABB leads the way in emerging markets

In 1995, ABB added another award to its list of honours when Percy Barnevik was named one of the two winners of the 'Emerging Markets CEO of the Year' (awarded by ING Bank and International Media Partners). This was an award for 'the chief executive of a company headquartered in the developed world whose expansion into emerging markets has best shown how these markets can contribute significantly to corporate revenues and profitability, and has benefited the countries involved.' Barnevik's citation was for having shown clear and strong leadership among industrialized companies in investing in emerging markets. While competitors followed more conservative investment strategies during the economic slowdown in 1988–90, ABB streamlined its operations in the major OECD countries and embarked on an expansion into Eastern Europe and Asia, in the former, converting previously State-owned enterprises into high-performance, low-cost 'industrial islands'. The citation also referred to ABB's strong investment in research and development and to its commitment to increasing the energy efficiency and lowering the emissions from its many infrastructure projects. These attributes not only made the company's investments in emerging markets more profitable, but also more environmentally sustainable.

Many ABB managers take pride in the way that ABB has participated in transferring wealth and technology to emerging markets and feel that this is very much something that distinguishes it from some of its competitors (see Tables 9.1 and 9.2. According to Percy Barnevik, the reason that the number of employees in Table 9.1 grows faster than sales is that the *added value* increases maybe ten times during this period.). Unlike other companies that import from other countries, ABB will build locally to develop the infrastructure there wherever this is appropriate. We have asked all the ABB managers we have met what they think constitutes ABB's real competitive advantage. Their answer is invariable. 'We are better at being local faster than the competition,' says David Hunter, former Head of Central and Eastern Europe, 'We are more comfortable with it'. Bengt Skantze, who has also worked in ABB's previous European regional management, enlarges:

The products must be right but that doesn't differentiate you any longer – all companies now have good products, although you still have to put a lot of effort into developing good products. The thing that really distinguishes us is our local presence, including a lot of small offices. It has given us advantages in many markets. We are the most internationally present group in our business.

227

Table 9.1 ABB's growth in emerging markets (overall figures)

Measures	1988	1997
Number of employees	20,000	70,000
Number of companies	100	300
Revenues (US$)	3 billion	8 billion

Source: ABB

Table 9.2 ABB's growth in emerging markets 1988–97 (individual market figures)

	1988		1997	
Countries	Number of employees	Number of companies	Number of employees	Number of companies
Czech Republic	5	0	5759	9
Poland	12	0	7738	13
Indonesia	37	1	1960	5
Romania	2	0	1449	4
Russia	7	0	1462	19
Turkey	334	1	750	2
Thailand	240	1	3739	5
Malaysia	212	4	880	7
India	3950	2	9630	10
China	249	2	4168	21

Source: ABB

The 'new Swiss' of Central and Eastern Europe

In ABB's first annual report in 1988, there was no mention of Central or Eastern Europe. Now, including minority interests, ABB has some 90 or more companies in 23 countries, including the Commonwealth of Independent States. It has some 30,000 employees, including 11,000 in Poland and 7000 in the Czech Republic. It has acquired or started activities in Romania, the Ukraine, Bulgaria, Slovenia, Kazakhstan and Uzbekistan and consolidated its businesses in Poland, the Czech Republic, Russia and Hungary. Orders received from the region have grown from $200 million in 1989 to $2 billion – 10 per cent of total European orders. It expects to double the order volume by the year 2000, if the region remains stable and progress in economic reform continues. In 1989, ABB obtained $50 million in components from Eastern Europe. By 1996, this figure was up six or seven times and ABB was expecting that figure soon to reach $700 million. Eastern Europe has not only helped ABB to reduce production costs, but has contributed to new product development (by, for example, helping ABB to manufacture more efficient large gas turbines through original jet engine technology from Uniturbo, a Russian joint venture).

Other companies have followed ABB into the region, but ABB is unique in the extent of its commitment. Dariusz Karwacki, General Manager of ABB Dolmel in Poland, told *Fortune* magazine in 1994, 'The other companies have focused mainly on the market opportunities. Only Barnevik has seen production potential here too' (Hofheinz, 1994). Percy Barnevik said, 'Gone is the era when Western Europe and North America were ABB's natural home bases. Poland and the Czech Republic have global product development responsibilities and are supporting newly acquired companies in Russia, Ukraine and Central Asia' (Moss, 1996).

Eberhard von Koerber, until recently President of ABB Europe, describes ABB's achievements:

> *Eastern enlargement has already been a success for ABB. In our global approach to business, we no longer differentiate between Eastern and Western Europe. ABB's Europe combines its resources in Portugal, Switzerland and Germany with those in Poland, Bulgaria and Russia to compete in the world economy. Thanks to enlargement, ABB Europe is much stronger now than it was in 1988, and the ABB Group is more competitive* (von Koerber, 1997).

Table 9.3 Revenues and employees per region (%), 1997

Regions	Revenues (%)	Employees (%)
Europe	55	65
The Americas	20	15
Asia/Middle East and Africa	25	20

Source: ABB Annual Report 1997

Poland was the first and fastest development programme in Central and Eastern Europe and has been a particularly successful story for ABB. ABB's original acquisitions there started to reach Western quality and productivity standards within 18 months. Within just 4 years, ABB's Polish operations were generating $220 million of revenues and were making a small profit on sales within Poland and on exports. ABB was selling Polish-made gas turbines in the US and using Polish-made high-voltage switchgear, turbine blades, rotors and other products in sophisticated power plant equipment assembled in Germany and Switzerland at half the cost of products wholly manufactured in Western factories.

Now, with more than 10,000 people including joint ventures on the payroll in Poland, it is by far the biggest operation in the region with close to $500 million in business, having started with $40 million. Order intake grew from $48 million in 1990 to $700 million in 1997. In the same period, ABB Polska's exports grew from $10 million to $200 million. A 1997 article in *Newsweek* calls the workers of Central and Eastern Europe 'the new Swiss', and describes how investment and jobs are migrating from West to East as big Western multinationals and small companies discover a combination of both high quality and low costs (Nagorski and Engel, 1997). Workers and managers in all sorts of industries there are working at anywhere from one tenth to one fifth of the pay of their counterparts in Western Europe. One of ABB's Polish managers, head of a rotor production unit in ABB's generator factory in Wrocław, showed *Newsweek* magazine the certificates awarded by his parent company that testify his products meet the same tough standards as those produced in ABB's Western plants: 'They show that we can do our job as well as the Swiss,' he says proudly. A technician at the Wrocław plant told *Newsweek*, 'Our mentality has completely changed. Before, we just put in our time. Now we see the link between what we produce and the state of our wallets.'

ABB has also played an active role as a 'good citizen' in the community. ABB Zamech, for example, provided medical equipment to a local hospital, helped to create a medical foundation and donated computer equipment to the local police department. Rolf Leppänen, a former ABB manager from Finland, notes, 'This type of communal activity was typical big company behaviour in Finland and Sweden 20–30 years ago and earlier, but has diminished significantly in the 1980s and 1990s with the end of "life employment" and restructuring. In Poland it is a powerful way to build trust between the community and the company' (Leppänen, 1994).

ABB uses Poland as a showcase to convince other East European companies about the benefits of joining ABB. When officials at the Nevskii Zavod power plant in St Petersburg hesitated to sign a deal with ABB, it flew them to see its operations in Poland. They talked with their future Polish colleagues and were impressed with how much local control ABB gave them. As a result, Nevskii Zavod signed up with ABB. Said General Director Vladimir Turkin, 'ABB was ready to give our people the opportunity to work. That is what set them apart from other investors' (Hofheinz, 1994).

To what does ABB owe its success in Eastern Europe? Percy Barnevik has said that success in the region depends on treating people as an 'enormous asset' while at the same time insisting that they achieve the same high standards of productivity and quality achieved by ABB in the West: 'It's very important that you don't start to see these companies as inferior, a sort of B-team. We make no Polish discounts – or any other discounts' (McClenahen, 1994). This, in turn, depends on investing heavily in training and development. Eberhard von Koerber states that one of the most important lessons learned in Central and Eastern Europe is the value of transferring know-how:

> *We say that our investments in know-how transfer have been more important to our business success in these areas than our investment in plant and equipment. Our*

experience in Poland has borne this out. Encouraging the entrepreneurial spirit in our Polish employees, giving them the business management tools and responsibility for bottom line results, showing them the benefits of our focus on speed and delivering greater customer value, have been the keys to our success there (von Koerber, 1996).

David Hunter, ABB's former country manager for Poland, commissioned a Polish university professor to make a study of the restructuring carried out by ABB in Poland to identify what had worked and what had been less successful. The study involved 1000 interviews throughout ABB's Polish operations. It was found that, in answer to the overall question, 'What is the score card for ABB?', the 'bottom line' was on the positive side in all cases. ABB had created a sense of urgency from top to bottom. The study showed that it was partly due to enthusiasm for new technology and new management approaches and partly, admittedly, due to fear – people could be fired for the first time in their lives. A negative finding was that, in turning the organization upside down, ABB had destroyed the existing culture in the organization – the company radio programme, the newsletters, previously existing informal relationships. 'Before,' says David Hunter, 'the Managing Director was the godfather who made all the decisions and everyone else did what he said. We had destroyed the culture and had not yet replaced it with a new culture.' The study also showed that in Zamech, its biggest acquisition, ABB scored high marks. According to David Hunter, 'A Polish team ran the restructuring. We didn't succeed in driving the restructuring deep enough, however. We concentrated on the top and were not getting the message all the way down.'

The study showed that in one acquisition – ABB Elta in Łodz (see page 122) – ABB had delayed too long in changing the existing general manager. The clear opinion from the interviews was that it is very important to make a change in top management immediately. David Hunter elaborates:

It doesn't matter whether the new management is local or foreign as long as it has a vision for the company and what must be done. People will tend to say 'Ideally, we would like one of us to run it, but if not, that's OK. Don't worry about continuity because the culture has been destroyed and we know the previous manager does not have power.' So we knew we had to get the message down and the consultants out.

The lessons from the study have not been made widely available in ABB, however – perhaps because they are 'too controversial'. Hunter says, 'There is a company saying, "If ABB knew what ABB knows, it would be unbeatable."'

ABB believes that the key to competitiveness is education and re-education. The challenge is for employees to move up the ladder of education and technology. You have to offer every worker a career. With this philosophy of education and career development in mind, in 1995 ABB opened a management training centre at Falenty near Warsaw (see page 327). David Hunter is obviously very proud of Falenty:

We advertised the centre and Polish politicians came through to see it on the opening day – we flew the Polish, Swedish and Swiss flags. It helped that we were seen to be spending significant money on training. It is a real facility, not a floating crap game. It is the only one, the only centre like it, in ABB. It is the only real campus.

In 1996, ABB recognized Poland and highlighted its commitment to Eastern Europe by choosing it as the location for its annual world conference at which it announced its results for 1995. This was a message to both Poland and the rest of the group. The event was attended by ABB managers from many of the countries in which ABB was operating and by some 230 journalists that ABB flew in for the occasion. The following year, as a further mark of the progress that ABB's Polish operations had made and the important position they now held in the group, ABB held a press conference in Poland, during which Percy Barnevik announced that ABB's ninth research centre would be set up in Krakow in southern Poland. He informed customers that ABB intended to put real high-tech roots in Poland based on local customers' needs, not just the needs of customers abroad.

The only thing left to do, says David Hunter, was to turn the operation over to the Poles, which it did in 1996 when it appointed a local Polish executive, Mirosław Gryszka, as country manager. Iwona Jarzębska, Director of ABB's Falenty management centre in Poland, describes the reaction of ABB's Polish employees: 'It is very important for us in Poland that ABB has now appointed a Pole as the country manager. It shows that they trust us and it is something we really appreciate.' As yet, only two other Poles are known to hold country manager positions in major multinational companies operating in Poland. 'Four years ago, Poles were not ready to take on positions of such responsibility,' says Gryszka, a long-serving manager at Zamech, 'That will change in the years to come' (Latour, 1997).

The Czech Republic is also a success for ABB. Most of its companies there are now profitable, despite a temporary hiccup in the largest company in 1997. It is a smaller market than Poland – $300 million revenues and some 6000 employees, although ABB has a higher market penetration in the Czech Republic than Poland. ABB is now also looking for growth in Romania. David Hunter says:

I would like to see ABB develop here in a similar way to Poland as the economy develops. The country operations are profitable. We need now to make some strategic moves to acquire some companies there in the near future. We can look forward to growth. It will not be as big as Poland but it will be as big as the Czech Republic for us.

In Hungary, ABB has 3 plants and some 600 employees. The Head of ABB's gas turbine factory in Budapest said, 'Even the simplest workers understand that they are part of one of the world's top companies' (Hofheinz, 1994).

Poland, the Czech Republic and Hungary are historically oriented towards continental Europe. ABB's biggest challenges in the region probably lie in Russia and the Ukraine, where it has not yet reached a critical mass and which are, as Barnevik has said, 'another ball game'. ABB believes that it has some good young local managers in Russia, but it has not yet developed the same business volume and sustainability that it has in Poland. It believes, none the less, that growth will come in the near future. David Hunter says:

> The biggest challenge is to sustain growth in the CIS and make the business prof-itable in the face of pretty confusing business conditions. We have to adapt our way of thinking and doing business, but they must change too. It has to be a mutual process. We have to monitor the transformation there and grow the business with it. We went into Russia based on our Polish experience but it hasn't worked yet. The economy hasn't taken off. The Ukraine is even further behind.

Hunter is nevertheless convinced that Russia and the Ukraine will come right.

Percy Barnevik also predicts that Russia will be one of the six or seven biggest countries in ABB in the long term. He says, 'To succeed in Russia, you have to like the Russians . . . If you don't like the Russians, if you can't create friends there, then you're not the right person to work there' (Hofheinz, 1996a). Many Western firms have been deterred from investing because of the country's perceived instability.

Barnevik is impatient with this stance. He admits that the recent instability in Russia may delay the growth even further. He says that ABB's strategy to go for brain power which can be used internationally, rather than local bricks and mortar, makes the company less vulnerable to reduction in local demand. The area of focus is oil and gas and here the Russians can pay in hard currency from what they export. Overall ABB's investments in Russia are only some 15–20 per cent of the investments in Poland.

> If you want to wait for a Western-style country, then you will have to wait for a long, long time – and then you will probably miss the boat . . . If you want to invest in Russia, you must do it long term. And I mean really long term . . . Rather than wait-ing for some imaginary future stability, you have to learn how to live in that society. But it is getting better. And the sooner you make your investments, the better off you will be – if you are ready to do it in the right way. If you are like some people who parachute in and come to the Embassy and quarrel about this and that, the Embassy can't help you. It doesn't help to talk about how much worse it is to do business in Russia than in Italy or America. You have to have the willingness to adapt and live with a different society than you're used to. But the rewards are huge if you do it right and long term. I am convinced of it (Hofheinz, 1996a).

ABB's principles for making activities in Russia work are similar to its approach in other countries (Hofheinz, 1996):

- **select the top management** use the younger people who are not too stuck in the old mentality;
- **introduce a massive training programme** send some of them to the West to work in the home company;
- **reorganize and pare down headquarters** into profit centres with new accounting and information systems;
- **carry out process re-engineering and provide new technologies** including computers and information systems – don't just give them 'know-how', make sure they 'know why' and tie them into ABB's laboratories so they become a part of ABB's global technology bank;
- **Create an incentive system** to motivate people and so that they know that, if they do a good job, they will be well rewarded.

ABB is also investing in the Central Asian republics ('another world again', says Barnevik), which it thinks have tremendous potential in oil and gas resources. Percy Barnevik has acknowledged that he is impatient with the pace of change in some countries and has said that change in Russia to a more stable situation could take up to five years. To arrive at a Western style market economy may take 20 to 30 years. But he has added, 'As long as you make steady progress, even slow, you have to live with that.'

ABB has modified its policies somewhat as it has expanded in Central and Eastern Europe. For example, one of the biggest problems that it faced when buying new companies there was surplus labour. It admits that it learned about this the hard way. It has found that most companies have twice or even three times as many people as they will need within just a few years of ABB-style restructuring. It is now reluctant to lay off people, knowing that this hurts ABB's reputation and that when somebody is made unemployed in the region, they have no protection outside the company and are doomed, very often, to real poverty. Latterly, the company has said that it will not buy a company where it sees a large labour surplus that it cannot engage. It may be possible to use the surplus people by bringing in new products or even by expanding existing product lines and selling more domestically and externally, although this may mean living with the surplus until quality improves and exports take off.

In Russia, ABB has also modified its policy of not taking minority positions in companies. This is decided on a case-by-case basis. Percy Barnevik says:

When you have someone you work a lot with in joint projects, I think it helps if we have a stake in them and support them. If you have an important supplier that you rely on a lot, and you're working with them to get quality up, it is natural that you take a stake there. Normally, the cost of doing that is not exorbitant. For $3 million, or $10 million or so, you can get a good position in the company. Then again, we have a certain desire to be a part of the establishment in Russia, to get onto the [cor-

porate] Boards, to have Board memberships so we can be part of discussions about the future (Hofheinz, 1996a).

As well as helping the firm to become a better partner, taking a monetary stake in a partner also confirms ABB's interest in them.

Win-win with Eastern Europe

David Hunter's move from country manager to regional management changed his perspective:

> *Being close to the BAs and the head of the power generation segment, I am a lot more involved and know more about the priorities and problems at the Group level. I can now see that things that come out of Zürich make more sense; I can now see the other point of view.*

For example, the Polish set-up has reached the point where it has to trim the operation to improve productivity. As Hunter says, it used to be:

> *'grow, grow, grow,' but now personnel costs are going up faster than productivity. If we let it get out of hand, it will damage productivity. The wage gaps between the Germans and the Poles are closing – the Germans are making a lot of improvements to get productivity – they are cutting the number of people and are catching up. We have to keep one eye on internal benchmarking.*

David Hunter worries, however, that ABB still has 'a long way to go to improve the transfer of technology between the traditional exporting countries and the developing countries.' He says:

> *We must become the best of the best. We have to improve our ability to make synergy. The technology 'giver' could be a German company when we start up a new company in the Ukraine. But it has no financial interest in this new company whose shares are owned by the local ABB company or an offshore custodian. Nothing accrues on the German company's balance sheet except perhaps licence fees. This is not always enough. It is a kind of giving process. They have to hope and expect that later conditions will improve for doing business together – either by the Ukraine company selling components to the German company or by giving a local presence that gives ABB an advantage over Siemens, etc. in a big project. Our biggest internal challenge is to become better at this process of giving and appreciating that a strong local presence can be a win-win situation. And also accepting that there will be a few situations where the giver won't be rewarded.*

One barrier to technology transfer has been the fear by Western employees of transfer of jobs to the East. 'People say it comes from the unions,' says Hunter. 'I don't think so. It is not so much a union problem. It is much more likely that it comes from middle management. Middle management is responsible for the fear factor.' Hunter's role up until recently as Head of Central and Eastern Europe, was to persuade people that ABB's operations in Eastern Europe are of benefit to the whole Group:

We should talk about win–win. It is not a zero–sum game. My job is to convince people that getting business in Eastern Europe is good for business in Baden and Mannheim. The stronger you get locally, the bigger chance you have to pull in business and develop the export potential from the big countries – Germany, Sweden, Switzerland, etc.

He gives two examples.

- **A large power plant rehabilitation project in Turow, south-west Poland, in the so-called 'Black Triangle'.** Says Hunter:

    If we didn't have Zamech, we would have lost that business because the Swiss had no real feel for how to deal with the customer. With Zamech's help, they got the business because Zamech knew how to make the moves. More contracts will follow and it should amount to $1 billion over 8–9 years – due to the fact that ABB had a local presence.

- **A new locomotive project.** The Polish government privatized the only large rolling stock manufacturer in Poland in 1995. ABB – and then Adtranz, its railway joint venture with Daimler-Benz – offered to buy the company, even though it was bankrupt, on condition that Poland made a big order for large locomotives. It was one of the longest, most complicated negotiations that Hunter says he has ever been involved in:

    Getting the Polish government and the Polish railway company to agree was very hard – $200 million was just the first part of the project. It established Adtranz as the number one supplier and pulled in work for the Germans, Swiss and Italians. Some content was sourced in Poland, but 60 per cent of the content was imported from outside.

Enlargement to the East – a decisive moment for Europe's future

ABB's managers in Central and Eastern Europe are proud of their contribution to the region's economic development, but point out that ABB is only one company. Hunter is adamant that Western Europe as a whole could do a lot more to promote prosperity in Central and Eastern Europe and should forget about 'temporary dislocations':

It should take the longer view. The average GDP per capita is less than $2000 in Central and Eastern Europe. Portugal has average GDP per capita of $10,000–11,000. If they reached Portugal's level now, it would be a huge boost to business. Central and Eastern Europe are now the biggest trade partner of the EU. If *we maintain trade patterns and grow GDP there, the trade potential would be bigger than the economy of Germany and its GDP. It will be huge. It could be accounting software and not transformers, of course, but it will still be big.*

How do you convince people to think like this? 'Argue, argue, argue. Persuade, persuade, persuade. The situation is much better than it was three or four years ago,' declares Hunter. 'The trend is positive, but it is not happening fast enough for me.'

ABB points to the fact that in its Agenda 2000, the European Commission concludes that an enlarged European Union internal market, with up to 500 million consumers compared to 370 million at present, will create substantial new output and employment opportunities. Liberalized markets, common regulations and standards and, ultimately, a common currency should encourage a more efficient allocation of resources and significant economies of scale. The result should be a high-growth/low-inflation environment, putting Europe in a significantly more competitive position. Enlargement to the East should lead to rapid gains in productivity and per capita income in Central and Eastern Europe. In particular, ABB expects that demand for infrastructure systems in energy, transportation and telecommunications will grow. Enlargement should fuel a virtuous circle in which both sides stand to gain considerably.

Eberhard von Koerber also believes it is a pity that, so far, business in Western Europe has played a too modest role in the enlargement debate as it has much more to contribute:

Success requires much more than capital investment. A crucial element is the transfer of management know-how and skills through training and exchange programmes between our companies. We integrate the new company as quickly as possible into our global marketing, technology, supply and finance networks where they have access to our entire worldwide base of expertise and experience. Our priority is to put the business into the hands of local managers as soon as possible, because it is they who know their customers best, who understand the business culture, who understand what their employees need, and who can help us expand our business as pioneers in neighbouring countries. In ABB Poland, for example, Polish nationals make up the whole management team. That is surely a major contributor to our success there (von Koerber, 1997).

During 1991–97, ABB invested over $100 million in providing its East European employees with some 400,000 person-days of training in seminars, workshops and on management courses. To support its long-term management development roles, it has built its own training centres in Warsaw, Brno and Moscow. Some trainees are sent to Zürich to do apprenticeships with ABB's business area staffs. When the expansion into Eastern Europe commenced, ABB also used its Swedish, Swiss and German plants to transfer skills to factories in Poland and the Czech Republic. Latterly, its Polish and Czech engineers and managers have trained staff in ABB's newly acquired businesses in Russia and the Ukraine. ABB's Nordic companies, in Denmark, Finland, Norway and Sweden, are also supporting businesses in Lithuania, Latvia and Estonia in a Baltic cooperation agreement. One observer goes so far as to say, 'Today, you might be forgiven for seeing ABB as more of a business school than a turbine manufacturer. In the last six years, it has trained some 7000 managers in Eastern and Central Europe – an output almost as great as the Wharton and Harvard Business Schools combined' (Hofheinz, 1996b).

Eberhard von Koerber also believes that another role for business is to publicly argue the economic case in favour of expansion into the East and offer counter arguments against those who take a short-term view. He says that it is not the case that jobs are being sacrificed in Western Europe in order to relocate them in the East. He agrees that jobs have been lost in Western Europe and that unemployment remains stubbornly high despite a return to economic growth:

> *But we have been losing those jobs since 1989. The restructuring we have seen in the West has been made necessary by a failure to maintain competitiveness in a global market, a problem that would have to be addressed even if the enlargement opportunity did not exist. On the contrary, I would argue that the opportunity to expand the EU eastwards couldn't have come at a better time because the net long-term impact of enlargement is positive for both regions. If living standards in the East can be raised to the level of that enjoyed by Portugal today, it is estimated that new business potential in terms of trade and jobs could grow to $220 billion each year. That is an enormous prize – one worth fighting for* (von Koerber, 1997).

According to von Koerber, 'the countries of the East are not our competitors but our partners in the race to be more productive' (von Koerber, 1997). He uses ABB's activities in Poland to illustrate his point. Of the $700 million in orders won in Poland by ABB in 1996, some $160 million were secured by ABB companies outside Poland, in Germany, Switzerland, Sweden, Denmark, Italy, Finland and the Czech Republic. If the results of Adtranz (ABB's railway joint venture with Daimler-Benz – see page 222 (Note 1)) are added, the total Polish orders won by ABB companies outside Poland was $360 million. ABB's Eastern and Western companies are therefore, he says, benefiting alike – 'a striking example of a win-win strategy' (von Koerber, 1997).

We asked ABB managers in the West how they felt about ABB's growth in the East. One European manager told us:

> *There will still be growth in Europe but not very high – 2 to 3 per cent. If we're going to be global we have to develop people in Asia and Eastern Europe and give people there the chance to take the company on to the next step. There will be pain, but most here will survive and their jobs will be more secure. The companies that don't do it won't survive because they are not close to the customer.*

Eberhard von Koerber believes that enlargement to the East is not only a sensible business or political and economic aim: 'For many Europeans, it represents unfinished business of a moral character (von Koerber, 1997). In his address to the Churchill symposium in Zürich in September 1997, held to commemorate the memory of Winston Churchill, he remembered that it was in Zürich in 1946 that Churchill had called for a United States of Europe. He quoted Churchill's words:

I hope to see a Europe where men and women of every country will think of being European as of belonging to their native land, and wherever they go in this wide domain will truly feel 'Here I am at home'. Unfortunately, he didn't live to see that day. Let us hope that our generation will (von Koerber, 1997).

ABB in Asia – going with the shift in the world's economic centre of gravity

In 1987, Asia was still mainly seen by ASEA and BBC as a remote export region. This perspective has been transformed by the opening of China, new accelerating economic growth in the whole region (up to 1997), including the huge Indian market, and the beginning of what Percy Barnevik has called the 'irreversible shift in the world's economic centre of gravity from West to East'. He says, 'Too many people think you can succeed in the long run just by exporting from America or Europe. But you need to establish yourself locally and become, for example, a Chinese, Indonesian or Indian citizen. You don't need to do this straight away but you need to start early because it takes a long time' (Wagstyl, 1997). Barnevik believes it can take at least ten years to create this insider position, and ABB has a significant head start.

As we saw in the case of the Bakun and the Three Gorges Projects described in Chapter 4, the opportunities (and sometimes the perils) are enormous and sometimes dwarf the imagination. For example, ABB estimates that Asia will need some 600 gigawatts of new electricity-generating capacity by the year 2010 to achieve its economic development goals. That is equivalent to more than five times the existing power-generation capacity in Germany, and the investment required involves hundreds of billions of dollars.
Percy Barnevik says:

The next century belongs to Asia. Over the past 20 years we have had the second Industrial Revolution going on there. The difference from our own in the last century is that now, 12 times as many people are involved and the speed is 5 to 6 times faster. The UK and Germany doubled their living standards every 40–50 years. The Koreans and the Chinese are doing it every ten years. Newcomers can jump over several generations of industrial development. If you are a European or an American-origin company and want to become a global player, you have to invest in this region (Dillon, 1998).

ABB's own participation in the new Industrial Revolution in Asia is reflected in sales growth from $2 billion in 1988 to over $5–6 billion today. ABB expects to see that figure more than double early in the next millennium. Employment has grown to some 31,000 people. In Asia, ABB has moved from an export-based business to more local value added, aiming to develop the kind of personal relationships that are vital to doing business successfully in the region. It is now largely, if not entirely, self-sufficient in Asia. When building a power plant, for example, India can supply steam turbines, Malaysia can provide circuit breakers and Thailand can manufacture the power transformers. In 1997, the region accounted for $5.4 billion in revenues, 17 per cent of the Group's total revenues. The ambition prior to the Asian crisis was that orders there would surpass $15 billion a few years into the next millennium. One senior executive says, 'We will take off in Asia. There is enormous potential, there is no discussion about that.'

Percy Barnevik points to the increasing role that the Asia-Pacific region as a whole will play in ABB's future – and in that of other firms:

We had 6–7 per cent of total sales from the region a decade ago. Today, we have increased that to 17 per cent. I expect that in 5 years' time, the sales figure will double. I think it may represent 30 per cent of the total Group turnover as a whole. And I think in 20 years' time, it may go up to 35–40 per cent. In a short timespan, there will be an enormous shift in the company's structure which I think is unheard of in economic history; not only in our company but also in other companies. An increase from 6–7 per cent to up to 35–40 per cent over a period of some 25 years is an enormous shift of the whole activity (Taneja, 1996).

The biggest long-term challenge for ABB is finding, training and developing local management talent in Asia. As in Eastern Europe, as a sign of its commitment, it has established a training centre for Asian managers. Although ABB's aim is always ultimately to have its local operations run by local managers, it still needs to base some expatriate Western managers there for the purposes of transferring technology and best practice. However, as Senior Vice-President Bengt Skantze says, 'We would like to move some good people out there but it is sometimes difficult. Some people don't want to go because of family situation, etc.'

ABB also has other questions to deal with that echo some of those in Central and Eastern Europe. Skantze says:

Other issues include support from the West. The most obvious thing is the resistance in the old units in Europe because they say we are taking jobs from Western Europe to Asia, building engineering there, etc. This is not quite true. Business increases both ends. It is win–win. The more activities we have there, the more we export. How do you make these people [in the West] accept that? It is a management challenge. It is difficult to generalize. How do you say this job is not available any more? Some types of work are just not competitive any more.

ABB now has some 20 joint ventures in China. It admits that at the moment, only a few of them are operating up to speed but some are highly profitable and set the example for others. Says one ABB executive, 'In Eastern Europe, we were more fortunate because we were able to get in early and get good existing companies where we could upgrade them to our way of working. But in China and other Asian countries, we have to take a longer way of developing'. Percy Barnevik believes that China's future is bright:

> I don't believe in all these prophecies about China falling into pieces. Nobody knows how China will look in 10 or 30 years from now. They have a lot of problems with constitution, corruption, congestion, pollution and inequalities. But the basic underlying strength of China is the hundreds of millions of people who have a high savings ratio, good education, business acumen and a rich heritage. They have important ingredients that made Hong Kong the world's sixth largest exporter. So, I'm convinced that China in the long run will be successful as it already is (Taneja, 1996).

As in other emerging economies, ABB wants to be an insider in China and build up the country from within as part of its global network. Barnevik recounts the time that he told a Chinese leader that ABB came as a Chinese company, only to be told, 'But you're not Chinese!' As he says, it can be very difficult to get across the idea of multidomesticity.

Is it easier to convince people of the virtues of multidomesticity in India, ABB's other Asian powerhouse? Barnevik reflects, 'We want to develop in India, export out of India. When I talk to the Indian prime minister, I am a foreigner, but our company is not a foreigner. So you've transparency, communication, understanding of situations and you have an insider' (Taneja, 1996).

India is certainly one of the countries where ABB also sees a tremendous future. There, the organization has moved from being a remote export market to become a global player. In 1995, as ABB reached almost $1 billion of business in India, it moved into a second phase of expansion that included taking an equity stake in power plants. Percy Barnevik said of the new stage: 'ABB investments have reached the critical mass . . . One particular thrust is to implement clean coal technology. We have to find ways for developing countries to improve power capacity without destroying the environment . . . I see India, also long term, as an export engine. The key thing is India itself, but you can get better by adding exports to it' (*Power in Asia*, 1995).

Barnevik has no problem with taking advantage of the huge difference in labour costs between East and West: 'Let's face reality,' he says. 'India's main competitive advantage is cheap labour. Our obligation is to pay the commercial rate in the environment in which we operate' (Dillon, 1998).

Barnevik believes that India is undervalued in the West in comparison with China:

Particularly in America, there is lack of understanding about India's potential. America has a love-and-hate relationship with China since the war and that has always made China a headline country. If you look at the kilometres and kilometres of text that newspapers write on the two countries, China may have five times more text than India. Because of the strong military and strategic importance of China, India is one of the most underestimated countries in respect of its potential in the Western world's eyes (Taneja, 1996).

ABB's Indian managers are proud of the company's progress. 'We have changed from being a local Indian company to becoming the Indian part of a global organization,' says A. K. Thiagarajan, former Managing Director of ABB India. The Indian company has technically upgraded itself and now relies heavily on the parent for drawings, etc. It is also expected to contribute to the rest of the group with design, engineering applications and software. It aims to increase its exports – to Bangladesh, East Africa and South East Asia – of high-voltage switchgear, software and power line carriers from 10 per cent of its sales to 20 per cent. Overall, its objective is to be a $3 billion full-range electrical engineering company in the next 5 years and to develop ABB India as a key member of the ABB Group, moving it from number 25 to number 10. 'In the year 2010, the USA will be number one in ABB, number two will be Germany, and then number three or four in the group will be India and China,' affirms Thiagarajan.

Just as ABB's Polish and Czech managers are supporting their Russian and Ukrainian counterparts, ABB's factory automation plant in Bangalore has now advanced to the stage where it is training engineers for Thailand and other countries in Asia. What, in addition to technological excellence, can other firms in Asia learn from ABB? H. K. Mohanty, Vice-President for Corporate Personnel at ABB India, replies:

Teamwork. There is a big emphasis in ABB on a team culture. Also, our belief in training and development and some of our personnel approaches such as the appraisal system. Our appraisal system is unique in India, it doesn't exist here. Indian organizations ask us if this is working. The conventional performance appraisal has shifted here to a development appraisal, including peers, not just supervisors.

A. K. Thiagarajan says of ABB's culture:

People work harder here than in any other organization I know. The organizational structure makes you do that. You have to work long hours and that can be stressful sometimes. Middle management get business responsibilities earlier than in any other company in India. As a result, people are more well-rounded than in any other organization.

ABB's commitment to development is not without its dangers – already, executive headhunters have started targeting ABB India's people.

Although ABB prefers to have 100 per cent control, in India it usually has to work with joint venture partners and has to take care in the way that it introduces its way of working. A. K. Thiagarajan says, 'This is difficult. The basics are very important. We switch the accounting system to ABACUS. In the older organizations, this takes time. We try to delayer, simplify and decentralize. We break down the organization into profit centres and take steps to build their competence.' Many such Indian organizations are used to a more centralized approach and people are not used to taking responsibility. 'We give them training and follow up,' says Thiagarajan. 'Communication is very important, we keep talking all the time at all levels. We are very impatient, we want results yesterday, that is an ABB thing.'

How does ABB India approach change in its joint venture partners? Thiagarajan describes the approach:

We bring in ABB technology. We go into the factory and look at the design. We develop things together with the ABB business area management. We replace the existing approach with the ABB way. Where necessary, we consider downsizing. We have a voluntary retirement scheme. By Indian law, you cannot dismiss people. We don't get as many people to leave as we would like. We have a consensus with the unions, we have to sell the idea to the workers and put it in terms of the survival of the organization. They must not think that we are ruthless. If you do downsizing or rightsizing, they need to see that we are doing it for all. And yet, we must do it. The right way – not harshly or ruthlessly. People must see that it is done for their survival and for the survival of the whole.

ABB India also aims to make its partners more marketing-oriented. Thiagarajan explains:

The joint ventures need tremendous improvements to revamp marketing. The aim is to integrate them into ABB's marketing eventually. We put in an ABB manager and a controller who make a review and an action plan. They have input from personnel, IT, the segment head – there is a tremendous amount of competence available in ABB. In the process, the joint venture becomes business and bottom line-focused and marketing becomes more aggressive.

ABB India's former Managing Director is optimistic about the future, although he is aware of the challenges facing the organization:

There are lots of hurdles and bumps and many difficulties, including political instability, but we have faith in the long-term. We must have continuing faith. We must organize and handle growth. This involves some problems, particularly management resources. We have large groups of managers who are mentally geared up for small businesses but who are now put in charge of global businesses – this is a big challenge.

ABB India's managers see their business becoming more complicated with the advent of global financing and power plant privatization. 'The skills are different. You have to handle large projects and know more about finance, risk management and handling global key accounts.'

So, how will ABB India look in five years' time? A. K. Thiagarajan believes:

it will be a more self-confident organization. It will be larger and more profitable. It will be a stronger member of the ABB group. Today, it is Sweden, Germany, the US, Switzerland, then Norway, Finland and a few others. Then it is India, Brazil and a few others. In five years' time, we will graduate to the second or first group. Our markets are growing, the number of employees is growing. The future is here.

Percy Barnevik is proud of ABB's achievements in India: 'When I came down to Bangalore, 10 years ago, the land was just being dug up. Today, I see that same plant selling more automation machines than all the other countries in the world. That gives you a feeling of satisfaction (Skaria, 1995).

Percy Barnevik talks of the challenges for the future in Asia:

Financial engineering is gong to be increasingly important as more of our large projects move to Asia . . . The differences between us will get smaller, and there will be equalization across the world. But it's not a situation where we in Europe go down and others go up. We will go up together. It is another win-win situation for Europe – that is my conviction (Gibson, 1995).

As Barnevik says, investments and transfers of technology to the East go hand in hand with more exports from the West.

Percy Barnevik describes what he calls 'the new world of ABB':

Gone is the era when Western Europe and North America were ABB's natural home bases and other regions were remote export targets with minor local operations. No longer are there any reasons to discount performance in countries like Poland and the Czech Republic for productivity, quality or anything else. They have global product development responsibilities and they are now in their turn supporting newly acquired companies in Russia, Ukraine and Central Asia. Our power equipment factories in Baroda and industrial automation centres in Bangalore, India, are like factories in Germany or the US. Our power engineering centre in Malaysia undertakes turnkey power plant contracts all over Asia. Our centres of excellence with 5000 employees in Brazil support surrounding countries in South America. Expansion into sub-Saharan Africa is being driven from South Africa where we have a broad range of technologies and 2000 employees. This is the new world of ABB, where we continue our rapid expansion to build new home markets and to participate in building these countries' infrastructure and industrial development. A special responsibility is to supply efficient and clean technologies to support a sustainable development and to help them avoid the environmental mistakes we made in the West, not to mention Central and Eastern Europe . . .

This new world of ABB also holds a key to growth for our companies in Western Europe, North America, Japan and Australia, where ABB still has the bulk of its capital, its technology and its highly skilled people. We need even more of our American boiler experts to go to India, to Central Asia, to Malaysia – not for two days but for two years. German companies must focus even more on 'adopting' new Chinese or Indonesian companies. The Swiss must accelerate the transfer of turbine technologies, the Swedes power transmission technologies. The build-up in these new markets is not a threat to the old markets. On the contrary, the bigger the local presence in the new markets, the higher the exports out of the old markets – it is a true win–win global strategy (Barnevik, 1995).

Looking beyond the Asia crisis

The long-term future may indeed be in Asia, but the economic crisis that hit there in 1997 inevitably raised questions about ABB's shorter-range plans in the region. The resulting currency weakness in the region and resulting economic problems reduced customer demand and put increased pressure on products imported from Europe and North America. Business observers noted that ABB's exposure in Asia was counterbalanced by its strong order book, but it was not impervious to the crisis. The big Bakun Dam Project in Malaysia was postponed, costing ABB $100 million, and an elevated train project in Bangkok, for which Adtranz was to supply the rolling stock, was cancelled.

CEO Göran Lindahl said in an interview with the *Far Eastern Economic Review*, 'Long term, I am very confident about Asia. The recovery may take a little longer than we expected at first . . . But I am convinced that the next millennium will be in Asia . . . Now is the right time to build up further investments for the demand that will come back' (Granitsas, 1998). Indeed, while many other companies have been cooling investment plans in Asia, ABB has been doing the opposite by creating new jobs and bringing in new technology. In October 1997, ABB announced that it was accelerating expansion in Asia. This was based on a belief that Asia will bounce back in the next two to three years and that the region, because its long-term need for infrastructure and industrial investment remains, will resume growth even faster than before. Up to 2001, ABB aims to increase its already sizeable presence in Asia by half, adding 50 manufacturing and engineering sites to the 100 it already has there.

We asked Göran Lindahl whether or not the Asia crisis would affect ABB's growth targets. He told us:

In five years' time we will say, yes it happened, but there is still high growth. We are where the growth will be; growth will continue. We are very well placed, with one third of our people in Central and Eastern Europe and Asia. Asia has 55 per cent of the world's people and a quarter of its power capacity, while Europe has 9 per cent of the people and 17 per cent of the world's power capacity. People in emerging markets can see satellite TV, etc. and they know how you could live. To build living standards, you need to have electricity available. The people there will demand electricity. I'm not worried about Asia. We will say it was a hiccup. With three billion people they want to see how they can improve living standards. You can't stop it.

A priority for the future is to achieve more local value added by, for example, building service centres in Asia to give the company full coverage of the region. Far from having dulled ABB's ambitions in the area, Asia is therefore still seen as crucial for the future. Indeed, experience of working in ABB's Asian operations is seen by some as a route to advancement in the company. Göran Lindahl himself spent some time looking after the group's interests in Asia.

The short-term news in Asia is not all bad, either. ABB may be able to take short-term advantage of the current situation. The depreciation of several Asian currencies makes producing locally even more profitable for ABB. One third of ABB's plants in Asia are in countries that devalued currencies during the crisis. All prepared export drives to take advantage of the currency depreciation. Svante Svensson, who is in charge of ABB's manufacturing at Bangpoo in Thailand, also told the *Far Eastern Economic Review*, 'I can't say that this downturn won't affect us, but that's not to say it will be all negative. This is a golden opportunity to be in the export market' (Granitsas, 1998). Furthermore, many of ABB's products do not require expensive imported components. In Thailand, for example, domestic content accounts for about 50 per cent for most of its products (which include capacitors, transformers and switchgear). (If domestic content is below 50 per cent, however, the higher cost of imported components cancels out the advantages of lower currencies.)

We asked ABB executives whether or not the continuing change of balance in the Group towards Asia would change the company. One European-based Swedish manager said:

Yes, but it is difficult to understand exactly how. It is tough for some people to accept. Ten years from now Asia will be the centre of the world. We know it intellectually but not in our hearts. In ASEA, we used to talk about the 'developing countries' like South Korea, etc. We thought they were small. But people don't understand that things have already tilted. South Korea's economy is bigger than Sweden's. The idea of the Pacific Basin was a bit intellectual – but it is a real thing. We accept it now – it is under way.

A key to ABB's success in spreading to new countries is its ability to mobilize skilled people in its existing operations to want to bring on ABB's people in the newly emerging economies. Percy Barnevik said that one of his big jobs as CEO was to strengthen the 'glue', making managers feel that they are part of a family. This means encouraging 'group-mindedness' with praise and bonuses for people who support ABB's operations in emerging economies.

Such support is already making a particular impact. Eberhard von Koerber says that the company is developing a new breed of ABB manager – 'East of Eden' – 'equipped with Western management tools, hungry for the taste of success and with a tremendous ambition to show that they have what it takes to compete. This has also set a fire under some of our Western managers, who find themselves having to run a bit faster to keep up' (von Koerber, 1996). Percy Barnevik gave us just such an example:

> *A challenge in these new countries is to really integrate them into ABB but often they are more eager than the old countries to really use the 'bible'. For example, you sit with a Czech guy and a German guy, and the Czech guy knows the bible [section on transfer pricing] almost by heart, like in the old days when I had to learn Luther's catechism in school – 'No,' he says, 'on page 17, it says that for the first refusal it is like that', while the German guy hasn't read it for three years! So you can say the newcomers are the eager proponents of the Group policy, they are really the banner carriers for the Group policy.*

Eberhard von Koerber points to another strategic dimension of ABB's 'exceptional presence' in the emerging markets:

> *We have established ourselves not only ahead of our competitors, but also ahead of our Western customers, who are now investing in these markets. With our local experience and supply capabilities, we can assist them in their local build-up, be it as their local EPC partner, or as their local full-service supplier, ensuring reliable operation over the long term, an essential precondition for profitability in capital-intensive industries such as petrochemicals or power generation. This is how we translate our vision for global partnerships with our customers into real action* (von Koerber, 1996).

Göran Lindahl believes that other companies will regret in the future that they did not expand as wholeheartedly into the emerging economies as ABB has done – 'because we are there where the customers are'. ABB, in its belief that exporting from the West is not enough and that a major stake in the development of Asia requires major local presence in the countries concerned, may be ahead of its competitors in the region. However, the latter are stirring. In 1998, GE signalled a shift in its strategy and a new focus on Asia. Business analysts had already been speculating that GE might turn to Asia, but with the opportunity to buy assets cheaply because of the financial crisis there, it was likely that GE would expand in the region on an unprecedented scale. GE was expected to spend up to twice as much to acquire assets as the $17 billion it had spent in Europe in the early 1990s and some very big deals were forecast. GE said it was very 'excited' about prospects in Asia and Chairman Jack Welch said, 'We are determined and poised to do the same thing in Asia we have done in Europe and other areas'.

However, GE is unlikely to go as far as ABB in its commitment to the East. ABB's aim is 'the massive transfer of knowledge from West to East through our product lines . . . The Group is gravitating eastwards to Eastern Europe and Asia' (Barnevik, 1996b). Barnevik says:

> *The demand for infrastructure investments has moved from West to East. The market for new power plants in the US has dropped 90 per cent, and 60 per cent of total global demand is now in Asia. These are unprecedented changes. You have factories where you don't need them, and where you need them, you don't have them. These changes in the environment require major internal changes* (Dauphinais and Price, 1998).

Looking forward, Percy Barnevik predicted:

> *The key difference in future will be the pace of change. Things have changed in the world before, but what is fascinating now is that today's changes are happening so fast. By the year 2010, the biggest home markets for ABB will include China and India, right up there with Germany and the US. Russia, Indonesia and Brazil will also work their way up to the top rankings. These changes will happen so quickly and will be of such a large scale that they will dwarf the developments in Western Europe, on which we focus so much of our attention today* (Barnevik, 1996a).

One result of ABB's global expansion is that, according to Barnevik, it is necessary to stop referring to ABB as a Swedish-Swiss group: 'We are a company with an international vocation. The Board now includes a Japanese member. Had we found someone just as qualified, it might have been a Chinese member' (*European Energy Report*, 1996).

At the time of writing, it appeared that the impact on ABB of the Asian crisis was, indeed, less than many had feared. According to the *Financial Times*, ABB's first quarter results for 1998 'allayed recent market concerns about its exposure to troubled Asian economies by reporting a double-digit increase in underlying order volume. The results, which came a day after Germany's Siemens issued a profits warning, suggest that ABB's new management team, led by Göran Lindahl, is starting to succeed in its attempt to accelerate the Group's recent lacklustre growth, in spite of the problems in Asia' (*Financial Times*, 1998). In this period, the company experienced strong growth in the Middle East, Africa and Latin America, but also saw a 16 per cent increase in Asian countries that were showing signs of a gradual recovery. The major restructuring exercise that ABB started in 1997 was also starting to reduce personnel costs and the project was expected to deliver its full impact in 1998–99. With the announcement of the news, ABB's shares, which had already outperformed the market thus far in 1998, rose SFr45 to SFr2,500 in a falling Swiss stock market. As Percy Barnevik himself told us, you cannot forecast the future, but there were some early signs that ABB's long-term confidence in Asia was going to be justified.

The re-emerging markets of the West

Percy Barnevik says that when he talks about growth opportunities in Central and Eastern Europe and in Asia, he is often asked by employees in the West, 'What's in it for us?' He refuses to accept the expression 'mature' markets for the OECD home markets and prefers to call them 're-emerging'. 'There are only two types of market: emerging and re-emerging,' he declares (Barnevik, 1997). There is a big potential, he says, in rebuilding the old industrial landscape in re-emerging markets. This is reinforced by deregulation and privatization, which create new demand and increased competition between ABB's customers who demand higher quality, lower prices, less pollution and better service. Demand for new industrial capacity is limited, but there is a growing need to revamp and modernize existing plant. As customers focus on their core business, they are outsourcing service and maintenance operations. This provides a further significant growth opportunity.

Re-emerging markets require innovation and creativity not only in products, but also in business approaches and financing. They demand new ways of approaching partnerships between suppliers and customers. 'This requires, above all, an attitude shift among suppliers from selling products and services to making customers more competitive and creating added value for them' (Barnevik, 1997).

In the industrialized world, there will be an increasing tendency to focus on high-tech and capital-intensive production. Export jobs are growing faster than overall job growth. Barnevik uses Switzerland to illustrate the implications of these developments. In 1987, ABB Switzerland had 18,000 employees in a loss-making, broad product operation. Today, half of the product programme has been closed or moved to Asia, Eastern Europe or other places, and outsourcing has reduced the vertical depth of production. As a result, sales have doubled since 1987 – that is, sales of the remaining capital-intensive and high-tech products have quadrupled. Employment has dropped to 11,000 people so sales per employee have increased 3 times in 10 years, or an average 13 per cent increase per year.

The change in the composition of the workforce is also dramatic, as 10,000 jobs were eliminated and 3000 new jobs, mainly engineers, were added. Of ABB Switzerland's employees today, 60 per cent are engineers, compared to 25 per cent 10 years ago. As Barnevik says:

It is like a new company. Big capital investments in multiple-operation machine centres and automation with robots have cut down process times for many components by 90 per cent or more. Some 84 per cent of total production is exported, half of that to Asia. Finally, after the transformation, return on capital employed has reached a very good level. From a business point of view, this is a success story. For example, nowhere can a high-precision turbine rotor be made cheaper than in Switzerland. The high salaries there don't have a major impact, since the share of personnel costs in the rotor's total product value is only 3 per cent (Barnevik, 1997).

What about the social consequences of these changes? Barnevik maintains that, while fewer people are employed, they are in more secure and better-paid jobs. Most of the 10,000 less-skilled people moved to smaller firms or into the service sector. He admits that some of them became unemployed or took early retirement.

A critical question, is how countries like Switzerland will create enough jobs outside their traditional industries to avoid social tensions, high social welfare costs, crime, etc. The industrial development I have described is inevitable. For industrial companies, it is not just a matter of improving results, it is a matter of survival. This is not unlike what happened to agriculture, a sector that 100 years ago accounted for 50 per cent of total employment but that today employs only 3 per cent of the workforce. The big challenge for these societies will be to stimulate job creation, particularly in the service sector, and to raise the education level to handle the ongoing transformation (Barnevik, 1997).

ABB looks to Latin America, the Middle East and Africa

ABB has also been looking at more recently emerging markets. Percy Barnevik says:

We should not let our heavy focus on Asia cause us to overlook the steady and encouraging growth in Latin America. Deregulation, privatization and the opening of borders have done wonders for economic stability and growth. For example, the President of Argentina said recently that his country, unlike some European Union countries, has achieved a level of fiscal strength that would allow it to meet the strict prerequisites of European Monetary Union – something nobody would have believed in their wildest imagination some years ago. There are also a number of countries in the MENA [Middle East and North Africa] region with good growth opportunities. Finally, one can even see some 'light at the end of the tunnel' in sub-Saharan Africa – not the least in attitudes. The tradition of blaming the old imperialism, experimenting with socialism and being dependent on foreign aid is being replaced by a belief in the market economy and an understanding that they have their destiny in their own hands. Maybe we will see in 20 years some of the 'old tigers' of Asia outsourcing to the 'new tigers' in Africa (Barnevik, 1997).

President Clinton's tour of Africa in 1998 – the longest visit to the continent by any US president – highlighted its move towards democracy and open markets. Although it still has serious economic problems, the 600 million people of sub-Sharan Africa are a huge market with enormous productive potential. 'The sleeping giant of Africa is awakening,' said one newspaper, 'and its vast potential can no longer be ignored' (Jordan, 1998). ABB's new CEO

Göran Lindahl points to the increasing importance of the region for ABB: 'In the Middle East and Africa we have 11,000 people and $3 billion in business. When US president Bill Clinton goes to Africa, we welcome him because we are there. In Africa, there is big potential with oil and gas and with the need for electricity supply in rural Africa.'

The benefits of global presence

To sum up, ABB has put enormous effort into building its worldwide business. It has said that there are 10 benefits to be derived from its global presence.

Upstream benefits

- Economies of scale in production.
- Broader product programme.
- Deeper core technology knowledge.
- Easy transfer of technology and production know-how across borders.
- Optimum level of local value added in production via interchange of modules.

Downstream benefits

- Global brand name.
- Economy of scope and pull effect from other related businesses.
- Export based on centres of excellence and/or competitiveness.
- Import pull instead of export push.
- Lower distribution costs.

ABB's ability to realize many of these benefits, however, depends on how well it can make the global dimension of its matrix work. ABB's global matrix has been the subject of much comment and speculation by management academics and business writers. CEOs of other companies wonder how the matrix functions and what they can learn from it. Let's move on and look at the matrix at work.

References

Quotes without references originate from the authors' personal communications – see page xviii for details.

Barnevik, Percy (1995) 'President's comments', *ABB Annual Report.*

Barnevik, Percy (1996a) *Percy Barnevik on Globalization.* University of St Gallen, Switzerland: presentation to the International Management Symposium, University of St Gallen, 20 May.

Barnevik, Percy (1996b) 'Engineering a worldwide advantage', *Europe's Most Respected Companies*, Financial Times & Price Waterhouse.

Barnevik, Percy (1997) *Global Forces of Change: Remarks to the 1997 International Industrial Conference, 'Inventing the Future'.* San Francisco: International Industrial Conference, 'Inventing the Future', 29 September.

Dauphinais, William, and Price, Colin (Price Waterhouse) (1998), interview with Percy Barnevik, 'Creating a federation of national cultures: reflections of Percy Barnevik', in *Straight from the CEO: The World's Top Business Leaders Reveal Ideas that Every Manager Can Use*. London: Nicholas Brealey Publishing, 37–46.

European Energy Report (1996) 'ABB spring surprises', 1 March (454), 19.

Financial Times (1998) 'ABB overcomes lower demand from Asia', 24 April, 29.

Frey, Jr. Sherwood C. and Schlosser, Michael M. (1993) 'ABB and Ford: creating value through cooperation', *Sloan Management Review*, Fall, 65–72.

Gibson, Marcus (1995) 'How ABB became Europe's best', *The European*, 5–11 October, 19.

Granitsas, Alkman (1998) 'In for the long haul', *Far Eastern Economic Review*, 5 February, 51–2.

Hofheinz, Paul (1994) 'ABB's big bet in Eastern Europe', *Fortune*, 2 May.

Hofheinz, Paul (1996a) 'Inside ABB', *Russia Review*, 17 June, 8–13.

Hofheinz, Paul (1996b) 'ABB at a crossroad . . . ', *Russia Review*, 17 June, 14–15.

Jordan, Vernon E. (1998) 'Africa's Promise', *The Wall Street Journal Europe*, 30 March, 6.

Kapstein, Jonathan and Reed, Stanley, *et al.*, (1990) 'Preaching the Euro-gospel', *Business Week*, 23 July, 34–8.

Latour, Almar (1997) *'The Hunt is On'*, *Central European Economic Review (The Wall Street Journal Europe)*, February V (1), 14, 16 and 26.

Leppänen, Rolf (1994) *ABB Action Recipe: Strategic Management in the Growth and Restructuring of a European Enterprise*. Helsinki: International Networking Publishing INP Oy.

McClenahen, John S. (1994) 'Percy Barnevik and the ABBs of competition', *Industry Week*, 6 June **243** (11), 20–3.

Moss, Nicholas (1996) 'Barnevik leads ABB on a journey to forge closer links with share-holders', *The European*, 7 March, 32.

Nagorski, Andrew and Engel, Reinhard (1997) 'The New Swiss', *Newsweek*, 25 August, 34–5.

Power in Asia (1995) 'Boost for ABB investments', 6 February, 1.

Skaria, George (1995) 'Interview with Percy Barnevik,' *Business Today* (India), 22 February–6 March, 100–5.

Teresko, John (1996) 'ABB industrial systems' (America's best plants) *Industry Week*, October, **245** (19), 32–6 .

von Koerber, Eberhard (1996) *Improved Performance: What Distinguishes the High Achievers?* Vienna: presentation to the European Petrochemicals Association, 1 October.

von Koerber, Eberhard (1997) *Enlargement to the East: The Decisive Moment for Europe's Future, Presentation to the Churchill Symposium*. Zürich: presentation to the Churchill Symposium, 18 September.

Wagstyl, Stefan (1996) 'Servicing: better profits to be made', Survey – Power-generating Equipment, *Financial Times* 26 June.

Wagstyl, Stefan (1997) 'A multinational cadre of managers is the key,' *Financial Times*, 8 October, 14.

10

ABB's global matrix – challenges and refinements

When you first create such a huge organization you have to make it transparent. You have to know where you make money, where you lose money . . . At that time, it was [also] important not to be regarded as a foreigner everywhere . . . So you can see a certain logic in a little exaggerated fragmentation, which was done deliberately for restructuring and for transparency – and in a little over-pronouncement of national entrenchment and the domestic role . . . Now, it is increasingly a matter of being low-cost, efficient, globally effective, and you have to adjust to that.

Percy Barnevik

Globalization poses big challenges for organizations and their managers. They have to spread resources around the world and, at the same time, build organizations that are able to respond more quickly to a wider range of external changes. More and more companies have been asking what is the most effective global organization design for them. What, for example, should be the role of the corporate parent or centre in a global company? A recent series in the *Financial Times* on 'The Global Company' pointed to a fundamental issue:

The tension between central and local management lies at the heart of the challenge of creating a global company. There are many ways of operating on a global scale. All require difficult choices between centralization and local autonomy. Any structure must cope with what is likely to prove the twenty-first century's biggest management challenge: combining worldwide reach with the flexibility and speed of reaction of a local competitor (Martin, 1997).

Percy Barnevik suggests that, while new product development gives a one- to two-year competitive advantage before competitors catch up, and while process innovation may give a more lasting advantage, the most difficult

253

competitive advantage to imitate is indeed, organizational. As Barnevik says, 'Globalization is a long-lasting competitive advantage. If we build a new gas turbine, in 18 months our competitors also have one. But building a global company is not so easy to copy' (Wagstyl, 1997).

ABB's solution, as we have seen, is multidomesticity with a very high degree of decentralization, small headquarters and a global matrix. It is also important to remember that the matrix works very differently for local businesses, like service shops, where the global influence is small, than for global businesses, like power plants, where even the business transactions are handled by the global BA. It claims that without the matrix, it would have been difficult for it to expand and build its global presence so quickly. However, matrix structures, as research has shown, can have their share of problems. Has ABB been able to avoid the traditional problems of the matrix? Has its matrix design changed over time? What is it like to work in the ABB matrix? What benefits does the matrix bring to ABB – do they outweigh the problems? And what are the future challenges in making it work even more effectively?

The matrix – for 'grown-up' organizations only?

The matrix structure became popular in the late 1960s and early 1970s among international firms faced with increased complexity and the need to manage more than one source of diversity simultaneously, such as different geographical markets and different products. As Philip Sadler, former chief executive of Ashridge says:

Complexity creates information overload, which can be dealt with in a number of ways – by decentralization of decision making, by installing highly sophisticated computerized information systems or by creating slack resources – buffer stocks or pools of manpower. The matrix offers an alternative approach by creating lateral relationships which cut across conventional lines of authority. Some enthusiasts see the matrix as the model for the organization of the future. Others see it as an expensive, overelaborate and confusing arrangement (Sadler, 1994).

As we have seen, ABB has combined three of these methods for coping with complexity – decentralization, computer information systems and a global business matrix – but reacts strongly against the notion of slack resources. Indeed, Tom Peters felt that one of the reasons for the success of the ABB matrix was an insistence on leanness that avoided a build-up of bureaucracy. ABB's leanness and its action-orientation may also avoid another endemic problem with the matrix structure – organizational politicking. We remember, for example, one senior executive from another company with an international matrix telling us that it is 'harder to spot the politicians in a matrix structure!' In contrast, one senior ABB executive says that ABB's spare organization and its policy of 'It is better to make mistakes than do nothing' is why:

> *I genuinely believe that there is so little political infighting here – people have so little time for it. It can paralyze an organization. I deeply believe that it starts because people don't have anything to do. When you are overstaffed, you're forced to protect your little kingdom to prove that you are valuable and needed. You fight against other little kingdoms. But it takes 80 per cent of your energy in protecting your company – when the enemy is really on the outside . . . Here, we all know what to do, we have no time to waste and fight, and we don't see any need to. Why should we have internal fights?*

If this were true, it would certainly accord with the view of organizational theorist Henry Mintzberg of McGill University in Montreal, who says that the matrix structure is for 'grown-up organizations' (Mintzberg, 1983). As an organizational attempt to 'have your cake and eat it, too' (he cites the words of fellow theorist Leonard Sayles here), it is 'for organizations that are prepared to resolve their conflicts through informal negotiation among equals rather than recourse to formal authority, to the formal power of superiors over subordinates and line over staff' (Mintzberg, 1983). As Mintzberg points out, although the matrix is a most effective device for developing new activities and coordinating complex multiple interdependencies, it is 'no place for those in need of security and stability.' As the matrix sacrifices the principle of unity of command, it can create 'considerable confusion, stress, and conflict, and requires from its participants highly developed interpersonal skills and considerable tolerance for ambiguity' (Mintzberg, 1983). This raises the question, in a global organization, of how a matrix will be accepted in different cultures. German employees, for example, traditionally have a high need for stability and lack of ambiguity and this may have added to ABB's difficulties there in the early days after the merger.

Mintzberg raises the question of whether a tilt in the balance of power between the different sorts of managers amounts to a reversion to a traditional single-chain hierarchy, without the complexity-handling benefits of the matrix (an interesting issue in the light of the most recent changes in ABB's own matrix). A perfect balance, on the other hand, without cooperation between the different managers can lead to so many disputes being pushed up the hierarchy for arbitration that top management becomes overloaded. The cost of administration and communication can also be very high in a matrix system which demands that people have to spend more time in meetings and communicating than in a simpler authority structure.

Resulting slow and costly decision-making processes were the reason some early experimenters with matrix organizations, such as Dow Chemical and Citibank, abandoned the matrix in favour of more conventional single-line reporting structures. ABB, however, defends its matrix as the only structure that can help it handle its complicated business environment. As one BA manager told us in an earlier research project in ABB:

> *In principle, nobody likes a matrix. Most people like to have one boss. But in the fast-moving world in which we live, with a fast-growing company, mergers and acquisitions, and many highly competitive markets, there is no other way to run this business. On the one hand, we consist of a collection of small, local, flexible units, each run by a profit centre manager. But the business is so big that it would be hopeless to run it without any coordination, both to control costs and to stop companies duplicating efforts and competing with each other in the same export markets.*

Some companies have turned to the matrix again. Indeed, according to *The Economist*, the renaissance of matrix management owes much to the advocacy of Percy Barnevik, 'who seems to have succeeded in operating such a system without dulling the imagination or restricting the initiative of his front-line workers' (*The Economist*, 1995). Barnevik once said that the matrix 'is a fact of life. If you deny the formal matrix, you wind up with an informal one – and that's much harder to reckon with' (Taylor, 1991). When still chief executive, Barnevik was often asked how he handled the organization. He said, 'People get the feeling there is built-in conflict. In reality, while it is not perfect, it works well in most cases' (Brown, 1994). He admitted that decentralization sometimes leads to overlaps and redundancies, but says they are outweighed by the advantages of entrepreneurial spirit and speed. He also acknowledged that ABB pays 'a certain price in the form of higher communication costs than other companies that are more homogeneous and concentrated in one country. However, the communication investment is a relatively small price to pay for the speed, flexibility, and many synergies we gain through decentralization' (Dauphinais and Price, 1998). He said it is important to recognize that the global and local roles are not conflicting but complementary and people must fully understand and accept these roles. The global BA manager decides 'the global charter', where to build or close plants, who will develop what, market allocations, strategy, technology, etc. He also pushes internal benchmarking, quality standards, global supply, etc. The local manager, whether a company manager or a country manager, works within that charter. He 'owns' the customers and he should run his operation to maximum efficiency and quality. Both roles are important and complementary. When both understand their roles, it works well.

As Henry Mintzberg pointed out, matrix systems often create a demanding environment for managers. Looking for cracks or strains in the matrix is a favourite sport of ABB-spotters, although ABB managers themselves generally agree that the matrix has been a fundamental reason for the company's success so far.

Erik Elzvik, Head of Corporate Development says:

ABB is a special type of environment. We drive down responsibility. Our identity is out there in the companies at the same time as we are a global company. For ABB, there is no other organization that could suit it better. We have a complicated product strategy. Our difference is in the way that we cover markets, locally and globally. Others are not able to do both. There is no other way to do it with all the complexity when you have projects with several countries involved. It would be simpler if we made chocolate. There you can have one factory in one country and sell it elsewhere. We need an organization with a double impact. Competition is built in – it keeps people on their toes. It is also very helpful in acquisitions. The drive comes in from the business area. Local advice and know-how come in from the country.

Managing the global process

As we worked on this book in 1998, an internal process of investigation, led by CEO Göran Lindahl, was underway in ABB as to how to take the organization's structure forward and refine it for the changing business environment of the future. Meanwhile, we asked managers to talk about how the matrix had worked up until then. What were the strengths on which they wanted to capitalize and what were the problems that they wanted to address? When we interviewed CEO Göran Lindahl in April 1998, he told us:

You must realize that ABB has a unique set-up. Nobody has ever tried to do this. US textbooks talked about the matrix in the 1970s, but nobody ever tried to do it by giving distinct responsibilities to people. We have tied the matrix to extreme decentralization. We have 5000 profit centres with profit and loss responsibility. Our decentralization is unique. The average size of a profit centre is $7 million. Each has fewer than 50 people on average. So we are built on 5000 perceived companies. Here you have our uniqueness. When we make money, we make it separately. Each one is not much by itself when compared to the overall corporate turnover of $35 billion. If one fails or a technology fails, it doesn't have an impact. But we have to know the future of the strategy and that is where the business areas come in.

As Lindahl said, the profit centres are close to the customer: 'All customers are local by definition. The profit centres deal with customers, with local behaviours, the local network, etc. The business areas are concerned with the global process – R&D, investment and divestment.' Lindahl explained typical examples of the 'global process' as follows:

- Research and development

    If we want to build motors in China, we take a universal design produced in Germany. We can use this design all over the world. R&D is carried out in one place, but the cost is spread over 10–12 places. R&D therefore costs less than if we did it all over the place. This is a business area responsibility.

● Investment

> In motors, we might have ten factories in ten different countries. If we decided to open a factory in Vietnam, the BA manager looks at capacity, at the gap in capacity between where the factory could be put and the capacity he has. He might say, I have more capacity in Latin America but in Brazil I have no motors. There is a factory there already so he doesn't need to put up infrastructure and it costs less. But then the manager in Vietnam is very disappointed. The country or factory manager sees their mandate and fights for that. This is the whole idea of the matrix. The business area manager takes the global view. But before he makes a decision, he must have a dialogue if he wants to create support and buy-in. It is healthy because there is discussion, people have to put facts on the table.

● Disinvestment

> If the business area manager sees that the market in the next five years will not support ten factories, he might decide that three factories in three different countries have to go. A factory manager might say, 'I agree we have to reduce capacity, but we should not close my factory, it is the most important', etc. Therefore the business area must have a global view.

Lindahl also saw the way that ABB secured performance targets by means of its budgeting process as a crucial feature of the ABB matrix. Each BA puts together a global strategic plan that is approved by the CEO. The plans form the basis for the CEO and Executive Committee to agree targets for return on capital employed, gross margins and growth for each segment and region. The segments, in turn, break down their overall targets by BA. Different BAs have different market possibilities, so some are given higher targets than others. The BAs break the targets down by business units (the companies), which set targets for their profit centres, which, as Lindahl says, 'sit in the marketplace. The profit centres have to consider how they can support the target – "Do I need more resources, workshops, etc? What are the customer needs?" They then feed their views back upwards. The budget process goes round two ways as, at the same time, regional and country holding company managers set their own top-down targets.'

Company managers therefore received two sets of targets – one from their BA boss, responsible for a product business worldwide, and one from their regional boss, responsible for the performance of all ABB companies (from all the BAs) in that particular country or region. If the two sets of targets were in conflict, the company manager had to negotiate with their two bosses to resolve the difference and secure agreement on the targets. All company budgets had to be jointly approved by the company president and the BA and country managers to whom they reported before they could be submitted to the Group management for approval. Both bosses assessed the performance of individuals and both had to agree on the promotion of individuals.

The BAs and regional country managements have had differing priorities, of course. The BA manager has been typically concerned to build global market share and has looked for aggressiveness in securing orders or for manufacturing efficiency. If performance falls behind, it is within the BA's remit to move production to a high-performing unit in another country. The regional country manager has looked to optimize country performance and respond to local pressures and may have been more concerned to reduce working capital or have been under trade union pressure to secure or increase employment. One area where company management was likely to feel increased pressure from both sides of the matrix was in ABB's environmental management programme whereby BA managers are expected to build environmental objectives into their strategic plans and local country managers are expected to promote ABB's environmental policies and programmes in their countries.

The benefits of the matrix

So what are the benefits that the matrix and its double impact have brought and will continue hopefully to bring? In summary, the matrix has provided a number of (some perhaps still more potential than actual) strategic, resource, learning and process advantages because of the way in which it:

- turns a scattered local presence into a 'global' home market;
- promotes economies of scale and scope;
- allows high-pay/low-pay synergy; and gives access to cheaper inputs;
- facilitates cross-fertilization of ideas; and provides a framework for West-East/North-South 'mentorships';
- encourages high performance by means of healthy competition and stretch targets;
- forces dialogue and builds 'complex thinking' into decision-making processes.

A 'global' home market

The global extreme of the strategy continuum favours comparative advantage based on the home market and competitive advantage based on cost.[1] The multidomestic extreme favours comparative advantage based on government policies and competitive advantages based on product differentiation. ABB, with its Swedish-Swiss parentage and Swiss head office, does not have the advantages of a large home market like its US competitor, GE, or even its German rival, Siemens. ABB therefore has to build as many compensating advantages as possible.

In fact, ABB often competes effectively on a global basis against firms that do have a large home market. This results from its attempt to optimize operations in each country by 'pooling' all its business operations from the different business segments and BAs in each country under a local parent company. This gives ABB large market shares and a substantial presence throughout the world, which, together, approximate to large home market advantages. Although firms with large home markets may have cost advantages, this is offset because they may develop an outlook that is focused primarily on their home markets and see little incentive to develop abroad (especially some US firms). ABB's local manufacturing presence may also give advantages over firms that export from their home market.

Economies of scale and scope

All of ABB's entrepreneurial companies and plants could, of course, try to make their own way in the world, but the resulting duplication of operations would be costly. If one person oversees all the businesses and plants and establishes ground rules for such factors as design and distribution, it can work to the plants' mutual advantage. They can specialize in specific products and services and, at the same time, tap into the world's best technologies. They can gain economies of scale and command better prices from their suppliers. They can also call on their partner plants in ABB's global network for assistance and so be better able to serve their customers. ABB claims that the economies of scale resulting, in particular, from the integration of its Central and East European companies into its global production network cut prices on some major products by as much as 50 per cent.

Percy Barnevik illustrates the possibilities:

It is a challenge to manage this structure, but the payoffs are considerable. We can see how it works by looking at our transformer business, for example. We have 52 transformer plants in 26 countries. Each of them is not that big, with 250 people generating orders of about $40 million a year. But together they are responsible for $2 billion in orders a year. If you coordinate them all at a global level, you can win some pretty significant economies of scale and scope. For example, each plant specializes in one type of product for the global market, with one kind of transformer being built in Geneva, another in Norway and another in Vietnam, etc. So each plant gains global economies of scale in production. At the same time, they are able to use common design modules, standardization in parts and manufacturing processes, and global supply management. We reduce engineering hours and manufacturing hours. We used to have 20 porcelain suppliers in the world, now we are down to 3. But we buy seven times more from each of them to reduce costs, and we work closely together with them at the design stage to improve quality . . .

Here's how that gives us a competitive edge. If you are competing against other small *companies in these countries and if you are as good as they are in quality, produc-tivity and so on, then the global economies of scale I described above should yield a 10 per cent average cost advantage over the long term. That adds up to $200 million in the case of our transformer business. This, in a nutshell, is the idea behind our 'big and small, global and local' approach to business* (Barnevik, 1996a).

High-pay/low-pay synergy and access to cheaper inputs

The matrix makes it possible to connect the marketing, technical and financial strengths of high-pay countries with the lower labour and capital costs of less-developed countries, both on a global level and within regions. Barnevik explains:

Within the different regions that we operate in, you have the US and Mexico, where you try to use the relative advantage of the two neighbouring countries: labour-intensive and capital-intensive. You have them in East and West Europe. The pay difference is one to ten. Working together in joint projects makes one stronger. Similarly, in Asia, there is Japan, Australia, and some of the big countries which have high-pay levels and major emerging markets. I think the combination of high-pay and low-pay countries in all these three regions is a competitive way to grow for the companies concerned (Taneja, 1996).

Another advantage of the matrix[2] is that, by means of its deep local roots, ABB's BAs can get an inside track to the best talent a country has to offer, cheap access to raw materials via global sourcing and the ability to access capital at the cheapest level possible. This financing advantage also extends to financial markets, as, by maintaining relationships with markets and banks in a number of countries, ABB can take advantage of differential market premi-ums and credit conditions. This also applies to exchange rate differentials. By controlling export production throughout the global production network, BA managers can take advantage of currency fluctuations. This should be another factor that facilitates the aim of being a low-cost producer.

Cross-fertilization of ideas and West-East, North-South mentorships

The matrix allows for managers to be inspired by their peers. Percy Barnevik once said:

I think managers underestimate how much people really want to be stimulated. One way to do this is to expose people to the best practices. The best managers at ABB get moved around. The idea is to have your best people taking their best practices with them and exposing newcomers. If you have a person in that factory in Scotland who does an excellent job, you send him down to Thailand, where you can be sure he is going to bring with him his genius. That's ten times better than to have managers from Thailand travel to Scotland and have a seminar or something (Karlgaard, 1994).

261

Another way in which cross-fertilization is encouraged is by means of 'mentorships'. With these, ABB's Western and Northern companies adopt ABB's new Eastern and Southern ones. Mentoring between individuals is a well-established principle in ABB's companies in Sweden (and ABB Sweden's mentoring scheme covers both white- and blue-collar workers). ABB's matrix allows it to apply mentoring at an organizational and global level. One way to encourage this is to measure the performance of management in the Western company by the performance of the Asian company for which it is a mentor. Qualitative bonuses should then reflect that performance. Costs of training should be included in budgets and industrialized company leaders who contribute to growth in emerging or transition markets should be recognized and promoted.

The learning can be two-way. Swedish researcher Christian Berggren notes that, unlike 'ethnocentric globalist companies', which look for people and ideas that match their cultural values, ABB is not dedicated to diffusing its home culture standards to its subsidiaries. On the contrary, he says, the mandate is to locate 'best practices' wherever they can be found in the world. ABB is a more open culture, more oriented towards learning. Maybe, he says, 'that is a small-country advantage' (Berggren, 1996).

High performance by means of healthy competition and stretch targets

The matrix has directly contributed to higher performance by virtue of the way it has reconciled the agendas of the different parties. On all-important decisions about strategic priorities, major investments and restructuring operations, managers have had in the past to present, defend and probably adjust their proposals to fit the often conflicting aims of two matrix bosses.

A particular example was given to us by a UK profit centre manager in the former industrial and building systems segment. He said:

> Objectives tend to be stretched because of the matrix. The business areas say 'Go for volume'. The countries say 'Go for profit'. So you have discussions within those limits. We are a sales group mainly. We import products from our factories abroad. The factory wants the company to go for volume almost at the expense of profit. But volume does not necessarily increase incremental profit. The country has to make sure we get profitability and that the result margin is good. The factory doesn't care . . . What we are trying to do is apportion value added across the chain – R&D, product development, etc. Somebody at the end of the chain sells it in the country. People at the end should take less value than the people doing the work up front. But the country can't survive on a 1 to 2 per cent margin, even though that's the value we're adding. We couldn't keep the infrastructure in place. So we must have sufficient value to cover our costs and make a profit. The factory must supply to us not just at cost but at a cost on which we can make a margin. So this is one of the things that we have to discuss in the negotiation. The business area sees the whole chain.

ABB managers have been at pains to point out that the tension created in this filtering and refining process is constructive. Said one line manager:

It is healthy conflict. ABB believes in conflict as long as it is curtailed. It makes sure you consider an issue from two perspectives. So we are not just pushed to going for volume like lemmings running toward a cliff. There is always someone else with another point of view. Healthy conflict works because it generates stretch targets. The targets are always being pushed forward.

Percy Barnevik explains the reasoning behind the constant pushing forward:

You reach your target and you get a new one! Is that pestering people so that they feel uncomfortable with having new targets all the time? I have had discussions with Central Europeans about that. You should not generalize about nationalities too much. There are of course differences in cultures, but if you take Germany after that terrible history of the wars and inflation in the 1920s, and the ten million people who have been driven away from the East, I think they have a more than average obsession with stability. To have stability is a plus and change is often perceived as a threat, as something you don't like and you try to avoid. Maybe the American mentality like Jack Welch, where you have stretch targets, can come over for the Germans as sometimes unreasonable. In Germany they made a lot of improvements and they increased profits from almost nothing to ten times and made at the peak DM400 million profit, helped by the unification, and they were proud and happy and all that trouble in Mannheim was behind us. Then they got a target of 1 billion. In five years you can make a billion. Then people said 'Now we have done what he said, we have achieved this percentage of return on capital, now comes a new target, he's never happy!'

Somebody even said that maybe I had some trouble in my childhood, that I was always unhappy. So they thought that I must have psychological problems, that I couldn't be satisfied, I was always wanting more. That is one way of seeing it, of course, but at the same time you have to convince people that standing still is losing ground because the world is moving, Siemens is moving, and these opportunities are happening. You have to build in a change culture, then change becomes a natural thing. I don't mean to redo the organization constantly. We have for five years now kept the organization the same since 1993 and now after ten years, it is time for a change again. You have to be careful not to change around organizations too frequently or have revolving doors for management so they don't get the chance to perform and live with their results. But when it comes to targets, ambitions, improvements, and the customer focus mentality – where you really climb the ladder level after level – you keep moving.

Constant improvement has certainly brought some dramatic changes at ABB. Says Barnevik:

I remember when we were cutting times with time-based management in the early 1990s, we cut production time for a motor from 86 days to 40 days to 30 days to 20 days to 10 days to 5 days. And people were saying 'Five days! To just cut half and half and half, how long can that go on?' But there's really no limit. You get IT, you get new ways of working with customers, you move away from batch thinking, so by having these big targets you get people to ask themselves, 'How can I close the gap, how can I now work differently?' You try to stimulate people's gap-closing mentality. Not by pounding them or pushing them or making them unhappy, but feeling a certain joy constantly to see things to strive for and to be better than their competitors, in gaining customers. That change mentality is an uphill battle. Because deeply rooted in some nations (and everywhere to some extent) is the flight towards stability. But in the target area I don't buy it, you just have to try to overcome it and make people feel comfortable with it. When it comes to organization, changing foundations and leadership, there you must be careful. Nevertheless some people are bound to say that Barnevik is too impatient, he should slow down a little more, I am sure there are some people who think that.

What is a 'gap-closing mentality'? New CEO Göran Lindahl explains that stretch targets represent the difference or 'gap' between growth (the stretch target) and 'business as usual'. It is up to managers to close the gap between the stretch target and business as usual by 'gap analysis'.

One effect of the matrix is certainly to concentrate companies and profit centres on operations. Says one senior manager:

The people who perform are the company managers. There are people in the matrix who are responsible for business areas, countries, and regions, but the business is done by someone who has full-time responsibility for a company. This is 80 per cent of the work. He doesn't sit in endless discussions about strategy. He knows exactly what he should do. Top-level strategy is important, but execution is done by thousands of people. There are 100 people at the centre, but out there are 200,000 people executing it. Now, I cope with a broad range of issues and I travel, there are always different problems from one day to the next, but in a company it is the same thing day after day – focused, focused, focused.

Dialogue is enforced and 'complex thinking' is built in

Referring to the example that he described above of the BA faced with a choice between locating a factory in Brazil or Vietnam, Göran Lindahl said:

There is healthy competition. It forces a dialogue, sometimes a battle. People are forced to talk about their contribution to the overall bottom line – which is the most important thing. If the manager in Vietnam thinks there will be 15 per cent growth there, there is a danger of the hockey stick effect [that is, overly optimistic forecasts]. Results in most cases are the result of healthy competition inside the Group. In the decentralized process, it provides a checking balance so there is no 'central' view. It is important to understand this – we have delegated responsibility to the units and it must be decided between the units.

ABB's operational managers agreed with Lindahl's perspective. Said one:

You always have two bosses, but it's not oppressive. It's clear that the BA doesn't get involved with day-to-day issues. We run the day-to-day operations; the BA input is strategy. The BA says here are the targets; you're allowed to argue and you can go back and then agree. They monitor financial and strategic performance. For example, if you want to be market leader, the BA will monitor it. It will carry out benchmarking for a customer improvement project. After eight years you accept that there will always be some conflict. This is normally healthy because it delivers change. If you have one boss, there is no chance to argue. We create submatrices. I work with a financial controller but she reports to another boss as well. If she disagrees with me, she can go to her boss. If she worked for me, she would have no chance to disagree. There is dialogue and a chance to discuss it.

We think that the ABB matrix has fulfilled a fundamentally important role. Our previous research led us to suggest that an underlying trait of many successful international managers in today's multifaceted global business environment is a capacity for *complex thinking* – thinking through different dimensions of a problem or situation rather than just one dimension, considering a number of possible solutions rather than just one solution, and being open to information that might contradict previously held assumptions. It seems to us that many successful international managers have learned from experience to do this either consciously or unconsciously. The ABB matrix does not leave it to chance. By forcing managers to always view important issues from at least two perspectives, it *institutionalizes* complex thinking.

Percy Barnevik has always said that the conceptual part of building a global group – the organization charts, policies and guidelines – are only 10 per cent of the task. The huge challenge, the other 90 per cent, is practical implementation – making it work. So, what are the crucial factors that have emerged in making the matrix work? Some of them are as follows:

- fostering group unity
- shared values
- insistence on mutual adjustment
- accountability – no corridor people
- short lines of communication
- horizontal linkages
- rewards for performance
- rapid implementation of change
- a flexible blueprint

- ABB's 'global optimizers'
- competitive advantage from multinational teams
- leadership – setting the tone from the top.

Fostering group unity

ABB's top management has given a lot of attention to the challenges of developing and maintaining group unity. It is aware that it needs to counteract the centrifugal forces that can pull any global company apart. In ABB's case these stem from its own deliberate policy of far-reaching decentralization, its profit centre-driven orientation and its multidomestic stance with strong national roots and loyalties. To these are added local pressure and attention from employees, trade unions and the media. ABB has also had to merge many different corporate cultures among its acquisitions in just a few years.

To support and build group unity and combat fragmentation, the company sees the need to enhance teamwork, particularly in 'cross-company-border-business area' teams (see 'Creating multinational teams for competitive advantage', page 278). It also talks of the need to reward 'group behaviour' and mix people from different parts of the company, by rotating people, creating mixed nationality teams and avoiding, where possible, national 'clusters'. The company must speak with 'one voice', says Percy Barnevik.

Priorities – what comes first at ABB

1	Customers	Thousands
2	Group	1
3	Country/global BA	150
4	Individual profit centre	5000

Source: ABB

Defining and intensively communicating shared priorities is a particularly important way to counteract the fragmentation of effort that decentralization can bring. Says Barnevik, 'Because we have many profit centres, people can tend to suboptimize and become narrow-minded. For this reason, we have emphasized shared priorities: the customer first, then the Group and only then the individual profit centre' (Dauphinais and Price, 1998). (The customer is given top priority in such statements but it is interesting to ask whether what the ABACUS accounting system measures first and foremost is sometimes something different.) Barnevik believes in setting the tone for cross-border cooperation from the top and rewarding people who promote the global Group and support other people. (The ethics of cooperation and communication have sometimes, however, been taken too literally, with people scrupulously inform-ing everybody about everything. ABB has invested in advanced electronic communication systems to alleviate the resulting information overload. See Chapter 12 for ABB's implementation of information technology.)

Shared values

As a major element in sustaining Group unity, ABB places great emphasis on what Percy Barnevik has called ABB's global 'umbrella' culture – the 'glue' of shared values that integrates and holds the company together and makes it stronger than it would be going its separate ways. This emphasis started with the policy bible originally presented at the Cannes conference in January 1988. But, says, Barnevik:

> *the most important glue holding our Group together is the customer focus philosophy – how we want to be customer-driven in all respects. The values describe how we want to create a global culture, what can be done to understand each other, the benefits of mixed nationality teams and how to avoid being turf defenders. Our policy bible is not a glossy brochure with trivial and general statements, but practical advice on how we should treat each other and the outside world* (Kets de Vries, 1994).

ABB says that its overall corporate purpose is 'to contribute to environmentally sound sustainable growth and make improved living standards a reality for nations around the world'. Percy Barnevik insists on the importance of this non-commercial dimension of ABB's shared values:

> *To continue the momentum of change, it is important that our people feel pride in something beyond the numbers. For example, we have pioneered investments in Eastern Europe, spearheading East-West integration. I don't want to claim that we knew more than anyone else, but I was absolutely convinced that Eastern Europe would open up. Consequently, because we were the first, we had the pick of the best Polish companies. Many of our people are proud of participating in that process. The same can be said about our work in the environmental field. I would like to create and develop an image of us helping to improve the world environment. For example, transferring sustainable technology to China or India, where they have a tremendous need to clean up their coal-fired power plants . . . Our employees can look at work like that and see that we contribute something beyond mere shareholder value. This is particularly relevant for attracting young people to the company. By and large, they are not happy just to work for a big company with high profits, they also like to see a purpose that goes beyond numbers. It is important that a company be perceived as changing the world in a positive way* (Kets de Vries, 1994).

Are the shared values and the 'culture of change' well established ten years after the merger? Barnevik says:

> *It is of course something which is never finished, but I think these values that the cul-ture is trying to promote will come. You can say that the ten years since the merger,*

the 18 years since I came to ASEA, is a very short history. If you go out in the world and interview ABB people, you may be surprised that they give such a coherent feedback. It doesn't mean that everybody says hurray, and thinks that everything is fantastic, but the values are there. Even if you are in Russia or the Ukraine, people have studied the bible there, they understand it, they believe in it. I also remember there was a general article some years ago, with a guy in Mexico who said that the blood running in his veins was red like ABB. He associated with the company. I think we have come fairly far, but there has to be a never-ending process to reinforce it, to keep the corporate glue living and vital and not to be worn down.

Shared values cannot, of course, solve every tension between the different agendas that may exist in the matrix. So the values are backed up by two basic operating principles:

- insistence on mutual adjustment
- clear accountability.

Insistence on mutual adjustment

Percy Barnevik worried that 'maybe it is wrong to talk about contradictions' and emphasized that the matrix's purpose is not to promote opposition, conflict or infighting (McClenahen, 1994). He insisted that the matrix boosts global market clout because of the coordination, even as the multidomestic structure empowers ABB people because of decentralization. ABB's policy guidelines say:

The roles of the two dimensions of the matrix are complementary. They are interlinked and interdependent, and good communication skills are required to promote a widespread exchange of views. Any arising conflict at the interface between regions and business area/segments must be resolved constructively. Only if the matrix works smoothly can we reap the benefits of being global (economies of scale, technological strength, etc.) and of being multidomestic (a high degree of decentralization and local roots in the countries in which we operate).

The main way in which integration of the different interests takes place is via the planning and budgeting process. A potential problem in the ABB matrix is precisely that tendency identified by organizational theorists for disputes to be pushed to the top of the organization. ABB makes it clear that this will not be tolerated. As Göran Lindahl points out, the centre has delegated responsibility to the units, which must decide on issues between themselves. He remembers that when he was in charge of the power transmission segment in the early days of ABB's restructuring, he received many issues that came up from the businesses for his decision. He always pushed them back down for further debate.

ABB managers now recognize the imperative. One said to us:

There is an unwritten rule. You can always escalate things. If two people don't agree on something, they can go up to the next level. But if the same two come twice, they both get fired – or so the rumour says! That's why decisions get taken and problems are resolved at a lower level.

The question of how conflict is resolved in ABB's matrix is one that has intrigued many observers and which some regard as the key issue in judging the effectiveness of ABB's structure. Some are not prepared to take at face value the assertion of ABB managers that they are able to resolve amicably most tensions at lower levels. If the advantage of the matrix is that it ensures that business issues are approached from more than one perspective, the downside is the amount of time plus the costs of meetings and travel that reconciling those views can sometimes take. With events moving ever faster in its business environment, this is likely to have been one of the reasons for the important modifications that ABB made to the matrix in the summer of 1998 and which we discuss later in this chapter.

Accountability – no corridor people

In the ABB system, profit centre managers are accountable. They agree their goals and know what they have to do. Percy Barnevik has often talked about being obsessed with the idea of creating a small-company, entrepreneurial climate *within* a big group. He says:

We are willing to suffer some extra costs, some difficulties from fragmentation, if we can create small-company speed and flexibility, with employees living close to customers, understanding the importance of their own individual efforts for the success of their profit centre, instead of feeling hidden away in a big bureaucratic organization . . . I have seen 'corridor people' who survive by floating around and never sticking out their necks. In ABB's transparent organization you cannot hide. You are visible and accountable. That is not a threat, but an opportunity. In ABB you are allowed to make mistakes. What is not allowed is not to correct them or to be passive (Dauphinais and Price, 1998).

Definition of roles is critical. Barnevik says:

Making our kind of organization work is a lot more demanding. You can mess it up easily. If you have poor business area managers who don't understand the system, it may become clogged. Decisions will be pushed upward. It is important that within this matrix you give a clear mandate to the various people in the system. People must have a well-defined role. For example, you can say to a guy at the generator shop in the United Kingdom, 'You are going to make generators for the whole world up to ten megawatts.' Now that is pretty clear. Or, 'You will go for these 12 export markets, forget about the others, I will take care of that.' If the person coordinating globally has his role clearly spelled out, and the person running a local shop does as well, they will support each other. When the local company

269

sees the advantage of belonging to a global business area, everything goes more smoothly (Kets de Vries, 1994).

Insistence on mutual adjustment and accountability are in turn supported by important structural aspects of the matrix:

- short lines of communication
- horizontal linkages.

Short lines of communication

Unlike many matrix organizations, if issues do need to be sent up the organization, decision making is not too badly delayed. Says one operational manager:

> *One of the good things in ABB is that you can have an influence on many policy decisions. If I don't agree, I can take it up to a higher level quickly. For example, I once didn't agree with the BA leader about purchasing policy. The segment told him to sort it out and he came over to the UK to do so. This would be impossible in other organizations where there are so many layers between you and the top of the organization. We have a much shorter line of communication. As long as the business area sees we are performing correctly, we are left to do what we want to do. We are free to devise our own strategy. If we are performing well, we get a pat on the back: 'Keep up the good work'. If we are not performing well, there is a lot of pressure on us to explain deviations from forecast.*

ABACUS, the ABB accounting information system, provides the fast feedback (Barnevik calls it 'fastback') that backs up accountability. Said one profit centre manager:

> *ABACUS is a unifying factor. It allows you to enter results and comments/criteria which is all fed back to Zürich. We all have ABACUS-driven timescales and have to put the figures in by a certain date. You can see what is happening by business area, by company, by profit centre. If you are failing to perform, you will get a call. Not for one or two months' performance, but for three to four months. They will come back to you with comments and questions. It is a very good way to run a global business.*

Horizontal linkages

Many observers have seen the ability to create horizontal linkages as being one of the key characteristics of ABB's structure. BA managers certainly give a lot of attention to managing horizontal connections, such as functional councils that discuss common problems and spread best practice of leading subsidiaries, company steering committees that maximize cross-organizational learning, BA Boards that bring together general managers of key companies, and *ad hoc* task forces. Yearly strategy and technology meetings enable managers from all over the world to meet, exchange experiences and learn from each other. ABB managers are also expected to take on additional responsibilities. A profit centre manager might, for example, have the add-on responsibility of being customer focus manager for their company and might also work on customer improvement projects as part of the customer care team for their BA involving people from a variety of different countries. While this adds to their duties, it helps to prevent isolationism and narrow perspectives and provides forums in which managers can debate and resolve conflicting differences of interest.

Rewards for performance

ABB's compensation system is designed to reward performance. ABB's bonus scheme, in particular, rewards performance against budget targets. Individual managers agree their bonuses – generally awarded against earnings after financial items and order intake – with their superior managers during the annual budget process. Bonuses might also include performance on qualitative objectives such as special projects. (If customers are ABB's top priority, we would also expect that part of their reward would be based on such measures as surveys of customer satisfaction.) The aim of negotiating bonuses during the budget process rather than defining a bonus formula beforehand is to avoid managers trying to bias budget targets to secure higher bonuses. Individual bonuses are adjusted to the difficulty of achieving the targets so managers who commit to very ambitious targets may earn some financial reward, even if they do not fully achieve their targets.

Percy Barnevik says:

Generally, I believe strongly in differentiation of base pay based on responsibility and performance. I also believe strongly in performance-related bonuses. The higher the level of manager, the higher the share of variable compensation. This type of compensation to a large extent relates to the direct area of responsibility for the manager. It is useful in addition to have some option programme for the high-level management which is based on the total company performance over the longer run. I have also good experience from long-term profit-sharing programmes for all employees (Dillon, 1998).

What do line managers think that ABB rewards? Says a profit centre manager:

ABB rewards success. If you do well, they will give you something that is not running well – to see if you trip up probably! If something doesn't turn round, then they will close it – but they will usually give someone a chance to turn a business round. Success is the most important thing. We don't tolerate failure. We can't afford to have a profit centre leader who is not profitable. So it is ruthless. ABB develops people vocationally and develops skills for the job. If you are successful, you are rewarded. If you fail in ABB, it makes efforts to find out what the problems are and turn them round. But there are two choices – up or out. My personal rule is that I won't allow

271

people to fail for two years. And I expect to be judged that way, too. I'm the last sur-
viving member of a new team that came in 1993–94. I'm now the only one left in
the same position. The others left or were demoted. So we are judged too.

This manager contrasts this approach with other companies that he has known where he says profit centre managers would be allowed to 'carry on almost regardless of results'.

Rapid implementation of change

It has always been one of Percy Barnevik's principles that tough decisions should be taken as early as possible and should be implemented as quickly as possible. Looking back, he says, 'As regards speed in execution, I must generally say that those times we postponed decisions to investigate more, I usually regret that we did not move even faster.' A BA manager agrees that the speed with which changes are implemented is a crucial factor:

Decisions taken early are normally the good decisions. Things that drag on are nor-
mally not so good. We have lots of examples of things that have gone well and not
so well and the difference is mainly to do with time and speed, where good intentions
have not materialized in actions taken. We were very quick in reorganizing after the
merger. We got people together from around the world and explained what we had
decided, who should be manufacturing and selling what and what technology we
should use in future. That was a good example of speed. But, if decisions about
which factory should specialize in certain products are not followed up quickly
enough and things are allowed to slide, then you are not able to take full advantage
of the scale effect.

A flexible blueprint

From the outside, and from much of what has been written about ABB, it appears that the matrix is a standardized formula that applies across the whole of ABB's many businesses. In fact, the way it works depends on the nature of the businesses, which range from 'superglobal' to 'superlocal'. Percy Barnevik has argued that the matrix allows the pursuit of both standardization and quality strategies depending on the nature of the business. He once said that he uses 'a loose, decentralized version of it – the two bosses are not always equal – that is particularly suited to an organization composed of many nationals' (Rapoport, 1992).

One study of ABB's matrix says that it is doubtful it is designed to generate productive conflict across two equal dimensions. While country managers would dominate in locally oriented businesses such as electrical installations and service, the BA managers would dominate global businesses such as the power plant business:

Rather, the matrix serves to present a diversified and fragmented business like ABB's in a simple manner. By drawing the matrix, we create the illusion of simplicity. In fact, the matrix derives its operational value not from the structure that it imparts to the company, but from the fact that it doesn't imply any rigid structure at all. Instead, it pushes responsibility for strategic decision making to the highest level. All that an operating manager has to recognize is in which type of business he is. If he is in a global business, he obviously takes the counsel of the BA manager first. If he is in a local business, he follows what his country manager dictates (Kellogg Graduate School of Management, 1992).

Percy Barnevik elaborated on the different ways in which the matrix works in his discussion with us:

You must remember that you cannot mechanically say, 'This is a model' because within ABB you have billion dollar transactions, involving huge power plants, refineries, high-speed trains, and then you have mass-produced $5–10 small pieces that you sell to wholesalers. You have local people in Stuttgart for whom the world is 25 miles around Stuttgart. They are servicing customers in Stuttgart and have nothing to do with the UK or even Hamburg, like a very local restaurant business.

. . . Then you have this global business like a combined cycle plant where every transaction, every customer order is dealt with on a global basis. You have to adapt the general principles to the customer distribution channel of the business. For the matrix people that meant that some business areas have a very strong global business dimension, almost like a company inside the company on the one extreme (for example, oil and gas are run like a company inside the company even legally). At the other extreme, you have the business area where people don't have much to do with each other because they run separate service shops in every country. The only global role they have is to maybe exchange people and give them tips – tell France, 'maybe the Spanish have a good idea for doing it'. This is more a sort of benign benchmarking, helping and comparing notes. It is remote and there is very little involvement – none whatsoever in operations.

This explains the remark made to us by one profit centre manager in an ABB service unit that, while he had read that networking was an important competence of the international manager, in his business he rarely needed to network with other ABB operations to do his job successfully.

Isn't this range of organizational possibilities within the matrix too complicated to manage? Barnevik says:

You have to handle that spectrum, which in itself is interesting because other companies can then associate with this part of ABB or that part of ABB and don't have to have everything. Now you can say 'isn't that very complicated to run with such a spectrum of different types of businesses?' It is complicated for a few people at the top who have to understand it all – the Executive Committee and myself – but it is not complicated for the motor man in Saarbrücken. He doesn't need to under-

stand combined cycle plants or refineries. He understands standard motors. For each of these players, you have to make it simple, simple, simple – and people sometimes mix that up and believe that it is extremely complex and that it takes an intellectual giant to fit in there and understand this spectrum. It doesn't take that at all. If it did, then it would be bad organization because we have average people.

Barnevik says that ABB adapted the organizational concepts all the time during the ten years after the merger:

You don't make a drawing and then it is fine forever. You learn from experience, of course. As we grew, we refined and improved as the environment changed around us. All of a sudden you have 30,000 people in Eastern Europe, and you start to have Asians to integrate. How do we bring technology to these new areas? This became a huge, looming issue. Are we organized properly to do that? Should we strengthen the global dimension in the matrix in some areas, so that people are really working together here between Asia, Europe and America? Privatization happened. All of a sudden you didn't have these national State monopolies any longer, now it was public bidding across borders. You had all those things to adjust to, so you learned as you went and refined and improved the concepts all the time. But a general trendline over time is reinforcement of the global BA role and reduced power for country managements, as the world and customers globalize around us. The extreme importance of national managers at the beginning, even with four country managers sitting in the Executive Committee, is gradually being reduced as we get established. But the operations continue to be run in the many small profit centres close to the customers.

The role of ABB's global optimizers

Much depends on ABB's 'global optimizers' – the BA leaders who manage the intersection between global coordination and the company's local entrepreneurs. This is a demanding role. In Chapter 6, we described ABB's BA leaders as 'global coaches'. One BA manager told us:

If you can manage in a matrix, you can manage anywhere. You have demands on yourself from all sorts of people. You have to rely on your powers of persuasion, and take time to build relationships so that you know who you are talking to and can adjust your way of talking to them. Your wider outlook and knowledge of what is happening globally should give you an advantage.

Such BA managers are usually highly experienced and rely heavily on a strong personal network:

I have been around a long time and have worked in different countries and management positions, so I've created a network of contacts both outside the company with customers and inside the company in various countries. Without this network, it would be very difficult to be successful, particularly in a matrix organization. It provides a lot of information and makes it much easier to get things fixed and agreed when you know the people you are dealing with.

Tom Peters described the BA leaders as follows: 'Business area chiefs live by persuasion. They are on the road and away from the political centre almost all the time. They earn their spurs by being helpful and only seek higher-level conflict resolution assistance at their peril' (Peters, 1992). After the changes made to ABB's matrix in 1998 (see later in this chapter), the role of the BA leaders would become even more crucial.

Competitive advantage from multinational teams

ABB's BAs also depend on their ability to create and manage multinational teams successfully. Researchers into such 'transnational' teams have indeed suggested that such teams are 'at the heart of the globalization process' and that multinational team effectiveness precedes company effectiveness (Snow, Snell, *et al.*, 1996). Getting such teams to work well is therefore a central concern for a global company. ABB certainly sees the creation of these teams as a fundamental challenge.

The 35 or so BA managers come from countries such as Brazil, Canada, Denmark, Finland, Germany, Italy, Sweden, Switzerland, the UK and the US. Each BA manager leads a team of local managers who have responsibilities for day-to-day operations in different countries. For example, a German based in Switzerland with global responsibility for a BA may have among his team local managers in Italy, Germany, Sweden, the US, Norway, India, Saudia Arabia and the Czech Republic.

Barnevik believes that, as business becomes more globalized, the competitive advantages of multinational teams increase: 'Any single-nationality corporate culture will run into problems as soon as it aims to integrate larger operations from other countries' (Barnevik, 1994). Overcoming the initial hurdles takes a lot of painstaking effort, but, once this is done, multinational teams can offer major benefits:

> *Their combined understanding and insight into global and local business problems are much deeper. Benchmarking of operational performance on an international scale becomes routine. Rotation of specialists across borders to transfer best practices runs into far fewer problems and, for example, international supply contracts across borders and joint development projects become the norm.*

Barnevik believes that ABB can profit from the unique use that multinational teams can make of their complementary skills and backgrounds. When expanding into Central and Eastern Europe, he points to ABB's ability to exploit Finnish and German experience in dealing with Russians, long-standing Austrian relationships with Hungarians and Slovenians and traditional Scandinavian links with the Baltic States and Poland. Now that ABB is established in Poland and the Czech Republic, new team members can, as we saw in Chapter 4, help with building the Group's presence further East. In other regions, ABB can use Chinese-speaking team members from Singapore, Hong Kong or Taiwan in developing activities in China, or Brazilians and Argentines in Latin America. An important side benefit, says Barnevik, is that ABB can recruit future global managers from the world.

Barnevik says that, 'Multinational teams do not happen naturally – on the contrary, the human inclination is to stick to its own kind. If, in selecting a manager, the choice is between a compatriot with a familiar background and a foreigner whose credentials appear strange and whose language is difficult to understand, objective criteria tend to lose out.' Barnevik believes that competence is the key selection criterion, not passport. It is sometimes necessary to interfere in the selection process, to force people to overcome the 'foreigner hurdle' and safeguard the idea of multinational teams. The value derived from the combined different backgrounds makes it well worth taking some risks.

Barnevik points out that few people have by natural instinct the ability to work well within such teams: 'It takes patience, understanding and ability to communicate.' One important route to developing effective team members, he says, is to transfer employees to other countries – young West Europeans to Asia or America, or North Americans to Europe, Asia or Latin America. When, after some years, they return home, they have acquired a deeper insight into different cultures, and may have learned another language. This may be costly to do on a large scale, but such transfers are important for the development of effective multinational team members and global managers. Barnevik points to the imperatives:

> *The common denominators in these efforts are communication, understanding and patience. There is no question that the price to pay for a high degree of 'multina-tionality' is a major investment in two-way communication and consensus-building across borders. Even after making full use of technical means of communication, a significant amount of time must still be invested throughout the organization in face-to-face meetings and teamwork. In the final analysis, openness, trust and respect are the key words in all this. At the end of the day, all people are 'local', with their roots in some home country. It therefore takes a major, systematic and sustained effort to bridge the borders, build the multinational teams and thereby create a truly inter-national organization. But it is well worth while.*

We asked Barnevik how you can get over what he calls the 'foreigner hurdle' when creating a global team. He re-emphasizes that mixing nationalities among the global '5 per cent' of managers is a practical business necessity:

> *Because there you have the problem, and those 5 per cent are not unimportant. If they do a bad job and favour their own countries and they can't convince people, if they have to beat them over the head every time, people don't respect them for how they divide up the products [among the countries]. You need the best and you really do need them to work together as a team. The problem is that bosses tend to attract*

clusters of people from their own nationality, not because they are racist, but because they feel comfortable with people they know best. You get a German cluster or a Swedish cluster. If, for example, you appoint an Italian to head up transformers worldwide and he proposes four other Italians as his immediate reflex, then you cannot react by saying, 'You should take that Swede or Mr Smith from America, and we put them into the team'. You cannot do that because if you make the guy responsible, he has to pick his people, he has to trust them, he has to be responsible for the team. You cannot just dump on him what you think is politically correct to get a mixed nationality team. But what you can do is to say, 'You are not allowed to appoint the Italians now, because we demand that you travel to the United States and there we'll have three candidates for you to look at, and I can promise you all three can do the job. But you have to be comfortable, you have to interview them, you have to be convinced yourself'. Then you say 'I know a Swiss-German, a Swede, a Norwegian, so you have to look at these 12 individuals'. Now it was a matter of making these countries in turn make available the best people, not try to hide them by saying, 'No, I need this Swedish guy in Sweden, I don't want them to sit down in Milano and help the world'. So you really had to make the givers come up with the good candidates, and you had to make the team leader look at them. In that way you could overcome the hurdles and make sure that you got mixed teams and then the Italian had, of course, to be deep down convinced that even if they had to speak English with a German, rather than Italian with an Italian, that discomfort was small compared to the advantage of reaching out to these regions and having that global competence available when running into trouble and having to overcome obstacles later on. There are always pros and cons.

New CEO Göran Lindahl is also an enthusiast for multinational teams and the benefits of diversity: 'When I put up a management team in the early days, I always requested three nationalities', he told us.

Leadership – setting the tone from the top

Much of the foregoing essentially boils down to the crucial role of leadership in making the organization work. Percy Barnevik defines leadership:

The essential qualities I feel are – number one is the ability to track, keep and develop the right people. To create a team spirit, to really tie them to you and make a proper selection of key people. That's a must. Number two is to provide a mission to the people; to make them rally behind that and have a common sense of purpose. That is extremely important. I think you need to combine all these qualities with executive and operational capabilities. You have to live with the business constantly and you have to be fast in decision making on whatever level you sit (Taneja, 1996).

If you as the CEO preach customer focus and people development, the most important thing is that you yourself visit key customers and develop the people reporting to you. You must visibly reward people who enhance the corporate values and you must not accept the ones who work against them (Dillon, 1998).

Creating multinational teams for competitive advantage

- Start at the top – internationalize the top team as a signal to the rest of the organization.
- Make competence the key selection criterion, not a passport.
- If necessary, interfere in the selection process to overcome the 'foreigner hurdle' and safeguard the idea of multinational teams.
- Request team leaders to interview and consider candidates from other nationalities.
- Encourage local operations to put up candidates for multinational teams.
- Take some risks in selecting team members.
- Even when using technical means of communication, don't forget to invest significant time throughout the organization in face-to-face meetings and teamwork to build trust and respect.
- Communicate the need for communication, understanding and patience.
- Transfer people to other countries and regions early in their career to give them appreciation of other cultures and to develop potential multinational team members.
- The costs of creating and laying the groundwork for multinational teams are an investment in building competitive advantage.

Top leadership is not just about missions and setting the tone. ABB's top managers talk about 'fingers in the pie' management – the need to stay closely in touch with the business. This is because top leaders may sometimes have to take direct action to adjust the company's direction in the light of changes in the business environment. A particular example is the way in which Barnevik in the early 1990s prepared the company for the economic downturn he saw coming. Says Barnevik:

> Decentralization does not mean abdication. You still have to know what is going on. When I went out in the spring of 1990, I could see the writing on the wall. We still had good orders and good margins, but enquiry rates were falling. We had all these young and enthusiastic people who did not stamp on the brake immediately. In that situation, you don't just sit back and say, 'It's your thing, let's see what happens' (Brown, 1994).

Barnevik set out some guidelines for leadership in ABB.

- Provide a vision to create corporate pride. It is not enough to say ABB will be the 'biggest' or 'most profitable' company. Rather, ABB is:
  - the leading electrical engineering company in the world;
  - pioneering the East European build-up;

- supporting the build-up in Asia – transfer of technology; training; ABB is an engine for economic development;
- a contributor to world sustainable development – supplying clean technology to East and South; clearing up in Eastern Europe; leading in product lifecycle stewardship.

- 'Walk the talk' – set the tone from the top. Every manager must set the example for those reporting to them. For example:
  - customer focus – visit key account customers **yourself**;
  - management development – develop **your own** subordinates by means of periodic development talks and career plans with job rotations;
  - cost-reduction campaigns – reduce top management's own costs.

- The communication challenge demands direct communication with many people (Executive Committee members themselves each meet 5000–6000 people physically each year).
  - respect language and cultural differences;
  - send memos on positive things;
  - talk on negative things immediately.

- Decentralization is not abdication – intervention/coaching is not centralization.

- Speed in action is critical:
  - get over negative changes early on;
  - avoid the 'investigation trap';
  - solve problems at the lowest level possible.

- Globalize the organization:
  - mix nationalities – in joint teams, for example;
  - combat the 'we-they' syndrome;
  - force new personal alliances;
  - develop global managers (see Chapter 11).

- Enhance cultural sensitivity:
  - listen and show respect;
  - understand the 'language problem' – be patient because people are at different levels of fluency in English;
  - be open and generous in borderline matters.

- Develop an operational and 'hands on' mentality:
  - avoid the 'ivory tower' problem;
  - live with the business and understand the business;
  - dive deep down and come up.

- A leader must inject confidence:
  - economic incentives and a top-down control system have limited effects;
  - confidence leads to cooperation and, thence, to competitive advantage.

Early challenges for the matrix

The matrix has not come easily. ABB's people have had to work their way up a steep learning curve. Says one manager:

> *In 1988 the matrix in ASEA was only four or five years old. Both ASEA and BBC needed more decentralization than before. Maybe it went a little bit too far. There were 15–1600 legal entities. At the same time, the number of business areas went up to 65 plus 6 to 8 business segments. Then there was the regional split-up, based partly on personalities. There were many more interfaces in the early period.*

The fundamentals of the matrix have not changed, however. One senior manager says:

> *We have sometimes tried to redefine the scope of responsibility of business area managers. But they haven't changed in substance. The local organization is responsible for plant, employees, customers. The BA is responsible for setting the framework and deciding that in this country we will do this, we'll produce components there. Not much has changed in this respect.*

One of the strengths of ABB's approach to its matrix is that, although the basics have not changed, the company will adjust arrangements to try to make it work more smoothly or alleviate strains in the system. For example, there is no doubt that the matrix, as originally conceived, put a heavy load on some key people. When we first met the ABB matrix in the early 1990s, ABB still had eight business segments for which different members of the company's Executive Committee were responsible. An Executive Committee member might then have been expected to hold both a global and a local role. For example, the leader of the then industry segment (selling components, systems and software to automate industrial processes) was based in the USA and combined responsibility for the worldwide activities of the five BAs in his segment with responsibility for overseeing the activities of all the ABB business segments in North America.

This highly demanding dual role was matched at the next managerial level below. For instance, the leader of the drives BA, one of the five BAs in the industry segment at the time, was based in Milan. He was responsible for devising and implementing a global business strategy for that BA. To that end, he coordinated 8000 employees and production in 15 countries, including a number of global centres of excellence for particular products. At the same time, as President of ABB Industria, he was responsible for watching over the activities in Italy of all the other BAs within the industry segment. He reported both to the industry segment chief in the USA and to the President of ABB's Italian holding company.

A major issue for this BA manager was how much time to spend on his global, strategic role and on the local, more operational responsibility: 'This double working cannot last forever. I used to be in favour of having two jobs, but there is a lack of time. It is not practically or physically possible to work 100 hours a week, 2 times 50 a week.' In such a situation, managers might veer towards one of the roles at the expense of the other. Some might prefer to concentrate on the strategic global role while others may prefer the local dimension, which may involve more contact with local customers or with people issues. More problematically, the double global/local line role sometimes made it difficult to maintain objectivity when the very purpose of the BA role was to decide on specialization, shifts of resources and production, and allocation of markets between the units within a BA.

ABB made a small modification to the matrix very early when, in 1990, it reinforced management with extra staff at the BA level and, at the same time, increased the BA managers' responsibility for technical development. It also launched, with the aid of outside consultants, a vast internal 'customer focus' programme to help mobilize thousands of managers. Some observers saw this as an 'admission' that ABB had not yet succeeded in what Barnevik had always considered to be the biggest challenge in running a group of ABB's size – motivating middle- and lower-level managers and promoting corporate values (Dullforce, 1991).

It was still early days, however. At the time of the merger, ASEA's people had been starting to learn to operate in a matrix, but it was a whole new world for BBC's people and those in ABB's new international acquisitions. Barnevik says that he insisted on no major changes in the matrix for five years. The first imperative was to break the organization down to achieve transparency. Looking back a decade after the merger, he says:

1993 was a year where, after five years, we made certain changes. When you first create such a huge organization you have to make it transparent. You have to know where you make money, where you lose money. In big functional companies, things are hidden. Losses are covered up by profits in other places, allocations are done on the basis of who can afford to pay it. There are all types of skewed, strange factors. Transfer prices give the wrong picture. You think one guy is a hero, but he is using transfer prices and, in reality, he is a burden. Therefore, that layer-cutting transparency and fragmentation into 5000 profit centres was a necessary thing to do even if we sometimes maybe went a little far. But that is easily corrected over time. Once you really had the overview and knew it, then you could put profit centres together. Did you really need to have 60 business areas or was it enough to have 36 so that you had a little more critical mass?

Barnevik remembers:

I felt after five years that it was time to do some of this move up to the middle of the road. With all our basic concepts still applying, we adapted, cut costs and adjusted. If you look at a ten-year period, we made one single adjustment half way. We said that for the first five years we won't change anything because then it was a matter of winning customers, and winning in the marketplace. Get customers. I wrote down every good idea that came up, but said, 'Sorry, we don't disturb the organization now with changes. You are right, maybe these units should be put together, maybe that centre of excellence should be in Germany instead of Italy, but let's sum them up, remember them, and then we take it all in one shot and implement it'. We had, for example, the four big countries – Sweden, Germany, Switzerland and the United States – as members of the Executive Committee. So the German country manager was a member there. Does that make sense to have a local guy be a group manager? No it doesn't. But at the time of the merger it did make sense, when you had to win the Germans, and the German guy had to stand up in Berlin and Frankfurt and say, 'I am in charge of Germany. I am a German, you can trust us as a German company, Brown Boveri has been around for 100 years. And I am sitting, by the way, in the Executive Committee of the company, so I have my say up there protecting Germany's interests'. At that time, it was important not to be regarded as a foreigner everywhere. We had to keep these 20–30 home markets, and be Finnish in Finland, Swedish in Sweden. So you can see a certain logic in a little exaggerated fragmentation, which was done deliberately for restructuring and for transparency – and in a little over-pronouncement of national entrenchment and the domestic role.

Barnevik tells the story of meeting the prime minister of France not long after the merger:

I was trying to convince him that we were a French company. I was speaking English to him because his English was better than my French and he took me for an American, which I always like. He started to complain about agriculture immediately (he was a minister of agriculture before), American soybeans, subsidies in the mid-West, and I said, 'You are worse in France, don't complain about the Americans!' So I finally said, 'I live in Zürich, Switzerland, Mr Roucard'. So he said, 'You Swiss are the worst of all, your farmers have the highest subsidies in the world, you put the prices twice as high as they ought to be'. I defended the Swiss, I talked about the Alps, and the farmer tradition, and the tourist industry, but he didn't stop. I finally said, 'I am a Swedish citizen'. So he made a small pause and said, 'But in Sweden you have nothing to be proud of in agriculture,' and then he said 'Mr Barnevik, how many home countries do you really have?' I said, 'Right now I have 23, and I defend them all'. So he said, 'Now I understand what you mean by multidomestic!' But at that time, you were French or you were Japanese or you were an American. Nobody would dream of calling Siemens American, even if they had a big company in America. Mitsubishi was Japanese, by birth and origin. And all of a sudden here is a company saying, 'We are Finnish, we are British, we are German, we are

Swedish'. In each country we had a 100-year history: 'We have grown up with this country, we are a citizen of your country, we are run by locals.' We have a Czech company from the time of Napoleon, 200 years old. We have 150 companies more than 100 years old. They have a proud heritage, and for us it was even more important to retain that at the time of the merger than to optimize globally and have the Swedes or Americans going into Germany and giving the commands, optimizing this and that . . .

Now that this period has passed, and the world is more global, you can talk about the European market, not a collection of national markets. This is a new ball-game in the markets. Now, it is a matter of being low-cost, efficient, globally effective, and you have to adjust to that. Even in this short history, you can distinguish certain periods. What I said before 1993 was that we didn't want to touch the organization in order not to dilute people. Because, rather than making the best out of the situation, it would have been easier for people to say, for example, 'I want more [market] allocations, I want to sell to more countries, why shouldn't my Scottish transformer plant cover all of Asia, not only three countries? I'd like to build a bigger transformer like they do in Norway, why should the Norwegians build all the big ones, we are better than they are?' Sometimes it was wrong, sometimes it was right. But we said, 'OK, let's do that at one time later on so that we don't disturb you with borderline issues'.

New challenges for the matrix – large projects and regionalization

So, 1993 was a major milestone for ABB's matrix. For it was in that year, that the 'first-time' shake-up in ABB's structure took place. ABB's top management by now realized that some aspects of the matrix were too complicated. It was difficult at the Executive Committee level, for example, to combine regional and business responsibilities. One manager explains: 'The business segment managers had regional responsibilities as well as global segment responsibilities. This sometimes led to a conflict of interests. When deciding where to put plants, no matter how objective they were, they were often biased to the local country.' This conflict produced pressures for the company to split the regional and segment responsibilities.

At the same time, by 1993, ABB had changed considerably. It had acquired over 60 companies around the world, some of them – such as Combustion Engineering – were huge. It had expanded into Central and Eastern Europe, buying up companies and injecting modern technology and Western management approaches. It had started an ambitious expansion programme in Asia. The massive restructuring programme had closed dozens of plants and eliminated more than 40,000 jobs since 1990. The Group's non-recurring charges were typically running at over $100 million a year, although Percy Barnevik said that he was impatient for the day when ABB no longer had to make such charges against its results. Whereas ASEA and BBC had been marginal players, ABB could now say that it was the world's largest power engineering group. Likewise, while at the beginning it had still been very much a European-oriented company, its $29 billion in annual sales were increasingly spread among the world's three main economic regions. Percy Barnevik recognized that the Group's expansion meant that some top managers were 'choking under the complexity of their responsibilities' (Rodger, 1993a). ABB needed to streamline the matrix to try to move even faster.

Changes in ABB's business environment and the emergence of a new competitive scene also necessitated modifications to its structure. Percy Barnevik had pushed the merger of ASEA and BBC in anticipation of the impact of the single European market, but even he was surprised at the speed with which 'huge rather protectionist' regional trading blocks had emerged. The elimination of protectionist barriers between West European countries was accelerating and the integration of Central and Eastern Europe into the European bloc was proceeding apace. For a group producing heavy infrastructure equipment, these changes had big implications on the way it should do business. One result was more public bidding by utilities across borders. Another consequence was the faster growth of large turnkey projects, which, by 1993, were accounting for a quarter of ABB's $29 billion turnover. Developing countries had always tended to purchase infrastructure equipment on a turnkey basis because they did not have all the requisite engineering skills themselves. Now developed countries were also moving in that direction as privatized utilities cut back the huge in-house design and engineering organizations that previously existed under State ownership.

ABB's top management saw that its management structures needed some significant modification for the new environment.[3] The matrix had been reasonably successful in preventing individual ABB companies competing against each other (although we remember one Swedish manager in Västerås telling us in the early 1990s about the problem of different ABB business units approaching the same customers in Sweden without knowing about each others' activities). It had been less successful thus far in bringing together resources from different ABB businesses for making bids on big turnkey projects. Decentralization had been highly successful in making the company responsive to local customers, but created challenges for this increasingly important type of business. For example, various Group divisions supply most of the technology and equipment needed to build steel-rolling mills and pulp and paper mills, but dispersed know-how and marketing efforts meant that ABB was less able to make effective bids for such large integrated projects. Percy Barnevik set a big management development challenge for the future when he said, 'We want integrated system thinking' (Rodger, 1993a).

Streamlining the matrix

Percy Barnevik realized that these new trends in the business environment and the far-reaching changes that ABB itself had undergone meant that a new approach had become vital (see Figure 10.1). To strengthen its competitiveness in bids for complicated turnkey projects, in 1993 Barnevik restructured ABB's Executive Committee and reduced the number of business segments. The Committee was cut from 12 to 8 members, including Barnevik and 7 executive Vice-Presidents, and the number of segments, which had already been reduced to 6, were folded into 4. Instead of directors having both regional and line responsibilities, in the new Executive Committee this was simplified and regional and line responsibilities were split. Whereas Committee members previously had responsibilities for both countries and products, now they had one or the other.

The new reorganization also created three regions: Europe, the Middle East and Africa, the Americas and Asia, each with a Committee member located in a headquarters for each region – Brussels, Stamford (Connecticut) and Hong Kong. Four other Committee members each took global responsibility for one of the four individual business segments into which ABB's activities were now consolidated: power plants, power transmission and distribution, industrial and building systems, and transportation. Committee members with regional responsibilities were to be accountable for sales, while those with product responsibilities were to be accountable for production, manufacturing, R&D, and distribution.

The slimmed-down Executive Committee aimed to clarify responsibilities and 'optimize transnational decision making', said Percy Barnevik. He pointed out that this was particularly important in electrical engineering where growth

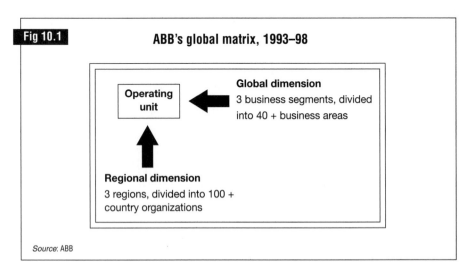

Fig 10.1   **ABB's global matrix, 1993–98**

Operating unit

Global dimension
3 business segments, divided into 40 + business areas

Regional dimension
3 regions, divided into 100 + country organizations

Source: ABB

was starting to come increasingly from the sale of whole industrial plants, high-voltage substations and distribution plants, rather than from individual pieces of machinery. Composite plant construction requires parts from many countries and that, in turn, requires close cross-border cooperation:

> *The purpose of the reorganization is to facilitate integrated system thinking, encourage teamwork by eliminating borderlines, and thus concentrate more effectively on the needs of customers and markets. With our reinforced product segments and new regional structure, we will become more effective in dealing with the challenges of the 1990s. The new organization will strengthen the operating advantages of our matrix and enable us to react even faster to market developments.*

The restructuring of the Executive Committee also aimed to help ABB adapt to the emergence of large regional trading blocks. ABB is a global company, but at this point also saw a need to be regional as each of the major world regions had unique challenges and environments. It needed to be a regional player because there were regional common issues that could not be left to each individual country. It found that it was facing more and more cross-border issues that could not be resolved by one local country manager or by one global manager. Utilities and railways used to be national, but, increasingly, utilities were buying into each other and trains were running into different countries on each other's tracks.

The creation of regional directors also reflected the emergence of increasing trade within large blocs and less trading between them. Percy Barnevik said that this was regrettable, but 'if you want to be a global player, you have to have a major presence in each.' While he pointed to an increase in intraregional trade within each area of the triad, he said that he was not that optimistic about the growth of trade between the blocs of the triad. He worried that:

> *A lot of so-called 'voluntary trade agreements' and quotas and other things are holding this trade back. It will grow, but if you want to be a global player, you have to be an insider in Asia, in the Americas and in Europe. That is why ABB was organized . . . into three global regions, with a US headquarters for the Americas, a Brussels headquarters for Europe, and a Hong Kong headquarters for Asia* (Barnevik, 1996a).

Each of the regions had its own imperatives and opportunities. In North America, the opening up of markets under the North American Free Trade Agreement (NAFTA) made establishment of one region for the Americas a logical step. This also enabled the Group to accelerate plant rationalizations between Canada and the US – 15 plants would be closed as a result of the acceleration programme. Treating the Asia-Pacific region as one division ensured focused attention in the area of the world with the greatest growth potential.

The growing unification of Europe also required that the Continent be treated as one market. Europe, said Barnevik, must now be viewed as one region – no longer divided into East and West – if cross-border corporate issues were to be properly addressed. He identified some changes of special significance for ABB in Europe that its strengthened European cross-border management would help it to exploit more effectively: the creation of the enlarged EU, the further opening up of Central and Eastern Europe, and changes in customer behaviour. He expected the larger and more open markets resulting from the creation of a single market comprising the EU and Norway (the European Economic Area) to produce cross-border regional and trans-European development projects in the energy and transport sectors. He also predicted that large EU-backed infrastructure projects of interest to ABB would attract EU grants of $128 billion and EU loans of about $174 billion over the next 5 years. In addition, ABB would be among bidders for other large projects worth $10–20 billion annually – mainly in Spain, Portugal, Greece, Ireland, southern Italy and eastern Germany. Barnevik also foresaw more public works opportunities and expected that open public procurement, privatization and deregulation would revitalize Europe's development business.

The reduction in the size of the Executive Committee had a particular impact on ABB's original homelands. Until then, the Group had appointed executive directors with responsibility for Sweden, Switzerland and Germany – the countries where ABB's main plants were located. Barnevik said that these directors inevitably sometimes defended their 'parochial' interests rather than those of the Group as a whole. This was no longer appropriate in a Group with operations as widespread as ABB's. When he was asked if he expected to be criticized for having only one Swiss member on the new Executive Committee, Barnevik declared, 'I hope we will not have this zero sum game on nationality. Now people move up here on the basis of qualifications' (Rodger, 1993b).

In addition to restructuring the Executive Committee, ABB also created a top management council consisting of 70 managers who meet 3 or 4 times a year to review operations and discuss strategy. It includes the Executive Committee members, senior functional heads, a number of BA and country managers, and key regional and corporate staff members. ABB insisted that this was a discussion group and not a new layer of management – which would have contradicted its philosophy of a flat organization.

Bringing the BAs to the centre

One intended effect of the restructuring was to push more tasks down to the next layer of management below the Executive Committee – the BAs. The BAs were themselves to be the subject of important changes. First, most of the BAs were taken out of line responsibilities to focus on their global strategic role. They were now responsible for global profit targets and for promoting the Customer Focus programme across their BAs. As one manager explains:

We have moved business area leaders out of line responsibility for a particular profit centre. There are pros and cons to them having line responsibilities. The positives are that if you sit on a big unit, you know the problems, you understand what's going on and you can call on resources. But the negative is that people suspect you of not being neutral with respect to other profit centres within the BA.

Another major change concerned the location of the BA leaders and their (small) staff. One of the features that Tom Peters felt distinguished the ABB matrix was that the BA leaders lived 'where it makes sense and move when it makes sense.' Writing in 1992, he said, 'In the traditional matrix, business area equivalents are typically berthed at mecca – i.e. corporate headquarters – and often win debates by mere proximity to top execs. There are no business area heads/teams at the Zürich headquarters, and neither grass nor excessive self-esteem grows readily under the feet or between the ears of business area staff members' (Peters, 1992).

Pre-1993, as Peters noted, the BAs were based all over the world, but there was increasing concern about their effectiveness as teams. As one manager says, 'They were travelling a lot to stay in touch with operations, but how do you get teamwork?' So, in 1993, it was decided to move most of the BAs to Zürich. One senior manager explained the move:

At first it was felt to be good if the BAs were out there close to a big plant, close to the local environment and the bosses of one of the bigger units. It was also a sign of globalization, that nothing was centred. But the conclusion over time is that, despite the benefits, they tend to be a bit isolated out there, sitting in an office with a few people, and not in the local organization. In Zürich, they can talk to people here and can cooperate with other BAs. Also, when they are in Zürich, they are seen as coming from Zürich, from head office, which gives them a little more weight. It is tough out there, they have to take difficult change decisions – for example, we can't make two motors in Finland or Sweden any more. Even if they don't close a factory, it is still a big change for the local organizations. When they're out there, they represent the global group.

It was also hoped that bringing the BAs to Zürich would make them more objective and globally focused. Says one senior manager:

By bringing the BAs into Zürich, it divorces them from local company roots. One of the BAs was based in Sweden – they were all Swedes, sitting in Sweden close to their home [ABB] companies. There is a natural tendency to favour your own country instead of, for example, Italy or a new start-up company. By bringing the BAs out of their home market, such as Germany, which is a big market, it gives them a more global view. They don't have personal proximity, it makes them a little more independent of the big ABB countries, – Germany, Sweden, Switzerland and the USA.

One effect of moving the BA staff to Zürich was to boost numbers at the corporate centre. Observers frequently comment that ABB has a head office staff of about 100 people. This is not quite true today. At head office, about 140–150 people make up the global staff. There are also 70 people employed in a separate service company, including telephonists and receptionists, who support the global staff. ABB Financial Services also has about 120 people in its own head office in Oerlikon but that is more like an operating unit which happens to be situated there. They could as well be in, for example, London. With the addition of 100 or so BA people (the teams range from 5 to 6 people in some BAs to 10 to 12 in others which earlier were located in other places), this makes a total of about 400 people at ABB's corporate centre (although neither the BA people nor Financial Services are housed in the main head office building in Oerlikon). This is still relatively small for a global corporation of 213,000 people.

Getting a matrix to work takes time

When Goold, Campbell and Alexander studied ABB for their research on corporate parenting in the early 1990s (described in Chapter 7), one ABB manager in ABB's North American management team told them:

For the matrix to work well, you need debate between the regional and BA management. This depends on three elements: conflict, teamwork and trust. At the moment, we probably have too much conflict, both healthy and unhealthy, but that is because we are still a very young company. We are only now developing the shared values, common language and shared culture that need to underlie the matrix (Goold, et al., 1994).

It was only in 1997 that Percy Barnevik was to say that 'ABB has virtually finished building its global structure' (Wagstyl, 1997). When we talked with managers in the company in 1997–98, there was a definite sense that people were now much more comfortable with ABB's multidimensional structure. 'What has really changed now,' says one senior executive, 'is that people have become more used to operating in a matrix. The big difference now is in how cooperation works, much more through teamwork – this takes time to achieve.' Percy Barnevik believes that ABB's matrix has even greater competitive potential: 'After nine years, ABB is far from fully exploiting the advantages of its organizational structure. But I believe this is the winning recipe in the long run' (Dauphinais and Price, 1998).

What could make the matrix work even more effectively in future? Says one executive:

The BA managers typically have a staff of 4 to 6 people and 25 plants around the world. They have to know what's happening. They can't supervise them as the organization is locally decentralized, but they must be aware of the issues and must be there sufficiently. What we could do more of is to move people around between business area and country management so that they see both sides. It tends to be that, if you stay in one or two types of job, you become very effective either in the local or the global role, but maybe you don't see problems from the right side.

Percy Barnevik summed up the challenges:

No one believes in decentralization more than I. For the last few years, I have purposely gone overboard on it. Otherwise, we could never get people out of their protective nesting systems that are inherent in big companies. But we've done that, so now we have to pull inside, do some consolidation, use technology to get control and efficiency (Karlgaard, 1994).

In sum, 1993 was a watershed year for ABB's strategy and structure. After five years, mergers and acquisitions became relatively less important, while integration, standardization and economy of scale now started to attract more attention. A shift in the ABB matrix had taken place. The global product dimension was starting to assume more importance than the local and national dimension. Certainly, some ABB managers worried at the time that the changes to the matrix represented a recentralization of the company. This was apparently so in Germany, which had always been a very independent part of the Brown Boveri organization in pre-ABB days. An article in the German *Manager-Magazin* in 1994 quoted a 'disillusioned top executive' who described ABB as 'a command economy worse than the Prussian military'! However, Barnevik believes future steps will be towards further globalization with increased roles for global BAs.

Large-scale projects – a new dimension for the matrix

By the mid 1990s, as we have seen, large infrastructure projects worth several billion dollars were an increasingly important part of ABB's business to the extent that they were starting to constitute a third dimension to ABB's matrix, in addition to its regional and global legs (see Figure 10.2). ABB and its predecessor companies have always been involved in large projects, but, during the1990s, partly because of economic growth in Asia, there was a huge expansion in the scale, scope and complexity of such ventures. When ABB competes on large projects in Asia, it goes in as a team of high-tech system suppliers from Western Europe and the US, plus low-cost equipment suppliers from Poland, Romania, Thailand or China. Its competition is Japanese companies in partnerships with their own low-cost suppliers in China, Malaysia, Vietnam and other countries. ABB believes that this is the only way it can compete and be profitable in these highly competitive markets.

Traditionally, power equipment suppliers delivered minutely specified turbines to technically highly competent national authorities. Customers in the

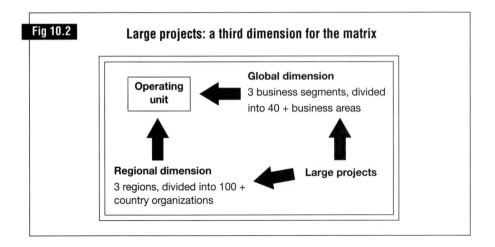

Fig 10.2   **Large projects: a third dimension for the matrix**

emerging economies are less concerned about technical specifications than with getting their suppliers to guarantee lifecycle costs and price per unit of energy. Power engineering firms are now having to deliver complete turnkey power plants where the turbine might comprise 15 per cent or less of the value.

Privatization is creating similar market changes in the developed markets. Deregulation of the industry and the growth of independent power producers is increasing the pressure for flexible financial solutions. Decreasing credit availability from traditional sources and high national budget deficits in some countries are creating the need for new financial structures.

In order to provide competitive solutions, it is no longer enough for suppliers to excel in power-generation technologies. Increasingly, they will be judged on the basis of price, the ability to devise appropriate financial solutions and project management skills. Suppliers still need a thorough understanding of individual components and the underlying technologies, but, more and more, they will be expected to demonstrate a much broader range of abilities for the power plant as a whole as customers develop projects requiring close involvement and support from vendors.

Large projects put particular demands on ABB's managers and organization. They are bigger in scope and scale and are high-risk. They demand a concentrated effort during a limited period of time – power plant projects that previously had a time horizon of 4 years now have to be delivered in 15 months. Large projects cut across the geographical and business dimensions of the matrix as they involve different regions and countries and bring together different BAs and segments. High-quality communication and cooperation are critical. To meet all the time and product requirements of large projects, ABB has to put together internal and external consortia. The result, as Christian Berggren has identified, is that 'a quasi-permanent project structure is imposed on the company's business and country structure' (Berggren, 1996).

Percy Barnevik has described the organizational and managerial consequences:

The teams are changing, but the control system has to be permanent. Every month, there is a project review, and no cover-up of any major problem is allowed. ABB needs 500 global managers for its international organization. But on top of that, we also need 350 global project managers. Running a large-scale project is like being the president of a big company. These managers have to squarely focus the interest of the group, and have the power to override objections from several national companies, if it is necessary for the project (Barnevik, 1995).

ABB intends to give more attention to developing managers to run projects in future. One senior manager says, 'We need better project managers. Our experience of projects is definitely increasing and we are upgrading the status of project managers. Sometimes they are more important than country managers and profit centre managers. It is a more demanding task than running a factory, even if fewer people are involved.'

David Hunter, formerly Head of Central and Eastern Europe, points to the challenges from his regional perspective:

We must improve our ability to manage and implement cross-border projects. We have a tendency to be weak here because we are so decentralized. There is always a tendency for ABB companies to be only concerned about their own company's welfare – this is human nature. There are usually several entities operating together on a project. We have a policy of open books. We insist that they open their books so no one tries to hide profit. And we insist that they share the profit (and the loss) according to the risk assumed. It is an imperfect process, but we must keep working on it . . . We must be more aware even than today of customer needs. In ABB it's very easy to get inwardly focused because there are so many problems. We are good at technology with customers, but we can improve in speaking with one voice to customers and especially to key customers. We are gearing up for global account management now – so there will be Mr ABB responsible for a particular customer globally.

Large projects bring other demands, too. They put increasing emphasis, for example, on 'financial engineering'.

Emerging markets do not always have the resources to fund large projects. For example, a Middle East city may want an urban transit system but is not able to pay for it. The supplier in such an instance may be required to construct the system, then operate it for some years, taking the revenue from ticket sales. This shift of orientation ('from selling to financing', as one manager describes it) calls for long-term customer relations, more creative approaches and the need for more 'systems thinking'.

Large projects present particular challenges for ABB and its matrix. As ABB approached the next millennium, not all observers were convinced that all was totally rosy in the matrix. Some worried that in several BAs, ABB was not achieving optimal economy of scale or capacity utilization. The scattered and fragmented power plant production network, for example, compared unfavourably with GE's much more consolidated operations (we tackle Percy Barnevik on this question later in this chapter). They were concerned too that ABB's dispersed structure often makes the transfer of technology and production know-how across borders highly complex and that, despite ABB's best intentions, it is not always easy to achieve the direct, personal contact between engineers that facilitates such transfer. Perhaps, as we have already noted, the biggest concern was the question of conflicting goals and priorities in the matrix. Were these counteracting the other advantages that the matrix had brought? ABB was mindful of such issues – hence Göran Lindahl's change project which came to a head in the summer of 1998.

ABB Financial Services

Financing has become a vital part of project development and customers increasingly seek suppliers who can provide total solutions, from feasibility studies and engineering to total project management and financing. This is where ABB's Financial Services segment (AFS) comes in. Its business objective is to give sales support to the ABB Group and supply financial services to internal and external customers on a profit centre basis.

AFS aims to provide one-stop financial shopping across the whole project life cycle – from bid development and the selection of ABB for a project, the structuring, development and financial closing of the project, plant construction and into the operational phase. One-stop shopping means that ABB can sell equipment that can be packaged with internal financial advisory services, equity investment and debt financing as needed.

Jan Roxendal, President of ABB Financial Services, says, 'More and more the client looks for total solutions rather than equipment. He doesn't want to own it, he just wants to use it. So we are looking at a different ownership structure which will become more common and we must understand how to deal with it.' Roxendal sums up the challenges: 'The market is forcing ABB to reconsider its way of doing business. Infrastructure projects are more and more "finance driven". Our markets are now largely in emerging markets. High quality financial input is critical for efficient project sales. Financing must be integrated into the commercial package from the beginning of the project development. Imagination, creativity and flexibility are vital to achieving our mission. We have the skills and resources but *teamwork* is necessary to succeed.'

Technological leapfrogs

ABB was investing $1 billion annually worldwide on tangible assets in the 1990s, but Percy Barnevik says that its big investment has been in research and development, applications know-how, and software. ABB now spends about 8 per cent of turnover on R&D ($2.6 billion in 1996) – 'nearly Silicon Valley levels', as one observer put it. More than 90 per cent of this is in the business areas and therefore close to the customer. (GE spent $1.9 billion on R&D in 1996 or 2.1 per cent of turnover; in 1996–97, GEC-Alsthom, as it was then called, spent 391.2 million ECU or 4.1 per cent of sales on R&D.)

While ABB says that it works systematically with payback calculations, it also believes it is important to make enough resources available for speculative and risky R&D where meaningful payback calculations are difficult. Percy Barnevik was concerned that not enough 'technology lifting' projects were in the pipeline and that budgetary constraints may have stopped some ideas. The Executive Committee therefore decided to make extra money available for very risky but high potential projects, the so-called 'HIP' (High Impact Program). 'The impact', says Barnevik, 'was really great – not only with the many new promising R&D projects but also because of the signal it sent to ABB's 20,000 R&D engineers'.

ABB says that it still needs to get more fruit out of its research efforts and CEO Göran Lindahl has promised some 'leapfrog' steps in technology. This policy started to pay off with the announcement in 1998 of a big breakthrough in power generation – the world's first high-voltage generator. Called the 'Powerformer', it can supply electricity directly to the power network without the need for transformers, thus radically changing a 100-year-old technology. ABB claims that the Powerformer dramatically improves reliability and efficiency, substantially reduces operating and maintenance costs, and saves about 30 per cent of the capital cost. Through its higher efficiency and lower operational losses, it also reduces the demand for natural resources and thus benefits the environment.

Developing innovative technology is, for ABB, a key to making its customers more competitive. 'So is getting those solutions into their hands quickly and at competitive costs,' it declares. This is why building 'technology' leadership and targeting research and development at specific customer needs is a major aim. The company sees its cultural diversity as fertile ground in which to cultivate creativity. It believes, in particular, that it derives advantage from its ability to form multinational teams among its research engineers and scientists worldwide that can bring a variety of perspectives to bear on specific customer needs. Its eight corporate research centres bring together leading researchers in many fields and from many backgrounds to work on its core technologies.

At the same time as ABB streamlined its operations, it also streamlined much of its product base, with an emphasis on developing modular systems. The aim of modularity is to be able to deliver flexible systems that can be changed as customers' business requirements change. It is seen as a more cost-effective solution for customers and, because it means ABB can standardize module design, it allows the company to deliver customized whole-system solutions while improving economies of scale in production. Modularity reduces lead times on power projects. Modular turbines, for example, start working for the customer even faster enabling power producers to generate electricity and revenue. Automation technology, in particular advanced control and instrumentation systems, allow customers in capital-intensive industries to improve return on investment for both their new and existing plants.

From a 'regional' to a 'global' structure

The concerns of those observers who worried about tensions in ABB's matrix and the time and overhead involved in resolving conflict, were at least partially answered by the surprise announcement in August 1998 of important changes in ABB's structure.

In perhaps the biggest shake-up in ABB's history, the large Industrial and Building Systems segment was to be divided into three new segments – Automation (including industrial robots); Oil, Gas and Petrochemicals; and Products and Contracting (dealing with industrial engineering processes). The Power Transmission and Distribution segment would become two separate segments – Power Transmission and Power Distribution. The Power Generation and Financial Services segments remained unchanged.

The composition of ABB's Group Executive Committee now consisted of the President and Chief Executive Officer, the heads of the global business segments, and the Chief Financial Officer.

ABB's new Group Executive Committee

Göran Lindahl	President and Chief Executive Officer
Renato Fassbind	Chief Financial Officer
Kjell Almskog	Head of the Oil, Gas and Petrochemicals segment
Jörgen Centerman	Head of the Automation segment
Alexis Fries	Head of the Power Generation segment
Sune Karlsson	Head of the Power Distribution segment and Head of the Power Transmission segment
Armin Meyer	Head of the Products and Contracting segment
Jan Roxendal	Head of the Financial Services segment

Simultaneously, ABB's regional and subregional organizations in Europe, the Americas and Asia were dissolved 'after having fulfilled their mission to coordinate ABB's expansion in their respective areas.' Country organizations would remain, 'continuing to build ABB's "multi-domestic" presence in markets around the world.' A new Group function will also be established to exploit the potential for implementing group-wide global processes, standards and programmes. Customer contacts and sales organizations were unaffected, with ABB's key customer accounts, sales coordination and other customer focus programmes continuing unchanged.

CEO Göran Lindahl told the press: 'This is an aggressive move aimed at greater speed and efficiency by further focusing and flattening the organization. This step is possible now thanks to our strong, decentralized presence in all local and global markets around the world. This should be seen as a leapfrog move in response to market trends, to make sure we can serve our customers better and build more value for stakeholders.' The new structure would increase ABB's speed in responding to market demands and lower costs, making the group more competitive. Lindahl also said that ABB is more than a power engineering group. By splitting the group into eight core businesses (including the 50 per cent in Adtranz), it should allow investors to focus attention on its role as a world leader in fast-growing businesses such as automation where it has a $6.4 billion order book and 34,000 employees.[4]

These developments involved some job changes. Some people who had been closely involved in the growth of ABB moved to new responsibilities. For example, Alexis Fries, who was previously head of the Asia region, took over Power Generation. Eberhard von Koerber, previously head of the European region, continued to work with the group as Senior Advisor to Lindahl and corporate management and as chairman of the Board of ABB in Germany, and Sune Carlsson, head of the industrial and building systems segment, was offered the job by Percy Barnevik of helping to turn round SKF, the Swedish bearings group.

Overall, industry observers expected the changes to cut management costs, simplify management lines and give more market visibility to businesses that had been buried in larger segments. As the *Financial Times* suggested, however, the importance of the changes was not the impact on costs but on culture: 'Country managers will henceforth report directly to main [Group] management, speeding up decisions' (*Financial Times*, 13 August 1998).

We had the opportunity to discuss the new structure with Göran Lindahl after the changes were announced. We asked him what had led to the changes. He explained that ABB's key principles of decentralization to profit centres, a flat organization, and the matrix structure with global business areas and strong national identities had proved successful for the company in the 11 years of its existence. The challenge was to make a basically good organization even better for the next millennium – an era which will be characterized by an increasing trend to a globalized environment. Lindahl describes it the following way:

If you look at the world during the 11 years of ABB's existence, you can see that we have had a very clear move from a nation state-oriented market place through regions to a globalized environment. In 1988, when ABB was established, the Berlin Wall was still there. When it came down we had been working for two years already. Before that there was the old pattern of countries protecting their 'national monuments', with their established trading patterns. When the Wall crashed in '89, suddenly we saw lots of trends. First of all, in the early 1990s the European Union became more than a paper product and people started to discuss it as a reality and started to believe in it. Then people started to talk about the integration of Eastern Germany into Germany and the possibility of the Eastern European countries joining the European Union. There was a higher degree of administration from Brussels which started to look into legislation and fiscal policies, etc.

Then you saw a trading block emerge out of the European environment, which went a little bit beyond the EU, and included some of the Eastern European countries, primarily Poland, the Czech Republic and Hungary, followed by the Baltic States. At about the same time you had the creation of the NAFTA [North American Free Trade Agreement] region, with the US, Canada and Mexico. And these countries now began to discuss how to approach Mercosur, the Latin American Trading bloc, so that started to emerge as a second regional development. And thirdly, we saw the Pacific Rim, which we now call Asia, emerge also as a large block primarily driven by South East Asia and to a lesser extent by Japan, because it was already an industrialized country.

Lindahl describes how the emergence of these three blocks led to the first change in ABB's organization in 1993 when it changed from a national structure to a regional structure.

Until then we had the larger countries of ABB – Sweden, Germany, and the US – represented in the Group structure. Then in 1993 we took out the three countries and put in the three regions. We also had several functions on that level where, for example, marketing was a functional responsibility at the top; we also had R&D. We then saw that you couldn't organize yourself any longer according to functions; you had to do it according to markets and the customers out there.

After that we have seen that, firstly, Asia has become more than a region, that it interrelates to a large extent with the rest of the world, primarily Western Europe and North America, but also with Latin America. China sells to Canada and the US. So there we saw that the regional borders tended to disappear. We have seen the same in Europe. Europe is now more than the European Union; it is also Central and Eastern Europe, a larger block with relations with the Middle East, and Turkey with its 60 million people. That is the trend of globalization, and it has happened more and more. This has led us at ABB to ask ourselves: What is now the next natural step in our organizational development?

The next transformation is to a global structure, says Lindahl. 'We concluded that we have to take the full consequences of globalization and that means

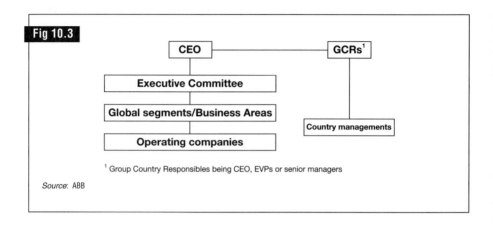

Fig 10.3

¹ Group Country Responsibles being CEO, EVPs or senior managers

Source: ABB

that we must globalize our organization also. That means that we take away the regions.' Country management will now report to Group Country Responsibles (GCR) who are drawn from ABB's group management (CEO and executive vice presidents) and other senior managers.

Lindahl points out that ASEA as the forerunner of ABB took the first step towards a globalized structure when it established sales and marketing arms in countries all over the world 15–20 years ago. The second step was globalizing technologies, when some ten years ago ABB started to look at the possibility of putting productive assets – added value manufacturing, design, service and engineering – out there. That, says Lindahl, was globalizing technology through joint ventures, greenfield establishments and partnerships of various types.

> *And now we are taking the third step with globalizing the structure and also globalizing the leadership. We have tried to create what I would call universal leadership that covers all the value systems of our customers and employees. We are coming out of a Lutheran and Calvinistic value system; we need to have a value system that is acceptable to Muslims, for example, or at least respects their value system. You have to do this if you want to be a truly global player. That goes hand in hand with the organizational development.*

One feature of increasing globalization is 'brutal' price pressure which requires continuous cost-cutting, superior efficiency and fast decision making. Taking out the regions and having country managements report to Group management will take out some direct costs such as those incurred in travel and meetings. The reorganization was also expected to lead to better coordination for projects and plants.

Has the matrix been scrapped as some reports suggested? No, says Lindahl, 'we have changed the balance, putting more power into the global dimension.

If there is a disagreement between the local and global dimensions, the global will have the pulling power. It is another adaptation of the matrix. If in doubt, we will always decide on the basis of Group profit – before it could be on the basis of country profit sometimes. If you are in a boundary-less world, then you need maximization of the global.'

The role of the country manager will continue to be that of building relationships with local governments and authorities; developing local customer relations; ensuring a structured ABB customer interface; and taking care of human resource development. They will also now be responsible for implementing global processes and common functions in their country and ensuring compliance with ABB directives. Company and Business Area unit managers now report to the global BA and have to meet BA targets and budgets for results and profitability. Segment and BA management will approve the selection of local Business Area unit managers – a significant step in a global direction.

What will change for the country managers? Lindahl says, 'Before, you could take the mandates as given. Today, you need a mandate that is agreed between the local and the business managers. I wanted to take away the "legislation" and see that decisions are always based on Group business needs.' Lindahl believes that in ABB's new organization, it will be critical not to exercise power but to have dialogue and create bonds between Business Areas and countries. The matrix still depends on fostering good relationships. When people properly respect each other's know-how, skill, and experience, the 'informal handshake matrix' will be stronger than any formal matrix. But, in the end, global priorities and decisions will prevail. Lindahl acknowledges that the way it works will depend on the business. ABB still has some very local businesses as well as global businesses. 'There is no one simple answer,' he says.

Lindahl points to the risk in a matrix of duplicating functions, such as business control. Now there will only be a single control function. Lindahl also says that by globalizing processes such as supply management, the company can increase its muscle by, for example, combining sourcing for factories in different countries. But he emphasizes that the countries are still very important. 'You still have to do business through the local organization.'

Where the newly created segments are concerned, Lindahl points to external and internal advantages. Externally, investors 'will compare us in future with Honeywell or Siebe Automation, etc. If I can say we can be compared with such companies, people can more easily take the risk and invest in ABB. The advantage internally is that we can attract the best people because they can see we have a value system that they like.'

Lindahl places the changes in the context of the three strategic initiatives that he has carried out since becoming CEO in 1997 to prepare ABB for the future. The first was to focus ABB on its core businesses and divest some non-core areas (ranging from electrical wholesaling to refrigeration). The second was the October 1997 restructuring in response to developments in Asia with the aim of using the low-cost environment there to promote even more efficient production (described later in this chapter). This latest major restructuring towards a more global organization is the third initiative.

The consensual style in which the changes were effected is significant. Göran Lindahl says that ABB used a new concept of management development and organization development.

> *Normally, when you carry out a massive change, you call in one of the big consultancies and they work with the management team, and then you announce it, and then you have to start to do the job and you use the consultancy. We have not used any consultants. We used our own skill, but we have also done it in such a way that over quite a long period of time the top managers of the Group were involved in the process. So it was not a surprise for people in the organization. It is not a breakthrough, but it is new, at a time when people want to have participation. They take ownership early on because they were involved in it. I personally talked to a huge number of people. Because, if you make a change, and some of them are directly concerned in it, you need to give people respect and therefore you talk to them personally. And you don't want to do that by telephone.*

The chief executive carried out extensive discussions with the company's 70 top managers. Then they were given a questionnaire with 40 'very specific and very provocative' questions. People had to respond in writing but they could do so anonymously so there was no 'tainting' because people wanted to try to 'satisfy' superiors. 'This has never happened in ABB before,' says Lindahl. He obtained 90 per cent support for the decision to remove regional reporting lines. The speed of the changes are also in keeping with ABB's reputation for speedy implementation. 'We have gone with tremendous speed,' confirms Lindahl. The 70 top managers are very good messengers of the changes and the decentralized nature of the organization is an advantage. 'A lot is done out there. When you push the button, it doesn't have to go through the hierarchy.'

Are the changes evidence of a five-year cycle in ABB's organizational development? Lindahl says that the fact that they occurred in 1998 was more of a coincidence, although he does believe that organizational structures have a life cycle of five to seven years and that, with the exponential changes occurring in the global business environment, the cycle tends more towards the shorter end of the scale. 'You have to revitalize,' he says.

Creating long-term value for shareholders –
the ultimate measure of performance

Sumantra Ghoshal and Christopher Bartlett have said that Percy Barnevik will 'survive in public memory . . . The reason will not be the strong strategic and financial performance of ABB under his leadership', but because he 'has created a fundamentally different model of how a large company can be organized and managed' (Ghoshal and Bartlett, 1998). This is true, but how have ABB's strategy and structure actually translated into financial performance so far? What does ABB believe are the key measures of financial success? How does Barnevik himself want to be judged on his own track record of financial performance?

Back in 1988, right at the beginning of ABB, Percy Barnevik set stretch targets of 10 per cent for profit margin and 25 per cent for return on capital employed. As Table 10.1 on the following page shows, those targets have proved challenging for the Group overall to achieve, although the Group's operating margin trend over ten years has been upwards (ignoring the restructuring charges in 1997; see Figure 10.4).

One of the major challenges that ABB faced – in addition to industry-specific problems and cut-throat competitive conditions in the power business – was the need to cope with a general economic downturn in the early 1990s before it was fully trimmed into shape. In 1991, 60 per cent of the company's

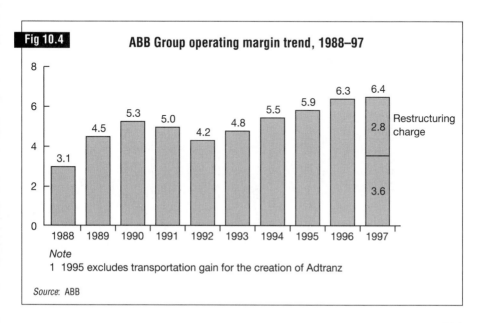

Fig 10.4   **ABB Group operating margin trend, 1988–97**

Note
1 1995 excludes transportation gain for the creation of Adtranz

Source: ABB

Table 10.1 ABB Group data, 1988–97 ($million)

	1988	1989	1990	1991	1992	1993	1994	1995	1996	1997
Revenues	17,562	20,260	26,337	28,443	29,109	27,521	28,758	32,751	33,767	31,265
Operating earnings after depreciation	543	918	1,386	1,417	1,219	1,311	1,574	2,181	2,113	1,137
Orders received	17,572	21,348	28,938	29,209	31,153	28,644	30,827	35,163	33,884	34,803
Expenditure for research and development	1,255	1,361	1,931	2,342	2,386	2,271	2,353	2,627	2,638	2,657
Number of employees	169,459	189,493	215,154	214,399	213,407	206,490	207,557	209,637	214,894	213,057
Ratios										
Operating earnings/revenues	3.1%	4.5%	5.3%	5.0%	4.2%	4.8%	5.5%	6.7%	6.3%	3.6%
Return on equity	12.5%	16.8%	14.5%	13.9%	11.8%	1.8%	20.2%	28.4%	22.2%	10.3%
Return on capital employed	11.6%	15.1%	17.3%	14.7%	14.7%	15.4%	16.9%	21.8%	19.9%	12.2%

Source: ABB Annual Report 1997

geographical spread of business, mainly in the OECD countries, was in recession, although growth continued in Eastern Europe and Asia. Despite the problems, the company still posted higher profits and turnover than in previous years. In 1993, Percy Barnevik chided a journalist who questioned the company's profitability, declaring:

> I think you have misinterpreted the company's development pretty fundamentally. If you go back to 1980, you will see that ASEA's profits rose ten times between 1980 and 1987. When we bought Strömberg, we transformed the loss to a return on capital of 25 per cent in 3 years. In the first three years of the BBC merger period, we doubled our profits. Then, in 1991–92, we had the disastrous recession in Scandinavia. This cost us hundreds of millions of dollars. Despite this, we made up these losses elsewhere. In 1993, with Scandinavia still not reviving, we had the recession in Germany, France and Italy. Another important factor is that we show our figures in dollars. If we had been a Swedish company, we could have shown our profits 30 per cent up. But, if the dollar goes up against soft Scandinavian currencies by 30–40 per cent, the optical effect is a reversal. Throughout this period, we also managed to drive up our operating margin from 6.5 per cent to 7.2 per cent. So, contrary to your assumption, I am extremely happy with our profits progress in this deep, long recession (Panni, 1993).

In the past, ABB, as a capital goods manufacturer, has been late in the economic cycle with three good years followed by two less favourable ones. Barnevik believes that many business analysts misunderstand the impact of the cycle:

> I grew up in the steel industry where the cycles are bigger and also in the pulp and paper industry. For some strange reason, when the cycle is up, the stock market is positively surprised. And the more the business cycle is down, the more they are negatively surprised. They never learn the cycle. We tried to ride the cycle and then put [our performance] in the context of the cycle. We had a bad downturn in 1991–92 in Western Europe which was a large part of ABB. We were able to keep up the pre-tax profit, but we struggled like hell, just to keep it for three years. And then, of course, people said, 'Barnevik, you said that you would achieve that target, and we see now three years in a row you have not improved your profit'. Then came 1994–95, where we doubled the profit in two years and then we did as good a job in 1995 as we did in 1992. We increased our profit 45 per cent. It is just that you had the market with you. I think that over these ten years we have grown some 17 per cent a year and we had 2 big write downs [for restructuring], where we closed a number of plants, to make a big shift into low-pay, low-cost countries, but apart from that we have been on a fairly steady climb if you put it as an average over full business cycles.

(The historical pattern may be changing, with an increase in ABB's service and retrofit business, thereby reducing the cyclicality in the group.)

Some observers have also asked whether or not the very policy of multidomesticity – which has given ABB its unique 'insider' presence around the
world – has affected its financial performance. Do the smaller manufacturing
units implied by a multidomestic approach mean that ABB is unable to match
the kind of efficiency, through economic purchasing, operating efficiencies
and low error rates, that GE can attain with its large factories? Barnevik
acknowledges that there are always tradeoffs to be made between local presence and global efficiency:

> *There was no question that in the early 1990s after the merger, we were fragmented,
> and I explained to you that it was by design. To get the transparency, to really
> change, you had to break [operations] up. And we are still maybe the most decen-
> tralized company of our size in the world. But you may not now have 1200 but 900
> companies. It also means that a local manufacturing presence in that country and
> that product was more important ten years ago than it is now. Italy now has pro-
> curement rules, where it is illegal to buy Italian goods for the government if you can
> get cheaper American or German or whatever. And if you are not the low-cost sup-
> plier, you don't get the order. The whole game has changed. Now you must be the
> low-cost producer. And certainly while [clients] like you to have factories in every
> country, wherever you are, they don't buy from you if you are not the low-price
> supplier plus, of course, consideration of quality, service etc. The changing environ-
> ment means that ABB has to adjust to that new world. I think we have behind us
> that 'persuasion period' where we had to persuade people we were really German and
> Finnish and so on. You cannot afford to have more plants than is rational.*
>
> *So that means that Germany may supply the world with certain things, but they
> will not produce at all certain other things, and of course the smaller country you are,
> the more specialized you become. Strömberg in Finland is a good example, going
> from being a mediocre, zero result company, providing practically everything, selling
> 70 per cent in Finland, and supported by all types of arrangements. There they now
> produce 15 per cent of that assortment for the world. They make three times more
> than they did before, but Finland has another role now. They are not the General
> Electric house of Finland, they are the world supplier in a niche. And that is, of
> course, what the Finnish government and key customers in Finland appreciate and
> they understand.*
>
> *So, that is one of the reasons why we had to close all these plants in 1993, and
> 1997. Because we have a new ball-game now. We are still [fragmented] compared
> to GE, which has practically everything in a few big plants in the US. In Jack
> Welch's eyes, we are still enormously fragmented. Even when you consolidate and
> look at these two, big suites of restructuring, there is always a balance to be domes-
> tic to the local country, and you must never give up that local dialogue, and being
> close by for servicing, and at the same time have a back-up from further away. But
> it has to be low-cost and high-quality, and it has to be innovative. It is a balance of
> combining these two things all the time.*

The competitive situation in the power segments remained severe and prices fell by 7 per cent in ABB's power-generation segment annually in the mid 1990s, the reason being that many players gave priority to market shares rather than profitability. ABB claims that it has frequently refrained from tendering for projects involving substantial pressure on prices. Some of its competitors had operating margins of 1–2 per cent or were incurring losses. Against that background, the performance of ABB's power-generation segment was very good.

Percy Barnevik says that firms must learn to exploit cost-saving opportunities in emerging countries to survive the constant downward pressure on prices. He cites the example of ABB bidding against Mitsubishi Heavy Industries to build a power plant in the Philippines: 'We have 60 to 70 per cent Eastern European content. The Japanese have 60 to 70 per cent Chinese content. What really happens is that beneath the umbrella of ABB and Mitsubishi are Romania, the Czech Republic, Poland, and Russia, meeting China.'

This does mean restructuring in Western Europe and North America. ABB had already been shifting the balance of employment by moving jobs to Asia and Eastern Europe at a rate of some 1000 jobs per month. During 1990–97, it reduced employment by 62,000 people, mainly in Western Europe and North America. At the same time, it added 57,000 new jobs, mainly in Asia and Central and Eastern Europe.

In 1997, however, moving early to forestall the Asian crisis, new CEO Göran Lindahl dramatically sped up the process by announcing ABB's intention to restructure in Western Europe and the US, including the reduction of 11,700 jobs (16,500 including Adtranz) and accelerate expansion in Asia. The aim was to speed up local expansion in Asia and improve the productivity and competitiveness of operations in higher-cost Western countries. ABB's core competence centres would remain in Europe and North America, but there would be a further shift of resources to emerging markets and Central and Eastern Europe. Thirteen factories would be closed along with several downsizings. Lindahl said:

We will take immediate action to increase our productivity in some of our operations in Western Europe and the US to ensure that we remain competitive in future. Some of these actions will be difficult in the short term, but the issue is not going to go away on its own . . . By acting early, we reduce the threat of significantly larger employment effects in our Western operations over the longer term.

The countries mainly affected would be Germany, Italy, Spain, Sweden, Switzerland and the US. These actions were to be implemented over 18 months and involved a $850 million restructuring charge against the company's 1997 results. The average payback of the actions was forecast to be two years. The company expected that ongoing restructuring would lead to substantial decreases in the West in 1998–99, while employment in the East would rise by 30,000 up to 2000/01. In addition to restructuring charges, one other impact on ABB's reported results has been the impact of a strong US dollar, the currency in which ABB reports its performance. In 1997, for example, while orders received as reported in dollars increased by 3 per cent, in local currencies they rose by 11 per cent.

One of ABB's senior managers said to us: 'We are not the most profitable company in the world and we have never claimed to be so. In some areas, we have actually done very well, although I think it is possible to get more out of the Group.' Given the market and restructuring challenges it has faced, we would say that the company has performed remarkably well on a year-by-year basis. However, while ABB's top management regards short-term performance as important, it is long-term measures that count even more.

Long-term shareholder value as the ultimate measurement of success

When, in 1998, we asked Percy Barnevik about his views on ABB's financial performance, he told us:

> *There is one ultimate measure of financial success and that is long-term increase of shareholder value. To create long-term shareholder value, you must satisfy your customers, motivate your employees, work well with your suppliers and be a good citizen. It is not really any contradiction between shareholder value and objectives for all these other constituencies. The biggest contribution ABB can make to society at large is to serve customers' needs, to grow and to be profitable.*

ABB's introduction of shareholder value in Switzerland at the time of the merger was a big change in thinking. Says Barnevik:

> *Shareholders were almost looked upon as bondholders. I remember a CEO in one of the big German companies there who had not been paid a dividend for ten years. They [companies] didn't see shareholders as owners, they didn't work for them. Unfortunately, many people in continental Europe misunderstand shareholder value. They think that because you measure a share every day, even every hour, every minute, that is short term. But we talk about long-term shareholder value. If we invest in China with a five-year payback, if we are building a presence in India, then we are building shareholder value. Not by increasing profit next year or next month. It has nothing to do with whether it is either short or long term. You can be both short term and long term. But shareholder value is the ultimate long-term measurement.*

Barnevik says that he does not believe in 'fluffy' talk about different stakeholders and that it can even function as an 'excuse machinery' for poor performance:

I publicly oppose this stakeholder mentality where you say that to judge this CEO we should ask how he handles customers, his people, his suppliers, is he a good citizen? You have all these stakeholders. To really create shareholder value, you have to treat your people well, you have to motivate them, you have to give a good service to your customers. If you are a bad citizen with a bad reputation you don't get the best people. You don't get the public orders. If you treat your suppliers like dirt, you don't get the best ones.

What I am saying is stay clear of the messy stakeholder stuff and say that, long term, you are measured on your financial performance and how you build value. Not by being tricky short term, but by building long-term value. You can only do this by doing a good job with all the other stakeholders. If, on top of that, you at the same time can participate in the development of emerging markets, in integrating Eastern and Western Europe, by being a case for that, contributing to sustainable development, then they are valuable side benefits. And what I found fascinating at ABB was to contribute to all these things while we were building shareholder value. There is no contradiction.

So, long-term creation of shareholder value is what you want to be measured by. Those who came in 1980, and bought ASEA shares, they got 87 times by the end of 1996 after 17 years, and if you instead had bought a portfolio representing the general stock index, you would have got 36 times the value in that period.

A focus on long-term shareholder value does not mean that ABB's top management neglects to monitor the short-term performance of its different businesses. Says Barnevik:

If you have a five-year project in a country, that means that you don't expect payback for five years' time because it is long term. But you must follow the progress every month, every quarter, and if they start to slip against the plan, you must intervene well before the five years. So you need to have fast feedback, to react on signals – this doesn't mean that you are short term. It is about controlling, being up to date, fast and speedy – so you can react in time also with regard to long-term projects.

The chief executive's role in communicating with investors to promote long-term confidence is vital in Barnevik's eyes:

The job I had to do with my shareholders was to tell Wall Street that my Eastern European venture in 1989 was not a disaster, because they thought that the Communists would come back and risk the shareholders' money. They said, 'Barnevik is a European and is all charged up with these emotions, thinking with his heart not with his head.' So I had to explain to them, 'I really think we can make a lot of profit here', which we then did in Poland, the first country. Again, it is about communication. And then you ask, 'Can you convince Wall Street?' Sure. If you know your thing, if you are convincing, and have good arguments, you can make these short-term shareholders understand and believe in you. Some may sell the shares, others will say 'I think ABB and Barnevik has a track record, this is a company that knows what they are doing, we would like to stay in there'.

A closer look at the development of the share price of its two parent companies, ASEA and BBC (respectively renamed ABB AB and ABB AG in 1996[5]), shows how ABB's investors have benefited. Calculations by Investor, the Wallenberg holding company, indicate that the annual total return to ASEA/ABB AB shareholders during 1980–96 was 30.1 per cent, compared to 23.5 per cent for the Swedish stock market. This means that 100 Skr invested in ASEA on 1 January 1980 would have increased in value by 87 times compared to 36 times for the Swedish stock market index (see Figure 10.5). The average annual increase in the share price was 42.7 per cent during 1980–87 up to the merger and 19.8 per cent during 1988–96 after the merger. (The Swedish stock market index rose by 17.1 per cent per annum over the latter period.) Turning to the Swiss parent, the average annual share price increase for BBC/ABB AG during 1988–96 was 21.9 per cent, while the Swiss market index rose by 14.1 per cent annually (see Figure 10.6).

It is also interesting to compare the share price development of ASEA/ABB AB shares with the share price development of the 20 most actively traded shares on Stockholm's stock exchange during 1980–96. The average annual increase in the share price of ASEA/ABB AB was 30.1 per cent, making it the third best performer after other Wallenberg sphere companies Astra (37.1 per cent) and Ericsson (31.4 per cent).

How does ABB AB's share price compare to its main competitors worldwide? Investor's own calculations show that, during 1980–96, ASEA/ABB AB outperformed GE, which today has the world's second highest market capitalization, although, of course, from a much lower starting point. The average total return for ASEA/ABB AB during this period was 30.1 per cent compared with GE at 21.6 per cent and Siemens at 9.3 per cent. (Investor also points out that the Swedish krona weakened against both the US dollar and the Deutschemark over this period.)

As a final measure of shareholder value, Investor also calculated the added value in absolute terms (in excess of the local index) that was created in both share categories during the periods 1980–96 and 1988–96. The added value during 1980–96 was 66,685 million Skr and 35,700 million Skr (Swfr 6660 million) for ABB AB and ABB AG (see Tables 10.2 and 10.3) respectively, or more than 100 billion Skr in total. As Investor says, 'As ABB internally have a clear focus on creating value for the shareholders, this is an important measurement for both management and the employees of ABB.'

ABB believes that it can boost shareholder value by linking it to the reward system for key managers. At the end of 1997, it announced the launch of a new management share option programme that would give its 400 senior managers

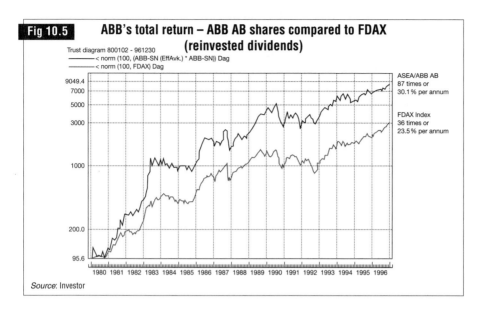

Fig 10.5 ABB's total return – ABB AB shares compared to FDAX (reinvested dividends)

Source: Investor

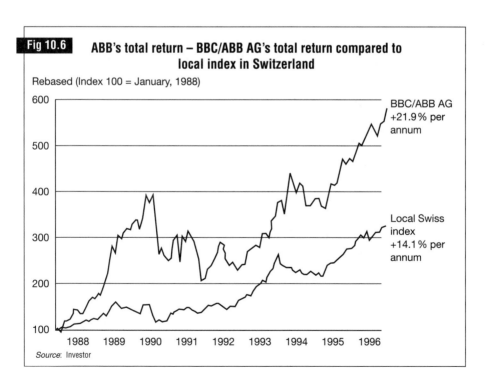

Fig 10.6 ABB's total return – BBC/ABB AG's total return compared to local index in Switzerland

Source: Investor

Table 10.2 ABB's total return – ASEA/ABB AB share price development

	Value creation ABB AB
ASEA's market capitalization at 30 December 1979	about 1,300 MSEK
Market capitalization at 30 December 1996	72,219 MSEK
Value of reinvested dividends, etc.	41,716 MSEK[1]
Total value if one invested in ASEA (including reinvested dividends)	113,935 MSEK
Average total return per year (%)	*30.1%*
Value at 30 December 1996 if one invested 1300 MSEK in index 30 December 1979	31,226 MSEK
Value of reinvested dividends (in index)	16,024 MSEK
Total value if one invested in index (including reinvested dividends)	47,250 MSEK
Average total return per year (%)	*23.5%*
	113,935 MSEK
	–47,250 MSEK
ABB AB's value creation in excess of the stock market average	66,685 MSEK

Note

1 It is assumed that all dividends are reinvested in ABB shares. For example, it is assumed that the Incentive shares were sold immediately and that the money was reinvested in ABB. It is also adjusted for the dilution due to options, etc.

MSEK = million Swedish krona.

Source: Investor

Table 10.3 ABB's total return – BBC/ABB AG share price development

	Value creation ABB AG
ABB AG's market capitalization at 30 December 1987	about 2,500 MCHF
Total value if one invested in ABB AG (including reinvested dividends)	14,860 MCHF[1]
Average total return per year (%)	*21.9%*
Value at 30 December 1996 of 2500 MCHF invested in Swiss index 30 December 1987	8,200 MCHF
Average total return per year (%)	*14.1%[2]*
	14,860 MCHF
	–8,200 MCHF
ABB AG's value creation in excess of the stock market average	6,660 MCHF
Value creation in SEK	35,700 MSEK

Notes

1 It is assumed that all dividends are reinvested in ABB shares. It is also adjusted for the dilution due to options, etc. The total return is based on figures from S-E Banken.

2 Total return of local Swiss index. It is assumed that dividends are reinvested in index. The total return is based on a diagram from ABB's investor relations.

MCHF = million Swiss francs.

MSEK = million Swedish krona.

Source: Investor

worldwide options on existing ABB bearer shares. This succeeded a management option programme introduced in 1993 and was intended to 'enhance ABB's long-term performance and the creation of greater shareholder value' by focusing managers' minds on shareholder returns. It was intended to have a continuous programme with annual option launches covering some 100,000 underlying shares. The duration of each year's launch would be six years.

ABB's new CEO, Göran Lindahl, is firmly committed to increasing shareholder value in future. When asked why shareholder value is important for ABB, he says, 'It is the ultimate proof of our success, that people want to put their capital into us – that we can add to shareholders' value. If we lose the stock price, then people will invest in something else.' How does shareholder value fit with stakeholder value? ABB is clear that the stakeholders for whom it aims to increase value are its employees, customers and shareholders. Lindahl says, 'You can either choose to do it against society or with society.' ABB prefers to do it with society.

A snapshot of ABB in 1997–98

In this book, we are trying to take a longer-term look at ABB, but let's take a snapshot of some of the key events and trends, both for the ABB Group as a whole and for its business segments, from its 1997 results, reported in February 1998.

ABB Group key events, 1997

- Continued order growth (11 per cent up on 1996 in local currencies) driven by:
  - growth in large projects (large orders increased by 37 per cent compared with 7 per cent increase in base orders).
  - Latin America and the Middle East and Africa showed strong growth;
  - Enhanced focus on marketing and sales.

- Asian turmoil triggered accelerated restructuring programme and speeded up local expansion in emerging markets.
- Power segments kept earnings at about the same level as 1996 on a comparable basis despite shortfall in revenues and negative currency effect.
- Industrial and building systems segment improved results over 1996.
- Increased emphasis on 'sales, sales, sales', including increased resources (personnel, training and so on) and focus on processes, structure and channels. The objective is profitable growth by means of enhanced market penetration.
- ABB's Powerformer is a 'revolution in electric power generation'.
- Service and retrofit saw good growth in all segments, with regional build-up of service business, including additional internal resources, implementation of new concepts and acquisitions.
- Automation is a core competence in ABB with $6.7 billion in orders received.

- ABB sales to oil, gas and petrochemicals markets reach $3.5 billion.

Power generation – 1997 highlights

- Strong increase in orders received, indicating increased hit ratio with better price quality.
- Successful year for ABB's advanced GT24/GT26 gas turbines.
- All BAs increased service and retrofit volumes.
- Increased speed in restructuring programme – strong emphasis on steam power plant business in Germany.
- R&D investments remained high.
- Continuous investments in the global sales network.
- Operating earnings about the same as 1996, despite shortfalls in revenues and negative currency effect.
- A year of consolidation and building up of profitable backlog.

Power transmission and distribution – 1997 highlights

- Orders increased 9 per cent on a comparable basis, double-digit growth in local currencies.
- Expansion in emerging markets continued. New operations in Asia, Africa and Central and Eastern Europe.
- Large power transformer factory to be closed in the US.
- Continued high level of investments in R&D – numerous new products and systems.
- Excluding Bakun costs, operating earnings increased 4 per cent in US$ and 14 per cent in local currencies, despite shortfall in revenues.

Industrial and building systems – 1997 highlights

- Increased profitability by means of reduced sales and administration costs:
  - more efficient sales process;
  - economy of scale in administration;
  - strong cost focus.

- Strong increase in large orders.
- Strong growth in oil, gas and petrochemical and service BAs.
- More than 20 acquisitions and joint ventures made.
- Many products and technologies launched during the year.
- Earnings increased despite lower revenues.

Adtranz – 1997 highlights

- Substantial increase in orders received – up 14 per cent with higher price quality:

- – success in UK rail market – more than 400 vehicles ordered and options for more than 800 additional cars.
- Major restructuring programme initiated:
  - – employment reduced by 1200, excluding acquisitions.
- Significant turnaround in the US and continued improvement in the UK and Portugal.
- Most projects awarded prior to 1996 now in delivery phase – all significant quality problems solved.
- New vehicle concept and standardized design developed.
- Fast entry into Eastern European market by means of major acquisitions in Hungary and Poland.
- Earnings negatively affected by restructuring costs and overcapacity – employee reduction now well under way.

Financial services – 1997 highlights

- Sales support activities continued to expand – a total of $8.6 billion of financing arranged for ABB's industrial units.
- Substantially higher fee income resulted in high earnings in leasing and financing.
- Continued improvement of underwriting result led to higher earnings in insurance, despite lower insurance premium levels.
- 'Treasury centres' earnings lower than 1996 because of lower volatility in European interest rate markets following the EMU convergence process.
- Energy ventures and structured finance reported high earnings.
- Income before taxes for the segment reached $297 million, slightly below 1996, mainly explained by a stronger US$.

ABB's market environment in 1998

- Despite short-term uncertainties, Asia continues to represent significant growth potential, driven by a need for infrastructure.
- Demand will rise in the Middle East and Africa due to low existing power-generation capacity and the need for interconnecting grids.
- Deregulation in power and oil and gas sectors is creating opportunities in the Americas – especially high growth is expected in Latin America.
- Continuing high infrastructure needs in most of Central and Eastern Europe will continue to benefit ABB as it has strong local presence in these areas.
- European economies have started to improve. Export and domestic demand are expected to drive increasing industrial output.
- ABB outlook: excluding the impact of the 1997 restructuring charge and assuming that average exchange rates against the US$ in 1998 remain about the same as in 1997, net income in 1998 is expected to increase.

ABB's longer-term targets

- ABB's longer-term targets are reaffirmed, despite increased uncertainties in the market environment.
- Annual growth of at least 6 per cent on average over this business cycle.
- Further considerable reduction of working capital in relation to revenues.
- Substantial increase of net income margin to 6–7 per cent of revenue from 3.8 per cent in 1996 (excluding restructuring charge).

Source: Presentation by Göran Lindahl, Zürich, 26 February 1998

Notes

1 Suggests a study of ABB by the J. L. Kellogg Graduate School of Management at Northwestern University, Chicago (J. L. Kellogg Graduate School of Management, 1992).

2 Highlighted in the Kellogg study.

3 The 1992 study of ABB's international strategy and structure carried out by the J. L. Kellogg Graduate School of Management at Northwestern University, Chicago, suggested that ABB's attempts to coordinate its business globally were sometimes counterproductive and that there were potential gains in efficiency if countries with homogeneous markets were organizationally moved closer together by means of the identification of 'regional centres' with similar markets and customers. Kellogg recommended the establishment of regional centres that could relieve BA leaders by task-sharing, helping to overcome knowledge and time constraints, and promoting quick reaction by 'competent and autonomous subsystems'. Cost-efficient cross-country standardization and coordination could be agreed independently of the BA leader and could reduce the number of potential communication links.

4 In October 1998, ABB purchased Netherlands-based Elsag Bailey Process Automation, the world's largest process automation company. This move took ABB deeper into knowledge-based industries and aimed to reduce its dependence on traditional heavy engineering.

5 In 1996, Barnevik announced that the consummation of the founding merger was virtually complete. The disclosure at the annual Group press conference announced a streamlining of the company's supervisory Board structure, designed to simplify decision making and strengthen links with shareholders. The shares of ABB were not publicly traded as ASEA and BBC still each owned half the stock. The shares of the two parent companies were traded on stock exchanges in Europe and the US. To highlight a new sense of unity, the parents would be renamed – the Swedish half would henceforth be 'ABB AB' and the Swiss half 'ABB AG'. It was hoped that the streamlined structure would make the Group more attractive to investors and that American and other investors would be less confused. In anticipation of a future flotation on the New York stock exchange, the individual Boards of each parent were reduced to 4 members each and each group of 4 became members of a streamlined 11-person ABB Board. Barnevik became the single Chairman of the new Board, retaining his post of Chief Executive and signalling that a new chief executive would be appointed. Co-chairmen Peter Wallenberg and David de Pury resigned their positions. Barnevik indicated that he wanted to have an Anglo-Saxon-style split between a non-executive chairman supervising the business and a chief executive in day-to-day charge. The remaining merger issue was the adoption of a single share structure (this was

delayed by negotiations with Swiss tax authorities on shareholders' tax liabilities arising from a stock merger).

References

Quotes without references originate from the authors' personal communications – see page xviii for details.

Barnevik, Percy (1994) 'Making local heroes international', *Financial Times*, 17 January, 8.

Barnevik, Percy (1995) Lecture at University of Linköping, 30 August (quoted in Berggren, 1996).

Barnevik, Percy (1996a) *Percy Barnevik on Globalization*. University of St Gallen, Switzerland: presentation to the International Management Symposium, University of St Gallen, 20 May.

Barnevik, Percy (1996b) 'Engineering a worldwide advantage', *Europe's Most Respected Companies*, Financial Times & Price Waterhouse.

Bennis, Warren (ed.) (1992) *Leaders on Leadership: Interviews with Top Executives, Harvard Business Review*, Harvard Business School Press, xiv.

Berggren, Christian (1996) 'Building a truly global organization? ABB and the problems of integrating a multi-domestic enterprise', *Scandinavian Journal of Management*, **12** (2), 123–37.

Brown, Andrew (1994) 'Top of the bosses', *International Management*, April **49** (3), 26–32.

Dauphinais, William, and Price, Colin (Price Waterhouse) (1998) interview with Percy Barnevik, 'Creating a federation of national cultures: reflections of Percy Barnevik', in *Straight from the CEO: The World's Top Business Leaders Reveal Ideas that Every Manager Can Use*. London: Nicholas Brealey Publishing, 42.

Dillon, Frank (1998) 'Barnevik's global vision', *Decision* (Ireland), May, 12–18.

Dullforce, William (1991) 'ABB ASEA Brown Boveri: first the creation – but the fruits have still to be fully realized', *Financial Times*, 5 April.

European Energy Report (1996) 'ABB springs surprises', 1 March (454), 19.

Financial Times, 'The Lex Column', 13 August 1998.

Ghoshal, Sumantra and Bartlett, Christopher (1998) 'Fired into the firmament', *Financial Times*, 5 February, 15.

Goold, Michael, Campbell, Andrew and Alexander, Marcus (1994) *Corporate-level Strategy: Creating Value in the Multibusiness Company*. New York: John Wiley, 163.

Hoffmann, K. and Linden, F. A. (1994) 'Kommando zurück', *Manager Magazin*, November, 34–45.

Houlder, Vanessa (1996) 'Technology: quiet revolution', *Financial Times*, 26 March, 18.

J. L. Kellogg Graduate School of Management (1992) *ABB ASEA Brown Boveri Group's International Strategy and Structure*. Chicago: J. L. Kellogg Graduate School of Management, Northwestern University, 8 December.

Karlgaard, Rich (1994) 'Interview with Percy Barnevik', *Forbes*, 5 December, **154**, 65–9.

Kets de Vries, Manfred (1994) 'Making a giant dance', *Across the Board*, October **31** (9), 27–32.

McClenahen, John S. (1994) 'Percy Barnevik and the ABBs of competition', *Industry Week*, 6 June **243** (11), 20–3.

Martin, Peter (1997) 'A future depending on choice', *Financial Times*, 7 November, 16.

Mintzberg, Henry (1983) *Structure in Fives: Designing Effective Organizations*. Englewood Cliffs, New Jersey: Prentice-Hall.

Panni, Aziz (1993) 'Reaping the harvest', *EuroBusiness*, October, 72–6.

Peters, Tom (1992) *Liberation Management: Necessary Disorganization for the Nanosecond Nineties*. London: Pan Books, 47.

Rapoport, Carla (1992) 'A tough Swede invades the US', *Fortune*, 29 June, 76–9.

Rodger, Ian (1993a) 'ABB managers strip for action', *Financial Times*, 25 August, 19.

Rodger, Ian (1993b) 'ABB seeks to win more projects by reshaping board', *Financial Times*, 25 August, 15.

Sadler, Philip (1994) *Designing Organizations*, (2nd ed.) London: Kogan Page, 134.

Sampson, Anthony (1995) *Company Man: The Rise and Fall of Corporate Life*. London: HarperCollins, 243–44.

Skaria, George (1995) 'Interview with Percy Barnevik', *Business Today* (India), 22 February–6 March, 100–5.

Snow, Charles C., Snell, Scott A., Canney Davison, Sue and Hambrick, Donald C. (1996) 'Use transnational teams to globalize your company', *Organizational Dynamics*, Spring, 50–67.

Taneja, Narendra (1996) 'Managing a vision', *Tycoon* (India), August, 24–31.

Taylor, William (1991) 'The logic of global business: an interview with ABB's Percy Barnevik', *Harvard Business Review*, March–April, 91–105.

The Economist (1995), 'Survey: multinationals', 24 June.

The Economist (1996) 'The ABB of management', 6 January, 64.

Wagstyl, Stefan (1997) 'A multinational cadre of managers is the key', *Financial Times*, 8 October, 14.

11

Developing ABB's people and 'corporate glue'

*It is fantastic how much business is really about people issues.
You never cease to be surprised whether you are a lawyer or an
engineer, or if you have a business education, that the question
really is: can you communicate, ignite people, be believable, build
trust? We talk about having bright strategies. But at the end of the
day it comes back to execution. Can you create a culture,
leadership, make people buy in, and feel part of it?*

Percy Barnevik, 1998

As mentioned earlier, CEO Göran Lindahl sees developing human resources as one of the two key priorities for ABB in the future. During recent management meetings he has emphasized the importance of attracting and developing new talent, a responsibility the company has firmly placed with line managers since the merger. Lindahl has also begun to take the development of ABB's corporate culture the next step. People from different parts of the globe – in particular, from Asia – have been asked to join a task force to reinterpret and enrich ABB's corporate guidelines, which had been written down in the 'Cannes bible' in 1988. CEO Göran Lindahl has said that one of the major challenges around the millennium is to globalize leadership and ABB is trying to create a 'universal leadership' that addresses the values of all the people who work for it.

How has ABB's approach to management development evolved over time? And what is expected of the ABB manager in the first place? In this chapter, we look at the profile of the people in ABB and how they are developed by the company. We then look at the culture of the organization by exploring how life has really been for people on the inside – rather than simply considering the company's attractive catchwords. We move on to the principles of the

317

culture that has been created since the launch of the famous Cannes bible in January 1988, and ABB's approach to change.

The people of ABB – a new breed of superhumans?

So, how would you like to work for ABB? How, indeed, would you like to run ABB or one of its businesses? How do you think you would measure up to the challenges?

ABB makes strong demands on its people. They are expected to work extremely hard, perform well and be technically very good. The performance of the profit centre is reported on a monthly basis, a practice that is used to create both internal competition and healthy internal benchmarking or cooperation. Profit and loss responsibilities encourage people to feel ownership and have meaningful autonomy deep down in the organization. Still interested in the job? Read on.

ABB tries to set high standards for its recruiting. Arne Olsson, Head of Corporate Management Resources, explains what is expected of every professional joining the organization:

- a good education;
- strong analytical skills;
- good communication skills;
- an interest in, and openness to, other cultures;
- energy to drive the business.

For Olsson, these guidelines mean that people need a good solid basis before they can learn to become ABB's corporate entrepreneurs and innovators, able to work well in its very decentralized organization with its in-built tensions.

New kids on the block

ABB managers will tend to take and leave their responsibilities at a younger age than their average European or Asian colleagues. For Arne Olsson, the key concern is to find and develop enough young talent for the organization. This is understandable given that, since the days of ASEA, the company has relied heavily on the energy of younger generations to achieve its ambitious goals:

ASEA had no problem with putting young people in important positions. If you compare this with countries in continental Europe, and the difference between the age profiles of the two merging companies in ABB at the time of the merger, this reflected very different philosophies and cultures. It was not unusual in ASEA that young people were put in demanding positions. But in large Swiss or German companies, people in the same positions were, on average, perhaps ten years older.

After being offered the corporate role for management resources, Olsson remembers turning up for one of his first meetings in Switzerland and being greeted by a Swiss manager who was greatly surprised at his young age. Heavily supported by Percy Barnevik, he has been pushing for younger people in ABB ever since.

In ASEA days, Percy Barnevik encouraged young talent by creating an informal group of 'speaking partners' to discuss strategy, acquisitions and organizational changes.[1] These young people had a formal educational background with university degrees in engineering and/or business administration and had been in the company for five to six years: 'It was a tremendous exposure for them and they all landed up in high-level positions. He always pushed to find and surround himself with bright young people and talent', Olsson remembers.

With his early departure from ABB's executive scene at 55, after 17 years as CEO of ASEA/ABB, which shocked the Asian community, members of which tend to begin their executive careers at this age, Percy Barnevik has also set the tone for his generation to retire and renew itself, leaving the stage for younger people. A number of managers in ABB – particularly people who had built up the company since the exciting merger days – today are very conscious of the explicit request for senior executives to leave early.

Understandably, succession planning is a major issue for everyone at ABB. It is considered a central part of a manager's responsibility. 'An important event recently was our big Management Conference in Montreux (November 1997). Göran Lindahl says we have to push more for developing people because the age profile of upper- and senior-level managers is getting older. People who were involved in the merger are now 50 or more. It takes time to develop managers, and we will now intensify the process', says Arne Olsson.

From engineers to business people

In line with its greater customer focus and in order to make its matrix really work, ABB has shifted from looking for engineers to recruiting more rounded businesspeople. When ABB was formed as a result of the merger, it inherited two management populations that had traditionally been composed of engineers. The matrix, and the management policies that came with it, required these engineers to behave differently. It was now time to act as entrepreneurs and innovators, which was a major transition for many. Now, the company is increasingly looking for businesspeople with a more rounded set of skills.

In 1998, an ABB manager said:

In 1990, typically a manager was an ex-engineer who had been promoted because he was a good engineer and had an engineering mindset. ABB recognized the need to have entrepreneurs to grow the business, people who liked individual responsibility and challenge. Now it needs more business-oriented managers, not even engineers. Now it's not just entrepreneurs who are needed, but people with wider business skills. There is more emphasis on marketing and financial skills now. The people I see now are business managers. Eight years ago it was engineers and in between it was entrepreneurs.

The perspective of Fred Bystrand, Vice-President of Information Services illustrates how this new trend takes ABB's move away from functional thinking one step further: 'I always say to my people that we are not here to have fun or play around with Information Technology, but to build IT solutions for supporting the business. That is our sole reason for being here.' He describes the profile of the new CIO the company has been trying to recruit:

The person should be more of a business person than an IT specialist. Otherwise we might end up with an IT kingdom of its own. The person has to understand IT and the possibilities it gives, but not a technology freak using technology for the fun of it. It needs to be a teamleader who can drive the technical aspects and business people alike. We are looking for business-oriented people who can build the IT solutions that the company needs.

Part of this shift is the greater value the organization needs to place on project managers. The profile and the skills of these project managers have not been recognized in the past. As one manager says:

The share of large projects in the business is going up. The challenge is to really value project managers, and not just the line managers. They might be running a gas turbine project or a substation project. They are running big businesses, and they face big challenges. Projects are higher risk than steady ongoing business. They face tougher conditions, and they don't have the cushion of a large organization around them. They are on site having to face straight up to the customer. Perhaps we don't value them enough.

How international do you have to be?

In a company where business can be 'superglobal' or 'superlocal', it needs people who can run both types of operation. Are all ABB managers international? The answer is clearly 'No'. The company looks for people who can be either the one or the other.

Depending on their position in the matrix, the job will require ABB managers to work in a spectrum of internationalization that reaches from doing a very local job in a radius of 25 miles around Stuttgart with no inter-action outside their home county on the one extreme, to a global role travelling the world on the other. At a local level, managers have very well-defined sets of responsibilities, clear accountability and ample freedom to act. In contrast, people at the top and at BA level have to deal with great levels of complexity and ambiguity and have or exercise little formal authority to achieve their goals. These global managers lead the stimulating yet manic and stressful life of the typical international manager.

ABB does not have many global managers. In 1991, Percy Barnevik said, 'We need maybe 500 or so out of 15,000 managers to make ABB work well – not more.' Yet he recognized that they were rare in ABB at the time – one of the company's biggest priorities was to create more of them. The need for inter-nationalization was tightly articulated: 'I have no interest in making managers more "global" than they have to be. We can't have people abdicating their nationalities, saying "I am no longer German, I am international." The world doesn't work like that. If you are selling products and services in Germany, you better be a German!' (Taylor, 1991). Today, these words captured by Taylor in a world-famous article for the *Harvard Business Review*, are still considered valid in ABB.

The critical positions that require a global outlook are the cross-over points of the company's matrix:

We do need a core group of global managers at the top: on our Executive Committee, on the teams running our business areas, in other key positions. From these strate-gic positions, these global managers oversee their small units formed into the business and country segments. The need for cooperation is written into their job responsibility areas, so that these people operationalize in practice what the organi-zation aims for strategically.

Global responsibilities (of the BA managers)

- Develop worldwide strategy.
- Produce economies of scale in R&D, supply management, production technol-ogy, financing.
- Deliverables: market allocation, transfer pricing, know-how transfer, risk management.

Local responsibilities (of country managers)

- Develop customer-based regional strategies.
- Produce 'economies of scope' in customer focus, labour relations, HR development, government contacts.

Source: Robert Feller, Vice-President, Corporate Management Development

Percy Barnevik's ideas on what he looked for in ABB global managers have become a classic of management literature. His rationale was simple and compelling: 'How are global managers different?'

Well, global managers have exceptionally open minds. They respect how different countries do things, and they have the imagination to appreciate why they do them that way. But they are also incisive – they push the limits of the culture. Global managers don't passively accept it when someone says, 'You can't do that in Italy or Spain because of the unions' or 'You can't do that in Japan because of the Ministry of Finance.' Instead, they sort through the debris of cultural excuses and find opportunities to innovate. For Barnevik, 'You have to acknowledge cultural differences without becoming paralyzed by them.'

Beyond these specifications, the company uses a thorough competency model to clarify what it looks for from its international managers. Robert Feller, Vice-President for Corporate Management Development, worked with the relevant management population to identify the profile of the international managers (see 'Profile of the ABB top executive', page 323). Feller describes the following four types of needs to which people in ABB who operate internationally must respond.

- **Roles and relationships.** By this Feller means managing without formal authority inside the ABB matrix and across borders and organizational boundaries, and the associated abilities to coach and persuade people, build relationships across countries and cultures swiftly, adjust one's way of communicating flexibly, balancing local pride and global needs, and being responsible for tracking talent and sharing expertise.
- **Critical issues and success factors.** For international managers in ABB, the critical issues are to overcome fragmentation and internal focus, achieve the shift from product to project business, increase value added in emerging markets and implement change fast. The company sees trust and cooperation across borders, excellence in project management, multicultural sensitivity and respect, coaching and empowerment as the success factors to achieve all the above.

- **Basic values and beliefs.** What drives people in ABB, and what newcomers are asked to adhere to, is the belief that in order to achieve a unified organization that is greater than the sum of its parts, ABB needs to exploit its diversity to the full. A deep value in the company is the need to be action-oriented, work at a fast pace and respond to changes quickly. For ABB, managing change successfully means acting as a learning organization. Developing this capability is seen as a key leadership task. The company also believes that people learn by doing, taking responsibilities and being accountable for results.
- **Key leadership activities and characteristics.** Feller sums up four leadership activities:
  - producing shared visions, smart strategies and a sound agenda;
  - attracting and maintaining the large network of resources necessary to accomplish a sound agenda;
  - motivating key people to work on the agenda and overcoming the inherent difficulties and obstacles of achieving all the above.

The characteristics that underlie these activities are industry and organizational knowledge; relationships inside the firm and in the industry; reputation, track record and credibility; analytical abilities, strategic and multidisciplinary thinking; strong interpersonal skills, integrity and motivation.

Profile of the ABB top executive

- Reactions to quick changes at local and global level to show:
  - analysis and structuring of complex, dynamic business situations and thinking in business scenarios;
  - understanding of international economic interdependencies influencing our business;
  - open-mindedness in responding to new types of customers and their expectations and needs;
  - creativity, fantasy, curiosity, courage and speed to come up with new approaches to a business challenge.
- Networking across corporate and cultural borders to show:
  - an ability to listen and integrate others' views and interests into one's own approach;
  - an ability to manage and participate in complicated business projects as leader, follower or peer in cross-border teams;
  - an ability to achieve one's goals with and through the matrix with cultural sensitivity and social competence;
  - an ability to communicate in several languages.

- Taking business responsibility in a large organization by:
  - accepting responsibility and being/remaining accountable;
  - giving responsibility to empower people and make them accountable;
  - ensuring compatibility between the corporate message and operational management in one's organization.
- Taking social responsibility:
  - having an attitude and understanding that ABB operates in a social context;
  - feeling responsible for, and taking charge of, our impact on the social environment.
- Moving from management to leadership:
  - from technical, mechanistic skills and short-term focus towards vision, credibility and empowerment of the organization;
  - combining 'competence' and 'know-how' with 'relationship-building' in one's business style and approach.

Source: ABB, Torino Group Report, 1998.

A number of ABB's BA managers have participated in Ashridge's study of the competences of international mangers, where we detected a shift from expatriates to multicountry managers – people responsible for looking after many countries at the same time. The research is summarized below.

A competence model for the 'multicountry manager'

In 1992, ABB participated alongside other international companies in a piece of research conducted by Ashridge Management Research Group (Barham and Wills, 1992). At the time, faced with the increasing competitiveness of international business, people were anxious to ensure that they had the management capability to handle the challenges. The question we looked at was: 'What are the skills and characteristics required of managers in the highly demanding and fast-moving international business environment of the 1990s and beyond?'

The particular type of international manager coming into prominence at the time of the study was the transnational manager: the type of people who would be running or participating in ABB's BAs. This is an international role, managing across a number of countries and cultures simultaneously, either globally or regionally.

The findings of the Ashridge study produced a view of international competence that includes both 'skills' and 'underlying characteristics'.

'Doing competences'

The interviews revealed three aspects to international management competence. The first involves active 'doing' competences, which involve observable skills and knowledge bases and consist of four main roles:

- championing international strategy;
- operating as cross-border coach and coordinator;
- acting as intercultural mediator and change agent;
- managing personal effectiveness for international business.

'Being competences'

The job of the international manager is challenging and makes heavy demands on both the individual and their family. Nevertheless, many people clearly thrive on the challenges. Our research suggested that successful international managers often have a philosophy of life or 'being' that enables them to do so.

This second aspect of international competence relates to the 'underlying characteristics' that facilitate the demonstration of skilled behaviours. It underpins the active side of the job and concerns the way that the manager thinks and reasons, the way that they feel, and the beliefs and values that motivate them. It consists of three mutually sustaining parts:

- complex thinking
- emotional energy
- psychological maturity.

Complex thinking is a particularly significant characteristic of the international manager. This is the ability to consider issues from a variety of perspectives, see several dimensions in a situation rather than only one, and consider more than one solution.

'Becoming international'

'Doing' and 'being' are combined in a career-long process of 'becoming international', but there are some crucial moments in any individual's development where there is very high potential for transition in their 'being' – in effect, an experience after which the world never looks the same as it did before. These may include a new job (in particular, an international assignment), a secondment, membership of an international project team or participation in a management programme.

Whether or not such a transition takes place may depend on the way that the experience is facilitated. A key element in the learning process is often missing in the work and development experiences of busy international managers – this is the need for reflection in order to understand and make better sense of an experience, draw out the learning and assimilate it in new behaviour.

Successful international managers do not consign what others consider to be everyday episodes or interactions with other people to the wastepaper basket. Instead, they reflect on them and glean as many lessons from them as possible. The opportunity to reflect in dialogue with another or others, in 'learning relationships', is particularly valuable. These others can be peers, coaches or mentors, so long as they allow the manager to explore different interpretations of events and behaviours. International managers often seek out the help of 'culture guides' when working in new countries, and they might consciously apply this strategy to help them learn and reflect on a wider plane about their work.

(Excerpt from Barham and Heimer, 1995)

Developing the ABB manager

In ABB, responsibility for management development lies with line management. Barnevik emphasizes:

In an organization of our type, where you have to bring together cultures from around the world and rally them around, it takes a strong leadership to do that. And to be a good leader, you have to track, keep and develop good people . . . There are colleagues in the Executive Committee and 500 global managers. Your ability to track, keep and develop a big team with these people is crucial to running such an organization. You can be the world's best speaker – charismatic or whatever. But, if you don't have the ability to develop all these people, you won't be successful in execution (Taneja, 1996).

ABB uses a number of formal and informal ways of developing its people, and giving them a sense of how they fit. While most of the activity is driven by the line, the company's personnel function is active in offering a number of leading-edge approaches. It is noticeable that even in HR, a field that generates many concepts and often elaborate processes, ABB works in its own minimalist, pragmatic style. There is no emphasis on grand models or textbook approaches. Arne Olsson puts it this way: 'Exposing talented people to demanding assignments and providing feedback and support – that is the key to management development.'

ABB has been noted for the way in which it gives younger managers tough assignments. Alexis Fries, 43 years old, was put in charge of ABB's Asia-Pacific region (and has latterly been put in charge of the Power Generation segment). CEO Göran Lindahl says, 'Demands on managers for international jobs are much greater. You need people who are very geared up and can handle the intensity' (Peterson, 1998).

In the years following the merger, ABB concentrated on helping people to settle into their new roles, and overcome the in-fighting typical of large mergers. The dramatic reduction in head office staff in 1988 left the personnel function very small. It defined its role not as a corporate HR function (the classic functions such as compensation and benefits are run in the countries), but as a 'management development' function. The emphasis was to build up personnel and management development functions in the countries. Decentralization is so strongly part of the way the company works, that ABB only runs one major corporate management development programme – the Business Unit Program, described later in this chapter. Local initiative in Poland has led to the creation of a management development centre at Falenty, near Warsaw, which has been attracting ABB managers from the East and the West.

Falenty: an ABB university

In Poland, as in the rest of Central and Eastern Europe, ABB faces two critical challenges. On the one hand, it has to build internal strength by training and developing local managers. On the other hand, it also has to create a corporate bond that will help to retain talented employees who are in demand by other organizations in these expanding markets. To address these challenges and meet the enormous demand for training, in 1995 ABB set up a management development centre at Falenty, just south-west of Warsaw.

The centre consists of conference and training rooms, a library and a 47-room hotel with catering and recreational facilities. Each year, over 1000 employees come to Falenty to attend management programmes or map out their career development. Falenty started out by running programmes only for Polish ABB managers to help them adjust to ABB's regime of decentralization and profit orientation. Iwona Jarzębska, who was Director of the Falenty centre before taking up a secondment to ABB's head office, describes the challenge: 'The profit centre approach was a big change for people who grew up in the West. But think of the tremendous change for people in Poland who had grown up in the "safe" environment there. Not all were able to make the change and this was not just a question of older age groups.' In addition to its new Polish employees, ABB also found that, with the opening up of the region, ABB managers from Western Europe wanted to come to Poland to take part in the programme. Participants are now roughly 50 per cent Polish and 50 per cent from the rest of Europe.

The flagship programme is 'Skills for the Future', a short MBA-type, 'very exciting' programme for 'high potential' staff from Europe that lasts six months. The programme consists of six one-week modules – one a month. Each programme has 25 participants. The programme started in 1995, so, by the end of 1997, Falenty had run 4 programmes for about 100 people in total. Participants work on projects between the modules and have to present their findings and

recommendations at the end. Iwona Jarzębska says that 'one of the really interesting things to see is that they stay in touch and talk to each other after the
programme ends – they form a network across boundaries and borders', which is
exactly the power of such a centre. In another two-day simulation called 'Decision
Base', participants create mock companies and fight for market leadership.
Participants often find, however, that through constant exchange of experience,
they actually learn the most from each other. And this interchange of learning is
again another aim of the centre.

The centre aims to develop skills at all organizational levels so, in addition to its
executive programmes, it also runs courses for first-line supervisors and managers,
and customized programmes for supply specialists, secretarial, sales, marketing
and human resource professionals. To quote from the centre's promotional
brochure, 'In Poland and thoughout the world, ABB maintains its global characteristic while preserving the local identity of its companies. The promotion of local
management allows ABB to integrate its unique corporate culture with the values of
the countries and regions in which it operates. ABB's Polish companies and the ABB
MDC [management development centre] are exemplary cases of this strategy.'

ABB has invested considerable resources in Falenty. The centre costs the company about $12,000 per participant. ABB thinks it is worth every penny. While most
companies in Poland lose 40 per cent of their workers every year, ABB's loss is half
that. And those managers it keeps are developing skills comparable to those in the
rest of the ABB Group. Other companies investing in Poland, such as Daewoo of
Korea, have been so impressed by ABB's approach that they have sent teams to
Falenty with the aim of setting up similar centres, perhaps with the help of ABB
consultants (Latour, 1997).

Eberhard von Koerber, formerly President of ABB Europe, describes Falenty as:

> a kind of ABB university where we strive to convey our common vision and strat-
> egy for the global ABB Group. We also use Falenty as a meeting point for
> managers all over ABB, where they work together in teams, sharing ideas and
> experiences, developing solutions together, and seeing with their own eyes the
> huge benefits of working together across cultural borders. I believe this serves as
> a model for action beyond our company as well. The implications of such 'coming
> together' for a united Europe of the future are very significant. Business and gov-
> ernment can do more to bring people from East and West together in business, the
> arts, education, sports and other areas. There is no more effective way to break
> down decades, and indeed, centuries-old cultural barriers and stereotypes (von
> Koerber, 1997).

References

Latour, Almar (1997) 'Homegrown Talent', *Central European Economic Review* (*The Wall Street Journal
    Europe*), February **v** (1), 18 and 26.
von Koerber, Eberhard (1997) *Enlargement to the East: The Decisive Moment for Europe's Future,
    Presentation to the Churchill Symposium*. Zürich: presentation to the Churchill Symposium,18
    September.

In typical ABB fashion, Arne Olsson, who is in overall charge of developing ABB's managers for senior posts, runs a small head office team together with three senior colleagues, who, between them, cover the globe. Their charter is to:

- support the creation of good processes in the local companies for management resource planning (identifying management talent);
- expose people to international assignments early;
- offer management seminars.

Olsson says that he is responsible for:

> *management resources, not corporate HR. Why don't we call it corporate HR like other companies? Because the company is very decentralized and we have very small central staff units. Here there are four senior people plus secretarial staff. There are three 'global management resources' staff – management planning, international assignments and management seminars – plus personnel services, which is the service organization. There are 10½ people in management resources, including secretarial staff. Therefore there is no way in the world that we can run HR as you would in a large company. You would need more staff. If someone asks me about the rules for company cars in our large German company, for example, I would say I don't know anything about it – why should I know – to manage that requires knowledge about local practice; it may involve local German tax issues, etc.*

The main focus of the function is on developing the international breed of manager who can work as part of the 5 per cent of key managers running the company. Olsson, who has been responsible for the function since the days of ASEA, adapted his basic approach to management development by adding a stronger emphasis on internationalization since the merger in 1988. He says, 'My concern is who are the young talent? How should we encourage their development and drive local processes for management development? How do we do that with local people with such a small staff?'

The light touch – driving local processes

Management resourcing and development is wholly owned and delivered primarily at a local level in ABB. In line with the corporate policy on decentralization, each country has its own way of working, and there is no formalization or standardization. The process to ensure that it happens is an annual management review focusing on succession planning and resulting in a systematic approach to management development. Arne Olsson says, 'It involves sitting down with country managers and business area managers to review performance and potential, and to discuss who can run what. The reviews develop lists of candidates for typical key positions, identify management talent early and are a starting point for individuals' development action planning. We discuss key people in their organization, the first two levels and possible successors to them.'

ABB's pragmatism shows in every aspect of the approach:

The important thing is not what specific binder or diskette you have with information on people. What is important is to have a local process to ensure management planning happens. Out of it comes a list and a reasonable understanding of possible candidates. We have a central database of more than 1000 people. In a large organization one has to have some kind of systematic approach to searching internationally for management candidates in order to ensure a mapping and an evaluation process that lifts the level of accuracy considerably higher than the 'telephone directory method' or informal networking. But make it simple and practical and take a line manager's perspective – there are too many sophisticated plans in glossy binders only collecting dust. To find a good balance between the traditional HR process on the one hand, and the pragmatic line manager's approach on the other hand, is where the real challenge lies. The size of the organization, its complexity and its multidomestic presence are things that don't make that challenge easier.

Many job appointments in the company are said to occur through the networks rather than formal job advertisements. Olsson says that it is the result that matters rather than the process used to identify people:

To make sure that something is going on on a local basis is the important thing. We have a pretty informal and decentralized structure. The Germans and the US have their own format of documentation – that is not the most important aspect of it. What comes out of the process is a categorization of people with ratings, etc. Exactly how you arrive at it in terms of documentation, etc. is not so crucial. An HR function can easily become too focused on the formal process itself. You have to ask if it pays off and is worth it.

Olsson has, however, been concerned to make sure that ABB has a process for systematically tracking management talent and making information about management candidates available to top and line managers. A large company does need to install some mechanisms and procedures to make sure that the Group has an overview of management candidates in the entire organization. This avoids people with management potential being 'locked up' in one part of the organization, having little opportunity to be considered as candidates for promotion in other parts of the organization. But isn't it a daunting task to search for management candidates in such a huge organization? Olsson suggests that a systematic approach to internal searches for management candidates should consist of the following steps, which reduce the complexity to manageable proportions.

● **Define the key elements of the organizational unit concerned.** What kind of business is it? What kind of customers does it have? Is it a standard product manufacturing business or an organization handling large projects? The purpose is to understand the business concerned as a starting point for defining what suitable candidates should look like in terms of professional background and experiences.

- **Define the candidate profile.** Given the job context above, define the experiences and skills needed to handle this specific job.
- **'Zooming in on those search or target areas within the organization' where you will most likely find suitable candidates.** The first and second steps above provide the input for this process. Narrowing down the search or target areas requires a good understanding of ABB's business activities and its organization. Nobody can be familiar with all the businesses of ABB and here discussions with senior line managers should help to define search and target areas of interest.
- **Take a close look at which managers and management candidates in the companies concerned could be shortlisted for the job in question.** The search and target areas have now been defined, so the task is reduced to proportions that can be handled and this is the next step. It involves considering on what levels these candidates should be found and to what extent they meet the criteria established. Studying three to four companies in this way should generate a final short list of a small number of names to be presented to management for consideration.

Olsson warns that there is a risk in being too systematic and too analytical. He says that successful appointments are sometimes made on the basis of a CEO or other top manager having a gut feeling or instinct that somebody is the right person for the job and that 'The one approach does not exclude the other – we should have both'. But Olsson definitely thinks ABB could improve its search process by being more systematic.

Another aim of the search process is to avoid what Olsson calls the 'there is nobody available' phenomenon. The best candidates do not perhaps get on to a short list because, as soon as their names come up, they are eliminated from further discussion with the comment that they 'are not available.' The search process aims to compensate for this reflex by ensuring that the most competent candidates can at least be listed in a first step and then be discussed and evaluated by upper-level management from the point of view of a company's priorities.

HR directors, says Olsson, are responsible for ensuring that the most competent candidates are shortlisted for key jobs. 'Every promotion,' he says, 'sets off a chain reaction of promotions on lower levels and opens up possibilities for exposing talented people to new challenges.' This also addresses the risk that young, well-educated people may leave after a few years with ABB because they do not get jobs they consider to be challenging enough.

Can careers be planned?

There is much debate in organizations today about how far careers can still be planned. How does ABB see this question? Arne Olsson says careers can be planned in the sense that it usually pays off to have an idea about where you are heading, but they cannot be planned in the sense that there are many factors beyond your control – a person does not develop as expected, their personal situation does not permit the planned career development, or development opportunities do not open up as hoped. What is important for the individual in general is:

- having a solid professional platform – a good education, knowing something really well;
- knowing what you are good at;
- selecting the right boss to work for;
- hard work and performance.

What would Olsson tell young people, in particular, about what they need if they want to work for ABB? 'A good education. Good basic knowledge of engineering, finance or business administration, etc. Good solid stuff. Strong analytical skills. Good communication skills. Some people are more talented than others in communication but communication skills can be developed by training and working at it. An interest in and openness to other cultures. And energy to drive the business.' He elaborates:

I tell people that they need a good solid professional platform to work from. You must spend real time in learning something early in your career – whether it's accountancy, designing gas turbines, financial analysis, etc. You have to know something very well. Having a solid platform develops analytical skills – you learn how to search for information, it gives you a frame of reference and helps to develop conceptual skills and acquire tools for work. It helps you think things through for the future – you know how to attack a problem, to go the roots of a problem, and analyze it – you can then apply this skill in other areas. It gives you something that's yours. So you are not just a skater, skating on the surface. It's good for your self-esteem – what you know, nobody can take away from you. It's helpful, but not important, exactly what you did learn. You need to know what you are good at, to be able to select the right boss to work for – and, of course, be prepared for hard work and performance. You have to improve your skills in areas where you are weak and keep in mind that it usually gives a bigger payoff to further develop what you are already good at.

The key to career development in ABB is performance. This means doing the right things (compare this, says Olsson, with doing things right); getting things done; being prepared, when need be, to put in long hours; effective work habits; and delivering first-class work. People should also be open to alternative career directions. The basic questions for people as their careers progress are 'What are you really good at?', 'Are you putting those skills to full use?', 'How can you further develop those skills?'

Olsson believes that managers develop 70 per cent on the job, while 20 per cent of it comes from the influence of others (the boss, colleagues, subordinates and so on) and 10 per cent comes from courses and seminars. He also believes that selecting the right boss to work for is a key factor in career development: 'Your boss plays a major role in your personal development through exposing you to demanding, "stretch" assignments; giving feedback and coaching; being a role model; and acting as a carrier of company culture and values. With an exposure to stretching assignments and appropriate coaching, most people have a potential to develop.'

To managers and HR people responsible for career development, Olsson gives some general guidelines:

> *Don't make firm commitments about career development – promises that cannot be kept erode your credibility and create hard feelings. Don't give away a seat to somebody until the chair is unoccupied. Be honest. Real life is full of compromises – career planning is to strike a balance between individual learning and development and for the company to get a reasonable return on investment.*

Screwing on a wide-angle lens – international assignments at ABB

An increasingly important aim of career development at ABB is to expose people to the international scene early on. Percy Barnevik explained the rationale for international assignments in his classic *Harvard Business Review* interview:

> *Global managers are made, not born. There are many things you can do. Obviously, you rotate people around the world. There is no substitute for line experience in three or four countries to create a global perspective. You also encourage people to work in mixed nationality teams. You force them to create personal alliances across borders, which means that you sometimes interfere in hiring decisions* (Taylor, 1991).

Percy Barnevik says that one of the biggest challenges in ABB is that national feeling is very strong:

> *Even if you talk about being global, Germans and Englishmen and Indians tend to cluster together. So we work very hard to breed global managers who really have lived in different cultures . . . The more you can create the sort of organizational creature that thrives in different cultures and ties it all together, the better. That is the bottleneck: there aren't so many such global managers and you have to work hard to develop them* (Skaria, 1995).

Arne Olsson explains how international assignments are used in ABB to develop international managers:

Business area people are the key people in this process. This global organization is a fantastic platform for developing people internationally. We have operations in 140 countries, including large operations in some big countries. Wherever you go you will find an ABB operation. We have close to 1000 expatriates in over 100 countries, plus people involved in on-site projects, such as the start-up of power plants.

This practice creates a continuous stream of people walking through ABB's operations all over the world (including the head office in Zürich).

International experience develops a 'wide-angle lens'

Arne Olsson believes that 'we should expose young people to international experience early in their careers. It opens their eyes. You can have a standard camera with a 50 mm lens. Then you get one with a 35 mm or 28 mm wide-angle lens – you suddenly get another kind of picture and you are surprised at what you see.'

For the company, this is about 'business development by people development'. Says Arne Olsson:

You can achieve this by picking good sales engineers or product specialists to send out abroad to support the local business – developing the business while at the same time providing opportunities for people development. In this sense most international assignments are business driven: the starting point for the planning of the assignment is a business need, a business problem to be solved.

Following the company's strategic integration of emerging markets, there is also a strong push for the reverse movement to the classic stream of Western managers eager to gain experiences in the East. ABB also took the initiative to bring 150 bright young people per year from Asia to Europe and the USA for 4–7 months 'to get a sniff of operations in a big Western ABB operation.' However, Olsson has found that some European countries often find initially a number of reasons not to cooperate, suggesting problems with lack of office space, unions and internal reorganizations. A good example of another 'let's use this opportunity' attitude was shown once by the Finnish company:

There was one young production engineer from India. My colleague in India phoned me up and said that this is a good guy who could be important for the drives business in future. The Indians had picked two ABB companies where they wanted to send him. I tried to arrange this with two [ABB] companies which gave various reasons for why they could not receive the Indian engineer. It's a matter of attitude. I called the Finnish company – they immediately said 'This is very interesting. We want to develop our sales business in India. Give us a day to see how we could organize something.' Next day they called to say, 'Yes, we will take him. When can he come?' They saw it as an opportunity to get a business ally in India. Take good care of a trainee from Asia, invest some personal time beyond the training programme as such and you have a friend and business supporter for life.

In the future, Olsson predicts, the company will see more of this kind of reverse flow of people on international assignments – 'We'll see Russian, Chinese, Vietnamese, Philippine engineers coming to Europe for learning experiences as well as adding their know-how here.'

Successful international assignments at ABB follow some of its few practical criteria:

- send the best people you have;
- give them international exposure early on in their careers;
- don't try to export personnel problems.

ABB tries to send open and flexible people, and hand picks some of its best people. Preparation for these assignments is not considered in great depth. Apart from sending people on the occasional course, they are also given video-tapes or half a day of preparation, including their families. The reason for this reticence is the difficulty of really preparing people before they go: 'It is like trying to prepare someone for a management position – the frame of reference is not there. It is easier to have some preparation 3–4 months after arrival.' A pragmatic solution, ABB-style.

Value-added management development

Management development at ABB is treated exactly like other business activities. It is driven by the same tight results orientation as operational and strategic management. Without a business imperative, there is no development. The organization tries not to mechanize management development, or make it system-driven. Management development activities are characteristically:

- business-driven;
- focused on the job and results;
- line managers are involved; and
- outcomes are assessed.

Managers are primarily developed on the job. After the need has been identified, adequate people to act as development partners or coaches and development opportunities are sought. Here, the characteristics of the direct boss are deciding factors. If the manager is demanding and perceived as a good coach, development is more likely to be on the job. Some exposure to general management is almost inherent in the nature of the organization. In our interview with Göran Lindahl, he said: 'In their first years at ABB, everyone receives a mini-MBA, whatever their background. What I mean is that very few people really can become or continue being specialized. People cover a big range of topics in our structure. They are invited to all sorts of activities which make them look at an issue from different angles.'

Arne Olsson says that the way to prepare people for general management is to expose them to several functions:

Companies are made up of different functions – finance, engineering, sales and marketing, production, etc. To run a business is to manage a multitude of functions. If you can, you need to experience the different parts of the business and follow a logical development from one area to another. For HR, the job is to encourage people to get exposed to different aspects of the business – sales and marketing, running a project, etc. If you look at successful managers – and not just in ABB – they have very often worked in different parts of a business. Göran Lindahl spent six or seven years as a development engineer, which gave him a very strong technical platform. He was exposed to people management early on by running a high-level laboratory. Then he was put in charge of a sales and marketing function which exposed him to customers, commercial issues, contract negotiations, etc.

ABB's management development philosophy

Managers develop:

- 70 per cent on the job;
- 20 per cent by the influence of others – their boss, colleagues, subordinates;
- 10 per cent as a result of courses and seminars.

Make sure to:

- pick the right boss – a good professional who will expose you to stretching assignments, coach you, support you;
- further develop your strengths;
- improve your skills in areas where you are weak;
- prepare for general management by taking responsibility for different functions or running a project.

Source: Arne Olsson

For international managers the mixed nationality teams created by BA leaders to solve problems and build a culture of communication and trust are an ideal training ground. The matrix allows people to manage global businesses from different parts of the world and bring mixed groups of people in different constellations to different locations. From the perspective of the individual, this produces a constant 'culture simulator', where the experience is always fresh, and no complacency can occur as long as people stay in the circuit of this cultural lab, or 'whirlpool'. In 1991, Percy Barnevik described the effect of the cultural whirlpool on him: 'I experience this every three weeks in our Executive Committee. When we sit together as Germans, Swiss, Americans and Swedes, with many of us living, working, and travelling in different places, the insights can be remarkable' (Taylor, 1991).

David Hunter, ABB's former Head of Central and Eastern Europe, previously worked for Westinghouse. He contrasts the two organizations:

The difference in atmosphere in coming to ABB was immediately apparent. ABB has a global culture. In a typical meeting there are at least four nationalities around the table. This was unheard of in Westinghouse. Today I attended a meeting of the power generation business involving its operations in Switzerland, Germany and the Czech Republic. There were three Czechs, a Dutchman who is the Controller for the Czech Republic, three Americans, three Swiss, a Norwegian who is the Country Manager for the Czech Republic, and an Irishman who is taking over as Country Manager in January. This cultural stew is typical for ABB. Westinghouse was not like this, not 20 years ago or even today. ABB is so global in nature, our problem is the opposite. We have to work hard to control the decentralization we have.

The Business Unit Programme – developing managers for international cooperation

Robert Feller, the head of Corporate Management Development, is responsible for the more formally organized management seminars at Group level. He is responsible for the Business Unit Programme (BUP), ABB's most significant corporate management development programme.

Robert Feller describes the ambitious purpose of the BUP, which is to develop the next generation of international general managers, to trigger change and impact business results. It is also designed to help discover, influence and develop ABB's identity and culture.

The Programme involves more than 100 managers from all businesses and continents each year and follows ABB's principles of management development very closely. It firmly links management development to business by assuming that people are mainly developed on the job, and that a demanding boss with good coaching abilities plays a key role. As with all management development activities at ABB, it is business-driven. This means that, firstly, there is a specific and real business need, and a concrete task relating to it. The following step is to match up Programme participants with the projects. Line managers are closely involved in the process to develop ownership and highlight that the activity is treated as any other business decision. Feller considers the sustained high level of involvement by senior executives, and the Executive Committee of ABB, to be critical to the success of the Programme, creating the motivation of participants and coaches.

The BUP concept

With more than 100 projects per year, the 18 month-long programme is based on the principle of action learning via individual business improvement projects (BIPs). Rather than serving as analytical exercises, the focus of these projects is on implementation and change management across borders.

Senior management involvement achieves two outcomes. Top executives help nominate participants, identify the projects, coach participants, evaluate progress and generally improve the BUP process. This in itself creates a development opportunity for top executives. Second, it helps to foster open communication and fast decision making across hierarchical layers to speed up the success of the projects and, ultimately, organizational learning.

Two one-week modules – with a gap of six months in between – provide participants with practical experiences on how to structure and run a change project, cross-cultural experiences, teambuilding (by means of activities such as outdoor exercises), greater understanding of international business within ABB and exposure to top executives. While the project work is carried out individually, the modules are designed to capitalize on cross-fertilization between participants and the senior executives. The management developers organize learning around personal and business issues raised by the participants, rather than formal, prearranged inputs.

Feedback is ongoing throughout the 18 months of the programme, where learning on a cognitive and an emotional level is explicitly combined. A coach supports each participant and takes responsibility for the project's strategic relevance: 'The typical coaching role is to give advice, follow up progress, stimulate innovation, be a sounding board and ensure the relevance of the improvement project chosen. A significant amount of mutual learning and trust evolves from the coaching function. In ABB, some 220 coaches are engaged yearly advising the same number of improvement projects' (European Training Foundation, 1997). At a results review meeting, and a final status report meeting, the outcomes of the projects are reported and checked (see Figure 11.1).

Fig 11.1	**The structure of ABB's Business Unit Programme**

Time in months

-2	0	+6	+12	+18
Preparation	Module A	Module B	Result review meeting	Final status report
• Description of projects • Coach and participant agree purpose and goals	• Overall purpose and goal refinement • Strategic positioning • Detailed action plan to module B	• Reports on progress and learning • Final implementation plan • Presentation to ABB executive panel	• Presentation of results and learning to ABB executive panel • Evaluation of BIP	• Written final status report • Results achieved • Return on investment

Source: ABB

Examples of BUP projects

Feller cites a few projects that have been completed on the BUP:

- improving engineering efficiency within the main centre of the business unit – cranes and harbour systems;
- developing the market and stimulating the demand for turnkey HV sub-stations business among private-sector customers in the northern states of India;
- developing a profitable power generation after-sales service in Venezuela, thereby creating a key advantage for new sales and developing skilled resources;
- adapting a company structure to improve time to market for new products.

During the first module, these projects are positioned for each participant (see Figure 11.2). Feller recommends that most of the projects should be in the shaded area between 'innovating' and 'stretching' projects to provide real learning for participants, while some may be 'strategic'. He makes a conscious effort to take people out of their comfort zones by ensuring that they are not in the well-known and structured area of the matrix, which relates to their 'daily job'. Outcomes of the projects can include increased market share, increased revenues and profits, reduced costs, and the encouragement of new thinking and innovation.

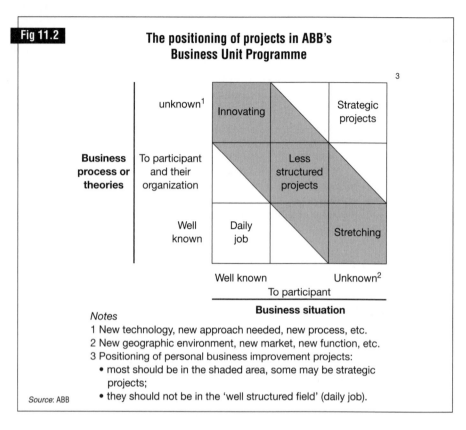

Fig 11.2

The positioning of projects in ABB's Business Unit Programme

Notes

1 New technology, new approach needed, new process, etc.

2 New geographic environment, new market, new function, etc.

3 Positioning of personal business improvement projects:
- most should be in the shaded area, some may be strategic projects;
- they should not be in the 'well structured field' (daily job).

Source: ABB

Outcomes of the Programme

The Programme is evaluated at various levels. Participants, coaches and senior executives rate the success of the BUP at different stages of the process. This is followed by measurement of return on investment for each project at various times after their completion.

The Programme has attracted much attention because of its emphasis on real-life cases and its bottomline results orientation. It is seen as an excellent model for illustrating how HR professionals can work with managers to create an offer that is treated like any other investment decision.

In the HRD community, there has always been a reluctance to measure the real, bottom-line impact, or return on investment, of training and development. The focus has primarily been on evaluating the quality of speakers, material, visual aids and so on, rather than the 'learning gained' and its impact on performance and learning results. A results-focused approach forces us to evaluate the process as well as to measure the results, and make a judgement on the return on the investment. In the ABB Business Unit Program, the learning process is continuously evaluated, more or less in the traditional way (during 12 months), the results are measured (after 12 months) and ROI is assessed (after 18 months). ROI so far is dramatically higher than in traditional capital investment. Yet, in a life-long learning process, these are very short periods of time. Therefore, in ABB there is an additional three-year follow-up to evaluate the long-term impact (European Training Foundation, 1997).

ABB's cross-company learning partnerships

Together with BT, LG, Lufthansa, SKF and Standard Chartered Bank, ABB forms part of the Global Business Consortium, specially designed to develop the next generation of global business leaders. Run by the London Business School, this international programme is aimed at senior managers in country or regional management roles who need to have transnational capabilities. The Torino Group writes:

The emphasis is on participants learning from each other and engaging in strategic benchmarking with other consortium members. Five international managers from each company work with the other participants in three one-week modules which span Asia-Pacific, India and Europe. The company-focused approach brings energy to solving current business issues, while at the same time broadening global perspectives. The programme combines sound academic research and analytical tools with insights and inspiration from regional business and political figures. The key themes of the programme are creating global strategy, the regional perspective and the country platforms.

The learning methods developed for this partnership include:

specially commissioned case studies on each participating company; 'company perception exercises', in which participants from one company build a picture of a paired consortium partner; cross-company teamwork; competitive advantage task forces, in which each company teamworks on the implications of the learning for themselves; and a CEO forum in which findings and recommendations are made to the CEOs of each participating company (European Training Foundation, 1997).

You might have reached the end of this section thinking 'That is no big deal. I could have thought of that.' People development at ABB is firmly rooted in a pragmatic approach to development based on action learning, a school of thought that emerged initially in the UK and has developed strong roots in Scandinavia over the last few decades. ABB's activities are leading-edge because not many companies manage to practise them, not because the ideas are revolutionary. This comes from ABB's ability to focus very clearly on what it really believes in. Management development in the company achieves results and develops credibility by getting HR professionals with their expertise to work closely with line management.

341

We asked Arne Olsson what are the main things for the future that he worries about in his job? He listed three areas of concern:

First, to make sure that on a local level there are processes and management attention to ensuring a supply of talent. This is where it starts – it doesn't start here in Zürich. I hope it has the management attention because it is fundamental. What quality you get in the machinery now determines what you get out in 15–20 years' time for high-level jobs. You can improve people then but you can't fundamentally change them.

The second issue is how local management views issues of management development. We need to try to instil in line managers the belief that 'management development is my thing'. This is perhaps the biggest challenge. Given the culture of the company – and it is not just ABB – it is mostly engineers – they chose to be engineers, they love their jobs. You have to make them say and look and feel that developing people is 'my job' and not something to be delegated to some staff function. HR must have quality in terms of people and processes to support them. But the real HR managers are the line managers. How do we get more line managers to think like this?

Third, how to get more international transfers – how to get more young representatives from our companies in Europe and North America exposed to international business and how to get more young talented people from Asia and Latin America transferred abroad. We need to get a reverse flow of expatriates. There will be more of a reverse flow over time. Historically we sent expatriates out to the so-called export markets. That is now changing. There are some big [ABB] companies out there.

How will ABB do this? Olsson is clear about what will be necessary:

It starts from the top. The top has to give the message – it's about walking the talk. What Göran Lindahl said in Montreux to 400 ABB people [at the December 1997 management conference] was very important. The last part of the conference dealt with management development. It was not last because it was seen as a leftover or an afterthought, but to underline the subject so it left it in people's minds when they went home. It was a powerful signal – that management development is not just the responsibility of HR, but is a top management role. And it is not just top management in Zürich but the top managers in each country who are responsible. It also depends on the quality of the HR people and systems who support it. It starts with attitude and doing.

Olsson suits actions to words. He is indefatigable in taking the message about the importance of management development to ABB operations around the world. We met him at 7.00 in the morning for our discussion on human resource development in ABB. Three hours after our early morning discussion, he was leaving for Malaysia to run a seminar about management development for 30 of ABB's young Asian managers: 'It is very important for them to see someone from head office, it gives them a sense of belonging to a large, global organization. My aim is to emphasize to them the importance of management development for ABB' and, at the end of the day, hopefully make them feel responsible for developing their own people.

Life in the matrix – what is the experience of the ABB culture really like?

When looking behind the scenes in ABB, the impression is that this is the world's hardest-working group of people. Pushed in many directions, and driven by ambitious stretch targets, people obviously work under high levels of pressure. Many people struggled to recognize the company they worked for in the articles that appeared about ABB in the press and the international management literature. In conversation with us in 1998, Percy Barnevik recognized that by suggesting 'We should not make any retroactive "nice painting" of what happened. The merger was very strenuous and burdensome for many people inside the company. It sounds easy when you talk about it afterwards.'

Earlier, Percy Barnevik said that ABB is 'not a company made up of working maniacs . . . Even if I happen to work long hours myself . . . contrary to many Americans I take a four-week vacation.' ABB wants dedication, knowledge, and tenacity. 'I happen to believe that big organizations are basically bad for people. They create bad behaviours, and you get maybe 50 per cent of what you could get out. Bureaucracy and size take away concern, responsibility, interest. You don't see the customer' (McClenahen, 1994).

Yet, there are many people who volunteer very positive statements about what it is like working for the company. An American ABB manager says:

What I most enjoy about ABB is the people. It is a fascinating group of people. ABB is a revolving door of nationalities. Learning to read a Finn or a Russian is a great challenge. In spite of the frustrations, the overwhelming majority of people in ABB really love the company. It's fun in spite of the long hours. Even the Americans like ABB. They have a hard time with the matrix, but you can tell they are enjoying it when they make jokes about it – they are used to a centralized system.

For a Swedish manager:

What is great about ABB is the informal contacts. Everybody is doing the job in the best way they can. You just call people. Decisions are not made in a formalized way. You contact the person who can make the decision and you talk. It is built on trust and personal relations. It is a very informal company. In the US it is simple, in Switzerland we can be a shock to people, also in Asia-Pacific.

Clearly, the Scandinavian and American influence has shaped the general style of interaction: 'There is very open communication. If someone wants something you just call, there are no long letters. Göran Lindahl says 'if there is a problem, don't write long letters, you call; to thank a person, you write', says a manager in Zürich.

A British manager adds, 'The things that I most appreciate about the experience with ABB is openness, trying to work in teams in a multidisciplinary way. They are hard-nosed and can make difficult decisions.' He continues: 'There are no restrictions, no barriers apart from having to speak English. It's a meritocracy. It's not about Swedes or Finns getting the job. There is a Finn here, and he is here on merit. He was recommended, we brought him in. ABB rewards success.'

You get rewarded on success and managing your business successfully. If you deviate from forecast, you must justify it. Next year you have to make sure that they hear your point of view. It is rare that they will make you sign off a budget you don't agree to. They want ambitious people. Commitment is important. People are not tracked if they are not in the office as long as they are performing.

The principle of decentralizing responsibility to foster entrepreneurial initiative has worked so well in ABB that it can now extend beyond management itself. To give one example: ABB is a very lean organization, so some middle managers share the support of a secretary, perhaps on a half-time basis. As the above UK manager said, 'I do most of my work myself on the computer, I use Lotus Notes, etc., so I don't need somebody fulltime'. This manager therefore gave his secretary part-time responsibility as a profit centre for his unit's training activity, which involves some 400 training days a year for customers. The secretary had more than risen to the challenge and had quadrupled the training business from £36,000 to £150,000.

ABB constantly recreates its culture by means of its personal relations. To do that, the company relies heavily on face-to-face interaction. For some of the people in global roles, this means a lot of travel. The company is conscious about using its managers as the bearers of the corporate culture. It also uses corporate seminars, management meetings and local or functional initiatives to reinforce its values, beliefs and norms. In Financial Services, for example, a special scheme was created to strengthen cross-border cooperation. Jan Roxendal, Executive Vice-President for Financial Services, describes it:

We give special recognition by making people 'Financial Services Partner' to stimulate people to work across borders. There are about 35 [out of 859 people] and it has a certain exclusivity. They are entitled to take part in a bonus scheme based on Financial Services performance – it is not huge, but it is an opportunity to share value. To become a partner, you have to prove that you've been successful, have contributed to synergies for ABB or Financial Services, or have generated a good profit. Mindset is important too – sharing values, being supportive of developing Financial Services in ABB. You have to be a team player and contribute to discussions. The composition reflects seniority, but gives an opportunity for experts to participate. It's a good network – we keep it loose. We meet twice a year when we discuss common issues or market-related issues.

ABB's group directives are known to fit into a binder. The rest is considered to be initiative. As one manager said: 'We are very decentralized. We have guidelines and policies, but no big books – they are documents of 10–15 pages at the most. And we have meetings – Board meetings – where we discuss where we are and where we should go.' The emphasis is on face-to-face conversation and re-creation of the way ABB works rather than formalized rules. Using Board meetings to repeat and reinterpret the key messages of ABB's corporate culture[2] implies an adult relationship in which small units are given the responsibility to make their own decisions, with the input of their Board directors. Unlike corporate indoctrination seminars, the culture is vitalized without asking people to passively consume it. The emphasis is on local initiative, and the Board meetings constitute an institutionalized coaching relationship.

As in any other company, power and politics play their roles. Some people still experience very clearly the power hubs as being Sweden, Zürich and Mannheim. Others feel that there is a greater homogeneity: 'The culture allows people to express their opinions openly but they must work in the Group interest. People who try to fulfil individual objectives at the expense of the Group will leave. We have strong individuals, but we should be like a soccer team, where people are strong individually but work for the team', says one ABB manager.

What do you need to work in the ABB matrix? 'Develop big ears and listen', says one manager. Why is this important?

Because you must listen to different cultures – to see why a Pole or a Russian or a Chinese thinks the way they do. You have to understand different cultures if you work in a global company. In a matrix organization you must understand others' points of view, even if you don't agree. It demands compromise – you have to be willing to accept a compromise that is less than perfect for you. Global strategy is the distillation of thousands and thousands of local decisions made each day. If you don't listen and pick up the tell-tale signs of these, you can't make global strategy.

Another manager agrees about the need to listen carefully, but also emphasizes the need to take action: 'Open your ears, learn, but don't have a phase of learning and then doing. Take the initiative right on the first day, learn by doing. Take initiative, initiative, initiative. Don't do it like a busybody, but in a constructive way.'

There is little complacency in the company. Everyone we talked to had a number of issues they felt needed to be addressed, and could easily list the challenges they saw for the future. For example, 'How should ABB position itself in future?', or 'How will ABB get talent in the future?', 'How will the markets develop, will ABB move fast enough to seize opportunities?' or 'How should ABB compensate good people?'. We did not come across anyone who was resting on past success.

Service and retrofit – a cultural issue for ABB?

Service and retrofit (renovating existing plant) are an increasingly important business for ABB. Intense competition for new power stations has driven power equipment suppliers to expand their service business. ABB's challenge in Western Europe, for example, now that the days of big investments in power plants are over there, is to find new growth opportunities, and ABB is focusing more and more on service and retrofit in this region.

The liberalization of the power industry and the development of independent power producers has fundamentally changed the nature of the industry in general. Before deregulation, State-owned utilities bought high-specification power plants with a life of 30 years or more and handled a lot of their service requirements with their in-house engineers.

In today's increasingly deregulated and fiercely contested markets, both new independent power producers and traditional utilities have become much more cost-conscious. They may prefer to spread their costs over the life of a plant by spending more in later years on servicing. Or, they may cut back in-house service teams and outsource such services. They may also demand higher levels of service, partly due to commercial pressures and partly because of technological changes which have created new opportunities in servicing. Funds for new power projects are in great demand so there is also an increasing need to raise the efficiency of existing plants by better servicing. The growth of independent power producers in developing countries has also brought new demands for service, particularly in countries with few local skills.

A senior ABB manager reflects on the implications of the increase in service business for ABB: 'It means a big change. At least one third of the business is now service. It's a cultural issue. Service used to be looked on as a second-class thing. It was much better to sell products. But now we must put service on an equal level. We have to preach that service is our growing business and put the best people in service and put them on equal terms with other people.'

Mobilizing people for continuous change

In 1997, the *International Herald Tribune* asked Don Sull, a professor of strategic and international management at the London Business School, to pick half a dozen philosophers whose beliefs, ethics and teachings could be encapsulated in modern investment profiles. The only provision was that the philosophers should be as diverse in geography, historical period and school of thought as possible. Sull and a pair of investment advisers then created stock portfolios to fit each philosopher. The chosen philosophers included Sun Tzu, Marcus Aurelius, Niccolo Machiavelli, Benjamin Franklin, Friedrich Nietzsche and Mao Zedong. ABB figured on the 'buy list' of Mao Zedong (along with AlliedSignal Inc. and GE) as a company with a leadership that promotes cultural revolutions of their own by initiating wholesale shake-ups to renew their firms' missions and operations (de Aenlle, 1998).

At first sight, ABB certainly strikes us as an organization driven by a continuous attempt to do better. People inside the matrix talk about the tensions and difficulties of working within the matrix. Percy Barnevik's remarks about the German and Swiss-German tendency for resisting change have become legendary. No wonder that we had built up an image of ABB as being stuck in a permanent state of manic renewal! While the message about ongoing change comes out very loudly, we wondered about the reality of ABB's approach to change. It was Percy Barnevik himself who helped clarify this:

Generally you can say that you can burn out if the speed of change is too big and continuous, people don't get the time to digest and adapt. . . If you look at a ten-year period, half way we made one single adjustment. We said that for the first five years we don't change anything in the organization because now it was a matter of winning customers and winning in the marketplace. I wrote down every good idea that came up, but said 'Sorry, we don't disturb the organization now with changes. You are right, maybe these should be together, maybe that centre of excellence should be in Germany instead of Italy, but let's sum them up, remember them, and then we take one shot, and implement it.

There are other types of change, which are about raising your targets. For Germans, who have had dramatic periods of instability and inflation, this can come over as unreasonable. I don't buy that. Standing still is losing ground. Siemens is moving, the world is moving, the opportunities are all happening out there. You have to build a change culture, so that change becomes natural, but I don't mean changing the organization constantly or having revolving doors for management. They need to get a chance to perform and live with their result. By setting these big targets you get people to ask themselves 'How can I close the gap? How can I work differently?' And you get to new ways of working with the customers, you move away from batch thinking, and you can cut production time dramatically.

So, the message is: don't keep tampering with the organization but keep raising targets. While many ABB managers seem to thrive in this environment, other voices have suggested that the ABB culture of 'permanent revolution' makes it difficult for people to maintain momentum and excitement, and that it can lead to cynicism and lack of responsiveness.

ABB's approach to change is clearly top-down. Nothing brings this home more strongly than the big bang approach to the merger. There was a tried and tested masterplan, and policies top management believed in. At the same time, the company is willing to experiment and review its concepts in the light of what actually works. Percy Barnevik – most visibly responsible for shaping ABB's change formula and acting as role model in the past – showed strong signs of listening. This is particularly clear in his gesture of writing down the ideas that people generated in the first five years after the merger before implementing them in order not to disturb the organization and help it to settle down from previous change and upheaval first. This combination of forthright and listening leadership is the powerful mixture advocated by Binney and Williams for radical change (Binney and Williams, 1995).

The matrix model effectively transformed every central function and BA into an entrepreneurial hub that had to experiment with creating a firm within the firm rather than use authority. People were forced to be responsible for change and treat other people in the Group as clients. Change happened primarily as a result of people creating personal networks where they used their influence. Jan Roxendal, Executive Vice-President for Financial Services, explains how it worked in his segment:

> In the treasury activity, the most difficult thing for a big international group is how do you get control over the financial flows? You can do it in two ways. You can try and use force or you can try to get people to do it voluntarily. Force does not work – each unit thinks that it is their own money. We try to do it through our structure: treasury centres which deal with ABB companies on the market in a professional manner. We operate like banks with trading rooms, etc. We entertain them, treat them nicely, call them, building the network. Our strategy is to buy market share by offering them conditions above the market. The profit should come out of economies of scale, better market conditions and better feeling for the market trends.

Percy Barnevik's passion for decentralization left its mark, and his approach to change is a preference for speed in order to avoid uncertainty for people, confusion and loss of market share. Göran Lindahl's approach to change, if perhaps more consensual, also emphasizes speed. When, in August 1998, we asked him what he thought the biggest challenges would be in implementing the recently announced structural changes in ABB, he said simply: 'It's done'.

Applying the merger formula for rapid global change

ABB used its merger formula not only to bring ASEA and BBC together – every subsequent acquisition was integrated in the same speedy fashion. A manager of Adtranz, the biggest part of ABB in the UK, remembers when ABB bought the majority shares in BREL in 1992.

What happened at BREL in the UK is a good example of the ABB change process. BREL, the railway engineering subsidiary of British Rail, was in serious trouble when ABB bought a 40 per cent stake for a nominal sum in 1989. Its authoritarian and bureaucratic culture was inappropriate to the challenges it faced in an era of privatization. It was used to cost-plus contracting, orders were being delivered later and later, and the company had an adverse cash flow.

ABB appointed a highly experienced Swedish Managing Director who rapidly announced that a restructuring would take place in just six weeks. With a supergoal of reducing work-in-progress, the 30 per cent rule was applied to head office, new projects were set up under a one-roof concept, a strong General Manager was put in charge of manufacturing and procurement with responsibility for delivery, and profit centres were established. The new Managing Director also communicated a number of key messages about how people should work together in future, based on ABB's policy bible. The manager who was at BREL at the time, remembers: 'One of the key messages was "Be of humble spirit". That was one of the most difficult things for us. People had never heard anything like that before. For me, it was a very significant statement.'

The company's top 25 managers now had to work on developing a vision for the organization's future and the way that they would work together more collaboratively. They then had to take the vision down into their own teams, explaining what was happening and where the organization was going, considering plans for future improvement, taking stock of the difficulties and looking positively at the future. Workshops were held for individual teams to explore how to work better and manage the process more effectively. This proved to be valuable for getting individuals to buy into the process, practise good team behaviour and explore where the organization wanted to move to in terms of its culture.

There were some tough decisions to be made. The manager that we spoke with recalls:

We had to rationalize the business, especially rolling stock, as British Rail was not placing any orders. We had to close the York factory and it meant a lot of redundancies in Derby. We did a lot of work trying to get people focused. Despite being redundant, they delivered things and left with their heads held high.

Performance improved rapidly: 'There had been some problematical managers, but their relationships with customers improved. There was a greater customer focus, more empowerment and the management teams worked better together,' says the manager. The new cultural environment that had been created helped. The 'best people' had been retained to be the organiza- tion's memory. Relationships with trade unions improved. On the shop floor, job demarcation had disappeared and there was only one job classification. Other changes included the adoption of a coaching approach with the project teams and the introduction of cross-disciplinary work with the manufacturing teams.

The UK manager we spoke to believes that one reason for the success of the restructuring was that BREL, especially the rolling stock operation, 'had seen the abyss, so anything was an improvement.' But he is unhesitant about the strengths of the ABB approach:

> *The thing I most appreciate about the experience with ABB is openness and trying to work in teams in a multidisciplinary way. ABB invested for the future to keep the core of the business, whereas BREL would say, if there is no income today, get rid of it. ABB very clearly set out an agenda from day one which took the business forward. It was a very positive approach.*

In acquisitions in emerging markets, the method is similar. The Elta case described earlier illustrates how ABB created a sense of urgency from top to bottom in the organization. Global managers have the job of disseminating the new competitive model to the new acquisitions:

> *The power transformers industry traditionally competed on cost and volume, ABB competes on flexible, time-based management. The ABB philosophy for managing change is show local mangers what's been achieved elsewhere, let them drive the change process, make available ABB expertise from around the world and demand quick results* (Taylor, 1991).

Communication, communication, communication

In his book *The Living Company* (1997), Arie de Geus talks about the impor- tance of seeing organizations as living beings, rather than machines. Percy Barnevik's language[3] is permeated by metaphors that seek their inspiration in living beings. Using a skilful mixture of directive 'telling' and listening, he also engages people by showing personal interest and using language that involves them. When he talks about acquisitions, he relates it to people rather than just numbers of companies:

> *Now, all of a sudden, 40,000 Americans were in the picture. Then the Norwegians came in with 10,000 people. It became a multigame that took it away from that bilateral focus that we had a little here at the beginning. . . All of a sudden you have*

30,000 people in Eastern Europe, you start to have Asians to integrate.

Another example of his engaging style is the way he integrates wider concerns:

We tried to indoctrinate 50,000 engineers to think about the lifecycle – what is the environmental burden when you develop something, when you develop logistics, inside the gates, outside the gates, up to the products' ultimate destruction or reusage? In that thinking we are also at the forefront, together with some people in the automotive industry. That is something we can be proud of.

Percy Barnevik uses catchwords to communicate his expectations of people very powerfully: 'Are you AC (after computers) or BC (before computers)?' People who have not grown up with computers feel painfully aware of the fact that a major revolution is completely bypassing them (but not their children). 'Are you a Giver or a Receiver?' For Barnevik, a 'Giver' develops people and has always enough resources for themselves and other parts of the organization, while 'Receivers' depend on a supply of talent from others. In a company where responsibility for developing talent is so clearly anchored with line management, being classed as a Receiver is an uncomfortable position to be in.

Very few business leaders have known how to use the media to reach their own objectives. Barnevik certainly does. Employees in India, for example, are proud of the increased publicity that membership of ABB brings. Percy Barnevik uses the international media like a giant megaphone, to amplify his message into the organization in order to socialize people into the culture and create change.

Yet, a lot of the messages had an uncompromising touch. This was probably necessary to build ABB into what it is now and change an entire industry in the process. This pioneering phase is now over. With his interest in involving people from emerging markets more actively in a process to renew ABB's culture (which has been formed primarily by European and US values), Göran Lindahl has taken on the challenge of creating a greater synthesis of the different approaches and management cultures around the globe. We asked Lindahl how he could keep the trust and cooperation in the management population that had been a striking feature of ABB's first decade (and, most particularly, its early years). For him, there are only two ways:

- by giving people genuine challenges;
- by creating genuine participation.

With the basic concepts of ABB in place, he has the highly demanding job of taking the organization into a phase of maturity without losing its edge and letting it fall into complacency.

Notes

1 Even today, Barnevik pushes this message . Now that he is at Investor, and responsible for a much smaller group of people, yet influencing a complicated international network, he is still intensely interested in the good questions young people pose him. Around seven to eight times a year, he speaks to large groups of students who, in Stockholm, treat him like a pop star.

2 In the Cannes bible of January 1991, Percy Barnevik defined the basic principles of the ABB culture as being meeting customers' needs, decentralization, taking action, respecting an ethic, and cooperating (see also Chapter 3).

3 Talking with Percy Barnevik, we were also struck by his verbal communication patterns. To the delight of advocates of neuro-linguistic programming, he uses redundancy, incomplete phrases and storytelling very effectively to make his message clear at a very deep level.

References

Quotes without references originate from the authors' personal communications – see page xviii for details.

Barham, K., and Heimer, C. (1995) *Identifying and Developing International Management Competence*', in: Crainer, Stuart (ed.) *Financial Times Handbook of Management*. London: Financial Times Pitman Publishing.

Barham, K.A. and Wills, S. (1992) *Management Across Frontiers*. Berkhamsted: Ashridge Management Research Group and the Foundation for Management Education.

Binney, G., and Williams, C. (1995) *Leaning Into the Future: Changing the Way People Change Organizations*. London: Nicholas Brealy.

de Aenlle, Conrad (1998) 'If philosophers managed portfolios, what would they be worth?', *International Herald Tribune*, 24–25 January, 15.

de Geus, Arie (1997) *The Living Company*. Boston: Harvard Business School Press.

European Training Foundation (1997) *Re-designing Management Development in the New Europe – Report of the Torino Group*. Luxembourg: Office for Official Publications of the European Communities.

McClenahen, John S. (1994) 'Percy Barnevik and the ABBs of competition', *Industry Week*, **243** (11), 20–3.

Peterson, Thane, et al. (1988) 'Europe's hotshots', *Business Week*, 6 April, 14–17

Skaria, George (1995) 'Interview with Percy Barnevik', *Business Today* (India), 22 February–6 March 1996.

Taneja, Narendra (1995) 'Managing a vision', *Tycoon* (India), August, 24–31.

Taylor, William (1991) 'The logic of global business: an interview with ABB's Percy Barnevik', *Harvard Business Review*, March–April, 91–105.

12

Harnessing the power of connectivity via IT

Globalization of business demands global organization. You can't begin to do that without IT . . . If you don't use IT to connect to your customers, it's like moving in the wrong direction on the escalator.
Percy Barnevik

Information technology (IT) is one of the two major priorities for the future that have been set by Göran Lindahl. For Percy Barnevik, who, after all, is a computer scientist by training and wrote his first computer program in the 1960s, IT is clearly a critical success factor for the company now, and in the future. He has said that global companies that are geographically far-flung and heavily decentralized such as ABB cannot function without comprehensive communication networks and computing power, as can be seen from his words above. Barnevik also says IT is an absolute must in order to have the freedom to operate across a wide spectrum of processes, such as manufacturing, engineering, development and sales. You can manufacture a generator in Brazil, with the design data in the US and you may sell it over in Asia – IT allows you to tie it all together, to operate in a borderless way so that people have access to all the most up-to-date information about manufacturing, engineering and sales (Barnevik, 1996).

As Barnevik leaves ABB, he can be proud that it is a leading-edge benchmark company in terms of its IT systems. Harnessing the connective power of IT is clearly a central feature of the globally connected corporation, but where did it all begin for ABB?

In his own minimalist style, Barnevik's master plan did not say much about IT *per se* (see Chapter 3). The entire focus was on ABACUS – the company's financial reporting system (see page 354). One ABB manager remembers when he joined the company from Siemens in 1990:

Siemens was very automated, and heavily into IT systems – there was a computer on every desk. Siemens Service was a $4.8 million organization, and ABB was a $3.5 million organization, but there was only one PC in the whole organization, and that was a battered old IBM. We had to go through two years of change at a time when IT was accelerating out there. The focus was not on IT at that time. I remember that, when I knew for certain that I was joining ABB, I phoned my new boss to ask him what software they were using so that I could read up on it and familiarize myself with it before I arrived. I heard later that he had said in some consternation to his secretary 'He's asking about software but I don't like to tell him that we don't have any computers!' But within 12 months we were well on our way to getting systems. They said 'As long as it is within budget, go ahead.' Now we have the latest PCs and software.

The route to progress

What was the route to progress for ABB? Fred Bystrand, Vice-President for ABB's Group Information Systems, based in Zürich, recalls that much of ABB's initial focus was, indeed, on ABACUS:

It was also the infrastructure for handling communication. It was given a big priority from the beginning, and it still has. The infrastructure was the base for handling reporting. It was the only thing we had to control the company. It started the ABB culture – don't send a lot of information to the head office that people only need locally, but let them concentrate on important problem areas with the option to drill down only when needed.

Manfred Kets de Vries saw ABACUS as the catalyst for making the centralization–decentralization paradox at ABB work. For Fred Bystrand, 'it is ABACUS that is holding us together.'

ABACUS is still working well today. It has proven itself – and probably paid for itself many times over – as the key system that knits ABB together, and is referred to enthusiastically by everyone we talked to as an essential contributor to the realization of ABB's strategy. While the technical background of the system has stayed the same throughout the years, it is coming up for significant modernization. In its early days, it had memo systems and dial-in connections. This has been replaced with network technology with relay of data and voice. ABACUS is still the only corporate system of its magnitude in operation in ABB today.

During the years following the merger, the IT function went through a painful restructuring process during which there was minimal activity at the corporate level. The movement was away from mainframes and centralized IT staff, to developing networks and IS companies in the US, Germany and

Switzerland selling their services on ABB's internal marketplace. In 1993, Fred Bystrand, at the time still at Sandvik where he had worked with Percy Barnevik for many years, received a call from Barnevik. 'Now it's time.' Bystrand joined the three people in the central group and took ownership of the infrastructure and the central network.

Once the mainframe had been eliminated, client server technology was introduced in the companies which went on to handle their own IT. The result was people 'playing in their own sandbox', with no support from specialists. Many of the initiatives from these years added significant costs to ABB's bottom line. At one point, the company had ten 24–hour customer support centres in different countries. Today, the ABB PC is an enterprise workstation connected to a server anywhere in the world, yet the network is coordinated by corporate IT. This still involves client server technology and graphic interfaces.

Presently, the focus of corporate IT is to take decisions about the network and IT security, Lotus Notes, Voice, Internet/Intranet, as well as base applications and vendor agreements. Says Fred Bystrand:

Corporate [IT] should be responsible for basics and making a global IT platform available. What we feel has to be done by us includes office automation and communication, and one source only making decisions about the Internet and e-commerce standards. In addition, it is about strengthening the IT direction of the Group.

By becoming involved in base applications, ABB's corporate IT group was able to reduce costs significantly. With a handful of people in the corporate head office, Bystrand coordinates his activities with people in the BAs and the 3700 IT people across the company, who are responsible for an overall IT budget of $700 million. The new framework that the company is working towards is the 'country concept' – each country should take care of its own infrastructure and applications, which should be standardized. The trend in ABB is already moving towards a country IT organization, and Sweden is leading the way with the first country CIO.

There are two overall systems with corporate coverage in ABB. ABACUS provides a quantitative picture, while Lotus Notes provides people across the organization with the possibility of finding out about what is going on in the company and exchanging information.

While ABACUS was very much driven from the corporate centre, the use of Lotus Notes developed in a completely bottom-up fashion. In the true spirit of decentralization, the corporate centre had not imposed Notes, but simply supported an initiative taken in the US power segment. 'We saw it as the chance to standardize. Perhaps today Notes would not be the most effective system, but it was the only groupware available at the time.' Fred Bystrand's pragmatic stance illustrates how balancing the centralization–decentralization paradox can work in practice. Instead of trying to analyze and come up with the best solution for the company centrally, the centre institutionalized what had already worked for people as the best solution. Following the success of the take-up of Notes, in 1993 it officially became the standard for groupware, and in 1994 the standard for e-mail in the entire company.

Locally, there are, of course, many more special applications of importance to the operating companies. 'Take a netting system for purchasing, for example. It cost us $1 million to develop and implement and it saved us $6 million in interest – 600 of our companies are using it, and it saved us $10 million in the first year,' says Fred Bystrand. 'There is another example in corporate research, where they have developed an encrypted system on Lotus Notes for tracking projects. It is very safe to use.' Linking up with clients through EDI is matter of fact for people in the company. The same is true for suppliers – they can be linked up with ABB via a supply management information system that tracks worldwide supplier information.

Percy Barnevik has pointed to the importance of IT in establishing an international network in R&D:

> *Diversity is essential to innovation, and we have nine research centres around the world with a multicultural mix of scientists and engineers. They network with other research institutions, absorb new ideas and hire good people. In Switzerland, where we have our biggest research centre, we have 20 nationalities. In Sweden, we have 16. These are of course individuals with quite an international outlook and that global network is very important for us to get the best talent and to generate new solutions for our customers* (Barnevik, 1996).

Given that the implementation of a standardized financial reporting system was one of the key priorities during the merger, it is the more remarkable that, until recently, the number one in IT has been doing his job on a part-time basis in addition to other responsibilities.

ABB's Lotus Notes success story

The use of Lotus Notes in ABB began in 1991, with an experiment in the US power segment: 'People started building simple applications and saw the tremendous power of Notes, not just e-mail. Compared to others it was more effective, also in terms of cost,' says Fred Bystrand, ABB's Vice-President for Group Information Systems. The 200 first users became 5000 by the end of 1993. The experiment was now ready to be taken to the Group level. In 1993, at the time of its first major reorganization, ABB decided to introduce Lotus as the corporate standard for groupware.

Fred Bystrand explains: 'In 1993, we had 16–17 different e-mail systems in the company and the IT people had to tie them together in an ABB-mailbox concept. Making Lotus Notes the mandatory standard for office communication solved this problem in a cost-effective manner.' The success of the experiment convinced people around the organization to invest in the system. One of the converts said:

Lotus Notes makes communication and exchange of information easier. It is unifying and helps getting lots of information across to people. Notes has helped us tremendously and we all find it very useful. We have been using it for two years and it has radically changed the way we work. It is like fax machines 12 years ago: they changed the way you worked because you could send things directly and know that people would get it the same day. I check my PC messages first thing – when I am out I can access them through my portable PC. It gives you a list of databases, tells you about new appointments and tells you when it has updated things. But you must be selective because you could spend the whole day on it.

With many business units all over the world, effective communication and coordination is a challenge. Fred Bystrand told us:

We said we need communication, so we had to invest. Notes functioned really well. An investment in infrastructure is often hard to motivate – other companies have problems investing – but with Notes we separated the infrastructure from its applications and it was easy. We recently added 20,000 users, and are now up to 100,000 users. And this figure is still going up.

Half of the company's 200,000 employees are regarded as potential users. Today, ABB is the number 2 user of Lotus Notes worldwide. ABB also sits on the Board of Lotus Advisers to influence future developments from the perspective of the client.

Managers in the business are conscious of the value added of Notes:

All the business areas and profit centres run Lotus Notes. It is used across the whole business vertically and horizontally. People can use and select the information right across the organization, they can dissect it by BA, country or region. You used to read about changes in the company in the Financial Times first of all, now you read it in Lotus Notes. If you read about changes before you see them in the press, you are not surprised.

One way in which ABB has used Notes is for creating a standard method across business units for capturing customer complaints and for tracking the status of the situations. This enables the company to document what complaints are being made and how they are being handled. Yet, what is it exactly that people do differently at ABB, since they have had Notes?

> One example of the usefulness of Lotus Notes is that we are working with other UK companies on a £1.4 million project. We are bidding jointly and I am leading the bid. I can send the bid to the other managers who can read it before it has to be in. That flexibility wasn't there before. We would have been faxing 40–50 pages.

Another example was the use of Notes by an international team looking at customer conflict resolution. A team involving people from the UK, Sweden, Switzerland and Finland put together the text over six months with only one meeting where they mapped the process. Notes cut costs and allowed them to get agreement more easily.

Notes implementations in ABB are typically driven by business imperatives, and are championed top-down by managers within the BAs. Mark Turell reports that some regions were well ahead of the others in getting value from Notes by developing advanced installations and Notes plans of their own. While it all started in the US and spread there very quickly, Britain and Germany followed enthusiastically. Other countries and regions were slower to embrace it or only adopted Notes to participate in global teamwork that was speeding ahead with the use of Notes (Mark Turell, 1996).

What's in the pipeline?

A number of new developments put ABB well on track to meet Percy Barnevik's challenge that IT will probably be the single most important factor for success for ABB, and, indeed, any global company.

ABB has recognized that decentralization has gone too far for IT. There are significant cost advantages, and, perhaps even more importantly, strong pressures for standardization coming from the telecom industry. In the future, ABB has to control what happens in terms of IT in the company more centrally. So far, the infrastructure has already been standardized – Lotus Notes is used for the Internet, groupware and e-mail, Microsoft Office and NT are used for office work. Yet, even more will need to be standardized in future.

Another driver for standardization is the regular exchange of PCs every second or third year. The replacement operation – on an obviously gigantic scale – becomes faster, easier and more cost-effective the more the configurations are standardized across the Group. Recognizing this need for calibration of its decentralized structure, and the need to shift some decision-making power, ABB has decided to look for a new Chief Information Officer, who would be reporting directly to the CEO. Given the excellent experience with Lotus Notes, it is now much easier to gain acceptance for IT standards in ABB. In this area, the corporate dogma of total individual freedom is waning as people learn about the advantages of shared systems. A lesson that still needs to stick, though – standardization is needed to avoid the problem of system updates (even with good documentation of the special configurations, changes can cause nightmares when systems are updated!).

ABB works very closely with a number of suppliers to ensure that the company receives value from its IT developments and implementations. The mutual influencing process takes different forms. The Vice-President for Group Information Systems sits on the supplier advisory Boards for Digital, IBM and Lotus, and is particularly active on the Lotus Notes Board. With companies such as SAP, Baan and J. D. Edwards, a number of key projects are in the pipeline for launching in the year 2000, including a global marketing system and an Activity-Based Costing system. ABB is also investing in ATM (an advanced new technology that joins up different packages of data and voice and sends it out in different packages and different directions), and wants to launch it at the global level. ATM can reduce costs and can be more effective than other technologies: 'It has been on its way for 5–6 years now. It is functioning well in some of our local areas and it needs switching the equipment for global use – it doesn't work globally yet.' And, of course, the topical area of knowledge management is not missing from ABB's list.

What are the company's next steps in terms of enhancing existing systems? 'An even better network, faster communication, high-speed lines and a more common desktop environment!' says Vice-President Fred Bystrand. There will also be more imaging, graphics and desktop video conferencing.

The corporate IT function of ABB thinks it can turn experiences such as the Lotus Notes success story into a way of implementing IT systems. Reusing systems that are successful in one part of the company in another is already a strategy of corporate IT – and, in fact, nothing more than ABB's culture of pragmatic sharing in practice. The next step would be for ABB to begin to build IT competence centres. As Fred Bystrand suggests, SAP implementations are a case in point:

> *It used to be that companies started from scratch, and every company installing SAP fell into the key implementation traps. We have to develop links to ABB systems, such as the ABB cost accounting principles. We are setting up a team of people who have implemented SAP 10–15 times before, and we send them out together with experienced project people when we have different requests. We have also built our own ABB base models to fit different types of company processes.*

Typical IT implementation traps

Fred Bystrand summarized for us his key learning points about implementing IT. All the following can get in the way of successful implementation:

- no management is involved – people say 'this is an IT project';
- no training of users;
- no testing before implementation;
- not having the correct data in the system.

'These traps have been known since the 1970s, and, of course, there are variations. What people never seem to learn is that if you are late, there are only two things you can do: add resources or delay the project. Otherwise, you get a system that you don't want, and you can have problems with production standstills.'

Using the Internet for business has been much talked about. One of ABB's first uses of the Internet was to set up a World Wide Web site in 1995. This, and the web sites that individual parts of ABB have established, give customers and other people access to information on ABB's capabilities, industry case studies and product data for key markets. Viewers can also visit databases of company news releases and general company information. ABB saw this as supporting its belief that the globalization of business requires global organization. The aim was to provide more and more information for the customer, 24 hours a day, when and where they needed it.

Since early 1998, using the web more proactively for business is becoming a commercial reality for ABB. People have stopped seeing it as an interesting possibility and have, instead, been using it to do business. A number of initiatives are under way. The company recently linked all its suppliers via the web – the common way orders are now placed with suppliers. In the future, this should completely replace EDI, as the web is considered a more effective means of communication. ABB has been using the web extensively for the dissemination of information on its products, companies and structure –an activity it will continue and intensify.

People in the company have also been working on a pilot linking customers to the company's systems via the web. As so often, the US is leading the way in this initiative, setting up a database on product information. This will allow customers to look at product drawings and reduces the need for archiving. Customers will also be able to look at order status, and track what is happening with their orders. Technically, the connection is established via the Internet, rather than a dial up, and the critical aspects which are receiving much attention from ABB, are security and access rights. Reliability is another issue – the company is concerned about the negative impact of system downtime when customers begin to rely on it. Although it has concerns about the reliability and security of the Internet, the company still clearly communicates the excitement of catching on to the vast possibilities opened up by it. It is too early to know exactly how ABB will be using the Internet in the next millennium. The company recognizes that the US is far ahead of Europe, particularly in terms of e-commerce. As the company progresses this new development, key questions it is asking itself relate to profitability and reliability, as much as what the different ways of using the Internet are.

An example of the use of the Internet is one of ABB's Swedish businesses – ABB Control, a worldwide manufacturer and distributor of low-voltage equipment. It recently launched a service selling consumer products directly via the Internet aiming to dramatically cut delivery times and achieve delivery within 24 hours. In the past, electricians wishing to purchase equipment needed to go through a wholesaler, who in turn would contact a manufacturer, who then contacted a subsupplier. This was a time-consuming process and it could take up to four weeks for the required part to be delivered. The aim of using the Internet is to simplify and reduce delivery times to customers and the company chose the Internet as a sales tool. The new Internet solution allows customers to select, with the click of a mouse, the components (such as mains breakers, earth fault breakers, automatic fuses and so on) they wish to include in the units they want to purchase. They can get price information as well as a picture of the finished product and have the unit delivered the next day.

It is the limits to IT progress that concern people, rather than the technology itself. In one of those memorable aphorisms that you hear repeated around the organization, Percy Barnevik talks about BC/AC – 'Before Computers' and 'After Computers' or the IT generation gap. The BCs, he says, are over 40 years of age, have not grown up with computers and are over-represented in the higher management ranks. He calculated that BCs at ABB made up 75 per cent of the company's 200 top managers, 60 per cent of the 5000 managers at the next levels and 40 per cent of its 50,000 engineers.

In 20 years' time, all managers and engineers will be AC, but companies cannot wait for that. Massive re-education is therefore necessary to convert BCs into ACs. As he says, speeding up the development of IT competence is the key for competitiveness today. IT development itself cannot be led by 'experts' but must be led by top management, must be integrated into the overall company strategy and must be the subject of the same economic scrutiny as other investments and resource allocations.

Then, now and tomorrow

IT has changed the way people work at ABB. If the company was international before, and operating across the globe almost independent of location, IT has accelerated this process even more. If there is a problem in a power station in Malaysia, for example, someone in the US can help resolve the problem by sitting in front of a screen. While colleagues in Malaysia take a camera with them, the person in the US can manipulate the data and look into the detail. The portable PC and Lotus Notes have made thousands of people in ABB virtual workers who can stay in touch wherever they are.

Barnevik's courageous and lucid style of putting all his eggs in one basket has worked for IT. His minimalist style provided a strong, mandatory structure via ABACUS, and, for the rest, there was freedom to experiment – driven by his passionate belief in individual autonomy and decentralization. Clearly, the company will need to centralize decisions much more in future, yet these decisions will benefit from a good base of experience of what has already worked for people around the company. The future approach to IT will, to a large extent, support the many bottom-up approaches and competences available and it is therefore much more likely to be embraced by people around the company.

References

Quotes without references originate from the authors' personal communications – see page xviii for details.

Barnevik, Percy (1996) *Percy Barnevik on Globalization*. University of St Gallen, Switzerland: presentation to the International Management Symposium, 20 May.

Turell, Mark (1996) 'ABB ASEA Brown Boveri: supporting the multi-cultural multinational', in Lloyd, Peter and Whitehead, Roger (eds), *Transforming Organizations Through Groupware*. London: Springer.

AFTERWORD

··

A seamless leadership succession

In 1996, *The Economist* asked, 'By trusting in multiculturalism and decentral-ization, Percy Barnevik has created a world beater. Could the firm hang together without him?' (*The Economist*, 1996). *The Economist* cited critics who suggested that ABB's relentless expansion had prevented it from putting down any deep common roots and that the company ran on 'nothing more sub-stantial than the adrenalin of permanent revolution.' While it noted the attention that Barnevik gave to developing a cadre of global managers whose job was to knit the organization together, the journal suggested that much of ABB's corporate glue came down to Barnevik's own relentlessness:

> *ABBers around the world speak reverently about his ability to get by on four hours' sleep a night and his familiarity with every nook and cranny of the organization. He reckons he speaks personally to 5500 of his employees every year. He spends only a couple of days at headquarters (often Saturday and Sunday); much of the rest of the time he is in an airborne office in a corporate jet . . . ABB's current structure has thrust an awesome amount of responsibility to the very top of the organization. The more global it has grown, the more it has relied on a strong leader to hold it together. The bigger test of Mr Barnevik's skills may be not how well the company performs while he is still in charge, but what happens to it after his departure (The Economist, 1996).*

That prediction was about to be tested. In October 1996, Percy Barnevik announced that he was stepping down as chief executive as he wanted to avoid the succession problems that many big companies experience when ageing bosses cling to power. 'With ABB well established on the road of long-term profitable growth, it was a natural time for this kind of transition. You should not stay too long in this kind of job,' he said. Barnevik, who was 55, said that he did not want to be like the UK's Lord Weinstock, who continued to run rival GEC until well into his 70s.[1] Barnevik, as we have seen, was suc-ceeded by a fellow Swede, Göran Lindahl, who moved up from his job as head of ABB's power transmission segment. Barnevik remained Chairman, a post he had held since earlier in 1996. Under his leadership ABB's turnover had soared from $18 billion in 1988 to $34 billion.

Certainly Barnevik had come to personify the company to many outsiders. Some pointed to the paradox of the coexistence of an emphasis on decentralization with 'a one-man show at the top' (Berggren, 1996). This is an exaggeration, but insiders readily acknowledge Barnevik's role. Asked to describe the essence of the company, one manager replied:

Leadership. Much of the company's achievement is due to Percy Barnevik. When he took over ASEA in the 1980s he saw that electric utilities were changing and that the industry was going from being local to global. He saw the globalization of the electrical engineering industry ahead of the others. It was not Weinstock of GEC who saw it. He knew that, if we are to be successful, we had to be one of the top two companies in the industry. He made ASEA lean and more global. Barnevik crafted this organization and vision in this little town – Västerås – in Sweden. It was outrageously ambitious – in an industry where the competitors were GE, Siemens and Westinghouse. In 1992, Barnevik said it was his ambition to be number one in all markets. Now, in 70 per cent of the businesses, we are number 1. In the others, we are number 2 or 3. If we are not, we get out. He has succeeded and therefore moved on.

Percy Barnevik's decision to step down as chief executive after nine years at ABB and eight years at ASEA showed his confidence in the future of ABB and his belief that, while a lot depended on him after the merger, the idea of continuous change was taking hold in the company. He points to the Executive Committee of eight people, all of whose members, he says, know what is happening. And he also points to ABB's strong supervisory Board, 'who are not just fee-collectors and are not afraid to disagree' (Sampson, 1995).

Barnevik has often said that his own role in holding the global group together has been much exaggerated. For example, he said (in an interview in India in 1995):

In this world of mass media communication, there is always a focus on the top . . . ABB tends to be Mr Barnevik. But I can assure you that we are not running a one-man show. We have in India, for example, Arun Thiagarajan, the President, as well as T. N. Shenoy, the Executive Chairman. They have to motivate the people here. It is important that we have a number of people like this in each country and also globally. The more the organization gets entrenched, and the longer it works smoothly, the less dependent it will be on me as a person. You must always have a person at the top to influence the policy and the strategy of the organization. So, as soon as Barnevik disappears, what do we do? The judgement of what I have done is not now; it is five years after I have left. But I do not deny that in the process of dramatic change, it takes strong leadership. All the conflicts between countries and companies can only be resolved with someone who has authority and respect. If you go to Germany, you will find that [Eberhard] von Koerber meets Chancellor Kohl. It is not that Barnevik is the main man (Skaria, 1995).

When we asked about the change of leadership, Percy Barnevik told us, 'One of the key responsibilities you have as the CEO is to develop candidates to replace you. If you do not have two or three reasonable candidates to replace you when the time comes, it is a bad grade for the present CEO and for the Board.'

Barnevik planned to remain non-executive Chairman of the Group's Board, but would no longer sit on the Executive Committee, the central decision-making body. He said he intended to spend more time as an international business leader, particularly in developing ties with the European Commission and governments in Eastern Europe, especially Russia. He is also active in a number of other Boards: Chairman of Swedish Investor AB and Sandvik, and Board member of General Motors and Du Pont, USA. Although the ABB Board meets only five times a year, he planned to spend a lot of time at the company and keep an office at the Oerlikon headquarters in Zürich. He intended to be an 'active' Chairman, involved in strategic issues beyond leading the Board work. He said, 'We are much less of a one-man show than many other companies. The top man is not alone – there is a group leadership. There are lots of "drivers" in ABB who are not in the spotlight.' Barnevik emphasized that the new CEO, Göran Lindahl, is leading the organization and he would not attempt to be a 'backseat driver'.

Göran Lindahl is an electrical engineer by profession, who first worked with Barnevik at ASEA. He joined the top management team first of ASEA and then of ABB at the time of the merger and took responsibility for the Group's power transmission and distribution business. He had also served as head of Asia-Pacific operations, where he had been responsible for some big power projects, including the Bakun Project in Malaysia. It was suggested by some observers that Lindahl's role would be more routine than Barnevik's, who had created the ABB merger and built the Group through big strategic purchases. Barnevik said that period was over and the future challenge was to achieve strong organic growth and expansion via smaller acquisitions. Göran Lindahl said there would be no change of strategy: 'We have created a platform. We must continue to strive for growth by going deeper into Europe, deeper into Asia, and America – not to mention Africa.'

What does the change in leadership mean for the company? One senior ABB executive told us:

Percy Barnevik is a very visionary man. He is extremely demanding and that is why he is successful. He puts all his energy behind his beliefs. And because of his very analytical mind, his beliefs are well-founded. Göran Lindahl has the same type of basic characteristics – dedication, working style, charisma. With his own way of working, he has established himself as the new leader of the company. And, of course, Percy Barnevik is still on the Board. It is very interesting to see the transition.

A lot of people outside the company were worried and said that the company depends on Barnevik. This is not the case. It is to the credit of both of them. Barnevik saw it was the right thing to do and that it was a good time to change because he was still young enough to be active on the Board during the transition. It was an orderly, early decision. And he had been around for 17 years. One of his basic principles is that change is good for the company. It shows in his own way of acting.

Percy Barnevik was vital at a certain stage of ABB's evolution – during the merger with BBC, to get the restructuring off the ground, to make the US acquisitions and build the global platform. As one manager says:

The company needed a visionary, entrepreneurial leader who could go in, make friends, and take decisions and risks. But the next stage is – how do you manage a business like this? It used to be a local business but GEC-Alsthom merged, lots of companies have been taken over or gone out of business. We are now at the head of all our business segments. We need a different type of leader. Barnevik knew when to get off. It now needs someone to drive it on, someone who knows the politics.

Some 18 months after the change of leadership when we talked with Percy Barnevik in his new role as Chairman of Investor, he told us:

I am happy that we could make a 'seamless' transfer after my 17 years as CEO of ASEA/ABB. Göran Lindahl was the chosen candidate, who knew the business deep down after some 25 years in the company and ten years on the Executive Committee. I happen to believe that it is a great advantage, beyond being a strong leader, that a new CEO understands the business deep down in any company. I am satisfied with ABB's strategy and direction and I am convinced that Göran Lindahl and his team will achieve the publicly stated objectives.

Percy Barnevik and Investor

In April 1997, Investor – the Wallenberg family holding company that controls 45 per cent of the capitalization of the Swedish stock market – announced that it had chosen Percy Barnevik as Chairman to take over from Peter Wallenberg, who was retiring at the age of 70. Barnevik was the first non-Wallenberg to hold the post in over half a century and had already sat on Investor's Board for ten years.

When Barnevik's appointment was announced, *Fortune* magazine said:

Percy Barnevik has been Europe's favourite manager for so long that he is known as the Continent's answer to General Electric CEO Jack Welch. Over the course of his career, Barnevik's dramatic success has unfolded in a series of acts . . . Yet one prize always eluded Barnevik: he never had command of a sprawling conglomerate as his old rival at GE did (Wallace, 1997).

If that was the case, Barnevik had certainly found his challenge.

Investor itself is little known outside Sweden, but it controls some very famous company names, including pharmaceutical manufacturer Astra, engineering concern Atlas Copco, domestic appliance producer Electrolux, telecommunications company Ericsson, car maker Saab, bearings manufacturer SKF, and forest products company Stora (Europe's oldest company). Under Wallenberg, Investor had quadrupled its portfolio to $8 billion in 6 years to the end of 1996, an annual growth rate of 20 per cent. Not all companies in the portfolio were equally high-performing, however. Astra, for instance, grew sales by 23 per cent a year during the previous decade, but Saab had lost $1 billion since 1990. As a result, Investor's shares sold at an average discount of 30 per cent to its underlying assets. It needed a revolutionary who could squeeze more value out of its holdings by bringing the laggards up to speed, getting rid of losers and creating a sense of urgency in the remaining businesses.

As *The Economist* said at the time of his appointment (in an article with an illustration depicting Barnevik as Superman swooping into an Investor Board meeting), 'Given Mr. Barnevik's record, it would be strange if he did not want to reorganize Investor fairly drastically' (*The Economist*, 1997). Barnevik said that his role was to help set an agenda for management at Investor's firms and then make sure that they live up to their objectives – 'There will be a certain degree of impatience, a certain degree of raising demands, a certain degree of benchmarking,' he declared. He calls this 'setting the tone' – asking difficult questions, imposing targets and a sense of urgency on Investor's companies. Barnevik decided to base himself in London, a major financial centre (he is said to regularly run 12 miles in Hyde Park), and commute to Stockholm, where Investor's head office is located. He also travels to Zürich where he maintains a small office as non-executive Chairman of ABB at the company's headquarters in Oerlikon.

Percy Barnevik is one of the world's great networkers. As if Investor and its companies were not enough to keep him busy, as noted, he is still non-executive Chairman of ABB and he sits on the Boards of such huge firms as Du Pont and General Motors (while the chairmen of Fuji Xerox and Royal Dutch Petroleum, among other companies, are members of ABB's own Board). He is Chairman of Sandvik and is a member of international advisory bodies, including the US-Europe Poland Commission (of which he is Co-chairman), the Competitiveness Advisory Group advising the European Commission and the European Union–Japan Industrialists Round Table. He is an adviser to the Russian government and takes part in meetings of such exclusive groups as the Bilderberg Group, an assemblage of the world's leading politicians and businesspeople. He is also a Charter Member of the World Business Council for Sustainable Development and a member of the Advisory Board of the Council on Foreign Relations, USA.

One of Investor's largest institutional shareholders said, 'With the arrival of Barnevik, we're at the front end of a whole new phase. Here's a guy who doesn't wait around for things' (Wallace, 1997).

We asked Percy Barnevik how he sees his role *vis-à-vis* ABB's new Chief Executive. He says:

The CEO is now Göran Lindahl and he is leading the company. In my role as non-executive Chairman of the Board I am leading the Board work with an unusually international and competent Board. The Board has its mandatory supervisory role and we strive to be contributors to strategy and business development. As Chairman, I am available and supportive whenever Göran and ABB needs me and I strive to be a good coach, just as I do in Investor, in Sandvik and in Skanska [a Swedish construction company] when I was Chairman there.

Barnevik is very sensible of the delicacy needed in his new role:

I know it is sensitive and sometimes it does not work when the former CEO becomes non-executive Chairman. I have therefore gone out of my way to disappear from the executive scene and I believe that nobody today, internally or externally, questions that Göran is 100 per cent in charge and leads the company. You can, of course, say, 'Why even risk that a fomer CEO as non-executive Chairman causes trouble for the new CEO?' Well, the advantage is of course that the Chairman as a coach and discussion partner for the CEO has a deep knowledge of the business and therefore can be valuable. Maybe the principle should be that the CEO does not become non-executive Chairman afterwards, but that exceptions are made when it can work well. I worked for 10 years inside Sandvik as an employee and I have now been the non-executive Chairman for 15 years and have related to 3 CEOs during that time. I feel it has been useful to have the thorough knowledge of Sandvik in my later Chairman role.

Where is Percy Barnevik going with Investor? He says:

Investor's business mission is to be an active lead shareholder in some 16 core holdings with some 700,000 employees and also to invest in new smaller companies where we have the competence and can contribute to development. Through the Boards, Investor puts a demand on performance to beat the stock index. If normal improvements do not help, restructurings or change in management must be considered. Ultimately, if nothing helps, we may look for another long-term owner and divest the shares.

This active ownership requires strong and competent Boards. In my first year as Chairman of Investor, I have been active to strengthen and internationalize the Swedish Boards where Investor is the lead shareholder together with a number of institutions, who also are important shareholders. Investor's role as an active lead shareholder or 'owner expert', is not new and Investor has consistently beaten the stock index whether you look at 5, 10 or 20 years. What I strive to do now is not to change direction but to press harder on the accelerator.

And what does it mean for ABB? Barnevik replies, 'Investor is the main shareholder in the Swedish part of ABB, ABB AB. As such, we put, of course, the same demand on ABB as on other holdings – to beat the stock index. I believe it is good for ABB, as it is for other companies, to have demanding and visible owners.'

What is Barnevik's own future direction? He told us:

My job right now is to chair the Boards of ABB, Investor and Sandvik, to contribute in the Boards of DuPont and General Motors and to participate in a number of international bodies. ABB and Sandvik are well under way under strong and focused executive managements, and the bulk of my time is presently spent on Investor and its big group of international holdings. While I nowadays am one or two steps away from the executive role, I find it challenging to influence such a big group of companies as those where Investor is lead shareholder . . . My nature is to be a 'change agent' and constantly strive for improvements and new stretch targets. Sometimes people who engage me get more change than they ask for!

References

The Economist (1997) 'Is it a bird? Is it a manager', 3 May, 77–8.

Wallace, Charles P. (1997) 'Percy Barnevik's next act', *Fortune*, 26 May, 70–2.

Göran Lindahl has done everything in ASEA and ABB from R&D to sales and marketing. He is said to know the organization inside out and to have what the Germans call *Fingerspitzengefühl* – flair or subtle intuition. Percy Barnevik acknowledges that Lindahl's breadth and technical depth far surpass his own knowledge. We asked Lindahl how he would describe himself:

Number one, I'm an engineer – I am deep in technology. So you will see ABB make leapfrog steps in technology. I will drive it from the top or it won't happen. Second, I'm a salesman in my personality. I've been fighting out there in Africa, in Brazil, etc. I've been woken up by a telephone call at 3 o'clock in the morning and at 9 o'clock have been on a plane to Malaysia. Not just selling, I negotiate. It is easy to sell if you accept any conditions. It is about pushing it through. Third, I have a deep belief and interest in achieving human involvement. We need to address it in such a way that people are excited about working for ABB.

Certainly, one immediate result of Lindahl's appointment was the increased emphasis on sales and marketing introduced in 1997, with the objective of securing growth via enhanced market penetration. Lindahl quotes a favourite saying of his as an indicator of his intentions: 'I used to tell people "Sell, sell more, sell even more!"'

How does Lindahl see the key challenges for the future of ABB? He drew us a diagram that explains that ABB strategy in the past has been to move into higher-margin businesses (from lower-margin businesses, such as installation, building and contract business, to higher-margin businesses, such as oil and gas) and to grow and expand geographically into new global markets (from Europe, to the US, to Asia and the emerging markets; see Figure 1). 'We have done this for ten years – what next?' he asks.

In reply to his own question, he points to the increasing importance of ABB's service and retrofit business and of the necessity for 'financial engineering'. However, he says that the big future challenge is innovation – not just in technology but in leadership. The two areas, he declares, 'which will have the highest impact on our operations for the next five years are human resources (HR) and information technology (IT).'

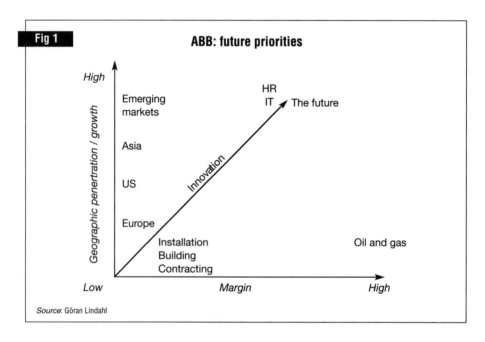

Fig 1

ABB: future priorities

Source: Göran Lindahl

Göran Lindahl's restructuring of ABB in 1998 was seen widely as confirmation that he had put his own mark on ABB and that he had established himself as a credible and forceful chief executive for the future.

Note

1 A review of a recent biography of Arnold Weinstock of GEC noted that while he had achieved great things earlier in his career, he had stayed on too long in the top job: 'The real lesson is, quit while you are still ahead.' (Morton, Alastair (1998) 'Delivering the goods', *The Spectator*, 4 April, 39–40.)

References

Quotes without references originate from the authors' personal communications – see page xviii for details.

Berggren, C. (1996) 'Building a truly global organization? ABB and the problems of integrating a multi-domestic enterprise,' *Scandinavian Journal of Management*, **12** (2), 123–37.

Sampson, Anthony (1995) *Company Man: The Rise and Fall of Corporate Life*. London: HarperCollins, 243–4.

Skaria, George (1995) 'Interview with Percy Barnevik,' *Business Today* (India), 22 February–6 March, 100–5.

The Economist (1996) 'The ABB of management,' 6 January, 64.

MEMORANDUM TO GÖRAN LINDAHL

To: Göran Lindahl, President and Chief Executive, ABB Group

From: Kevin Barham and Claudia Heimer

Re: **The future of ABB**

Dear Mr Lindahl

ABB has successfully completed its first decade of existence and has consistently been rated as Europe's most admired company for the last three years. It has been the world's favourite case study for many years, and occupies the corporate Mount Olympus together with GE and Microsoft. As you mentioned to us, ABB has a unique set-up – nobody has ever tried to do what you have done. Textbooks talked about the matrix in the 1970s, but nobody ever tried to follow it by giving distinct responsibilities to people along two dimensions. From Västerås and Baden, the company redefined the rules of the game for an entire industry.

While talking with many ABB people in different parts of the world over the last few years, we have not detected any visible signs of complacency in the organization. It seems to us that you have the interesting job of taking the organization into the future by making sure that, indeed, it does not fall into self-centred contentment.

You have been very much part of the success story, and you know the company deeply. From your perspective, you have told us about the challenges for the future of the company. You pointed out to us that they are:

- how to innovate in technology for the new millennium – you talked of the need for 'technological leapfrogs';
- how to continue to increase sales;
- how to use financial engineering to provide total solutions for clients, especially regarding large projects;
- how to attract young talent – the best scientists and leaders – and how to develop them;
- how to reap the benefits of IT.

While you identified HR and IT as the areas that are likely to have the greatest impact on the company in the next five years, you seem particularly focused on globalizing leadership in the company.

Two of your initiatives have made a clear start in this direction. You have introduced a refinement to the matrix structure which shifts decision-making power to the global rather than the local dimension.

You have also started to renew the ABB culture. In line with your interest in genuine participation, you recently invited ABB people from different cultures and religions to respectfully, yet critically, adapt the company's mission, values and policies booklet for truly global leadership. You recognized that, so far, the booklet has been based on what you call essentially

Lutheran and Calvinistic values and, without changing its essence, you are interested in engaging people from different cultures more fully.

We will watch with great interest how you take this forward. Yet, are people and IT going to be enough?

As you prepare to take the company into the new millennium, we see a number of challenges that relate to your past as well as your future.

- A few years ago, ABB started to move production from the West to Central and Eastern Europe and Asia. While it is intellectually well understood, this enlargement to the East is emotionally far from being digested and accepted inside the company. With all the work that has gone into creating a truly multicultural company, the strength of national feeling persists – and probably always will.
- Decentralization is part of ABB's trademark. The effects on the autonomy, accountability and the achievement of your companies are indisputable, although it might have been a little overdone in some areas – for good reason. However, does it mean that some of your central functions sometimes have slender resources with which to make an impact?
- ABB's capability for hard work has become legendary, yet people also need to rest and renew. If we were to think of the state of tension that the pace of ABB creates for people as a rubber band, is there a limit to how much people can take before it breaks? How can you ensure that you maintain its elasticity?
- The company has effectively communicated its emphasis on shareholder value. The message that you are focusing on *long-term* shareholder value has not yet reached out in quite the same way. Younger generations are interested in workplaces that are interesting *and* allow them to be successful, are ethically sound *and* ambitious. If you want to attract young talent in future, how will you have to modify the way you communicate about shareholder value?
- The ABB merger in 1987 was once described as 'to think the unthinkable and then act'. If the environment ABB has created is one of 'hypercompetition', by spotting discontinuities in the market and seizing the opportunities at great speed, how are you going to recreate your competitive advantage? Your competitors are moving, sometimes copying your ideas. Will you continue calling the shots? How will you keep them dancing?
- Finally, ABB is strongly committed to the principle of sustainable development, and you have set ambitious new environmental targets for BA managers. Will they be able to generate enough buy-in to translate these targets into their strategies and have the organization deliver on a large scale?

We look forward to finding out about the next big surprise coming out of Zürich!

Kevin Barham and Claudia Heimer

LEARNING FROM ABB

15 giant steps to a global organization

1 You don't need to have all the answers when trying to achieve change on such a grand scale as the ABB merger. It helps if you have the opportunity to try things out first on a smaller scale and review them to see what works well – it adds to your credibility.

2 Decentralization to profit centres around the world is the key to creating an entrepreneurial mindset. Decentralization does not mean that top management can abdicate. It requires control and 'fingers in the pie' management.

3 Stay close to customers around the world during a merger to reassure them and not lose market share. Customer focus is not a platitude – it should be at the heart of everything you do.

4 Don't delude yourself that you can forecast the future – you can only see breaks in trend lines, and you won't always see those. Instead of trying to cater for every eventuality, you need to be capable of flexibility and innovation. Look at your own organization – how can you improve that capability? Incidentally, what would it mean for you if your two closest rivals joined up?

5 Understand which parts of the business are more global and which are more local and act accordingly. However, don't assume that 'global' and 'local' are mutually exclusive – globalization is ultimately about serving local markets better.

6 Multiculturalism is not an ethical issue, it is a practical business need. Intervene to promote the principle of international teams where necessary. Globalization of the top team sends a powerful signal to the organization about its commitment to local markets and to working across borders.

7 Set challenging targets, but don't keep changing the formal organization. Give people the chance to focus on achieving results and stay around long enough to live with their results. Record ideas for change and implement them all in one go at the appropriate time.

8 Communicate, communicate, communicate to 'fire people up' – even at the risk of competitors listening. Use simple slogans. Keep repeating the messages internally and externally so you create consistency. Use the media as a foghorn into the organization and to give your people around the world a sense of pride and identity.

9 Globalization requires transparency and connectivity across time zones and geography. You can't do that without IT. Speeding up IT competence is the key for competitiveness today. As Percy Barnevik says, *every* company is an IT company in future.

10 Every manager, including the CEO, should aim to have two to three succession candidates ready at all times. It can be fatal if they don't.

11 You don't necessarily need lots of global managers – not everybody has to be global – but you do require a pool of cross-culturally capable people from which you can draw your global managers. You need people who are able to work effectively in multinational teams. Substantial investment in global management development is therefore a fundamental requirement in becoming and remaining a global organization.

12 Results-oriented learning on the job gives management development credibility and makes line management take responsibility for developing people. Aim for 'business development by people development' – make sure that there are good processes in the local operations for identifying management talent and expose people to international assignments at an early stage in their careers so they screw on a wide-angle lens.

13 Don't assume that all your organizational values are fully applicable across the world. Be prepared to test and modify those values to take account of new cultures joining the organization as you globalize.

14 Keep it *practical.* Concepts are only 5 per cent of the building of a global organization. Execution and the ability to engage people around the world are 95 per cent.

15 *Long-term* shareholder value is the ultimate measurement of performance in a global company. You can live with oscillating profits in certain parts of the globe, if you know you are investing in the future. It overcomes sloppiness when considering financial underperformance. Long-term shareholder value requires you to think holistically – you cannot achieve it without treating customers, employees and society around the globe well.

INDEX

··